SINGAPORE 2065

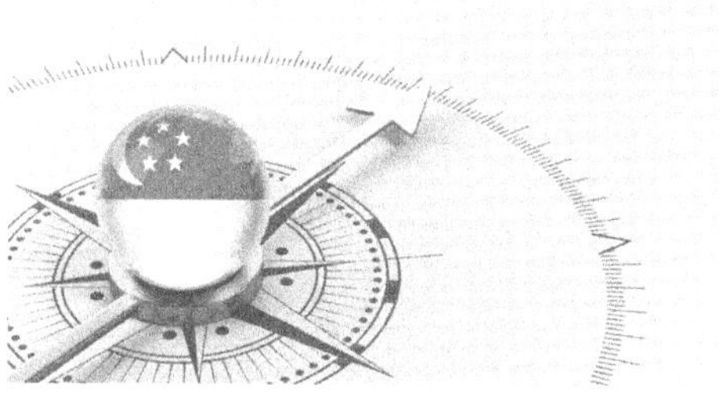

Leading Insights on Economy and Environment from 50 Singapore Icons and Beyond

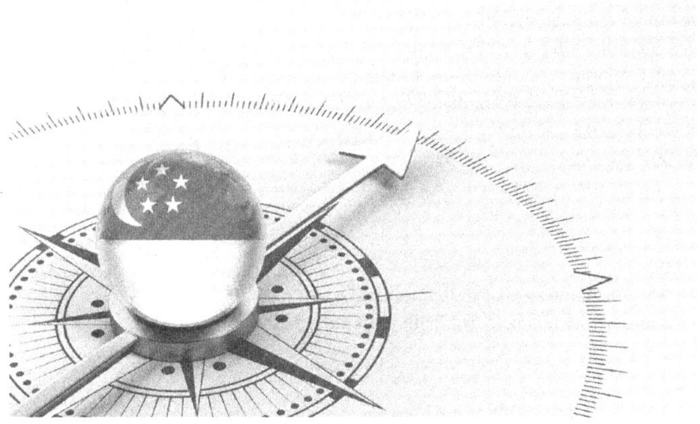

Leading Insights on Economy and Environment from 50 Singapore Icons and Beyond

Edited by

Professor Euston T. E. Quah

Nanyang Technological University
and
President, Economic Society of Singapore

NEW JERSEY • LONDON • SINGAPORE • BEIJING • SHANGHAI • HONG KONG • TAIPEI • CHENNAI • TOKYO

Published by

World Scientific Publishing Co. Pte. Ltd.
5 Toh Tuck Link, Singapore 596224
USA office: 27 Warren Street, Suite 401-402, Hackensack, NJ 07601
UK office: 57 Shelton Street, Covent Garden, London WC2H 9HE

Library of Congress Cataloging-in-Publication Data
Singapore 2065 : leading insights on economy and environment from 50 Singapore icons and beyond / edited by Euston Quah (NTU, Singapore & Economic Society of Singapore, Singapore).
pages cm
Includes bibliographical references.
ISBN 978-9814663366 -- ISBN 978-9814663373 (pbk.)
1. Singapore--Economic conditions--21st century. 2. Economic forecasting--Singapore. 3. Singapore--Environmental conditions--Forecasting. I. Quah, Euston, editor.
HC445.8.S5324 2015
330.95957001'12--dc23

2015018719

British Library Cataloguing-in-Publication Data
A catalogue record for this book is available from the British Library.

In-house Editor: Li Hongyan

Typeset by Stallion Press
Email: enquiries@stallionpress.com

Printed in Singapore

In memory and respect of Singapore's Founding Prime Minister,
Mr. Lee Kuan Yew;

Dedicated to my loving wife and children,
Juat Mei, Josh and Jo-ann

Endorsements

"A stunning collection of perspectives across the spectrum, Singapore 2065 presents a compelling look into the future through a series of thought provoking insights. This volume also celebrates the country's exceptional success, retelling the invaluable stories and anecdotes that have paved Singapore's tremendous journey over the last 50 years. As Singapore continues to chart into the next half century, Singapore 2065 *leaves plenty to ponder and will remain a valuable repository of knowledge for many years to come."*

Bertil Andersson
President
Nanyang Technological University

"Singapore 2065 *has brought together a diverse and intriguing range of ideas and insights from a rich cross-section of contributors: policy makers, researchers, close observers of Singapore, student leaders, and others. These essays reflect on Singapore's remarkable progress and development over the past half-century, and explore the opportunities and challenges that lie ahead. Over the next 50 years, the world will continue to be an uncertain place, offering exciting opportunities, but subject to bouts of deep uncertainty and disruptive events and trends. Ultimately, Singapore's continued success over the next 50 years will depend less on our material resources, but on our people, and specifically our key attributes of nimbleness, adaptability, creativity, resilience and the willingness to strive for a common purpose."*

Tan Chorh Chuan
President,
National University of Singapore

"Singapore's success came in large part from its continuous efforts to anticipate what changes are likely, not often looking as far as ahead as 50 years ahead, but certainly not afraid to try. Here are 50 minds stretching forwards into the 21st century — confirming that the city-state's spirit lives on. I am confident that our environment will have a better future thanks to the projections in this volume. Everyone who cares should read and think about them."

Wang Gungwu
Chairman,
East Asian Institute
National University of Singapore

"There are few issues that are more important than the economy and the environment in the 21st century for any country. They are especially important to Singapore, given its size and open economy. As the nation celebrates its 50th birthday, justifiably proud of its achievement, it is also timely to contemplate what the future might hold and what we need to do to ensure continued success as a nation. In Singapore 2065, *you will find food for thought. What is of particular interest is that the deeply thoughtful essays collected in this volume crisscross at different points, and also raise a number of fundamental issues concerning value and identity that are inextricably tied to Singapore's future development. This book certainly provides keen insight into the economic and environmental challenges we face, but it also compels us to reflect on the larger story of "Majulah Singapura" as we march into the future."*

Alan K. L. Chan
Dean, College of Humanities, Arts & Social Sciences
Nanyang Technological University

Contents

Foreword

Professor Euston Quah has brought together an interesting and diverse slate of opinion makers for this worthwhile book on Singapore, on the occasion of our 50th year of nationhood. Their perspectives of the future illustrate the challenges and opportunities that we face as a small country in a changing global environment.

We cannot tell what the world will be like 50 years from now, just as few expected how radically the world would change in the last half century. Even in Asia alone, few scholars expected that countries like South Korea and Singapore would have advanced the fastest in the last 50 years, or that China would in a shorter space of time emerge from inward-oriented socialism to become the world's manufacturing powerhouse, its largest consumer of resources and second largest consumer market.

What we do know is that the future will be very different from the past. The developed countries face the prospect of prolonged slow growth — restrained by debt and much smaller increases or reductions in their working age populations, possibly coupled with low productivity growth. Slow growth is also shaping a new and more fragmented politics, with less appetite for global cooperation and multilateralism. Climate change continues unabated. Turbulence in the Middle East is likely to persist for many years. Conflict and tensions based on religious and sectarian beliefs, now globalised, have become a defining challenge of the times.

Economic confidence remains intact in Asia, but here too progress will surely not follow a linear or unbroken path. And everywhere in the modern world, technology is reshaping the world of work. Robots are becoming cheaper, safer and more advanced, with improved sensors, machine vision and softer, lighter materials. They will lower costs for companies and consumers, but also replacing many jobs.

We embark on our next phase of development as a nation amidst these uncertainties, and the very real risk of disruptions in the regional and global environment. But we start from a position of some strength, coming out of the transformations we achieved in our first 50 years.

- Standards of living for most Singaporeans have increased five to six fold since the 1960s, even as the challenge of inequality remains. Our lower and middle income groups have seen substantial improvements in real incomes in the last decade alone. We have avoided the broad-based stagnation in living standards seen in many developed countries.
- Our education system has transformed Singaporeans' potential dramatically in 50 years, and is one of the best regarded internationally. We must work harder to sustain social mobility in the decades to come, but it is more alive in Singapore than most other countries.
- Home ownership in Singapore is a unique achievement. Even amongst households in the lowest 20% of incomes, over 80% own their own homes. Public housing neighbourhoods and urban planning have enabled ethnic and social integration to a degree unparalleled in other cities, and broadly distributed access to quality schools, healthcare to recreation.
- Our reserves, built up through years of prudent fiscal policies, now give Singapore a strategic advantage that we never had in earlier decades. Besides offering security for the future, it now means a steady stream of investment income in our government budget each year to spend on economic and social priorities — quite different from most developed countries, who are either having to raise taxes and cut expenditures today in order to service large debts or to impose an even larger burden on the next generation.

But it is the continual improvement in our human capabilities, in every vocation, and our ability to work together to achieve common goals, that is Singapore's most significant strength. We must keep evolving.

Our future will depend not only on adapting and perfecting what has been done elsewhere, but more and more on creating value through new skills and technologies, original business solutions and a spirit of experimentation in society. We must provide space for young Singaporeans to explore their interests and develop a deep sense of fellowship with their peers as they grow up in our schools. We must develop a system that supports learning throughout our lives, and help everyone acquire skills to work alongside and take advantage of new technologies.

We are making an even better Singapore, both more innovative and more inclusive. We must do so with the blend of imagination and practicality that got us to where we are today, and always with a sense of fairness. We can build a culture where everyone earns respect for the effort they put into their lives and the contributions they make in their own ways, but where we can also count on one another. This book is a valuable contribution to the healthy debate on the choices we must make as we go forward together.

Mr. Tharman Shanmugaratnam
Deputy Prime Minister and Minister for Finance, Singapore

Preface

As Singapore celebrates her 50th birthday in 2015, perhaps it is timely not just to rejoice in her significant achievements, but also to give thought to what is to come in the next 50 years, specifically what will happen to Singapore's economy and the environment in 2065 and beyond. *Singapore 2065* was borne out of this intention. Preparations for the celebration of Singapore's 50th birthday were very much in the news in 2014. This book was conceived while doing my routine exercises at my health club, with the television facing me and announcing the many programmes that will take place in 2015 for Singapore's 50th birthday. As many of the forthcoming projects and books will be focusing on a more reflective perspective of Singapore, I thought it would be unique to come up with a book inviting 50 Singapore icons to ponder the future of Singapore; not just the immediate short-term future, but rather the far future. I also intentionally selected a homegrown publisher, *World Scientific,* to take on the task of publishing the book. World Scientific has become an internationally recognised and successful publisher.

More than 50 years ago, the World Bank and most other observers predicted that Burma, the Philippines and Sri Lanka would be the blooming Asian economies of the new millennium, not Singapore! Today, as a nation with only 50 years since independence, Singapore has achieved much more than was ever expected, and as such we have become a narrative of economic success.

Singapore has no doubt come a long way from a backwater country very much dependent on entrepôt trade and bounded by many constraints, to the modern metropolis and economic powerhouse she is today We acknowledge the significant achievement of Singapore's founding Prime Minister, Mr. Lee Kuan Yew, in building a great Singapore. While we express our deepest sorrows in Mr. Lee's passing, we also rejoice in Mr. Lee's immense contributions to Singapore. Discussions on how best to remember Mr. Lee Kuan Yew, while extremely important, there is, in my view, no better way than to reflect and see Singapore's vibrant economy, thriving living environment in our dynamic metropolis as evident of his remarkable achievements. Furthermore, the garden city and painstaking efforts by Mr. Lee to ensure a clean and green Singapore, are all hallmarks of his belief and conviction that a country's growth must ensure sustainable development and that includes the conservation and protection of the natural environment.

However, can it be taken for granted that Singapore will maintain this position into the future? The short answer is no. This is because Singapore, with her very open economy, has to contend with the ever-changing external and internal environment. Nothing is static, everything is dynamic, and it would be interesting to know where and how these changes will take us. Concomitantly, with higher incomes, Singaporeans demand a higher standard of living and a better quality of life. The many factors that determine quality of life certainly include nature and the living environment, which pertains to matters such as optimal population size, air and water quality, the availability of open and green spaces, and congestion externalities among others. There seems to be a strong correlation between the environment and the economy. Further economic success and higher incomes will mean that every additional dollar earned in GNP (Gross National Product) will now provide less additional satisfaction (happiness) to Singaporeans, or even dissatisfaction for some. Therefore, society's focus may shift towards building a better quality of life beyond economic gains. But again, due to our ever-changing external environment, it cannot be taken for granted that incomes will remain high. Competition from countries in the region, dynamic trade flows, and changes in the large economies of the United States and China will continue to impact Singapore. Should incomes start to fall, one may see a regression, whereby there might be a reduced impetus to protect the environment, and a returned focus on income and employment stability. Moreover, the endless possibilities of technological advancements could alter the current relationship and trade-off between the economy and the environment, freeing us from our past constraints, and propelling us in ways we could never have imagined.

This book's focus is on Singapore's future economy and the environment. This is also very much in line with me being an economist, more specifically, an environmental economist. The book invites 50 Singapore icons and beyond to give their thoughts on these issues. The invited authors are given free rein to write on how they envision Singapore to be like in 2065, as long as they deal with aspects of the economy and/or the environment. The "Singapore 50" are well-known personalities, prolific writers and speakers, and mostly household names. These are individuals who inspire awe with the mere mention of their names, broke intellectual frontiers with their impactful works, and influenced national policies for the better good. Many of them are also frequently engaged with the media and are active in stirring up intellectual discussions. Readers will easily recognise their names. There are of course many other Singapore icons. Unfortunately, this book is unable to include many of these other prominent icons whose expertise lie beyond the fields of economics and environment, or who have been invited to contribute but have declined.

I have intentionally included a second group of authors whom I labelled as "Beyond 50". This group includes respected journalists who have written much on the economy and the environment, as well as a select few foreigners who are well acquainted with Singapore over the years, through their frequent visits and strong affiliation to the academia; all have also taught in Singapore universities. In addition, I have invited a small group of people who are young and dynamic, many of whom may be upcoming future icons. Some in this group are associated with me as part of my university core of research assistants, as well as former students at both the National University of Singapore and Nanyang Technological University.

In all, the entries in this book fall under three categories: careful and rational arguments; projections, calculations and simulations; and visionary thinking. This collection of essays covers not only convergent and divergent visions of Singapore's distant future, but also explores what can and need to be done now and over the near future, so as to avoid potentially negative scenarios, strengthen our comparative advantage, and put the nation in a favourable position 50 years down the road. In addition, statistics, notes and quick facts of Singapore's past and present have been included at the end of the book.

Predicting the far future has always been challenging and exciting. I hope my readers, whether now or in the future, will find *Singapore 2065* interesting, useful and insightful. And to the readers in 2065, if I may ask — have the visions in this book been realised? In the meantime, let us ponder, prepare for, and shape Singapore's future.

And as John Maynard Keynes wrote in his classic 1930s article, "Economic Possibilities for our Grandchildren," in the volume, *Essays in Persuasion:*

"My purpose in this essay, however, is not to examine the present or the near future, but to disembarrass myself of short views and take wings into the future. What can we reasonably expect the level of our economic life to be a hundred years hence? What are the economic possibilities for our grandchildren?"

Of course, speculating and predicting 50 years ahead is already a difficult and daunting task, let alone thinking about a hundred years — that may require another volume.

Euston Quah
President, Economic Society of Singapore
Professor and Head of Economics
Nanyang Technological University
Singapore

Acknowledgements

Foremost, I would like to acknowledge my team of committed research assistants, Christabelle Soh, Cristian Chen, and especially my chief research assistant, Tan Tsiat Siong. Over our frequent meetings at Scotts Square's Dome Café and at the Damai Club, Grand Hyatt hotel, Singapore since February 2014, we discussed, made comments and suggestions at great length, worked hard, and shared this memorable journey. I am also deeply grateful to my able secretary, Ms. Shida Baji, for her clerical, administrative aid, and coordinating efforts throughout this project. Not forgetting at NTU, Ms. Joey Kek, Ms. Julianna Yik, and Ms. Kum Wai Han, for effectively facilitating my administrative responsibities throughout the years. My gratitude also goes out to my secretaries at NUS, Lena and Khatini, for their valuable assistance. I also wish to acknowledge Ms. Ham Oi-Mun for being there for me during much of the early part of my academic career. These excellent secretarial and managerial staff have been crucial and highly valued in getting much of the work done and ensuring efficiency and timeliness. I could not have had a better team over the years than them.

I thank Mr. Chua Hong Koon (Publishing Director, World Scientific Publishing), who provided me with useful advice and timely reminders. I thank Mr. Max Phua (Managing Director, World Scientific Publishing), who enthusiastically supported this project right from the very beginning.

I also thank Ms. Li Hongyan (Senior Editor, World Scientific Publishing) for her excellent suggestions and attentive work as my desk editor.

In addition, I am thankful to Prof. Liu Hong (Chair, Humanities and Social Sciences (HSS), NTU), for his encouragement on and support for all my academic pursuits. A special mention goes to the Economic Society of Singapore Council and also to the Economic Growth Centre, NTU. It is from the many discussions on a myriad of economic issues that inspirations and intellectual capital were drawn. I also want to thank Ms. Christina Seet from the Economic Growth Centre and Ms. Vivian Tan (Manager, Economic Society of Singapore) for their generous help and support.

Most importantly, this book would not have been possible without all the contributing authors. I cannot thank them enough for sharing their interesting views, insights, and addressing what they think are the possible scenarios of the future. I hope the readers, whether now or in the future, will enjoy their inspirations and thoughts as I did. I would also like to express my sincere appreciation to Deputy Prime Minister Mr. Tharman Shanmugaratnam for his contribution of the Foreword and his presence at the book launch; Dr. Sng Hui Ying for her provision of Singapore's facts and statistics; Prof. Bertil Andersson (President, NTU), Prof. Tan Chorh Chuan (President, NUS), Prof. Alan Chan (Dean, HSS, NTU), Prof. Wang Gungwu (Chairman, LKY School of Public Policy, NUS) for endorsing and believing in this book.

Finally, to my wife, Mei, and my children, Josh and Jo-ann, for their unwavering support and enthusiasm for this project, which required much time away from the family.

To Singapore 2065, may Singapore continue to prosper.

Euston Quah
Singapore 2015

The Next Fifty

Some revitalise along a road less travelled,
Or trek around Kailas to stretch their legs,
Find echoes in silences of each valley's snow
Hushed serene by pure blue skies; or dream
Of char kuay teow to assuage frenetic Mondays,
Hot emails, confer calls, way off bottom lines.

What's new?

After rough beginnings, clash of ideologies, the
Slog of pioneer leaders and workers brought
High keyed rankings, lifted gross and per capita
GDPs, house ownership, IT and other networks,
Percentage of annual growth, we take stock at
50; model, predict and prepare for the next 50.

What's the future?

Can not, must not, will not be more of the same.
That much we know. But what else? We imagine
With discretion; project with adventurous logic;
Stretch science into fiction; fiction into science,
Past Vernes, Clarke; successive futurists, dreamers.
One in a thousand ideas is bull's eye. A low return.

What else?

KPIs and indices for chapter headings: economics
Stressed by giant neighbours India, China, techno
Innos, demographics, how we teleport, educate, train;
Distribute income, keep free trade; resources we can
Muster, how consume, renew leadership; openness
Of speech; rule by law; the nation's reputation.

How then?

The people, the people, first and last, now and to come,
Take our roads best proven; self-upgrade, adapting
Quick to sharp, daring times. Trek around cyberspace
With ease. Turn silences into mantras which create.
Put silicon into valleys. Above all, live and let live
The better life. Balance care for self and others.

What more?

As we update, renew and rearrange tiring skylines,
Tunnel and reclaim, let's pledge our Island, its little ones,
To tidy, living green, the firm corners of our compass.
Let then shimmer in light, set mood and spirit, unfold
Shadows, chlorophyll our air, distil flower and shade.
All this and more careful adventuring for posterity.

My take?

Among the many marvels Sarah, Ruth, Daniel,
David, Jonathan, Evan and Caleb is how mere
Thinking will drive machines to do our bidding,
At work and home, bettering the quality of life.
Whole communities. Perhaps by a microchip,
On a slim card, or comfy in their index finger tip.

Edwin Thumboo
Feb/Mar 2015

Excerpts of Quotes on Singapore's Future, from Founding PM Lee Kuan Yew, ESM Goh Chok Tong, PM Lee Hsien Loong

Lee Kuan Yew
First Prime Minister of Singapore (1959–1990)

"I think we have to go in whatever direction world conditions dictate if we are to survive and to be part of this modern world. If we are not connected to this modern world, we are dead. We'll go back to the fishing village we once were."

"Will Singapore be around in 100 years? I am not so sure. America, China, Britain, Australia — these countries will be around in 100 years. But Singapore was never a nation until recently. An earlier generation of Singaporeans had to build this place from scratch — and what a fine job we have done. ... But after that, the trajectory that we take will depend on the choices made by a younger generation of Singaporeans."

"What I fear is complacency. When things always become better, people tend to want more for less work."

"The perennial challenge is to remain competitive. To be competitive, we must remain a cohesive, multi-racial, multi-religious nation based on meritocracy. We have to strengthen our national consciousness at a time when the forces of globalisation are deconstructing the very notion of nationhood. All countries face this challenge. A country like America has over 200 years of history to bond its citizens. We have only 40 years. But so long as the succeeding generations of Singaporeans do not forget the fundamentals of our vulnerabilities, and not delude themselves that we can behave as if our neighbours are Europeans or North Americans, and remain alert, cohesive and realistic, Singapore will survive and prosper."

"I have always believed that a blighted urban landscape, a concrete jungle destroys the human spirit. We need the greenery of nature to lift our spirits."

Goh Chok Tong
Second Prime Minister of Singapore (1990–2004)

"Our present context is very different from that in 1984. Today, our people are far more educated and global in outlook. Asia is on the rise. We are witnessing the emergence of new cities across the world and especially in Asia — cities which compete for talent, ideas and capital. Therefore, being one of best cities in Asia alone cannot sustain our prosperity. To continue the football analogy, First Division or even the Premier League is no longer good enough — we now need to play in the World Cup. With globalisation, we should benchmark ourselves against the best in the world and aim to be one of the most liveable cities globally."

"Singapore can be distinctive in its ability to marry environmental sustainability with economic vibrancy. Singapore can be a city big on economic ideas but small on environmental footprint. We can build a vibrant economy which is environmentally clean and resource-efficient. We can be a hub, originating and exporting future technologies that can make high density living even more eco-friendly. We will make public transport our transport of choice. 80% or more of our buildings should be certified Green Mark. Singapore should be a city bustling with activity day and night, but yet contain rich urban biodiversity within our green areas and our coastlines."

"To stand out amongst cities and countries, Singapore must go beyond being clean, green and safe. It must be a vibrant place which boldly embraces talents and ideas. And most importantly, it must hold special meaning as Home for its citizens, both here and abroad."

"The economic centre of gravity is shifting from West to East. This could be Asia's Century. No doubt there are serious challenges. But I believe if we are innovative, realistic and skilful, we can overcome them. And together ride the Asian wave to prosperity."

Lee Hsien Loong
Third Prime Minister of Singapore (2004–Present)

"To have an eye on what lies ahead has always been the Singapore way. Even as we focus on the present, we must look forward and have confidence in our future. And perhaps less obviously, we must also know and understand the past and especially our past. … Because unless we understand our past, we will fail to appreciate what Singapore's success depends upon — why Singapore works the way it does. We will become unjustifiable pessimistic about our future prospects."

"We have to manage our numbers. We have to stay open and welcome those who are ready to contribute to Singapore and who are ready to make their home here. We must maintain our reputation for being a good place to live and work because we lose that at our peril. If people think that we are not interested in attracting investments, or that talent is not welcome here, or that we have turned inwards. I think that is the end of us."

"We are doing our best to develop Singapore as a liveable and sustainable city. Trying to manage the consumption of scarce resources, like water, energy, and pricing them properly so people have the incentive to save and not waste these resources. Trying to take the long-view: planning over generations, implementing programmes over several electoral terms and rallying Singaporeans to forgo some immediate gains for future dividends."

"We have all contributed to the Singapore Story. At the heart of the Singapore Story is our belief in Singapore, belief that we can turn vulnerability and despair into confidence and hope; belief that out of the trauma of separation, we could build a modern metropolis and a beautiful home; belief that whatever the challenges of this uncertain world we can thrive and prosper as one united people. Let this belief and spirit burn bright in each one of us and guide us forward for the next 50 years and more. Together, let us be the pioneers of our generation. Together, let us create a brighter future for all Singaporeans."

Unveiling Singapore 2065: A Summary

Euston Quah
Professor and Head of Department (Economics)
Nanyang Technological University, Singapore (NTU)

Cristian Chen
Graduate (Economics),
NTU

and Tan Tsiat Siong
Graduate (Economics),
NTU and National University of Singapore (NUS)

The essay contributions in this book can be characterised both by their varied approaches and diverse ideas, covering an extensive range of topics such as evolving economic structures, Singapore's place in the dynamic global economy, technological advancement and innovation, environmental sustainability, the future of education, our social compact and so on, to name a few. Some essays zeroed in on specific topics with impressive depth and technicality — usually an indication of an author's profession or area of expertise. Others took a more holistic approach through a balanced exploration of preferred key issues. Certain pieces even took on a refreshing angle, such as in the form of a heartfelt letter to young Singaporeans, a fictitious yet highly conceivable Singapore Budget Speech for 2065, and a captivating narrative that takes the reader through the picturesque surroundings of Sungei Buloh Wetland Reserve. In tandem with this book's key themes of "Economics" and "Environment", this overview categorises the key ideas of this book accordingly as such, then proceeds to go over poignant points discussed on the interrelationship between economy and environment, and a conclusion.

On Economy

Many contributors acknowledge the critical role of external circumstances in determining the wellbeing of Singapore's small open economy. They highlight Singapore's need to remain highly adaptable to unpredictable challenges, and to also maintain her competitiveness in order to not only survive, but also thrive amidst the ever-changing and uncertain global economic landscape. Various means to reach these ends have been proposed. These include but are not limited to: provision of quality infrastructure, able management of industrial relations, attracting global talents and investments, continual improvement in educational and skill levels, strong political governance, raising productivity levels, developing Singapore as a world-class international maritime centre, and cultivating the right mindset in citizens. The potential implications of global developments on Singapore's international trade and macroeconomic structures are also explored in several articles, which portend that Singapore may go through a continued decline in export manufacturing, but experience growth in service sectors such as the financial services.

However, despite the inherent vulnerabilities of an open economy and the challenges it faces, the advantage of an open economy lies in its ability to tap into a world of opportunity. The world's economic centre of gravity is slowly but surely shifting towards Asia, and there are potentially vast benefits to be had when Singapore shares the fruits of regional growth with her neighbours. Several propositions have been raised to place Singapore in such an advantageous position, such as developing Singapore as a regional and global hub, cultivating favourable diplomatic and economic ties with her neighbours, and creating critical ecosystems of business activity.

Given the inextricable relationship between technology and economic growth, and the breakneck speed at which new and improved technologies are phased in and out today, it is not surprising that the essay contributions are also abound with enthusiastic speculation on technological advancements, the kind which most readers would not simply dismiss as implausible. The predictions range from lifestyle-revolutionising and industry-shaking developments in 3-D-printing and "intelligent" cognitive technologies, to Singapore achieving complete self-sufficiency in food production and fully automated electromagnetic cars being as ubiquitous as the trees that line our roads. Some contributors also inevitably address the theme of technology while exploring issues on transport and infrastructure, such as envisioning the abolishment of private car ownership to be replaced by a nationwide implementation of a driverless taxi system, all the more a reminder of the undeniable pervasiveness of technological change in our world today.

Besides macroeconomic and technological affairs, social issues are also a much favoured topic of discussion, with one of the most recurrent subtopics being that of wealth and income inequality. Readers may be able to notice an apparent unanimous agreement that inclusive growth should be made an indispensable goal over the next 50 years, and that it is essential for Singapore to strengthen her social compact through various available channels such as education, philanthropy, volunteerism, social enterprises, community orientation and other means that help improve social mobility. These writers highlight that inequality may be further aggravated by rapid technological growth that is inherently disruptive and skill-biased, as lower-skilled workers become phased out by machines. It is therefore imperative that the government, firms, and citizens look out for each other, especially the needy and vulnerable, in order for Singapore to remain politically and socially cohesive.

Yet another social concern brought to the fore is that of Singapore's shifting demographic profile. Many authors elaborate at great length on the looming threat of Singapore's ageing population. This impending problem and its concerns are studied in multiple contexts such as healthcare, infrastructure, integrated living spaces, technology, financial security, and even the setting up of overseas retirement villages. The implications of an ageing population on Singapore's labour market are also explored by certain authors who foretell future unemployment problems due to a mismatch in skills, and also voice recommendations on Singapore's ideal retirement age. Accordingly, concerns on Singapore's ageing population are also closely intertwined with discussions on the projected size of Singapore's future population, dependency on foreign workers, and forging of the Singaporean identity.

On Environment

Readers keen on green will get to whet their appetites with essay contributions revolving around the natural environment. Various environmental-related issues such as climate change, rising sea levels, biodiversity and natural capital, recycling and product cycles, water and waste management, as well as environmental consciousness are extensively discussed across the chapters with much rigour and passion. Contributors assent that in the forthcoming years, energy production will be much more clean and efficient, especially through the adoption of renewable energy. Additionally, the development and management of the environment as a financial asset is also explored as a new area of opportunity for Singapore. Moving forward in the greater environmental scheme of things, Singapore's long-term objective is to achieve sustainable development.

On Economy and Environment

In line with the main themes of this book, most entries explore both economic and environmental issues. A common point frequently raised in this context is that measures of economic success are changing. In the next 50 years or beyond, Singapore's achievements will not only be benchmarked by her GDP growth, but also through a holistic consideration of other essential aspects such as liveability of the physical environment, magnitude of carbon emissions, extent of income inequality, and overall quality of life. It is also notable that the ever-present discussion on tensions between the economy and the environment garner different opinions, which include the compelling proposition that society should consider aligning the interests of the economy and environment holistically, instead of viewing them in terms of trade-offs.

The projections and hopes contained in this book range from the bold and visionary, to the pragmatic and down-to-earth. The sifted ideas mentioned in this overview are not an exhaustive coverage of the content of this book, and by no means do justice to the vivid projections and astute insights of all the authors. Readers will have their imaginations stretched as they get glimpses of a plausible future where Singapore exports water, foreign workers are bionic beings, and home is an apartment in a 500-storey building. Also, readers attuned to contemporary social issues will have their intellect stirred by compelling viewpoints such as the revolutionising of women's roles in society, and a future where an ageing population is viewed as an economic and social asset. With that said, informed readers will have no trouble finding something to pique their interest. Despite the multifarious topics and viewpoints contained in this book, an underlying theme is still indisputably that of Singapore in a world where the only constant is change.

Editor's Chapter: What Beckons Singapore's Future Environmental Landscape?

Euston Quah
Professor and Head of Department (Economics)
Nanyang Technological University, Singapore (NTU)

and Christabelle Soh
Recipient of the Lee Kuan Yew Gold Medal (Economics), NTU

The pursuit of economic growth has always necessitated accepting some degree of impact to the living environment. Conversely, the preservation of the living environment will always involve foregoing some measure of economic growth. This is in line with the basic fundamental economic principle that every choice entails a trade-off, and the sooner and better a society understands these opportunity costs and gains, the clearer and easier for policymakers to make informed decisions. The tension between the two — the economy and the environment — often results in governments having to prioritise one over the other, and in terms of resource allocation. Many would also argue that there is a clear limit to which natural capital as in green spaces and forests can be substituted for physical capital as in buildings and infrastructure.

In Singapore, economic growth has historically taken centre stage and has always been the backbone of the country's material progress. There

This chapter is adapted from an earlier article in *The Straits Times* titled, "Growth v Greenery: Where Will Singapore's Priorities Lie?" (March 4, 2014).

were good reasons for this. In the early days of independence, Singapore faced existential challenges. Real income per capita, the amount of goods and services that could be purchased with the average income, was only approximately one-twelfth what they are today. The unemployment rate was between 10–12%. That meant that for every 10 people looking for work, one (or slightly more) was unable to find any. The post-war population boom also meant that jobs had to be found for the growing number of young people. The late Dr. Goh Keng Swee famously recalled that "(I)n the first few years when I went home for lunch, I passed big schools and saw thousands of kids going home at 1 p.m. I kept on worrying where I was going to find jobs for them."

The emphasis on economic growth then can be easily observed from the policies adopted. Doors were opened and red carpets were rolled out to attract Foreign Direct Investments (FDI). The Economic Development Board was set up and specifically tasked to bring in FDI, a crucial mandate that has remained unchanged till today. Simultaneously, Free Trade Agreements (FTA) were actively pursued to expand Singapore's export markets.

However, economic growth was not pursued with the complete abandonment of environmental concerns. Even then, it was recognised that Singapore's small geographical area meant that the living environment was inextricably tied up with industrial activity. As such, the paradigm was that while economic growth was paramount and had to be pursued, some consideration would be paid to the living environment. An example of this was the land zoning that was carried out. More pollutive industries were located as far away as possible from residential areas. Also, standards on waste and pollutant discharge were enforced from the start, a policy directive uncommonly observed in developing countries. The planting of trees and general greening of Singapore were also clear efforts to preserve the living environment.

In more recent years however, with Singapore's increased affluence, this policy stance seems to have become less acceptable to the population. There have been calls to consider reprioritising growth and paying more attention to the living environment instead. The non-material aspects of the quality of life have gained more prominence as comfortable income levels become the norm. To a large degree, this is unsurprising. As incomes increase, the marginal utility of income (the addition to welfare that extra income brings) decreases, which tips the scales in favour of non-income determinants to welfare.

So what beckons Singapore's future environmental landscape?

"Economists" and "predictions" are two words that, when combined, induce polite scepticism at best and outright cynicism at worst; the latter being the more common response in the post 2008 global financial crisis world. This current sentiment is very nicely captured by the late American humorist Evan Esar: "An economist is an expert who will know tomorrow why the things he predicted yesterday didn't happen today."

As such, it takes a certain degree of courage to try to envision what Singapore's environmental landscape would be in the far future. Fortunately for the two authors, the far future is sufficiently distant for both not to be too bothered if the predictions do not pan out. This gives us courage to boldly make the following claims.

In the energy sector, three developments will converge to create two shifts in the way we obtain energy. The first shift will be in terms of the composition of our fuel mix. Currently, the bulk of Singapore's fuel comes from natural gas piped in from Malaysia and Indonesia. However, with improvements in technology to harness and store electricity, we expect to see a greater reliance on renewable energy, specifically solar energy. Singapore is well suited for solar energy given the perennial sunny climate. Prices of solar panels have also fallen dramatically since China's entry as a producer into the solar panel market. The obstacle that has prevented thus far more widespread adoption of solar energy has not been that of price, but rather of dependability — the difficulty of storing cheap solar energy produced in the day for use at any time. Hence, as electricity storage technology improves, we foresee a shift away from natural gas towards a greater use of solar energy.

The other development that will drive the shift in our fuel mix away from piped-in natural gas is developments in clean technology regarding burning coal and shale gas extraction. Coal and shale gas are very similar in that both are abundant and therefore extremely cheap. However, concerns for the impact they have on the environment have limited their growth. For shale gas, the concern is over the pollution caused (such as groundwater poisoning) in the extraction process known as "fracking" as well as recent scientific findings that the process may increase the probability of earthquakes. For coal, the concern is over the release of large amounts of carbon emissions when it is burnt. With technology that mitigates pollution from fracking and other natural disturbances, and improvements in carbon capture technology, the pollutive aspects of both fuels will be addressed and we expect to see a migration towards these cheaper energy sources. As things stand, Singapore is already exploring importing shale gas from the US.

The third development is the trend towards a more cooperative world as our neighbours become prosperous. As the region's growth accelerates from greater trade and investment links, friendlier ties will enable the full implementation of a smart energy grid with every ASEAN nation plugged in. This will allow for a greater stability in the electricity supply as energy deficits in one country can be made up for by energy surpluses of another, as well as greater efficiency as more energy will be produced by the producer with the lowest marginal cost. For Singapore, this will also mean a general shift in energy generation from internal to external sources.

Policy-wise, we expect a broadening of markets in which the economic principle of taxing negative externalities (costs to third parties that are unaccounted for) are applied. A good number of these taxes are already in place — cigarettes are taxed for the health cost imposed on passive smokers; road usage is taxed (via the Electronic Road Pricing (ERP) system) for the congestion caused; and there are taxes on car emissions because of the pollution created. For some existing markets, the scope of these taxes will be expanded to include the whole market. For example, to deal with congestion, every road will be priced. Additionally, smart gantries will adopt dynamic pricing of roads where the price of using a particular road would depend on the level of congestion on it — the greater the congestion, the higher the price.

For other markets, taxes will be increased or introduced to correct for other externalities such as those related to water consumption, waste generation, and possibly even noise creation. Amongst the new taxes, carbon taxes to mitigate global warming would have the furthest reaching impact since it would be the first (and possibly only) tax on a "universal" externality (all economic activities result in some degree of carbon emission). In sum, Singapore will move towards a state in which all externalities are internalised.

Of course, taxes are not the only policy tool. Complementary policies will also be developed for more complete solutions to the problems.

In the case of climate change, while carbon taxes will help reduce the carbon emissions and slow down global warming, adaptations will be made to accommodate the reality of an already warmer world. Existing policies such as higher building bases to prevent flooding and regulation on coastline development will be expanded. Buildings will be built further inland in response to higher expected sea levels and land reclamation may be curtailed until it becomes clear that reclamation does not contribute to flooding.

Similarly, for waste management, policies will be developed to complement taxes. Aforementioned warmer relations with our neighbours will enable Singapore to lease land from Malaysia and Indonesia for landfills for non-toxic wastes. Of course, the cost of leasing land will trickle down as higher waste disposal fees for consumers. This will, in turn, incentivise waste reduction and greater recycling. On a related note, new technology will allow the current offshore landfills that will certainly be full in the future to be developed as usable land for industrial or even residential purposes.

For water, higher taxes to reduce usage will solve the demand-side issue. On the supply side, improved desalination technology would make large-scale desalination feasible for Singapore. At the same time, NEWater technology will become sufficiently advanced for NEWater to become a cheap and abundant water source. Between the two, Singapore will finally achieve 90% water sufficiency.

Regarding congestion, expansion of the ERP will be accompanied by substantial improvements to the public transport system to encourage a further switch away from private car usage. Great investment will be pumped into developing a public transport infrastructure that is cheap, efficient, and most importantly, comfortable.

At an even higher level of policymaking, there will be a fundamental shift in the way we think about balancing priorities. Instead of the past guiding principle which sought to maximise economic growth within the constraint of not going below the minimum acceptable living environment, we will adopt a more holistic optimisation of welfare which recognises that society's welfare is neither static nor solely dependent on economic wellbeing and therefore requires constant adjustment of policies to achieve the optimal combination of economic and non-economic factors to maximise overall welfare.

This fundamental paradigm shift will also influence Singapore's population size, in that policy will be guided by the concept of an optimal population that can maximise the quality of life. The size of the optimal population will be dynamic and change according to the contributions of material and non-material factors to the quality of life.

The same thinking will also guide the amount of environmental goods such as green cover that is provided. Continued increase in affluence would diminish the value of additional income and therefore increase the relative value of environmental goods. In response, more environmental goods would be provided. Conversely, tough economic conditions would result in lower priority given to the environment. Success in the economy should not be taken for granted as external competition from other countries reins in.

To facilitate the prioritisation of factors deemed important, systems will be established to elicit the public's preference for environmental goods. One part of this would be requiring all proposed public projects to be accompanied by environmental impact analyses (EIA). EIAs have not been adopted thus far primarily because the valuation techniques used to put a monetary value on environmental goods have not been robust. Also, Singapore's early priority had been survival, which precluded "wasting" resources on EIAs. However, over the next 30 to 50 years, the combination of increasingly developed robust valuation techniques and the shift towards more holistic welfare optimisation will promote the use of EIAs. We would also have had the chance to learn from the experience of other countries in the region that have adopted the practice.

Finally, since the potential haze season is still upon us perennially, we make a final tongue-in-cheek prediction about haze in the far future — it will definitely still be around since fires during the hot and dry season are only natural as is the continued impact of the El Niño years. The only issue is whether man-made factors worsen or mitigate it. We would safely predict that because of all the earlier and ongoing efforts by the governments in the region, this perennial haze is bound to decrease substantially by year 2065.

Singapore's environmental landscape in the far future may not be quite a different one from today but certainly a dynamic changing one which utilises modern technology, pragmatism as it has with its cost-benefit analysis and efficiency-based decision-making encased within good governance.

Singapore 50

A Community at a Crossroads: The Perspective of a Community Leader

Azmoon Ahmad
Chairman
Association of Muslim Professionals, Singapore

Over the last 50 years, the Malay/Muslim community in Singapore has seen numerous programmes rolled out to empower it by intervening in key areas of education, employment, youth, gender, family and socio-religious life of Malay/Muslims. A number of the Malay/Muslim organisations and institutions addressing Malay/Muslim issues were set up as early as the 1950s.[1]

In the last two decades in particular, there have been constant discussion and debate about the community's progress through platforms like the National Convention of Singapore Muslim Professionals, which has been held at the beginning of each decade since 1990, aimed at charting the community's strategic directions.

The Malay/Muslim Community's Achievement

The Malay community has made significant educational and employment gains. Minister-in-Charge of Muslim Affairs, Dr. Yaacob Ibrahim, described the community's achievements during his speech at the Hari

[1] Young Women Muslim Association (PPIS) was set up in 1952, Muslim Youth Literary Association (4PM) in 1948 and Jamiyah Singapore earlier in 1932.

Raya Get-Together in August 2013 as having "scaled many peaks of excellence" (Ibrahim, 2013).

Indeed, the accomplishments of the Malay/Muslim community are remarkable if one was to consider certain characteristics which make its progress within the larger Singaporean society a challenge. Despite lagging for decades in terms of median household income, which limits the funds a Malay family could allocate to their children's education; and despite the lower educational attainments of Malay parents, which constrains their contribution to their children's academic pursuits, the community continued to improve their educational and occupational profiles. More are going to post-secondary institutions and better qualified Malays are entering the workforce.

Given the community's ability to thrive under less than favourable conditions, there is cause to remain positive about the social, economic and political affairs of the community as 2065 approaches. It is however worth highlighting potential pitfalls as the community navigates an uncertain future over the next 50 years.

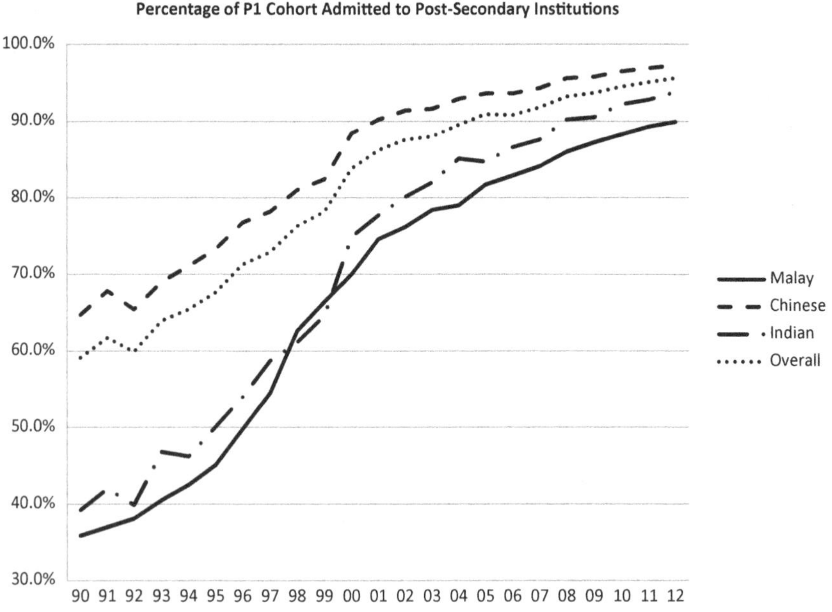

Source: Ministry of Education, Singapore

Redefinition of Success and Impact on Community

As the community was making progress, at the national level, success continued to be redefined, bringing about both benefits and challenges to the community.

On the one hand, the move towards according greater prestige for talents and skills that extend well beyond academic success led to the creation of multiple avenues for achieving excellence, which the community could capitalise on and which gives the less academically inclined a chance at doing well in life. Self-help groups conducting education programmes began to introduce fresh initiatives, offering, for example, experiential learning programmes to young children to nurture creative talents.[2]

On the other hand, the community's aspirations are by and large geared towards achieving academic excellence. Years of efforts at inculcating the importance of academic achievements made it difficult for both Malay/Muslim organisations and Malay/Muslim parents to shift gears and adapt to the broader definition of success. Passing examinations and getting into good schools remain the immediate concern, hence the failure to fully appreciate a system of multiple pathways.

There was no clear indication that, since the introduction of the Ability-Driven Education (ADE) paradigm in1997 (Lee, 2001), the Malay/Muslim community is taking advantage of it or that it complements the cultural or socioeconomic attributes of Malay/Muslim students. But the new landscape is here to stay and the push towards a system that prizes skills and talent is likely to gain momentum as 2065 approaches.

Work-and-Study Initiative

More recently, during his National Day Rally 2014 speech, Prime Minister Lee Hsien Loong talked about work-and-study paths for non-graduates. Citing the stories of several Keppel employees who rose through the ranks to land senior managerial positions, Mr. Lee conveyed a clear message that pursuing higher qualifications which are irrelevant to one's career is not the way to go, assuring instead that opportunities to obtain higher qualifica-

---

[2] Mercu Learning Point, for example, introduced the Integrated Project Work in 2008 to train children to apply the principles of problem-based learning, an initiative to encourage children to conduct active investigations on a topic instigated by questions or problems posed by the children themselves.

tions that are pertinent to one's ability to take on greater responsibilities in one's job will remain open throughout one's career path.

With the announcement by Mr. Lee, the drive to value skills and talent may gain traction in the long run. Changes are expected to follow in the areas of education and employment, based on the recommendations of the ASPIRE Committee which the government accepted.[3]

Employment Challenges of a Young Population

The emphasis on education is particularly important to the community not only because it is a conduit for social mobility but also because of its relatively youthful population (Singapore Department of Statistics, 2013), making it imperative to look into how best to equip the young to make telling economic, social and political contributions in the next 50 years.

As Singapore pursues its population growth policies and its vision of a global city, there will be a multifaceted impact on the community. Immigration of talents and high-net-worth individuals (HNWIs) will constantly infuse renewed vigour into Singapore's drive to maintain its competitive edge. Jobs will continue to be created, benefitting Singaporeans and the Malay community.

However, it is worth noting that the share of PMET jobs have increased to 52.7% in 2013 from 45.4% in 2003 (Ministry of Manpower, 2013) and will continue to grow in the next 50 years. It can be projected that new jobs created will be largely in PMET positions while the share of non-PMET employment categories will continue to shrink.

In the lower-skilled job categories, declining emphasis on the paper chase and assurance of work-and-study opportunities may slow down the pace of educational attainments made by the Malays, perpetuating their overrepresentation in the segment of workers with secondary and post-secondary (non-tertiary) qualifications. While there will be those who will advance into managerial and professional positions from lower starting

[3] The Applied Study in Polytechnics and ITE Review (ASPIRE) Committee, chaired by Senior Minister of State for Law and Education, Ms. Indranee Rajah, was tasked to study how applied education in the polytechnics and ITE could be enhanced. http://www.moe.gov.sg/aspire/aspire-report-online/.

points, questions remain about the chances of the rest scaling the rungs of the income ladder against a backdrop of competition from low-cost labour and high income inequality.

With only 28% of Malays in PMET positions (Singapore Department of Statistics, 2010) and the perpetuation of non-tertiary qualified Malays entering the workforce, the prospects of keeping pace with how the occupational composition at the national level is changing do not appear bright.[4] Hence, there are real concerns about whether the Malay community will face an employment crisis in the next 50 years.

The work-and-study initiative is however beneficial to the community in the sense that, considering that a significant proportion of post-secondary Malay students are in Institute of Technical Education (ITE), the ASPIRE Committee's recommendations promise career paths for ITE graduates, thus making it possible to nudge them towards higher income brackets.

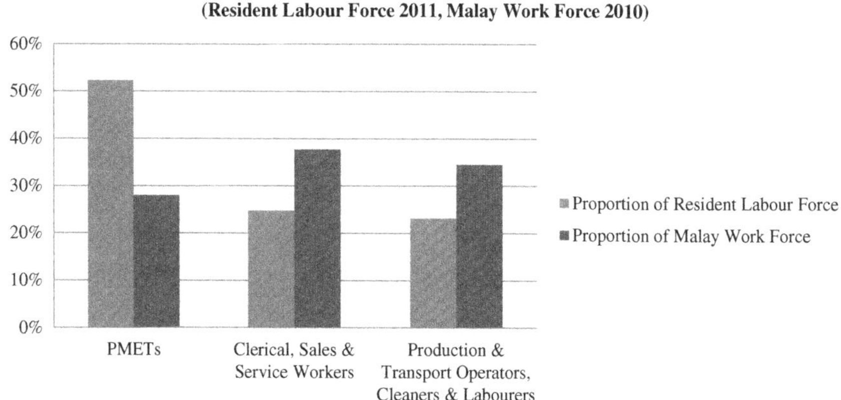

Sources: Census of Population 2010, Department of Statistics, Singapore; Labour Force in Singapore 2011, Ministry of Manpower

[4] While it can be argued that other communities may also see a slowdown in educational attainments with the work-and-study initiative that Prime Minister Lee announced, it is worth noting that the Malays are overrepresented in the ITE educational category. The work and study path for the Malays will be longer than for the others, hence requiring a longer time to land PMET postilions.

Immigration and Emigration of Malays

The improved outlook for the community's ITE graduates notwithstanding, augmenting the educational and occupational profile of the Malay community is likely to remain a major challenge. It is unlikely, for instance, that there will be a substantial inflow of Malay or *pribumi* talent from Southeast Asia, as Prime Minister Lee shared during his National Day Rally speech in 2010. Although he gave assurance that efforts will continue and that the government will not allow immigration to upset the racial mix, the rate of Malay immigration is unlikely to change sufficiently to have significant economic, social or political impact on the community in the next 50 years.

On the contrary, the likelihood of Malay emigration is greater, particularly among those who are better educated and higher skilled. Perceptions of discrimination and keen competition for employment opportunities will be among the primary motivators for seeking greener pastures abroad. The human capital flight will not augur well for the community's continued socioeconomic progress.

Income Inequality and the Underclass

The social landscape is expected to be harsher as population policies contribute to the growth of the middle class, sparking shifts in income distribution that aggravate income inequality. More households, of which many will be Malay ones, will struggle to cope with inflation as the threat of a permanent underclass developing looms not only over the community but also on a national scale. Social researchers have estimated that between 10% and 12% of resident households are unable to meet expenses on basic needs (Donaldson et al., 2013). The problem is likely to become more acute as Singapore heads towards 2065.

The government has taken a cautious approach in ensuring that social policies are calibrated so as not to undermine the values of self-reliance and resilience but it has been improving social safety nets over the years, with more measures being announced during the recent National Day Rally speech.

Affirmative Action

The improvements to social safety nets notwithstanding, there may still be a need to institutionalise affirmative action for society's disadvantaged, not one that is modelled after the much-criticised Malaysian National Development Policy[5] but one that promotes a diverse spread of people of various backgrounds in the workplace. Such affirmative action can be implemented without undermining the principles of meritocracy as Minister for Foreign Affairs and Law, K. Shanmugam, pointed out (Chia, 2009). He cited the example of former US Secretary of State, Dr. Condoleezza Rice, who benefited from Stanford University's selection criteria, becoming a professor at the institution. He said, "Assuming 10 people made the cut-off, try to look for some who are also from the Malay community."

Social Divide

It is of utmost importance that bold measures are taken to address economic problems as they could contribute to social tensions, pitting not only one social class against another or natives against naturalised Singaporeans but also, within the community, one group of Malays against another. This intra-community divide could be in the form of increased isolation of well-to-do Malays from the struggling ones, the emergence of subcultures that are at odds with mainstream Malay/Muslim culture, the polarisation of socio-religious orientations as prevailing socio-economic conditions give rise to suspicion of capitalism and modernism, all of which could undermine efforts to sustain the community's socioeconomic progress.

The Singaporean Identity

Conversely, the diversity that immigration introduces may address a thorny issue: there has been persistent disquiet within the community that

---

[5] The National Development Policy replaced the Malaysian New Economic Policy in 1990 but, like its predecessor, pursued affirmative action for ethnic Malays which included quotas for admission to public universities until 2002.

employment and workplace discrimination have debilitating effects on the job opportunities and prospects of Malay workers. An increasingly diverse population will bring about a new social order in the next 50 years, which may see the Singaporean identity of Malays emerging more strongly than their ethnic identity, thus countering negative stereotypes of the Malay worker. They will be part of the Singaporean core in the workforce (Faizal, 2013).

A stronger Singaporean identity will address the longstanding issue of the position of the Malays in the Singapore Armed Forces. More Malays are expected to hold what have hitherto been considered sensitive appointments, thus countering perceptions that Malays are unable to land key appointments in government institutions by virtue of their ethnicity.

Conclusion

Looking into the future, the outlook for the Malay/Muslim community may not be very rosy but, with the right initiatives, the strengths of the young could be harnessed to hedge against the risks posed by an uncertain future socioeconomic landscape. There have been many positive developments in the community, such as making educational and employment progress despite beginning from lower starting points. They point to the community's resilience in navigating adverse socioeconomic terrains to achieve desired outcomes. There is therefore a valid reason to remain optimistic about the community's future.

Note: Special thanks to Abdul Shariff Aboo Kassim from the Centre for Research on Islamic and Malay Affairs (RIMA) for his contributions to this article.

References

Chia, S. A. (2009). No Quotas But a Diverse Spread of People. *The Straits Times*. Retrieved July 2009 from http://news.asiaone.com/News/the+Straits+Times/Story/A1Story20090706-152905.html.

Department of Statistics, Singapore. (2010). *Census of Population 2010: Statistical Release 1, Demographic Characteristics, Education, Language and Religion*, pp. 76. Singapore: Department of Statistics.

Department of Statistics, Singapore. (2013). *Population Trends 2013.* Retrieved June 1, 2014 from http://www.singstat.gov.sg/publications/publications_and_papers/population_and_population_structure/population2013.pdf.

Donaldson, J. A., Loh, J., Mudaliar, S., Md Kadir, M., Wu, B., and Yeoh, L. K. (2013). Measuring Poverty in Singapore: Frameworks for Consideration. *Social Space*. Retrieved December 18, 2014 from http://ink.library.smu.edu.sg/lien_research/110.

Ibrahim, Y. (2013). Speech by Dr. Yaacob Ibrahim, Minister for Communications and Information and Minister-in-Charge of Muslim Affairs, at Hari Raya Get-together, 23 August 2013, 8.00 pm at Sheraton Towers Singapore. Retrieved February 1, 2014 from http://www.news.gov.sg/public/sgpc/en/media_releases/agencies/mcicrd/speech/S-20130808-1.html/.

Lee, C. K.-E. (2001). *Ability-Driven Education in Singapore: Recent Reform Initiatives.* National Institute of Education Corporate Seminar 2001.

Ministry of Manpower, Singapore. (2013). *Labour Force in Singapore, 2013.* Retrieved February 1, 2014 from http://stats.mom.gov.sg/Pages/Labour-Force-In-Singapore-2013.aspx.

Yahya, F. (2013). Developing a Singaporean Core in our Workforce. Retrieved September 2014 from http://lkyspp.nus.edu.sg/ips/wp-content/uploads/sites/2/2013/12/Faizal_Developing-a-Singaporean-Core-in-our-Workforce_011213.docx_.pdf.

Imagining Singapore, The Cognitive City

Janet Ang
Vice President
Systems of Engagement & Smarter Cities
IBM Asia Pacific

When Singapore was declared an independent city-state in 1965, no one would have dared to imagine that Singapore would be one of the wealthiest countries in the world.[1] With only trishaws as taxis and typewriters as computers, Singapore was then, a third-world nation with poor infrastructure, limited capital, unskilled workers, high unemployment, a meagre (Gross Domestic Product) GDP per capita of US$516[2] and a broken dream.

Acknowledging Our Blessed History

Fast forward 50 years and our little insignificant island has grown by leaps and bounds.

Today, we can humbly boast about having the world's best airport,[3] the world's second largest container port,[4] a GDP per capita of $69,000,[5] and

---

[1] D. Choo (2012, August 14), S'pore is Now Richest in the World, *Yahoo! Newsroom*. Retrieved February 24, 2015 from https://sg.news.yahoo.com/s%E2%80%99pore-is-now-richest-in-the-world.html.

[2] Retrieved February 24, 2015 from http://www.taxationservices.com.sg/incorporation/brief-introduction-to-singapore-economy/.

[3] The World Airport Awards (2014, March 26), Changi Airport in Singapore Has Been Voted the World's Best Airport by Air Travellers at the 2014 World Airport Awards, Held at Passenger Terminal EXPO in Barcelona, Spain (Press Release). Retrieved February 24, 2015 from http://www.worldairportawards.com/main/2014_airportawards_results_announced.html.

[4] Y. N. Lee (2013, September 28), S'pore Poised to Remain One of World's Top Maritime Ports: Maersk, *Today Online*. Retrieved February 24, 2015 from http://www.todayonline.com/business/spore-poised-remain-one-worlds-top-maritime-ports-maersk.

[5] http://www.singstat.gov.sg/statistics/latest_data.html#1.

being ranked the world's second most competitive economy by the World Economic Forum.[6]

For this, I salute the pioneer generation of our country, the ones who have laboured selflessly and tirelessly for all Singaporeans today, so that we can enjoy the lifestyle, infrastructure and employment of a developed country and a global city, in just 50 years. Special mention goes to Mr. Lee Kuan Yew and his old-guard colleagues for writing our Singapore story. They had the courage to dream big, creating a "First World oasis in a Third World region," and the leadership to make it happen.

From Efficient to Smarter

To date, Singapore has successfully leveraged science and technology to create highly efficient and productive capabilities in housing development, tax and central provident fund administration, town and city planning, education, policing and defence, unified ticketing and fare management systems in public transport.

We have come a long way from when I first graduated from the National University of Singapore and joined IBM Singapore as a systems engineer back in 1982, working with many of our government agencies to computerise the volumes of paper records into databases and automate manual processes into IT systems. It has been a privilege working with so many talented individuals within the pioneer IT community in Singapore to design and implement systems that have helped to transform Singapore into the knowledge economy that we are today.

Many of our government agencies are now best-in-class in the use of IT to drive productivity and efficiency. Several agencies in Singapore already use modelling and predictive capabilities to address key environmental concerns in Singapore such as air quality and dengue outbreaks,[7] and video and smartcard analytics to improve the efficiency of current modes of public transportation.[8]

---

[6] World Economic Forum (2015), Competitiveness Rankings. Retrieved February 24, 2015 from http://reports.weforum.org/global-competitiveness-report-2014-2015/rankings/.

[7] IBM (2012, July 3), Singapore's National Environment Agency Collaborates With IBM To Improve Environmental Services Related To Air, Weather And Public Health (Press Release). Retrieved February 24, 2015 from https://www-03.ibm.com/press/us/en/pressrelease/38241.wss.

[8] LTA (2014, June 2), LTA, SMRT, Starhub and IBM Collaborate to Improve Transport with Data for Singapore Commuters (Press Release). Retrieved February 24, 2015 from http://www.lta.gov.sg/apps/news/page.aspx?c=2&id=407a5053-0345-40f5-8d64-51fb31bfb2a0.

To this end, Singapore has become the poster child for a well-run and well-connected country with not just the "know-how" (design and technology of the physical and built environment), but also the "do-how" (operating systems and institutional mechanisms).

From Programmable to Cognitive

Technology has played a key role in the turnaround of cities like New York and London, and has certainly proven to be a key driver of growth for Singapore. In recent times, we have seen the development of future technologies like Leap Motion gesturing, Oculus Virtual Reality, Boston Dynamics' BigDog, Bitcoin, 3-D Printing, Bloom Energy, driverless cars, drones and Google Glass, and the like. I am sure we can all imagine the application of these future technologies in one way or another in the coming years.

But there is a much bigger shift in the evolution of technology that will shape every aspect of development in the next 50 years for Singapore and cities around the world. John Kelly III, Senior Vice President and Director of IBM Research in his recent book, *Smart Machines: IBM's Watson and the Era of Cognitive Computing*,[9] wrote, "The changes that are coming over the next two decades will transform the way we live and work just as the computing revolution has transformed the human landscape over the past half century. At IBM, we call this the era of cognitive computing."

Cognitive computing put simply, brings to us, the power of human reasoning, cognition, and insight at a scale vastly greater than what a human can comprehend and manage.

This is where IBM Watson comes into play. It represents a new era of computing based on its ability to interact in natural language, process vast amounts of disparate forms of big data in particular, unstructured data in text form, and is able to learn from each interaction between man and machine.

I believe that Watson and Cognitive Computing can and will have immediate and significant impact on how work will be done, how decisions

---

[9] J. E. Kelly III and S. Hamm (2013), *Smart Machines: IBM's Watson and the Era of Cognitive Computing* (Columbia Business School Publishing), New York, NY: Columbia University Press.

will be made with better insights, how lives might be changed in every aspect — from the way diseases will be managed, to how treatment pathways will be more personalised, to how expertise in every field will be scaled to provide more insightful, evidence-based advice, to how interactions between governments and their citizens, and enterprises and their clients will be more engaging.

In fact, connected devices such as the mobile phone, tablet and the Internet of Things, infused with intelligence are already fast changing the way we perceive data, innovate and operate. Unprecedented amounts of data are being generated every second. The opportunity to mine insights from all of that data to tackle the bold challenges in the world is tremendous!

Now, imagine a Singapore where everyone had their own personal cognitive assistant in the form of a handheld device — smartphone, watch, glasses, ring, bracelet, and any design one might imagine from the James Bond movies. These personal cognitive assistants would learn about us, interact with us, and feed us with information that could very much save our lives. With a personal cognitive assistant, you could even receive an alert about a gas leak in your house!

The Future of Computing — Augmenting Human Intelligence

Right here and now, the journey into the future of cognitive computing has already begun.

IBM Watson already sees application in various sectors including healthcare, retail, tourism, education and finance, among others, to solve broad classes of problems. The successful development of cognitive computing will enhance our daily lives, amplify personal productivity and "intelligence," and drive a new era of global economic competitiveness and innovation.

To bring this into perspective, consider the example of processing clinical trials, which can be an arcane process — it is done manually, which involves sorting through patient records to ensure that proper matches are made. Can you imagine if clinicians could quickly "sift through" millions of pages of clinical trial and patient data to match patients with appropriate clinical trials within seconds? Well, with Watson, it can do just that and potentially help to save patients' lives.[10] In fact, the Mayo Clinic has recently announced that it will be using Watson to do clinical trial matching for their patients.[11] With the dawn of genomic medicine, doctors, with the help of Watson, will be able to attack cancer and other devastating diseases with treatments that are tailored to the patient's own DNA profile.

Imagine also, being able to dish out relevant financial advice to your customers with smart assistance that analyse large volumes of data, including research reports, product information and customer profiles in order to understand your customers' needs and weigh their financial options. At DBS Bank, Watson is being trained to assist relationship managers to become "smarter."[12]

Imagine too, a time when we can be trained by the best professors and practitioners in any field by interacting with a system like Watson that has been trained by the very best clinicians, capturing and learning their knowledge gained from years of experience. At the Cleveland Clinic, Watson is already being put to work in this regard.[13]

Imagine the future of computing a step further, to make man and machine reasoning together. In today's complex world, it is not so straightforward to find right and wrong answers, as they are based on facts and reasons. So, imagine if systems could help us construct arguments and build opinions on variety of complex subjects, help us debate an issue and present to us the pros and cons in real time, understanding natural language and with factual arguments. These debates could be on anything ranging from complex government policies to social and environment issues. There is no end to the possibilities.

Don't get me wrong. I do not foresee a situation where machines would play the same cognitive role as humans. Instead, I encourage you to look at

---

[10] IBM (2013, October 18), MD Anderson Taps IBM Watson to Power "Moon Shots" Mission Aimed at Ending Cancer, Starting with Leukemia (Press Release). Retrieved February 24, 2015 from http://www-03.ibm.com/press/us/en/pressrelease/42214.wss.

[11] IBM (2014, September 8), Mayo Clinic and IBM Task Watson to Improve Clinical Trial Research (Press Release). Retrieved February 24, 2015 from https://www-03.ibm.com/press/us/en/pressrelease/44754.wss.

[12] IBM (2014, January 9), DBS Bank Engages IBM's Watson to Achieve Next Generation Client Experience (Press Release). Retrieved February 24, 2015 from http://www-03.ibm.com/press/us/en/pressrelease/42868.wss.

[13] IBM (2013, October 15), IBM Research Unveils Two New Watson Related Projects from Cleveland Clinic Collaboration (Press Release). Retrieved February 24, 2015 from http://www-03.ibm.com/press/us/en/pressrelease/42203.wss.

them as helpers. The opportunity here is not to replicate human cognition, but to use computers to help us reason over human-created data — our communications, documents, images and designs. By freeing the human from the most mundane and repetitive tasks, we will actually have the opportunity to maximise our logical reasoning capabilities, think more imaginatively and creatively and improve decision-making. The bold challenge in cognitive computing is for computers to augment human intelligence.

Imagine It, Decide It, Do It

In the next 50 years, the winner will be the one who is able to "make sense" of the massive volume of big data and add value by creating actionable insights. In the new era of computing, public service and government, as well as residents will be able to better understand how cities work and use that knowledge to make cities safer and more economically vibrant.

Going forward, Singapore will be competing with innovative cities like San Francisco (Silicon Valley), New York (Silicon Alley), London, Boston, Seoul, Hong Kong, Dubai and others. Innovation and speed is of the essence.

Singapore has a unique opportunity to be the world's living laboratory for developing new technologies and capabilities that takes us into the future of cognitive, now. I believe that PM Lee's Smart Nation initiative in particular would help drive brownfield and greenfield domain innovations. This gives Singapore the opportunity to lead the world in the use of Data & Analytics to improve people's lives by building ecosystems of public and private big data users that spur innovation, creating new national and industrial capabilities.

We must first train our future leaders and equip them with the latest technological skills to solve problems of tomorrow.[14] This includes our ageing workforce and closing their skills gaps to keep them relevant to Singapore's growth plans. We must institutionalise policies that protect intellectual property rights. We must invest in research and development, and promote entrepreneurship and the exchange of technology. We must build a thriving ecosystem of innovative, forward thinking start-ups and

[14] National University of Singapore (2014, October 14), IBM and National University of Singapore Partner to Offer Watson Cognitive Systems Education in Southeast Asia (Press Release). Retrieved February 24, 2015 from http://news.nus.edu.sg/press-releases/8216-ibm-and-national-university-of-singapore-partner-to-offer-watsoncognitive-systems-education-in-southeast-asia.

enterprises both private and public. We must continue to build on the strengths of a strong, trusting and empowered relationship between government and citizens.

As we turn the page on the last 50 years and look towards the future, my wish is that Singapore will emerge as a beacon for the evolution of future societies, infused with cognitive capabilities. Even more importantly, I wish for Singaporeans to remember our heritage and surge on with a continued respect for diversity, our Singaporean "can-do" attitude and a sense of ownership that will spell greater success for Singapore, our home.

The future forward begins now. We only need to imagine it, to decide it and to do it.

Local Politics, Global Townships

Zulkifli Baharudin
Political Observer

Singapore was never meant to be. But by a stroke of extraordinary luck and genius, we were blessed with exceptional people who guided our journey from a sleeping village to a bustling metropolis today.

For a vulnerable city-state without natural resources, our fortunes will forever be tied inextricably to the external world.

Singapore's biggest challenge lies ahead and nothing we have ever learnt can prepare us adequately for it. Ironically, we can find our place in the world only by navigating and connecting ourselves even more vigorously to the global world, guided by the same stars that have led us here.

As in the past 50 years, Singapore will go through major shocks because as a small city-state we will not be able to buffer ourselves against the vagaries of the bigger world.

How we respond to these shocks and the choices we make amidst a more diverse society will determine our future.

However, I will choose to dwell on a more optimistic scenario as we are somewhat programmed to think about the future in a more linear fashion as improving the future is what many human beings continue to live for. The future that I have envisaged is also based on the positive assumption that current efforts to reform the education system and initiatives to revolutionise the workplace with more emphasis on skills and knowledge as opposed to one based on pure academic qualifications will bear fruit. However, it is the cultural change towards education and the workplace that will be the primary determinant whether we succeed in transforming Singapore and be future ready for the new world. Besides, when faced with a major challenge, Singaporeans have been shaped to be pragmatic in making choices that will ultimately be guided by certain priorities that will ensure our survival and prosperity.

It is for this reason that I choose to take a more optimistic view in predicting what life will be like 50 years from now.

Like all developed nations, the trend that will have the biggest impact on Singapore will be our internal demographics and the global technological revolution. This will have a serious impact on the way we live, work and play.

Hopefully, if we are able to deal with these challenges well and plan wisely for the future, we can envision a day when Singapore becomes one of the most cherished global cities on earth.

While there are undoubtedly negative consequences of technology, the most positive view is that technology will continue to be a liberating force for men and women in the modern world. Singapore's natural adaptation to technology will enable it to transform the island into one of the most wired places in the world.

Unlike the past, a new generation of citizens, whose priorities include a sustainable high quality of life and a desire to balance between moral and spiritual aspects of life, will provide new colour and shape to our society.

The demand for greater participation will mean more bottom-up initiatives as opposed to top-down. New political norms will emerge with people becoming more deeply involved in the process and thus permanently shape the nature of local politics in the future.

Increasingly, Singapore will come to terms with severe demographic issues. At the risk of being one of the oldest populations on earth, a pragmatic population will learn to welcome immigration to rejuvenate Singapore to become a bigger, younger and a permanently immigrant society. This will have serious implications on the way we live, work and play. Immigration will change the colour and tone of our society, making the ethnic-based classifications we see today totally irrelevant. More than that, it will shape just about every aspect of our lives.

The transformation will not be as straightforward as political tensions between these constituencies will both scar and shape the norms and consensus for the future.

HDB living, which has been the centre of all of our social and economic activity, will be transformed to accommodate the trends arising from a new population, technological revolution, and above all, a new way of life as well as accommodating to the new political realities. This is where most of the far-reaching changes to our daily lives will take place. Local politics will be increasingly drawn to contesting demands for ageing in place and other societal norms brought about by a growing and more influential immigrant population.

Unlike the present where HDB estates are essentially satellite residential communities, a new Singapore will be divided into specialist clusters and corridors of excellence and innovation. The areas around Changi for example will be transformed into a self-contained and increasingly independent aviation city; Alexandra and Ayer Rajah will emerge as a global technological and innovation hub. One common feature of these global estates is their connectivity with other global cities in the world. They operate as part of a global ecosystem and professionally far removed from their neighbours in nearby towns who are similarly linked to other global ecosystems of their own. Here, Singaporeans, many of whom operate from their homes, provide a whole range of sophisticated services to the world over.

As people live and work in their homes, cars will become scarce. Public transportation will cater to all commuting needs. All essential requirements of living will be available in these self-sufficient communities that have complete healthcare and education facilities as well as public and recreational amenities. There will be little need to travel outside the cluster.

Politically, the challenge ahead is not what and how we envisage our future to be, but how we manage the conflicts and tensions that will arise as we weigh the priorities and compromises needed to realise this vision for our future. A more educated population will necessarily demand a greater say about everything that affects their lives. Independent global citizens whose livelihoods are increasingly determined by forces outside Singapore will make political governance complicated.

The participatory process in decision-making will have to be exponentially different. Lines between public and private sector developers will be blurred for building such a complex and integrated living environment. Rules for governing and managing such an arrangement will require new institutions essentially for self-regulation. A more independent community will be ready to manage their own affairs even in handling matters such as local revenues, taxation and even education that have been unchallenged for a long time as a domain of the government. Decisions by distant bureaucrats will not fit into this new reality. These new communities will demand new political institutions that are more responsive and apt in managing their lives. Direct election of their representatives to a national parliament will feature as a new political model. Familiar institutions like the Town Councils, Community Development Councils and Residents' Committees will occupy only the annals of our historical records.

Inevitably, the journey that we will have to take in moving towards such a future will require a change in mindset of an entire generation who are now in their early teens. For now, nothing that they are preoccupied with can prepare them adequately for such a task as where schools are still teaching them more about the past on the assumption that this will prepare them for the future. Instead, the focus must be to predict the future and prepare them for what is ahead. In a world where information is free, education cannot be about rewarding those who know only the facts.

This is where schools will see some of the biggest changes in the entire history of Singapore where teachers become facilitators and where the real teaching takes place at the various centres as they serve as incubators of learning and teaching. Students will learn from working professionals. They will be assessed more by their peers and professional mentors than by administrator-teachers. Continuous learning and teaching will be a permanent feature in the specialised communities as they become extremely crucial in the survival and sustainability of the global clusters. The responsibility for educating the young and continuously training all members of the community will truly be a shared responsibility.

The future that I have sketched is not in my view utopian but within the realm of possibility. But this scenario will not happen without painstakingly transforming aspects of our future living environment and successfully managing the complex process along the way. But this requires a common ideological consensus to be forged and a willingness on the part of every single member of the community to make the necessary yet potentially painful choices. This will require personal sacrifice never before expected of us.

But most of all will require all of us to be exceptional just like our forefathers. We have to be brave to take the leap of faith, trusting only our instincts and those of our fellow countrymen on this same journey. The only thing that can deny us from achieving the greatest success is in not believing in our own destiny.

With some luck, the same stars will emerge to guide us but once again, it will require the ordinary amongst us to each believe that we can lead extraordinary lives in the transforming and making of a new Singapore.

Sustainable Singapore: Taking the Long Term View

Vivian Balakrishnan
Minister for Environment and Water Resources, Singapore

When Singapore had independence thrust upon us in 1965, we suddenly became a city with no hinterland, few natural resources and potentially high unemployment. Development was an existential challenge. Fortunately, our pioneering leaders opted for a model of sustainable development, way before it was fashionable to be green. From the start, they believed that growth was a means to a loftier end — a higher quality of life for all Singaporeans. The first tree planted by founding Prime Minister Mr. Lee Kuan Yew in 1963, the Keep Singapore Clean campaign launched in 1968, the establishment of the Anti-Pollution Unit in the Prime Minister's Office in 1970 and the Clean Air Act passed in 1971 were key milestones and stand testament to our commitment to protect Singapore's environment. Mr. Lee strongly believed that "unlike other cities, which have the space to allow the better-off to distance themselves and create clean and green suburbs, Singapore's size forced us to work, play and reside in one small island. We do not distinguish between the affluent and the less wealthy neighbourhoods, but maintain a clean and gracious environment for rich and poor alike."[1] These choices have shaped Singapore into what it is today — a clean and green city in a garden, with a secure water supply.

[1] Lee K. Y. (August 2000), Address by then Senior Minister Lee Kuan Yew at the Nature Conservancy's Asian Pacific Council Inaugural Meeting.

In the next 50 years, Singapore will have to develop amidst global environmental changes. A key concern is the increasing strain on natural resources and the environment due to the increased global consumption of water, energy, food and consumer goods as a result of rapid economic development, increased urbanisation and a burgeoning middle class. Global real gross domestic product (GDP) today is about five times the level recorded in 1965.[2] If this pace of growth continues for the next 50 years, global GDP will reach US$250 trillion or more. This rapid pace of economic growth will largely be driven by urbanised cities. Over half of the world's population now live in cities and these cities account for more than 80% of global GDP.[3] This trend is likely to continue and intensify over the next five decades. More and more cities will grow in developing nations and, crucially, we will see a growing middle class in emerging markets. The McKinsey Global Institute (MGI) forecasts that the middle class in emerging countries will double its share of global consumption from one-third to two-thirds by 2050.[4]

The increased rate of environmental degradation and higher emissions of pollutants due to more production and consumption will exacerbate the pace of climate change. Singapore is especially vulnerable to climate changes as a low-lying island city in the tropics — we will be adversely affected by rising sea levels, rising temperatures and more extreme weather occurrences like intense rainfall or prolonged dry spells.

Singapore is a microcosm of these global trends and as we grow our economy, we need to be increasingly cognisant of environmental constraints. While our long history of long-term planning to manage our resources and our environment puts us in a good position to manage our natural resources, we must recognise that these came about from deliberate public policies and not by chance. Likewise, our future, and those of our children, should not be left to chance. This is evident in the following examples.

---

[2] Global GDP was estimated to be around US$50 trillion in 2015, based on the International Monetary Fund's World Economic Outlook forecast of 3.8% growth in 2015. Global GDP in 1965 was US$9.1 trillion.

[3] World Economic Forum (2014, August), A Report of the Global Agenda Council on Competitiveness: The Competitiveness of Cities.

[4] R. Dobbs et al. (2014, March), *Urban World: Mapping the Economic Power of Cities*. New York: McKinsey Global Institute. Retrieved February 25, 2015 from http://www.mckinsey.com/insights/urbanization/urban_world.

Water and Solid Waste Management

We have always been obsessed with water security. The Independence of Singapore Agreement included a guarantee for the supply of water from Johore under 1961 and 1962 agreements. Since the first Water Master Plan in 1972, we have diversified our water sources with the implementation of the Four National Taps strategy. The First and Second Taps of local catchment water and imported water are dependent on rainfall. For the First Tap, we have expanded our local water catchment to two-thirds of Singapore's land area and increased the number of reservoirs from 3 in the 1960s to 17 today. This makes us one of the few cities in the world to harvest urban stormwater on such a large scale. PUB has plans to further expand the catchment area further in the long term.

Planning ahead is as crucial today as it was in 1965. With a projected doubling of water demand from the current 400 million gallons per day (mgd), we need to continue to plan and build capacity ahead of demand growth, and put in place a robust, diversified and sustainable water supply. Our Third Tap of NEWater is produced by reclaiming used water to close our water loop.[5] The Fourth Tap, desalinated water, is today produced by our two desalination plants which are among Asia's largest seawater reverse-osmosis plants. Both NEWater and desalination are weather-resilient sources that provide a buffer of safety in times of dry spells. Today, NEWater and desalinated water can meet up to 55% of our water demand. We plan to increase this to 80% by 2060.

Our strategy of Four National Taps, coupled with Singapore's Deep Tunnel Sewerage System for collecting and conveying used water, illustrates how long-term planning has helped Singapore overcome a strategic vulnerability. In fact, a strategic vulnerability has become a global opportunity for our water companies.

Like water management, solid waste management is another area where Singapore's limited space for landfill means that we need to plan for the long term and constantly think of innovative solutions. This started as early as the 1970s, when we decided to use incineration plants to reduce waste volumes by up to 90%. In addition to reducing waste volumes, our

[5] NEWater is produced by further purifying treated used water from the Water Reclamation Plants (WRP). At the NEWater factory, treated used water goes through a 3-stage process of microfiltration, reverse osmosis and ultra-violet disinfection, making it ultra clean.

four incineration plants also supply around 1.3 terawatt-hours (TWh) of sustainable energy per year, enough to power 220,000 households.

In 2014, Singapore generated about 7.51 million tonnes of waste. This burden will grow over the next 50 years with growth and rising incomes, making it crucial for Singapore to close the waste loop. NEA is therefore exploring how incineration bottom ash (IBA)[6] from Singapore's incineration plants can be re-used for various applications without endangering public health such as road construction, concrete for buildings, and land reclamation.[7] This effort will help conserve space at Semakau Landfill — our only landfill — which is projected to last us till 2035 and beyond.

As we build our water and solid waste management infrastructure in the coming years, there will also be much scope to realise process synergies in the energy-water-waste nexus. NEA and PUB are planning to co-locate a new Integrated Waste Management Facility (IWMF) with the upcoming WRP at Tuas to optimise the processes at both plants. For instance, the IWMF's incineration processes could supply energy to the WRP, and the treated used water could be used to cool IWMF's processes. These will be completed by the first half of the 2020s.

Though built out of necessity, our planners and engineers have designed our infrastructure to not just meet Singapore's growing needs but to also ensure an excellent quality of life for Singaporeans. For example, PUB's Active, Beautiful, Clean Waters (ABC Waters) programme seeks to transform Singapore's drains, canals and reservoirs beyond their traditional functions of drainage and water storage into beautiful streams, rivers and lakes, turning them into focal points for recreational and community activities. Besides bringing people closer to water, the programme creates opportunities for them to enjoy and bond with water, so that they can better appreciate and cherish this precious resource. With innovative design and attention to operational details, Semakau Landfill is a place which is clean and scenic, with thriving mangroves. An April 2007 article

---

[6] IBA is one of the main byproducts of incineration plants, comprising the non-combustible residue of combustion in the incinerator. The other is incineration fly ash (IFA), which is the fine residue that rises with flue gases. IFA is more toxic as it often contains high concentrations of heavy metals, dioxins and furans.

[7] Chemilink, a private engineering company, is test-bedding the combining of IBA with marine clay to produce a material which can safely be used for land reclamation. This is being test-bedded at Semakau Landfill.

in the *New Scientist* even dubbed Semakau Landfill the "Garbage of Eden."[8] These are spaces for Singaporeans to enjoy, and to appreciate the importance of investing and maintaining a clean and healthy environment. This is a legacy for future generations to continue building on.

Climate Change

Climate change is another challenge that we are working to address. Singapore contributes less than 0.2% to global emissions and we have limited access to alternative energy options. But we have and will continue to play our part by taking steps to reduce our carbon emissions. Singapore is also acting now to ensure that we are resilient to the potential impacts of climate change. We have developed a Resilience Framework to guide our future adaptation plans. We have also established the Centre for Climate Research Singapore within the Meteorological Services Singapore to build capabilities in projecting future climate change and examining possible impacts on Singapore. Meanwhile, we have already started some adaptation efforts. We are protecting our coasts against long-term sea level rises — minimum reclamation levels have been raised by one metre since 2011. onwards. We are also addressing flood risks with a holistic "source-pathway-receptor" approach, working on flood protection along both the drains and canals ("pathways") stormwater travels through, as well as areas which generate stormwater runoff ("source") and potential flooding areas ("receptors").

Need for Everyone to Play Their Part

Beyond the Government's role in setting policies to improve Singapore's environmental management, the effort to conserve the environment must involve participation by individuals and organisations. There are many initiatives led by non-governmental organisations which exhort everyone to play their part to protect the environment. For instance, the Singapore Environment Council's ENVision exercise encourages conservation of the environment through daily actions like saving energy and water, reducing and recycling solid waste, or using greener forms of transport to reduce carbon emissions.

---

[8] E. Bland (2007, April 12), Island of Trash or the "Garbage of Eden"?, *New Scientist*. Retrieved February 25, 2015 from http://www.newscientist.com/article/mg19425991.600-island-of-trash-or-the-garbage-of-eden.html.

In 2065, I hope to see a Singapore where individuals are environmentally-conscious in their daily lives, and where companies incorporate the "triple bottom line" — People, Planet, Profits — into their operations. There has been much progress over the last 50 years, and more can and will be done by individuals, businesses and NGOs to make a positive difference.

The Future of Sustainability and Singapore

Our experiences in balancing limited natural resources with a growing economy can inform the solutions to global environmental challenges. First, innovative solutions can provide growth opportunities, turning environmental vulnerabilities into strengths. For instance, Singapore now has a robust water industry ecosystem, with 150 water companies and 26 R&D centres. Our waste management companies, such as Keppel-Seghers, also export their solutions to other countries. Second, in order to be innovative, it is necessary to grow capabilities and talent with both vision and know-how. For example, PUB's Academy@Waterhub and the Aquarius Programme aim to groom future leaders in the water industry, and our water research institutes here are world-renowned. Third, there is a need to engage the public actively. We already adopt an approach in Singapore where environmental sustainability is not just about what the Government can do, but is about what everyone can do. Looking beyond our borders, Singapore's efforts to increase awareness and dialogue of urban sustainability issues are embodied in the biennial World Cities Summit, Singapore International Water Week and CleanEnviro Summit Singapore conferences which bring together a broad spectrum of business leaders and policymakers.

Singapore's efforts on environmental sustainability, past and future, are building a liveable and sustainable home for people in Singapore. Today, the success of the vision of our pioneers has bequeathed a clean and green city with clean skies and sparkling waters. This is also why Singaporeans cherish our city and call it home. Over the next 50 years, we will have to work hard to build upon this reputation, and to be a city where people and companies grow roots because of its liveability and vibrancy, which offer opportunities for a high quality of life. Singapore's environment is and will be one of our most important competitive advantages, and part of a virtuous cycle which will provide the momentum to build a better Singapore.

Refashioning Singapore's Relationship with Its Hinterland

Manu Bhaskaran
CEO
Centennial Asia Advisors

Introduction

Singapore's economy has prospered since independence, powered by a dynamic manufacturing sector and the clustering of activities which make it a leading centre of finance, transportation, business headquarters and trading for the region around it and in some respects for the world. As we look at Singapore's next 50 years, this essay examines the potential challenges to Singapore's status as a regional and global hub and what Singapore could do in response.

In essence, there are substantial opportunities emerging which Singapore can profitably exploit but the challenges are growing as well. The expanding flows of goods, services, capital and people created by the rapid growth within China, India and ASEAN are huge positives. So is the widening integration among all these countries which will allow trade, financial and people flows to grow even more rapidly than GDP.

However, challenges are also real: in particular, competitors such as Hong Kong and Bangkok appear better positioned to create large, dynamic hinterlands which will give their hubs greater scale than Singapore. Singapore needs to look at ways it can work with its immediate neighbours to substantially expand the immediate regional hinterland around it. This necessitates a bolder strategy to ensure that Singapore's hub position remains competitive.

Considerable Opportunities from Asia's Expanding Economies, Synergies from Integration

The transformational growth of China and India is well documented and will create huge new flows of trade, investment and people that will benefit Singapore's hub. Another positive factor is how Asian countries are integrating at an increasing pace, yielding synergies that will provide an additional boost. The Asian Development Bank (ADB) estimates that the number of free trade agreements (FTAs) in Asia has surged from 54 in 2000 to 498 in 2014. Of note, while these FTAs and region-wide initiatives such as the ASEAN Economic Community (AEC), the Regional Comprehensive Economic Partnership (RCEP) and the Trans-Pacific Partnership (TPP) garner much attention, there are other modes of integration operating as well. These include sub-regional efforts encompassing just a part of a region such as the Greater Mekong Sub-Region (GMS) as well as the creation of cross-border economic entities such as the Iskandar-Singapore initiative and the more spontaneous, cross-border trading that one increasingly finds, for example, between border regions of Thailand and Laos. All these are supported by more projects to expand physical connectivity such as the Singapore-Kuala Lumpur and the Bangkok-Kunming high speed rail lines. All these point toward increased cooperation and integration among economies in Asia.

The Challenges to Singapore's Status as a Regional Hub Will Grow

While some of these sub-regional integration efforts are likely to be positive for the region as a whole, they could pose a challenge for Singapore in the future. As other Asian cities such as Hong Kong and Bangkok assemble and integrate into considerably larger immediate hinterlands than ever before, they will gain economies of scale and scope which could exceed Singapore's, especially given that there are no current plans to develop an integrated sub-region around Singapore on the same scale as Hong Kong and Bangkok potentially will have. It is instructive therefore to look at the Pearl River Delta (PRD) and GMS to better understand this potential challenge.

The Pearl River Delta (PRD) has emerged as one of the major concentrations of economic dynamism in China encompassing major cities such as Hong Kong, Guangzhou, Shenzhen and Macau. What is now changing is a massive push to increase physical connectivity within the PRD while also promoting more seamless integration there by encouraging the flow of labour and capital. Connectivity projects such as the Hong Kong-Zhuhai-Macau Bridge and the PRD Rapid Transit (connecting every major urban centre in the PRD) have already been built and will be supplemented by a web of high speed rail links and multiple expressways over the coming decade.

The physical infrastructure push is strengthened through policy initiatives to encourage more integration within the PRD. Hong Kong has greatly benefited from its Closer Economic Cooperation Agreement with China, an agreement which is now expanding to include integration efforts such as the Shenzhen-Hong Kong Economic Cooperation initiative which covers areas such as financial services, hi-tech and high-end R&D and transportation up to 2020. As we progress into the 2020s and 2030s, the PRD will be elevated from simply a destination for relocation of activities from expensive Hong Kong into a well-integrated economic zone with Hong Kong as its epicentre, substantially changing the value proposition that Hong Kong offers.

Bangkok, similarly, will be at the centre of the GMS, which consists of the two southernmost provinces of China, Cambodia, Laos, Myanmar, Vietnam and Thailand, have been growing rapidly. With its stated goals of strengthening connectivity and achieving economic efficiency through the facilitation of cross-border movements and integration of national markets, bridges and rail links have or are currently being constructed, and cross-border investments are flowing into the emerging economies of the GMS.

Bangkok has the most to gain from the huge growth that the GMS integration promises. It can leverage off Thailand's existing close links with the other GMS economies. For example, Thailand is one of Myanmar's strongest business partners, with over US$7.5 billion invested in Myanmar or almost half the total foreign investment Myanmar received in the 1988–2009 period. The International Monetary Fund projects the Cambodia-Laos-Myanmar-Vietnam component of the GMS to be the fastest growing ASEAN countries in coming years. Bangkok will be serving an immediate hinterland with a current population of 326 million, which is slightly more than that of the US, this would attract strong interest from MNCs that are keen on participating in this growing market.

Bangkok's global scale airport, its major port and the 10,600 km of roads for the three economic corridors of the GMS place Bangkok as the principal gateway to access the GMS. As Thai labour costs increase with growing prosperity, firms will outsource production to the GMS countries but retain high-value activities in Bangkok, and so increasing the attractiveness of Bangkok's cluster and encouraging foreign multinational companies to also concentrate more activities there.

With immediate hinterlands combining large populations with regions of high growth, Hong Kong and Bangkok will increasingly have a critical mass of high growth engines that Singapore will not. Already, Singapore's ranking as an attractive regional hub is being questioned. In a 2011 report of Asia-Pacific Regional Headquarters done by the European Union Chamber of Commerce in China, it was found that European multinational companies rated Shanghai, Hong Kong and Singapore as 1st, 2nd and 3rd respectively with Bangkok a distant 9th. One reason why Singapore slipped below Hong Kong and Shanghai was its distance from China, a huge hinterland. Over time, this disadvantage will grow.

Singapore's status of being the leading air hub could be compromised as well. While Singapore leads both Hong Kong and Bangkok in terms of the number of flights, Hong Kong International Airport leads in terms of the number of passengers handled as of 2013. As the GMS and PRD develop to a greater extent, a greater flow of people and air cargo would be expected, which could prove key in the respective developments of Bangkok and Hong Kong.

Consequently, Singapore Must Evolve New Strategies to Build an Immediate Regional Hinterland

Singapore should consider the creation of a Southern Malacca Economic Region (SMER) together with its immediate neighbours Malaysia and Indonesia, to maintain its long-term relevance in the global economy. The SMER will encompass Iskandar, Johore, Malacca, parts of the Riau Archipelago, Singapore, and parts of the Sumatran mainland, linking

Singapore, Malaysia and Indonesia, giving Singapore an immediate hinterland of 14.8 million people in an area of 115,144 km^2 and a GDP of almost US$300 billion. This will help Singapore to not just become a global city but also achieve development as a regional leader with sufficient market size to back its economic development.

Through integration, the main benefit for Singapore would be to solidify its position as a regional hub and to be able to attain economies of scale. Singapore can thus act as a centre for expansion. Local businesses often bemoan the small market size in Singapore, which results in a lower return to innovation. If such businesses are able to tap into the additional 10 million people in the SMER, this could possibly lead to a greater incentive for innovation. Multinational companies could also be persuaded to invest in the SMER by locating their regional headquarters in Singapore while outsourcing production to more cost effective areas like Malaysia or Indonesia. Given Singapore's excellent standing in world rankings, especially the World Bank Doing Business Index, this should not be difficult. Rapidly developing areas like Iskandar Malaysia could be a production base, with imports and exports handled through Singapore due to its status as a free port, lowering cost.

While the economic advantages of forming SMER are clear, political and policy challenges in the form of ethnic relations and divergent economic philosophies would no doubt inhibit the creation of the SMER. Thus, Singapore has to work with its neighbours to find ways to overcome these obstacles. The recent blossoming of Singapore's relations with Malaysia which has produced extensive cooperation to promote cross-border integration between the Iskandar Region in Johore and Singapore shows that the political will needed to promote integration in this part of the world can be found given the right leadership.

In conclusion, Singapore's regional hub status will face more challenges in future. To mitigate such threats, Singapore needs to constantly relook its strategies towards engaging with its neighbours. Securing Malaysia and Indonesia's cooperation in the creation of an immediate economic hinterland would help safeguard Singapore's long-term competitive position as a regional and global business and finance hub.

SG100@2065

Chan Chun Sing
Minister for Social and Family Development
Second Minister for Defence, Singapore

It will be a significant achievement by any measure if Singapore beats the odds of history and celebrates SG100 as a sovereign country. Few expected us to survive and thrive as an independent nation 50 years ago. Fewer should expect our survival and success to be replicated effortlessly in the next 50 years.

Our survival and success will depend on our speed and ability to adapt to the uncertainties and emerging forces that will shape the road ahead. These forces will impact the five fundamentals that are minimally essential for our continued success — security, opportunity creation, a strong social compact, a common identity and leadership.

Security

Security — defined as our ability to safeguard ourselves from existential threats and to access resources (e.g. water, energy and material) — is essential for our survival. The age-old dictum — that what we cannot defend is not ours — will always remain true. However, the existential survival of a small state like ours is an eternal challenge. Weakness invites predators, while success attracts others to covet what is ours.

Singapore as a small state will also need to navigate a new world order by 2065, where a number of major powers such as the US, China, and India will be jostling for influence and control on the world stage. A number of regional powers will also emerge to compete for regional influence. We have never been freed from big power dynamics and it will remain so. Our challenge thus lies in navigating the contests of the bigger powers carefully to maintain our sovereignty, secure our interests and access opportunities. Even if the region's security architecture matures, we must maintain the wherewithal to defend what is ours.

Barring significant breakthrough in solar or nuclear energies as safe, sustainable and dependable alternatives, our age-old need to secure energy supplies would remain. Independence from external water supplies must also be achieved by 2065, as our second Water Agreement with Malaysia would have expired by 2061. However, water security is very much dependent on our energy security. To survive, we need to continue securing these lifelines. To thrive, we must maintain and protect our links with the rest of the world, which is our hinterland.

Opportunity Creation

Beyond the geopolitical forces mentioned above, the combined forces of technological advancements, rapid information exchange, and the consequent ease by which increasingly fragmented groups can mobilise also suggest that the future international order in 2065 is likely to be more fragmented. An increasing number of smaller independent political entities will emerge, as they seek to be unshackled from large and lumbering political entities. Coupled with the pace of global urbanisation, these developments will result in cities being the main organising entity for competition. Cities which adapt most quickly to the changing international conditions will best survive the competition.

All these present both opportunities and challenges for Singapore. On one hand, the ability to embed ourselves in the emerging network of high-performance cities will create new opportunities for us. However, these smaller and more agile political entities will also intensify the competition for us. Many of them may be in our region too.

To thrive, Singapore must continue to create opportunities for talent to flourish. This means that we have to continually create the conditions to retain, attract and groom talent, regardless of origin, to contribute to our survival and success. We must engender a positive cycle where talent and success beget more talent and success. To enable this, we need a culture of continuous policy and business innovation. We will also need to embrace values that reward talent and hard work, instead of personal connections and ancestry.

Strong Social Compact

While we strive to retain and attract local and global talent to contribute to our success, our social compact also needs to be strengthened so that society remains cohesive in good times as well as tough times. This will be more challenging in future because economic development and intensifying competition from present and future cities will quite easily widen the opportunity gap between different groups in our society. It is also challenging because the more established a society becomes, the more ossified its systems can be and this will in turn exacerbate the differential access to opportunities. Hopefully, this challenge will not be compounded by racial or religious fault lines.

Ossified social systems usually end up with sudden catastrophic discontinuities that we must avoid. Hence, it is imperative that we build a society where all its members are willing to share the fruits of success and shoulder the burden of difficult times together. To build such a society, we must first endeavour to keep our society mobile, with an emphasis on rewarding effort and talent regardless of prior privileges due to inheritance or connections. While outcomes and access to opportunities can never be fully equalised, we must keep pathways continuously open for those who try, regardless of background or origin.

Secondly, we must also engender in those who have succeeded an appreciation of society's contribution to one's success. This must in turn translate into a sense of responsibility and care for the less privileged. This will help bind society together even if economic forces inevitably widen the disparities. It will also distinguish us from winner-takes-all societies.

Identity

Without a sense of national identity, there is no basis for the desired social compact that we have just discussed. However, as talent becomes increasingly mobile, we can expect more and more people to question whether the concept of national identity is already outdated; and whether one's identity can be derived from business corporations and personal causes instead.

In light of this, it may be increasingly challenging to attract Singaporeans and non-Singaporeans alike to stay and contribute when the going gets tough and opportunities are not as abundant as before. It remains to be seen if the current and future generations of Singaporeans can emulate the spirit of our Pioneer Generation, who identified with this country and were determined to rebuild this place for the next generation even when the chips were down.

In order for the successful to contribute to Singapore through thick and thin regardless of whether they are here or abroad, they must be inspired by the set of values that define the Singapore Identity, i.e. multiracialism, meritocracy, incorruptibility, justice, opportunities for all, rule of law, and country before self. These values must remain the cornerstones of our success and inspire generations to come. We must also aim to inspire a wider group of friends and supporters beyond our shores to support our continued survival.

Leadership

In a future environment characterised by complex geopolitical relations, intensifying economic competition and globally mobile talent, the ability to continuously bring forth strong leadership teams to harness the talents and efforts of our people will be critical for our success. Many better-endowed countries have floundered due to their inability to put together a strong leadership team that is able to do justice to the talents and efforts of its people.

The evergreen characteristics of a good leadership team remains — committed, competent, connected to the people, clean, cohesive and compassionate. Commitment to the Singapore cause rather than any personal agenda is vital. We need leaders who believe and can mobilise our people to believe that we can beat the odds of history. We need both the leadership and our people to remain cohesive, in order to take decisive actions to seize opportunities and avoid pitfalls. Our agility will determine our destiny.

It cannot be taken as a given that good leaders and strong leadership teams will naturally emerge. Even individually talented leaders need to be groomed to form cohesive leadership teams. Like every sector, talented and committed individuals will be attracted to serve in an environment that recognises and respects their contributions. Societies that foster a positive environment stand a better chance in attracting such individuals to come forward to serve. A negative political environment, once set in, will only attract power-hungry and self-serving leaders. This ruins society's ethos and perpetuates the negativity. We must seek to be different.

Conclusion

Future-casting is perilous. The only constant is change. If one can get it roughly correct and not precisely wrong, one should already be congratulated. Even if we achieve the five necessary enablers mentioned above, the question of whether they are sufficient for 2065 remains. Wars, pandemics and technology may fundamentally change the way societies are organised. Our challenge is thus to remain agile and continuously adaptable, so that Singapore and its values live on.

The Future of Singapore's Ageing Population: Ageing as Asset and Adaptation

David Chan
Professor of Psychology
Director, Behavioural Sciences Institute
Singapore Management University

The public discussion on Singapore population challenges has rightly focused on issues of liveability and quality of life due to the mismatch between population growth and infrastructure support. The strong negative emotions experienced and expressed in the population debate, particularly those that occurred since the release of the 2013 Population White Paper (NPTD, 2013), have surfaced many deeper issues for analysis. Examples include sustainable economic models, urban planning, manpower management, fair employment practices, social mobility and social cohesion (Chan, 2012, 2013a). Compared to these issues, much less attention has been given to the analysis of the so-called "ageing problem." This is somewhat surprising given that a rapidly ageing population is the starting point for arguments over economic and social issues concerning immigration.

In the discussion on population challenges, ageing is presented as a liability, primarily economically and probably also socially. But can ageing be an economic and social asset? More basically, how should ageing be conceptualised?

The conceptualisation of ageing is of fundamental importance to the population discussion. If we do not conceptualise ageing adequately, it will lead to inadequate inferences about what really matters in ageing issues and the related population matters. This in turn will lead to inadequate policies or programmes designed to address the purported problems of an ageing population. Thus, the facts and perceptions of ageing are practically important because they create both constraints and opportunities for the effectiveness of age-related public policies in virtually all domain areas.

In this article, I argue that the population discussion has overemphasised the negatives and neglected the positives of ageing. I propose that we replace the term "ageing problem" with "ageing issues" and construe ageing issues as an adaptation process involving all stakeholders including individuals and communities. More details on this perspective of ageing issues are available in Chan et al. (2014).

Beyond the Old-age Dependency Ratio

In the Population White Paper and related official statements on Singapore's ageing population, a central focus was on the adverse consequences that would result from increasing old-age dependency ratio for Singaporeans if there are no mitigation effects from procreation and immigration. The old-age dependency ratio is operationally defined as the ratio of the number of working Singaporeans (from 15 to 64 years old) to the number of older Singaporeans aged 65 and above. The conceptualisation is based on the assumption that it is appropriate to bifurcate Singaporeans into two groups with those below the age of 65 having to economically support those above it. The validity of this assumption is questionable on both economic and social grounds. It incorrectly assumes that upon reaching 65 years of age, Singaporeans are no longer able to contribute to society at large and will suddenly and automatically become a burden and dependent on those who are younger.

The age of 65 years is one of many arbitrary cut-offs that could be selected to indicate economic contribution and dependency. The official retirement age is a function of national and organisational employment policies, which can be changed. In addition, actual permanent retirement from any employment and economically productive activity is partly dependent on the individual's choice and circumstances, some of which may be influenced by the prevailing social norms and policies. In reality, many Singaporeans aged 65 and above are economically active and contribute either directly or indirectly, as well as significantly, to the vibrancy of Singapore's economy, while many aged 25 years or younger are still in the schooling phase of life, and not in a position to provide financial support to family members.

Moving forward in the population projections, older Singaporeans will become more highly educated and have a longer life expectancy. Together with advances in technology and medical science, adoption of healthy lifestyles, and re-design of work, it is highly likely that post-65-year-olds will be in sufficiently good health for a longer period of time, thereby allowing older Singaporeans to make productive and significant contributions, both economically and socially.

Older Singaporeans should have opportunities to stay well integrated into both the workplace, at their pace and in their chosen area of work, and the society, in various voluntary endeavours. Each generation of older Singaporeans will possess not only economic capital but also important social knowledge and skills related to history, culture and practical experiences that can be transferred to younger generations. These resources are valuable assets to society and contribute positively to social capital. When older Singaporeans are cast in more positive light, or have built strong family ties, intergenerational relations is enhanced and positive intergenerational transfers are more likely to occur, which in turn contributes to the development of social capital.

In short, population policy formulation and public discussion need to move away from a fixation on reducing the old-age dependency ratio and the conjecture that a high ratio will produce adverse consequences, while rethinking the current assumptions upon which the old-age conceptualisation perpetuates a counterproductive stereotype that ageing is inherently negative and incorrectly casts older Singaporeans in a negative light. This is counterproductive to addressing population challenges, and likely to harm intergenerational relations and negatively affect social capital.

In contrast to the negative framing of the concept of old-age dependency ratio and the underlying notion that constructs ageing as a liability, the view of older Singaporeans as an asset and valuable resource will lead to a different orientation towards social expenditure on the elderly. Social expenditure on the elderly should not be construed as a zero-sum cost or as the depletion of resources. This erroneous construal will lead to misallocation of resources and funds. Instead, it should be construed as a continuous investment in human resources, with efforts in enhancing health, work, community development and other elderly-focused initiatives regarded as strategic, goal-directed investment to enhance citizen wellbeing and developing intergenerational relations. This investment will have a positive multiplier effect that broadens and builds social capital (Chan, 2013b).

Mixed-use Infrastructure and Facilities

Facilities that are built to cater to the needs of the elderly and increase their wellbeing, such as senior activity and wellness centres, should be located within residential areas. This is consistent with "ageing in place" and it prevents social exclusion and increases social connectivity between elderly people and the rest of the population. However, wherever practically feasible, these facilities should be developed as part of a mixed-use infrastructure and facilities cluster as opposed to exclusively for elderly care. This will help prevent stigmatisation and isolation of the elderly and conflicts over land use in residential areas. The mixed-use and facility cluster should serve a complementary range of activities and services (e.g. childcare, senior activities, libraries, social enterprises, etc.) and enable accessibility to and foster interactions amongst different generations. These facilities could also be tailored to the specific needs of communities based on grassroots feedback, so as to create a sense of community ownership and belonging. In mixed-used facilities, elderly persons could take up work such as childcare duties and library services which may be employment or volunteer work.

Promote Social Interactions through Intensification of Land Use and Integrated Living

With increasing population density, there should be more efficient intensive use of land, combined with the provision of efficient infrastructure and quality mixed-use amenities that are well integrated, accessible and affordable. This will provide a highly effective physical environment that is conducive for high-quality living that promotes social interactions and therefore social capital. For example, well-integrated planning for mixed-use facilities and public and recreational spaces with equitable access for all groups will encourage social interactions among elderly and younger persons as well as among people of different ethnicities, nationalities and social backgrounds. Integrated living will also involve creating suitable employment opportunities in residential areas that are close to home. This work-home proximity will contribute to social interactions involving different generations and diverse groups, together with other integrative functions made possible by the work-home proximity. These functions include enhancing part-time work, flexible work hours and work-life balance; reducing commuting time and easing the strain on the public transport system; encouraging the elderly to remain economically and socially active; enhancing general and asset-based volunteerism in the work-home vicinity, which contributes to the sense of community in the neighbourhood; encouraging entrepreneurship and innovation in business; and creating value-added jobs for various segments of the population (Chan, 2013c).

The attractiveness of quality living in integrated mixed-use facility clusters will increase the housing and rental prices in and near these areas. It may be useful to consider implementing equitable policies that lower the cost for residents taking up job opportunities in their neighbourhood.

Given the multitude of social capital implications, we need to explicitly incorporate social and behavioural sciences in land use and infrastructure planning, so that the resulting physical environment will positively influence social interactions and behaviours and not create unintended negative social consequences.

Early and Targeted Health Screening and Promotion

Research has shown that individuals with poor health are more likely to have poor social relations and low social wellbeing. Many activities for developing social interactions and relationships, especially those involving older persons, presuppose a basic level of health among the individuals involved. Healthy functioning is a fundamental pillar for enhancing wellbeing and developing social capital. Although the life expectancy of Singaporeans has increased, this index of human development does not measure health conditions such as long-term chronic illness or ailments that Singaporeans may face as they grow older. The government should work with the private and people sectors to institute a comprehensive and targeted national health screening programme over the individual's lifespan beginning from a young age. The early screenings will enable the early detection of health risks and more effective prevention and management of health problems for an ageing population. This in turn delays the onset of old-age health problems, promotes health and prolongs the period of active lifestyle.

Conclusion

It is true that an ageing population presents policy challenges. It can be a significant economic and social liability if there are no mitigation effects from procreation and immigration. But it is equally true that an ageing population also presents policy opportunities. It can be an asset that contributes to building a vibrant economy and strong society.

More fundamentally, for Singapore to progress, we should not construe ageing as simply a population policy problem to be fixed. Instead, we need to approach ageing as a natural process that individuals, communities and the government should and can adapt to in order to enhance citizen wellbeing by developing economic and social capital.

References

Chan, D. (2013a, December 28). From Emotions to Shared Values. *The Straits Times.*

Chan, D. (2013b, February 4). Population Priorities and Perceptions. *The Straits Times.*

Chan, D. (2013c). Population Matters: Contributions from Behavioural Sciences. Paper presented at the Behavioural Sciences Conference 2013, Singapore, March 7, 2013.

Chan, D. (2012, May 10). The Heart of the Immigration Debate. *The Straits Times.*

Chan, D., Elliott, J., Koh, G., Kong, L., Nair, S., Tan, E. S., Wee, A., and Yeoh, B. (2014). Social Capital and Development. In Yap, M. T., and Gee, C. (Eds.), *Population Outcomes: Singapore 2050.* IPS Exchange Series, May 1, 2014.

National Population and Talent Division (NPTD). (2013). *Population White Paper: A Sustainable Population for a Dynamic Singapore.* Singapore: Prime Minister's Office.

Inventing SG100

Chen Show Mao
Member of Parliament
The Workers' Party, Singapore

In March 2014, Leon Perera wrote for *The Business Times* on what he could see of Singapore's economy in 2065: 3-D printing of small batches coupled with big data analytics will enable a degree of product customisation unimaginable today. Household robots will revolutionise the domain of personal services as well as household work, helping a much older workforce to remain productive till an older age. Space or near-space travel will revolutionise long-distance transport and accelerate globalisation. Stringent Green and ethics regulations will shift resources away from simply making and consuming more towards making everything greener, safer and fairer.

These are big themes — mass customisation manufacturing, a smaller world, higher productivity across all industries and in the home through robotics, more Green and ethics compliance across the board... To this we can add a shift in world gross domestic product share to Asia and Africa, a largely urban world, greater use of renewables, stronger protections for nature reserves as green lungs and so on.

In addition, with a smaller world, trade in goods and services will account for an increasingly important share of world gross domestic product, facilitated by increased globalisation wrought by advances in transportation, communications and information technologies, as well as the continuing trend of strengthening the rules-based multilateral trading system and increasing regulatory harmonisation, which encourage cross-border economic activities.

Many of these trends can benefit Singaporean businesses by helping them overcome the natural limitations of their small domestic market and scale of production. Similarly the trends enable the Singaporean worker, including the self-employed, based in Singapore to join the ranks and networks of employees and contractors of increasing numbers of multinational companies whose footprints cover Singapore.

Textbook factors of production for our economic growth include land, labour and capital. The small area of our land and number of people it can support for productive labour while we aspire to be "one of Asia's most liveable cities" are natural constraints on our future economic development.

Capital, significantly in the form of technology, enables us to coax higher economic growth from the limited resources of land and labour at our disposal. So does human capital, the quality of our labour resources, which may be improved by our investments in education, training and health.

Improvements in technology are taking place in many industries at substantial speed. Information technology is advancing at exponential rates by several measures. For our purposes, advances in technology may help us minimise our future trade-off between economic growth and environmental sustainability — by improving the efficient use of our constrained resources such as labour input (e.g. information technology) and natural resources (e.g. renewable energy) and by increasing the size of addressable market for our products and services (e.g. transportation, communications and information technology).

Fifty years ago, Nobel laureate Dennis Gabor wrote, "The future cannot be predicted, but futures can be invented" (*Inventing the Future,* Pelican Books, 1964, p. 161). What future can we invent for Singapore in another 50 years — what can we do to help bring about the future that we can glimpse now and hope to touch in 2065, keeping in view the future trade-off between economic growth and environmental sustainability?

For example, we as a society can do the following:

- identify and champion high-technology and Green economy industries as important pillars of our economic growth;
- encourage firms to adopt new technology for productivity growth;
- provide a social safety net for our workers who increasingly face the risk of redundancy as a result of accelerating globalisation and disruptive changes in technology, so that adequate retraining may take place and they will have the confidence and sense of security to put their labour to the best use;
- make investments in our human capital through education, training and health;
- renew and deepen our commitment to the open, rules-based, multilateral trading system for world trade.

In the future, as economies and polities mature, some of the key growth versus sustainability questions that vex us today will be taken off the table. For example:

- World population growth will level off... and growing aspirations for higher quality of life, many expressed politically, will help keep population densities in check in Singapore and elsewhere.
- Development will provide its own solution to some of the ill effects of growth, as we are seeing with pollution in China today.
- Technology will provide solutions that avoid some of the trade-offs we struggle with now, such as orbital solar panels for power generation, etc.

This is a benign view of the future. It could go the other way — environmental disaster leading to economic and political chaos. We need the right kind of leadership, politics and public attitudes to ensure the right evolution in the economy and environment. If we have these, problems can and will be solved, just as 190 countries came together to successfully resolve the problem of CFCs and ozone depletion in the 1980s and 1990s.

Singapore 2065 — Who Holds the Future

Jeanne Cheng
Managing Director
SP Services Ltd

As I sit down to start to pen my thoughts on what Singapore will be like in 50 years' time, Sir Winston Churchill's famous quote comes to mind — "The empires of the future are the empires of the mind."

Churchill, who passed away 50 years ago, said this long before the World Wide Web came into existence. His quote is now more relevant than ever before. Facebook is changing the face of the world. You no longer do research, you use Google and Wikipedia. You no longer send greeting cards to your friends, you whatsapp. News no longer spreads like wildfire, they go viral. And they are ignited not by a spark but a tweet or a blog.

The World Wide Web has created a new world, one that is vast, borderless, yet connected and instantaneous. We have transitioned from a bricks-and-mortar to a digital world in less than a generation. Technological innovations have changed the world order. Guess which are the world's most admired companies? According to the latest Fortune survey, Apple, Google and Amazon topped the list. These companies and the services they provide were not around 50 years ago.

With such rapid technological and lifestyle changes in the last 50 years, what will the future portend? In 50 years' time, will Singapore remain as one of the world's most competitive economies? In 2065, will it continue to enjoy one of the world's highest per capita GDPs, ranked third ahead of the United States and Germany?

The changes that Singapore experienced in the last 50 years are equally momentous. When Singapore became independent in 1965, it was a tiny red dot that most dismissed without much thought. Singapore had no land, no resources, just people that needed to be fed. There were racial riots and political tension that threatened the delicate multi-racial, multi-religious social fabric. Singapore had nothing and had to import everything, even water.

Fifty years on, Singapore now has NEWater, recycled from waste water and is no longer dependent on a single source of water supply. It has the world's best infrastructure, from airport to power systems. It staged Formula One's first night race, a prime spot on the world auto racing calendar. In a short span of 50 years, Singapore has achieved tremendous economic success to leap from a developing country to a first world economy.

A Survey of 50 Young Singapore Professionals

Just like our past, our future lies not in our might but in our mind. Many have written on Singapore's experience as the economic miracle of the 21st century. Most ascribed Singapore's success to the ability of its leaders in rallying its people to beat the odds. The Singapore in 2065 will be a nation built upon the hearts and minds of our future leaders. How Singaporeans in their 20s think and act in the next 50 years will shape the Singapore in 2065.

Therefore, to get a glimpse of the future, I surveyed 50 young Singapore professionals between the ages of 20 and 30, males and females working in Singapore and overseas. I asked the young people five questions relating to the sustainability of Singapore's competitiveness, the economic challenges Singapore will face moving towards 2065 and their hopes for the future.

Question 1 — Will Singapore remain as one of the world's most competitive economies in 50 years' time? 72% of the respondents said yes, 12% disagreed and 16% were uncertain. Those who were optimistic pointed to the investment made in education and skills development, the open economy and pro-business environment, competent and committed leaders, strong governance and transparency and Singapore's position as a key financial hub.

The pessimistic ones cited the rise of developing countries such as China, the lack of a talented workforce, labour and land shortage and falling birth rates. Those who were uncertain expressed concern over populist government policies, our lack of natural and manpower resources and the difficulty in retaining talent.

Question 2 — What are the most significant economic challenges that Singapore will face moving towards 2065? The top concerns are an ageing population (21% of the votes) followed by a widening income gap (17%), volatile international economy (17%) and tight labour market (16%).

Question 3 — What do you think are the likely changes to the global and regional economic dynamics? Most of the young professionals felt that Singapore will continue to benefit from strong international relations and regional ties. They also predicted that there would be a shift towards a multipolar world with several economic powerhouses, China being the key driving force. The rise of Asian emerging economies and economic protectionism creating an adverse trade impact were less of a concern.

Question 4 — What best meets your hopes for Singapore's future? Among the eight factors listed, a Singapore that is affordable to live in ranked as the top priority (23%), followed by a society with a stronger identity and greater sense of togetherness (15%), a society anchored on values such as integrity, meritocracy and family values (13%), a society with diverse definitions of success (13%), a Singapore with a fulfilling pace of life (12%) and a Singapore with a strong and vibrant economy (11%). A Singapore for Singaporeans and a society that takes care of the disadvantaged received relatively fewer votes of 8% and 3% respectively. One percent of the respondents wanted more freedom of speech and a more liberal society.

Question 5 — Although the young generation in their 20s have not suffered the same hardships as the pioneering generation, do you think they have what it takes to secure the future of Singapore?

88% of the young professionals interviewed were confident that the young generation could continue to do well for Singapore while 10% were not hopeful and another 2% were not sure. The young generation felt that with better education they were in a stronger position than the pioneer generation to secure the future of Singapore. As a technologically savvy generation, they were more skilled, creative and innovative. They also acknowledged that the strong foundation laid by the past generation would place them at an advantage. The young people felt that they too were working hard especially having to compete with foreign talent.

Those who were less optimistic thought that the young generation is too self-centred, too narrow-minded, not willing to work hard, taking things for granted and lacked a competitive spirit. A few who were not certain cited political diversity and mobility of the talented.

Youth of the Future

The responses given by the 50 young professionals through this mini survey give me reason to be hopeful about the future of Singapore. Our youth sees education and learning as key to achieving success. Notwithstanding the gripes we often hear about having to compete with foreign talents, the young people know that to stay at the top they need to compete. They emphasise the importance of an economy that is outward-looking, open and transparent. They believe in building a society anchored on values such as integrity, meritocracy and family togetherness.

They also see the perils of a society that is individualistic and shuns hard work. They acknowledge that a strong government and political stability are prerequisites to a strong economy. They know that talents are mobile and good leaders are needed to sustain Singapore's economic success.

Our youth show maturity and are pragmatic in their thinking. They feel the cost pressures of a developed nation and show concern over a widening income gap. They know that their generation will have to grapple with the problems of an ageing population and falling birth rates.

Fifty years on, the World Wide Web will be replaced by other technological advancements. But if our young generation work hard and look beyond, asking not what the future holds for them but believing that they hold the future, they will discover and conquer yet another brave new world.

I started this article with a quote and would like to end it by borrowing a line from Franklin D. Roosevelt — "We cannot always build the future for our youth, but we can build our youth for the future."

Instead of predicting what Singapore will be in 2065, we can help shape it by developing our youth today to meet the challenges and opportunities of tomorrow. I thank two young Singaporeans, Mr. Teo Kai Xiang and Miss Jacyln Chen Liting for their help in conducting the survey among the young people. I wish both of them and the present generation of the 20-somethings success in their aspirations for Singapore and fulfilling their dreams of the future.

Singapore: A Dreamland for Hardworking Singaporeans?

Chew Soon Beng
Professor of Economics and Industrial Relations
Nanyang Technological University, Singapore

Can Singapore be a dreamland for the hardworking Singaporean who will have retired by 2065? People from around the world are generally impressed by the economic achievements of Singapore as a country and as a society. However, after staying in Singapore for a week or so, they are shocked to find that some of our citizens in their 60s have to do manual work for a living. It is obvious that many of these Singapore elderly citizens do not enjoy manual work in their 60s. Some of them work with some degree of discomfort. But they have to work even into their late 60s and perhaps even into the early 70s because they did not earn enough during their younger days.

Singapore's per capita GDP is one of the highest in the world and people from low per capita GDP countries such as China cannot understand why old people have to work in their 60s. Of course, Singapore is different from many societies. We do not have a government-funded pension scheme for most public sector employees, not to mention non-public sector workers. But we have budget surpluses and huge national reserves on a per capita basis. Our universities rank high by international standards. But we do not score high on social dignity at all.

The issue is how can we prevent a situation where our hardworking citizens do not need to work for a living when they reach the official retirement age? Can this goal be achieved on a sustainable basis?

There has been much discussion on the advantages and weaknesses of our CPF scheme lately. Personally I think our CPF scheme would meet the gold standard for society security for Singapore provided the following conditions are met.

Each child has to be educated to reach his or her potential. Each worker will receive training to keep him/her gainfully employed. So far, I think Singapore has done this very well.

Each worker can be gainfully employed. Gainful employment means the worker is getting a family wage commensurate with his/her human capital. We have to a large extent achieved this, and we have Workfare Income Supplement (WIS) Scheme to ensure that our low-wage workers are sufficiently paid.

Each worker has to be gainfully employed for a sufficient number of years. This is the area that we need to beef up. This aspect is currently grossly insufficient for many Singaporeans working in Singapore. Singapore's official retirement age is 62. We are reluctant to raise the retirement age to 65. Without legal backing, our efforts in pushing the re-employment age to 65 recently has not been sufficiently broad-base, although the re-employment age has been raised to 67 for the public sector. All these efforts may come too late for some Singapore citizens who may lose their jobs upon reaching 62. Most of them have to get another job because they are still healthy and life expectancy is about two decades more than 62. When you change jobs in your 60s, you are likely to have to accept a downgrade in your career to a more physically demanding job. The pay will drop significantly. Many feel so humiliated that they stop working. This is a waste of human capital, especially when our society is facing a labour shortage and our citizens desire to work longer.

If the present situation of preparing for a decent life after retirement continues, we will continue to see many Singaporeans do manual work for a living after the official retirement age from now to 2065. How could we create a web of policy initiatives where hardworking Singaporeans can enjoy the fruit of their labour after the official retirement age?

Firstly, I feel that our official retirement age should be linked to the average life expectancy, keeping the difference between the two to 10 or at the most 12 years. In other words, although we do not want admit it, our employment system discriminates against older people. We have to remember that Singapore does not have a government-funded pension scheme. Ours is an individually funded pension scheme which we call CPF Life. Under the government pension scheme, if a civil servant were to resign before the official retirement age, he or she will lose his or her pension. But under our current employment scheme, a worker can resign without losing any pension as there is no pension to begin with. The linkage between the official retirement age and average life expectancy will provide added impetus to the adoption of the flexible wage system, the flexible medical scheme and effective training of mid-career workers on the part of their employers and the government.

Speaking of CPF Life, most low-wage workers do not have a sufficient balance in their respective Retirement Account. This is why many of these workers have to do manual work in their 60s. This is why citizens who are in their 50s are very concerned about changes in the CPF policy such as the minimum sum because they simply do not have sufficient savings in their CPF and bank accounts combined. They are afraid that they may pose a burden to their adult children who already struggle to pay their housing mortgages. The fear comes mainly because of the longer life expectancy which creates another concern: the impending hospitalisation bill which must surely come; it is a matter of when. This fear is not confined to low-wage workers alone, but also to middle-income employees.

How to ensure that low-wage workers have sufficient balances via continued employment? Currently we have Workfare for low-wage workers. We may want to adjust the amount of Workfare and ensure that a good portion of the Workfare will be deposited into their respective eventual Retirement Account. Coupled with effective training schemes, the desired goal is to encourage a young recipient of Workfare at age 35, for instance, to be able to meet the Minimum Sum in his Retirement Account as much as possible when he reaches the age of 55.

Of course, the Minimum Sum is meant for consumption at age 65 and this age will increase as life expectancy increases. How about the minimum sum in the Medisave account? At the moment, the minimum sum for the Medisave account is $45,500 but in 2012, the average balance in the Medisave account was around $30,000.

As we know, MediShield Life is now compulsory. And the annual premium and co-payments are likely to increase with each passing decade. Currently, our employers purchase a health insurance scheme to provide medical benefits to their employees. The additional medical coverage from the employers is not the best use of the wage bill. As it has been suggested by NTUC, instead of providing employees with medical benefits, employers could deposit the money they would have spent on health insurance into the respective Medisave account of their employees. I believe that a revamp of our employers' medical benefits scheme is inevitable.

When the government estimates the minimum sum for the retirement account and for Medisave account, the implicit argument is that these amounts are necessary to meet the daily expenses and medical expenses for our citizens in their twilight years. This in turn implies that most of our citizens would own a fully paid HDB flat (at least a three-room flat) by the time they reach the age of 55.

In other words, to make Singapore a dreamland for hardworking Singaporean retirees by 2065, the government has to optimise the parameters of the wage system, Workfare, the necessary investment in human capital, the price of land and hospitalisation charges subject to the linkage between the retirement age and the average life expectancy to work out the Minimum Sum for the retirement account and for the Medisave account respectively.

I do not advocate the EU style of welfarism. I believe that Singapore should never end up like London where many common Londoners live outside London either by choice or necessity due to high property prices, because Singapore, unlike London, is a city-state. The October 2014 student unrest in Hong Kong reflects to a certain extent the impact of high property prices on the average resident. But for Singaporeans who work hard to acquire a good education and remain employed with a lifelong learning attitude, they should have the option of not working for a living after the retirement age. I wish to state the premise of my position is that the growth trajectory for Singapore will be positive in all aspects from now to 2065. I rule out the situation of a vicious cycle where the life expectancy declines due to policy paralysis. However, maintaining a positive growth trajectory for Singapore over the next 50 years requires political stability and continuity of a strong and effective public sector. If the majority of citizens can see that they can enjoy the fruits of their labour during their working years and especially after retirement, political stability in the city-state can be maintained.

A Silent Revolution

Claire Chiang
Co-founder, Senior Vice President
Banyan Tree Holdings

The kind of revolutions with military might were the affairs of men. The silent revolution I am referring to is about how men and women are changing the way they wish to work. This revolution is invisible yet enduring, personal yet transformational. Where it happens is right at the core of our daily living.

The increase of dual income families has become a norm. The notion of men as breadwinners and women the homemakers is archaic. The work-centric need for survival which drove past generations is no longer a salient motivation factor as globalisation now offers amazing opportunities and distractions. The X and Y generations born after the 1970s want careers and family, personal gratification and work fulfilment. So the Baby Boomers bosses, those born in the 1950s and 1960s now begin to ask what mindsets and skillsets they must adopt to sustain workforce excellence and retention, since most Generation X and Y workers leave their jobs after one or two years. This is a high cost for the company.

In the last 100 years the challenges that women face have transformed drastically. Today, I will present a snapshot of four women in one century to illustrate this cataclysmic transformation at work.

My paternal grandmother, born in 1898, migrated from Hainan Island to Johore to join her husband as a rubber tapper. Uneducated and widowed a few years later after a bee killed my grandfather, she followed her son to

Singapore. Her stoic purpose was survival and keeping the family together. Stepping out of Hainan Island fired her revolution from within, just like millions of other women who left their hometowns to migrate to a new possibility. Singapore signalled a beacon of hope and a new beginning.

My mother was raised in Malacca and later in the 1930s, both mother and daughter moved to Singapore after my maternal grandfather abandoned them. She had to quit school to sell bread on the streets and later worked in a laundry. She met my father in Singapore and they went through the upheavals in the pre-independence and nation-building years and raised six of us children with a tight fist, by stretching every dollar to its maximum to provide us shelter and education.

My mother was the captain of the ship. Her challenging circumstances hardened her to teach us that no one owed us a living. She resonated the ethos of one of the earlier campaigns I remembered best in Singapore, that of "the rugged society." That was a period of resilience, toughness and endurance; we believed in hard work and we did our best. Pragmatic as wife and mother, while brokering property sales, my mother got us a shophouse with two rooms, quite a vast improvement from the one room in a longhouse we used to all stay in. Besides her many talents, what I found revolutionary was her focus on education. Against the then cultural backdrop which regarded daughters as "thrown away water," her investment in me was a transformational commitment which I owe a lot to.

For women my generation, I remember standing upright during school assemblies in the 1950s to receive the message from the Queen of England on Commonwealth Day, and I sang Negaraku, the Malayan national anthem before I sang Majulah Singapura in 1965. We were the first batch of beneficiaries of post-independence achievements, with choices for schooling and at work. Growing up in a city-state of 1.2 million people amidst expanding development opportunities, we shared a heightened sense of purpose and believed we all had a role to play to help Singapore succeed. Passing the PSLE, "O" Levels, "A" levels, University Degree, followed by work and marriage then raising of children were unquestioned benchmark achievements. It was an age of possibilities which led us over decades to the cusp of a digital revolution that is both exciting and bewildering. A new age has dawned on us.

My daughter, born in 1985, adept with the Internet and all things electronic, grew up in a safe city-state of 3 to 4 million people, while enjoying its economic growth by harnessing technology and social media to create many more possibilities we never even dreamt of. Her generation questions the meaning of work and life. Because of more choices being made available due to higher education and social mobility in Singapore, these choices bring also conflict as there is also no longer one "right" path to follow. My grandmother's fight was for survival, my mother's was progress, mine was for equality and my daughter's is for personal control and self-actualisation. The young people today are more likely to ask "What can I get out of work?" in order to find satisfaction in life outside of work.

The next 50 years will present even more conflicted choices for women as the rainbow of possibilities will glow even brighter, requiring a higher blend of reason and intuitive to set right women's hearts so that they know how much is enough to lead a good life. Young women feel they could lead, yet the (male) world thinks they are weak: and the (female) world thinks they are life warriors, yet these same young women are quivering in their hearts, needing reinforcement and sponsorship.

How do we moderate these psychodynamics among women and men to optimise women's talent and for those who desire a family, the unique situation of being a mother as well? Women are pulling out from the job market between the ages of 35–50 years because of family duties and the need to care for young children. Today the younger women quit because of the lack of flexibility at work. While the employment trend has shown less of a sharp drop after 35 years in employment and more of a rippling dip on a plateau engagement, we begin to see the shift from corporate engagement to individuals doing their own businesses.

A new silent revolution has begun with women opting out of corporate lives to be independent and flexible. More of them are becoming qualified professionals, savvy and entrepreneurial, earning more than before and wielding influence and impact. They realised successful work-life integration is not about getting what you want all at once all the time, it is about tweaking your plans to achieve small wins at different times, within a longer time frame. The final outcome is the total sum of an integrated life suffused with personal joy, marriage security, family bliss and work excellence.

These emerging women leaders will influence the texture of work relationships by entwining care and competition in their leadership style and agenda. This will shift and lift the revolution by women to include revolutionising the male partners to embrace mindset diversity and inclusiveness, if they wish to "lean in" and work with women as their bosses or partners.

Or, as corporates, women will learn to make timely calculus at different life-cycle stages to define the way they work by leveraging new communication and connectivity technologies like iPads, the Polycom "starfish" phone and other equipment for conference calls, Skype, Facebook and Whatsapp, among others and maximising the use of mobile offices that allow them to work anywhere.

Smart leaders exploit such technology by offering part-time employment, flexible working hours, working from home and other ways of work engagement to attract talented employees who wish to have a more flexible schedule. A June 2007 Goldman Sachs Sustain report on the sustainability of corporate performance analysed the competitive advantage in mature and emerging industries as they evolved in response to a rapidly changing globalising world. It reported that among factors on governance, social and environment standards, the rise of the new generation of workers who have the desire to align personal and corporate values is creating a different workplace culture from that of past generations. Leaders now need to provide now rewards beyond financial gain in addition to mentoring and coaching and a high-tech, flexible workplace.

With our falling fertility rate, there will inevitably come a day when all women will be viewed as a necessary part of the workforce. Their expectations cannot be ignored. This is a demographic impact which leaders need to understand by embracing its dynamic to develop a slew of workforce life-cycle management (WLM) practices to optimise resources for sustainability. Flexibility, work customisations, adaptability and off-site interactivity are some key approaches that enable workers to choose a variety of ways to continue working.

This inevitable revolution can only be completed by growing a group of work-life strategists, to help companies formalise a strategy to execute a flexibility culture. HR managers must move from the backroom to the boardroom to have a say in human capital strategies. Department leaders should learn to plan a flexibility schedule and set performance targets. This resetting involves letting go the need for "face-time" and being open in fixing work procedures. Working at home can be effective for some, and at the same time, it minimises corporate expenses by reducing office rental and utility costs. In short, the new workplace needs more options to help executives exercise choice and control and remain efficient and productive.

"Having it all" is about overhauling traditional ways of thinking and working, to embrace people's aspirations as the centrepiece in decision-making. This transformation is about driving economics to achieve what the heart desires. Women who have been the silent majority for so long have staged this revolution knowingly and unknowingly over centuries, and they will one day surprise the world. No longer will there be the question of "What if women ruled the world?", because they will. It will then be a better world.

Singapore in 2065: Geopolitical Certainties in a Changing Global and Regional Environment

Barry Desker
Distinguished Fellow
S. Rajaratnam School of International Studies
Nanyang Technological University

As we move towards 2015 and our 50th year of independence, there will be a flurry of books and articles recalling the challenges overcome since 1965 and the destiny which awaits Singapore. The bigger surprise has been the number of efforts at crystal ball gazing attempting to look 10, 25 and even 50 years into the future.

What is striking is how much our imaginations are prisoners of the present. Even though we want to look beyond today and aim to conceive of a world which will unfold in the years ahead, we are shaped by our memories and experiences. Linear projections are common. We struggle to grapple with the possibility of discontinuities, of changes which break existing moulds.

At the same time, our natural optimism leads us to plot a future which highlights Singapore's role at the forefront of nation states, a beacon of economic growth, social development and political stability. When we discuss the possibility of changes, the tendency is to think in terms of incremental shifts. Few consider the possibility of paradigm shifts, which should not be ignored.

This article, which takes a slightly different focus, argues that Singapore's future will be shaped by its geographical location. Even as we consider the possibility of incremental changes, discontinuities and paradigm shifts, there will be constants which will shape our responses to events as well as mould the perspectives taken by Singapore and Singaporeans. One key constant is geography, which influences the opportunities and challenges facing Singapore.

A frequently heard view in Singapore, especially among younger Singaporeans, is that we are part of a globalising world and that our economy today depends on trade and investment relationships with developed regions such as the United States and Europe as well as rising powers such as China and India. Proponents of this view would argue that unlike 1965, our role as an entrepôt has diminished and that Singapore has succeeded in overcoming the constraints of its regional environment. Such perceptions are reinforced by the ease of travel and communications, which leads Singaporeans to leapfrog the region. Singaporeans go abroad to study in the developed countries and now China, more learn French and German than Indonesian or Vietnamese, and many Singaporeans spend their vacations in distant lands, travelling to the region only on short visits for business or weekend breaks.

However, as then Minister Mentor Lee Kuan Yew observed in the 2009 S. Rajaratnam Lecture, "we must never delude ourselves that we are a part of the First World in Southeast Asia, a second and third world group of countries. Our region has its own special features. Singapore's destiny would be very different if we were sited in Europe or North America. We cannot transplant our island elsewhere. Therefore, a recurrent issue for Singapore is how to differentiate ourselves from our neighbours in order to compete and survive, and also get along with them. This is a perennial foreign policy challenge."[1]

Singapore is situated on a critical node of global trade at the strategic intersection of the Pacific and Indian Oceans. The narrowness of the Strait of Malacca and Strait of Singapore in the waters around Singapore created a choke point for international maritime navigation, a critical factor in

[1] Lee K. Y., *The Fundamentals of Singapore's Foreign Policy: Then & Now*, Singapore, MFA Diplomatic Academy, 2009, p. 7.

Singapore's successful emergence during the colonial era as an entrepôt and major British naval base. But location is not enough. Singapore's rapid growth after its founding in 1819 occurred because Singapore's status as a free port under British rule contrasted with the mercantilist protectionist policies of the Dutch who were the dominant colonial power in the archipelago.

Singapore's success led to the emergence of an informal economic zone centred on Singapore. Proximity to Singapore facilitated Johore's development of an export economy centred on rubber, relying on imported Chinese labour and capital from Singapore, even though political control and administrative authority remained in ethnic Malay hands. A symbiotic relationship developed between Johore sultans and British colonial governors in Singapore, symbolised by the magnificent residence of the Sultan on Tyersall Road in Singapore before the Second World War.

Freedom of movement occurred not just between Singapore and Malaya, which were seen as one entity under British rule, but also between Singapore and Riau. Although the Johor-Lingga sultanate had been divided by the Anglo-Dutch Treaty of 1824, Singapore emerged as the economic heart of the Riau Archipelago. The Straits dollar was the currency in Riau from its incorporation into the Dutch East Indies in 1913 until President Soekarno banned trade with Singapore in 1963. When I was on a visit to Riau with the Indonesian Coordinating Minister for the Economy Radius Prawiro in 1989, he recalled how as a young Indonesian finance ministry official in 1955, he was sent to audit the accounts of the local government in Riau and had to convert his subsistence allowance paid in Indonesian rupiah to the Malayan dollar. This pattern continues today. In September 2014, the local regional administration reminded hotels in Bintan that they were not allowed to use the Singapore dollar for transactions.

Even in the late 1970s, when I visited outlying areas in Sumatra, I was surprised that the owners of rubber plantations listened to shortwave broadcasts from Singapore which carried the daily price of rubber traded on the Singapore Rubber Exchange. The prevailing Singapore rubber price determined the price at which they sold their rubber to dealers. I was told that tin miners and rubber traders relied on these broadcasts even before World War II.

The reality is that our location will have a critical impact on how Singapore is perceived globally as well as the diplomatic, political and security challenges faced by Singapore in the future, just as it has influenced the past and present. Our geographical location also has a continuing economic relevance, especially as the sub-regions around Singapore become increasingly integrated into the Singapore economy and Asia's economic development acts as a locomotive for Singapore's growth. This combination of opportunities as well as vulnerabilities and risks arising from our geographical location will remain a critical factor for Singapore over the next 50 years.

The sharp exchanges between Malaysian and Singapore leaders in the aftermath of Singapore's departure from Malaysia in 1965 and the memories of Indonesian Confrontation in the early 1960s created an acute sense of vulnerability, which shaped independent Singapore's foreign and defence policies. Over the past 50 years, bilateral relations with both Malaysia and Indonesia have improved significantly. Nevertheless, during periods of stress in the domestic politics and economies of Singapore's neighbours, criticisms of Singapore come to the fore, including allegations of Singapore benefitting from the outward flow of funds from ethnic Chinese Indonesian conglomerates during the Asian financial crisis in 1997–1998, threats by Malaysian politicians to cut off Singapore's water supply and attempts to undercut Singapore's role as a logistics hub for the region.

Such concerns have led to Singapore's continuing interest in strong external linkages beyond the region. By developing global connections, promoting the use of its facilities by Singapore's partners and creating an environment which welcomed transnational corporations, Singapore used its strategic location to build an outward looking global city-state. In turn, Singapore's support for freedom of navigation through the Straits of Malacca and Singapore, which are used for international shipping, as well as freedom of overflight highlighted Singapore's role as a nexus of international trade, finance and communications.

While Singapore's location has facilitated its emergence as a global telecommunications network hub, major international airport and global seaport, alternatives and competitors will emerge over the next 50 years as our neighbours build up their capabilities and benefit from cheap, plentiful land. How Singapore responds to these challenges will provide a critical test for a new generation of Singaporeans. A visionary approach not rooted in the recent past would see such facilities as complementary to Singapore and would work towards integrating the use of these key transportation and communications infrastructures around Singapore.

Reimagining Singapore in 2065 should lead us to think beyond the boundaries of present day Singapore. There is no reason why the region surrounding Singapore cannot be integrated into a larger economic space providing scope for work, play and travel for Singapore as well as our neighbours. Movement towards this freer two-way flow of people and ideas will require a mindset change in Singapore as well as Malaysia and Indonesia. Policymakers will have to welcome the freedom of movement, not just of tourists but also of workers and professionals. The opening of borders will be a sharp discontinuity from the practices of the last 75 years. As Singaporeans become accustomed to commuting, we should not be surprised that more will live in Johore or in Bintan, Batam and Karimun, enjoying the space that will not be available in Singapore, just as skilled workers, managers and professionals may live in Singapore and commute to factories, shipyards and state of the art offices in the surrounding region.

The creation of an integrated economic zone around Singapore will be a reversion to a mode of relationships which resulted in Singapore's emergence as the preeminent trading, financial and communications centre in Southeast Asia a century ago. Successful implementation of such an approach will require the development of a group of policymakers familiar with the languages, culture and environment of our nearest neighbours — a significant challenge as trends in our educational system have resulted in a greater awareness of developed countries rather than the region around us!

An Inclusive, Liveable, Global City-State

Grace Fu
Minister, Prime Minister's Office,
Second Minister for the Environment and Water Resources
and Second Minister for Foreign Affairs, Singapore

Quality Economic Growth

Singapore in 2065 will be economically vibrant. Our restructuring efforts bear fruit, and we will continue to enjoy good economic growth driven by productivity increases. Wages rise across the board as re-designed jobs leverage on technology, are more productive and create higher value-add. All jobs are considered respectable occupations. Employers are open to flexible working hours and part-time work to attract and tap on our senior workers and women. More women will sit on company boards and hold senior positions across all industries. Inclusive and innovative work-places enable high local employment rates across all age groups.

In 2065, there is also a strong local workforce and sense of entrepreneurship in Singapore. There is minimal underemployment in the economy. This means that Singaporeans are equipped with the necessary skill sets and the economy has sufficient and suitable jobs for them. Singapore companies are competitive, strong and agile with good leaders at the helm. Singaporeans are competent and well suited for leadership positions in MNCs, including many which our companies have become. Singaporeans are adventurous and are willing to take more risks, attempting new business opportunities, and entering the global market with Singapore as the base. This results in a more outward-looking, entrepreneurial and innovative labour force.

Values and Mindsets

The global economy will continue to bring us challenges as well as opportunities in 2065 and beyond. It is our strong values that define our society and nation that will continue to see us through. With sustained economic growth, Singapore in 2065 will continue to be forward-looking with opportunities well distributed in a meritocratic society. We are able to overcome urban stresses observed in other major global cities, e.g. income inequality, social friction between different groups, etc.

We define success less by the material possessions we have in relation to others, but by the satisfaction from the efforts ploughed in and achievement of personal life goals. There is less emphasis on paper qualifications; instead, people have a deep respect for professional skills and expertise accumulated through real-world experiences. Aspirations remain high, as is the sense of achievement and success.

Our people continue to embrace diversity as an opportunity to generate ideas and innovate. Integration between locals, new immigrants and foreigners is good, with more having friends of different nationalities and races. Singaporeans are open to different perspectives, and accepting of diverse interests and social groups, leading to healthy, constructive debate in the social and political spaces.

Singaporeans also develop a stronger community orientation. More people are willing to forgo individual benefits for the greater good of the community. Local communities are close-knit, with neighbours supporting each other and rekindling the "kampong" spirit.

Environmental stewardship is strengthened with a stronger community orientation. Singaporeans naturally want to keep our environment clean and use our limited natural resources wisely. Good cleaning, binning and recycling habits are the norm. Residential communities feel responsible for shaping their living environment.

High Quality Living Environment

Singapore continues to provide a high quality living environment for residents in 2065. While Singapore's constraints as a small island city remain the same, our challenges in terms of land, water and energy are also opportunities which motivate us to think innovatively to plan and design our city. The environment continues to nurture and support the values and mindsets of an inclusive society.

All our public urban infrastructures are designed to be places of social interaction, active living and inclusivity. People from all walks of life can interact in and enjoy the parks, waterways, inter-linked walkways, hawker centres and community spaces.

Residents stay in sustainable eco-precincts capable of providing for their growing and ageing needs. Examples such as green roofs, water and energy efficient features form the prevalent architectural style for built infrastructures. More vertical kampongs[1] will also be built. These single developments will have quality facilities catering to different demographic segments ranging from young families with childcare needs, to senior citizens who are enjoying their active silver years.

Mixed residential, business and commercial developments are spread across Singapore. For instance, this includes the future North Coast Innovation Corridor comprising Woodlands, Sembawang and Seletar Regional Centres, as well as Punggol's Creative Cluster. Travel times are shortened; cycling,[2] roller-blading and scooting to destinations become safer and easier through the use of park connectors or dedicated lanes.

Technology remains the key driver to free up our land constraints, and transform our environment and lifestyles. Space use is transformed, for instance, through the creative use of our underground space.[3] The Jurong Rock Caverns facility, located 130 m beneath Banyan Basin on Jurong Island is just one example of how we can utilise underground spaces to provide strategic storage capacity for Singapore's energy security. It is the first such facility in Southeast Asia, and has helped free up 60 ha of land (equivalent to 84 football fields).

---

[1] A Vertical Kampong development is expected to be completed by 2017 in Woodlands. This HDB initiative will emphasise public spaces like a community farm, lush roof garden and community plaza, and also include studio apartments, care facilities and commercial facilities to give residents the convenience in a single development. Green features like underground bicycle storage, pneumatic waste conveyance, bioswales, rainwater harvesting and solar panels will also be included.

[2] LTA is piloting a bicycle sharing scheme at Jurong Lake District and city centre areas starting from 2015.

[3] For more information on the concept of an underground park in New York, please see http://www.thelowline.org.

Enabled by technologies (e.g. robotics, sensors, etc.), senior citizens live independent fulfilling lives, remain mobile and continue to be well supported by their families and communities. Barrier-Free Accessibility (BFA) guidelines continue to be the design principles to allow ease of mobility for all residents. Autonomous vehicles are used to help residents who have difficulties walking long distances.[4] With employees being able to telecommute and enjoy flexible work arrangements, the reduced need for physical workspaces frees up valuable real estate, and lowers overall business costs.

A Confident Future

Finally, Singaporeans in 2065 will continue to have a sense of optimism and confidence about our own future, as well as the future of Singapore. We have relevant economic skill sets, and continue to do well in the global economy. We are also supported by a strong network of family and community members who continue to see us through any difficult times. We feel a strong stake in Singapore, and continue to play an active part in moulding Singapore's future to be even better and brighter than before.

[4] NUS, Singapore MIT Alliance for Research and Technology (SMART), IDA and LTA are currently conducting trials where autonomous buggies can ferry passengers within Jurong Lake District, e.g. around a park.

Ecolink: Future Challenges to the Linking of Singapore's Economy and Environment

Geh Min
Immediate Past President
Nature Society (Singapore)

What will we do as the wisdom of our past bears down on our future? It is a story of ageless conversation, not only conversation among ourselves about what we wish and mean to do, but a conversation held with the land...

Barry Lopez

Singapore's first Prime Minister, Mr. Lee Kuan Yew, saw the economy and the environment as inextricably linked. This was not just an abstract vision but a pragmatic goal to be achieved with determination and efficiency. That it is a success is not in doubt.

Rich, clean and green are probably the three most common adjectives used to describe Singapore both by Singaporeans themselves as well as foreigners.

In Mr. Lee's own words, "After independence, I searched for some dramatic way to distinguish ourselves from other Third World countries. I settled for a clean and green Singapore," and on pronouncing on the success of this policy, that "No other project has brought richer rewards to the region … it was good for morale, for tourists and for investors," and "Greening is the most cost-effective project I have launched."

But as Mr. Lee recognised, a vision is only as good as its implementation. While the vision itself is even more relevant today than when it was first conceived how it is interpreted and implemented needs to be updated to fit current knowledge and future challenges, both known and unforeseen.

Natural Capital

Singapore's green cover, as measured by satellite imaging, increased from 36% in 1986 to 47% in 2006. The accuracy of these figures were verified by a timely study by NUS where satellite imaging was matched with ground truthing. Indeed, the study showed the green cover in 2010 was found to be 56% of the land area. This commendable achievement, in spite of a doubling of the population and an impressive growth in GDP is certainly reason for congratulation.

However, it would be valid to examine in greater detail the quality and sustainability of this green cover.

Primary forest, an ecological blue chip for its biodiversity and ecosystem services, is almost impossible to value in pure economic terms while a golf course, which is the ecological equivalent of a junk bond, was considered better able to generate economic value. This divergence has posed considerable difficulty to policymakers searching for the right balance but after an initial overemphasis on manicured "managed green" in the 1970s they have consistently if cautiously recalibrated their perspective to include more natural biodiversity and ecosystems. This enlightened approach has required some expensive U-turns such as the reconnection of Bukit Timah Nature Reserve to the central catchment area by an ecolink after its bisection by an expressway, the de-canalisation of many waterways and the reversing of land reclamation in Chek Jawa. Clearly they recognised the value of ecosystems services such as flood control, improved air and water quality, prevention of erosion and lowering of ambient temperatures that these ecosystems provide.

Inevitably, some oversights and mistakes have been irreversible. Mangrove forests which originally covered 13% of our landmass are now reduced to less than 1%. Most of this destruction was a result of land reclamation and conversion of rivers to reservoirs. From an economic cost-benefit analysis the exchange was well worth it. Our most valuable economic assets such as our financial district, our international airport and our petrochemical hub now occupy this reclaimed land.

But mangroves have now proven to provide ecosystem services such as protection from storm surges, rising sea levels and erosion as well as providing rich carbon sinks and natural land reclamation; all invaluable for climate change mitigation and adaptation. A better understanding of these ecosystems then would have given better protection to our economic assets and water supply by integrating mangroves into the original reclamation planning. Mangrove regeneration at this retroactive stage may be impossible in some areas and expensive man-made sea walls and dykes insufficient, as demonstrated by Hurricane Katrina and the Asian Tsunami.

The balance sheet for our natural capital or reserves is low on ecological blue chips (our primary forests are 0.28% of our total land mass) but encouragingly high in both spontaneous (29%) and managed (27%) vegetation both of which have potential for increasing their biodiversity and ecological value if managed wisely.

But what will the situation be 50 years later with a growing population and more pressures and demands on scarce land? Do we have the same policies, checks and balances that we have for our fiscal reserves to enhance their value and to protect them from devaluation and destruction?

What could be written off before as an "externality" can no longer be done so without huge economic and ecological losses as illustrated by the haze pollution from forest fires. Failure to develop an acceptable currency for ecosystems and biodiversity and a workable conversion rate between economic and ecological value will seriously impact on both.

Singapore should take the lead here as we did in the past. As Mr. Lee noted, "No other project has brought richer rewards to the region.... Greening was positive competition that benefited everyone."

But our greening cannot be based on past paradigms. It needs to be brought to a higher level to meet future challenges.

Social Capital

In addition to enhancing our natural capital Mr. Lee recognised that the environment can also grow our social capital: while our public housing policy gave Singaporeans a sense of ownership, a clean and green environment would give us a sense of belonging and pride in our country.

The shared environment is both a carrot and a stick for social behaviour. Clean and green spaces could inculcate and encourage responsible communal attitudes and develop a stronger sense of civic consciousness. But, as he ruefully noted, "The physical environment was easier to improve than the rough and ready ways of the people."

Worryingly, littering and other environmentally anti-social behaviour is still on the rise in Singapore. In the past this could be attributed to ignorant third-world behaviour but after 50 years of a first-world environment maintained by an army of cleaners and a plethora of anti-littering campaigns, signs and laws, Singaporeans cannot now be unaware of the rules of conduct with regard to cleanliness. Littering can only be seen as a result of social apathy or worse, a deliberate anti-social act reflecting a sense of social malaise or alienation.

On the positive side, the sprouting of numerous environmental initiatives by civil society begun after Chek Jawa has been on the rise. While many like Waterways Watch and Community in Bloom align well with government policies, others like Bukit Brown have had more chequered or contentious histories. How these differences between top-down and ground-up initiatives can be dovetailed into workable and equitable models will be a challenge.

The private sector too has not been slow in doing their share in creating and enhancing public spaces in parks, institutions of learning, libraries and even nature reserves.

But how quickly and to what extent we can grow our population in an already crowded space and what our carrying capacity for social integration is remains unknown. It is evident that apart from physical constraints, crowding causes more tension and stress and that could reach a tipping point which rips apart the social fabric. We are already seeing some signs of these tensions.

The issue of spatial justice, too, is a growing one as space becomes a premium. Riots in Istanbul in 2013 over the destruction of a public park for a shopping mall and frequent protests in China over perceived land grabs for private golf courses show how potent the environment and land use can be as flashpoints for perceived social injustice.

Singapore has been aware of this and has been generous with public parks and amenities despite allotting a significant amount of land to the private sector. This delicate balancing act will become more challenging in the future with a shrinking land bank and a growing population with higher expectations. *People now do not just want more public space but also more say in it.*

Singapore has achieved against great odds, the monumental feat of a first-world environment but we have yet to grow a citizenry who actively and responsibly participate in creating and maintaining this environment. No one can doubt this is not only a worthwhile but an essential goal.

An Eco-centric Future

Mr. Lee realised the importance of the economic-environmental nexus and even more remarkably, of establishing and maintaining this link from the start. At independence, Singapore was a poor nation with an uncertain future and no hinterland so it was natural that we should view and assess our progress from a predominantly economic perspective. 50 years later, we are now a prosperous nation which has achieved not just economic success but a clean and green environment and a growing sense of nationhood.

The challenges we face are not less than before but they are vastly different. Mr. Lee himself noted that this millennium's challenges will be environmental ones. We now need to chart our course from a more informed and coherent social and ecological perspective as well as an economic one. Failure to do so will not only threaten our future sustainability but do a grave injustice to our founding fathers' foresight.

Reference

Yee, A. T. K., Corlett, R. T., Liew, S. C., and Tan, H. T. W. (2011). The Vegetation of Singapore: An Updated Map. *Gardens' Bulletin Singapore, 63*(1 & 2), 205–212.

Progressive Shifts into the Future

Gerald Giam
Non-Constituency Member of Parliament
The Workers' Party, Singapore

Thinkers, technologists and entertainers of times past have attempted to paint a picture of what the world might look like in the future. The 1964 World's Fair in New York showcased jet packs, lunar colonies and picture phones, while the 1989 film *Back to the Future Part II* — one of my favourite movies growing up — featured ordinary folks zipping around town in flying cars and on hoverboards.

Not all of these materialised, of course. We do have Skype and telepresence, but personal jetpacks and hoverboards are, sadly, still not available in stores. Many "disruptive" new technologies did emerge, like the Internet, social media, consumer mobile communications and self-driving cars. These have revolutionised the way we work, play and interact with each other. While people once thought the fastest way to get around the city of the future would be to pilot a vehicle through the air, few anticipated the invention of transport or communications technologies which could dispense of the need for drivers or even physical travel.

Predicting the future is always challenging. We tend to see the future through our present-day lenses. Nevertheless in this essay, I will attempt to anticipate what Singapore may be like in the decades ahead, grounded in our immutable circumstances (like our geography), factoring in recent political and social developments, and throwing in a generous dose of hope.

The Singapore of the year 2065 will continue to be shaped by both the internal and external political environment of the day. Given Singapore's small physical size and population, the external political environment will have a significant bearing on our future progress. For example, if great powers like China and the United States were to engage in a conflict with each other within the next 50 years, dragging in their allies and forcing countries in the region to take sides, no amount of good governance in Singapore will be able to ensure the continued prosperity and security of our people.

The year 2015 marks the year that the Association of Southeast Asian Nations (ASEAN) has committed to establish a single market and production base among its 10 member states, through the ASEAN Economic Community. It is clear that ASEAN is not about to become an economic and monetary union along the lines of the European Union any time soon. However, the momentum continues in the direction of greater integration, spurred mostly by external circumstances, especially the rise of China and the competition and opportunities that it brings. If ASEAN member states are able to narrow the development gap with each other, the dream of greater integration could be achieved sooner. Currently, this looks like a bit of a fantasy, given the huge development gap between member states, and with some of the more developed members, like Thailand, even taking a step back in terms of economic and political development. Nevertheless, recent political and economic developments in two leading ASEAN member states, Indonesia and the Philippines, give some reason for guarded optimism.

Domestically, there has been a trend towards greater acceptance of political diversity, by both ordinary citizens and the incumbent powers. While some stalwarts in the latter camp can still be heard proclaiming that a political opposition is unnecessary because the governing party can check itself, this argument is rapidly losing its currency. Separate conversations I have had with many Singaporeans, whether young or old, rich or poor, and even among supporters of the present government, point to a desire to see more vibrant public discussions about issues that matter. Nevertheless, whether Singapore will progress, as most other developed countries have, into a two-party or multi-party state will depend on a variety of factors. These include the calibre and performance of the governing party and the political opposition, the social and economic situation of the day, and the appetite for change among the electorate.

Recent political developments in Singapore could be instructive of the social and economic policies which may evolve in the years ahead. The results of the 2011 General Elections (GE) struck Singapore's political landscape like a bolt of lightning. The landmark election saw the popular vote of the governing People's Action Party (PAP) dip to a historical low of 60.1%. The political opposition increased its elected representation threefold, from two to six.[1] Over the next two years after the GE, the PAP went on to lose two by-elections in Hougang and Punggol East constituencies, and their favoured candidate for President narrowly won the Presidential Election, garnering just 35.2% of the popular vote.[2]

The post-GE 2011 landscape has been dubbed by many observers as a "new normal" environment. Dr. Tony Tan, speaking in his private capacity just two months after the general election and a year before he was elected as President, observed that "the situation where you have one overwhelming party which has almost all the seats with little effective opposition ... is a matter of the past."[3]

With political dominance no longer a given like before, the PAP has been forced to take a long, hard look at its policies to address some of the unhappiness on the ground, in order to staunch a further slide in its electoral fortunes. This has meant reassessing some of the dogma that has underpinned many of its hard-nosed economic and social policies over the past two decades. The "new normal" environment has precipitated noticeable shifts in many economic and social policies in areas like population and immigration, housing, public transport, healthcare and care for the elderly.

In a newspaper interview in April 2013, Tharman Shanmugaratnam, the deputy prime minister and finance minister, intimated that the centre of gravity of the Cabinet had shifted to the "left-of-centre."[4] What caused

---

1 Elections Department Singapore (2011), 2011 Parliamentary Election Results. Retrieved February 25, 2015 from http://www.eld.gov.sg/elections_results2011.html.

2 Elections Department Singapore (2012), 2012 Presidential Election Results. Retrieved February 25, 2015 from http://www.eld.gov.sg/elections_past_results.html.

3 Speech by Dr. Tony Tan Keng Yam at the Singapore Chinese Chamber of Commerce and Industry Distinguished Speakers Lecture Series, July 15, 2011. Retrieved January 7, 2015 from https://www.youtube.com/watch?v=2CaMV1-kIQc.

4 Ask DPM Tharman: The Full Transcript, *The Straits Times*, April 20, 2013. Retrieved January 7, 2015 from http://www.singapolitics.sg/features/ask-dpm-tharman-full-transcript.

this shift is a subject of debate. The PAP would claim that it is constantly undergoing self-renewal, while many political observers and ordinary citizens have attributed it to pressure from the electorate.

Will these progressive shifts continue? Given Singaporeans' growing education levels and exposure to political, economic and social norms in other developed countries, they are unlikely to accept any backsliding to the authoritarian ways and the tight-fisted fiscal policies that have been the hallmark of successive PAP governments. Instead, there are likely to be calls for a greater levelling up of society, to ensure that no citizen is left behind in the wake of the country's economic progress. This will require stronger and more comprehensive social safety nets, particularly in the areas of healthcare financing, retirement adequacy, and support for the low-income, people with disabilities and the elderly.

To become a more "caring society" would require greater social solidarity and risk-sharing among our people — a realisation that we will be better off advancing together as a nation than leaving the more vulnerable members of society behind. In particular, I am hopeful we will see a transformation in the way that society views and treats people with disabilities. The proportion of the population with physical or mental disabilities will grow as our society ages. Recent years have seen more provisions being made for the disabled, including statutory requirements for building owners to incorporate physical accessibility features, better wheelchair accessibility on public transport, and more educational assistance for special needs children.

Yet these changes are only the beginning. There is much more that can be done to enable people with disabilities to fully integrate into society and workplaces. Some of these changes will entail higher public expenditure — for example, providing larger subsidies for special needs education such that parents pay the same amount, whether their children are disabled or able-bodied. Will society be willing to collectively carry these burdens, in order to ensure that all our people can fulfil their full potential as contributing members of society? This will be a mark of our progress as a nation.

History may not favour the survival of small city-states, but recent political, economic and social developments in Singapore give hope for optimism for our next 50 years. Predicting the future is tricky business. Shaping it is even harder. Yet the future of Singapore is for all its citizens to take hold of, and to shape for the better. We owe it to our children and future generations who will live to see the year 2065 and beyond.

Of Nutmegs, Values, and an Island Called Singapore

Heng Swee Keat
Minister for Education, Singapore

To look forward to the next 50 years of the small island of Singapore, we should first look backwards by about 400 years and at two other islands — Pulau Ai and Pulau Run.

In the early 17th century, these two outcrops in the Banda Sea were the most valuable properties in the world.

The islands drew fortune-seekers for one reason: nutmeg. Nutmeg was prized in Europe as an exotic flavouring and preservative agent, and even as a medicine. In the words of a contemporary observer, it was the "most coveted luxury in 17th century Europe." Nutmeg traders enjoyed profit margins of up to 60,000%.

For over 150 years, the maritime powers of the day fought over these islands. Rivalry between the English and Dutch was fierce, and the islands changed hands twice. When the Dutch seized Pulau Run in 1665, the English retaliated by taking New Amsterdam in North America.

Two years later, they negotiated a peace treaty. The English gave up Pulau Ai and Pulau Run. In return, they kept the island that held New Amsterdam. At the time, no one thought this a fair deal for the English — instead of nutmeg riches, they got a small trading post with less than 1,000 people, on an island more commonly known today as Manhattan.

Today, nutmeg is just another commodity, and Pulau Ai and Pulau Run are sleepy atolls. And Manhattan? Many today would call it the heart of the financial world.

What can we learn from this centuries-old story of islands on opposite ends of the world?

First, economic structures evolve. Single products are vulnerable to changing tastes, fads and the challenge of new and better products — it is not possible to build a lasting economy on the back of a single product, or a single sector.

Since the 17th century, we have witnessed a series of sea changes to the way individuals and whole societies work, trade, and live. Even just the last 50 years have brought unpredictable changes and greater volatility. In this period, we in Singapore assumed independence and found our legs. We also saw new systems of government as nationalism succeeded colonialism, followed by transnationalism and global citizenry; several global recessions; sea changes in biomedical science, nanotechnology, ICT and other fields; the digital revolution; and the perpetual drift of the global economic centre of power across the continents. Long and short economic cycles, and unpredictable structural changes are the norm.

In more recent years, the Global Financial Crisis of 2008 has driven home the lesson that real, sustainable growth can only come from the hard and continual work of restructuring, and ultimately from productivity growth. Policymakers around the world are beginning to take structural reforms to heart. If this continues in the coming 50 years, we have cause for cautious optimism.

The second lesson is that a zero-sum game, like what played out in the spice wars, cannot be a basis of sustainable economic development. It required brutal fights, domination of the islands, and for some to profit at the loss of others.

Post-Second World War, countries have at times transcended the zero-sum trap. We learned to cooperate through international bodies and agreements, we freed the movement of goods, ideas and people. The 1947 General Agreement on Tariffs and Trade (and later WTO) grew out of the vision that greater trade cooperation enables all to prosper. Countries continue to go through spasms of protectionism, but seen on a scale of decades, our combined progression has been upward and mutual. Trade and cooperation have been a crucial part of the global and historical growth story, indeed in the advancement of mankind.

In the last 50 years, those who embraced cooperation and plugged themselves into the global economy have prospered, lifting hundreds of millions out of poverty. From our early days, Singapore benefited greatly from this openness, including the spice trade. Singapore was for centuries an emporium of the world, thriving in the trade of physical goods, and a key node in the Maritime Silk Road.

By keeping ourselves open to the world, Singapore was among the Asian success stories whose experience encouraged many more, including China and other developing nations, to join the global grid.

The third, and most important lesson is this: ideas and values are of timeless worth. There may be times when single commodities outvalue them, but in the long run, it is the indomitable and intangible that not only enrich whole societies in their pockets and their spirits, but endure over centuries. And what differentiates a good idea from a valuable nutmeg tree? While commodities come in limited supply, good ideas can be shared limitlessly. In the sharing and propagation of good ideas, they generate further good ideas, wisdom and wealth, and uplift whole societies. They are a classic public good, and those societies that can best grow this public good are best placed for success and longevity.

There is one more characteristic of good ideas that distinguishes them from nutmeg — good ideas can sprout anywhere.

These three lessons bring us back from the Spice Islands and Manhattan Island to another, smaller and younger, island — Singapore.

The story of Singapore to date has been one of evolving with time, staying open to all, and being a home to good ideas. These are approaches that anyone can adopt; no one society is destined to succeed or fail at evolution, openness or good ideas. Indeed, all around us, we see others great and small experiment with these approaches. I believe we will see great accomplishments from our neighbours, our competitors and our friends when they stay nimble, open and creative. And we will welcome their successes even as we seek to chart our own way for Singapore.

As for Singapore, though small and bare of natural resources, this city-state can aggregate the talent, capital and ideas that can catalyse innovation and creativity. The world is not flat but spiky. Increasingly, the life-changing innovations of our time come from the major global cities that bring together talent, wealth, and a dream to improve lives.

Singapore has, like every other city on earth, the potential to do this well in the future. Our particular strength is our diversity in race, religion, culture and ideas that allows us to be a Global-Asia node. But we must keep on keeping our minds open and our reach high, even as we stay grounded in our values.

Nobody could have anticipated the changes we have seen in the last 50 years. I certainly could not have. In my earlier jobs, working hard to respond to some of these changes, such as the tumultuous Asian Financial Crisis of the late 1990s and the Global Financial Crisis in the late 2000s, I learned that we must build strong fundamentals and stay vigilant and adaptable if we want to thrive in this age of transformation.

In the next 50 years, we shall see accelerated transformations of economic structures and technology. We shall see very important geopolitical and demographic changes play out in ways that the world has yet to experience. We can choose to close our doors and minds. Or we can choose to harness our creative impulse, our will to adapt, and ultimately our instinct to bring everyone forward together, as we have done in riding through all the changes of the past, regardless of the seeming insurmountability of challenges.

In Singapore, we must be ready for and embrace change. We must stay open and connect with the world, and enable everyone to be the best they can be. We must also always have a mind on the long term, and not take shortcuts or opt for short-term fixes that would land us in trouble later. Economic growth and economic restructuring are hard work, but we can do it and we do not shy away from hard work.

In the future, the global economy will be defined more by ideas, innovation and creativity. We can be a living laboratory for these changes, and usher in an era where advanced manufacturing and new services, powered by technology, powered by ideas, will enhance people's welfare. And we must invest in research and development, and protect and advance the use of intellectual property.

Singapore's progress over the last 50 years is best explained by our transparency about the values we stand for, and our actions to show this. We are a people and a government who can be trusted to keep our promises, who can be relied upon to work hard, do our best, and ensure the predictability in public policy that will make others feel safe for decades to come. We stand for integrity, social harmony, hard work, self-reliance, good governance, openness to the world, humility to learn, generosity to share, and commitment to building and supporting a fair and just society.

This has brought us prosperity over the last 50 years as local and foreign investors took us at our word, and as union leaders, workers and employers work together in a relationship of trust to create fair outcomes for all.

Going forward, we shall keep investing in education. To prepare for the unpreparable, our education system must seek to create multiple pathways, promote multiple modes of learning, and develop talents in multiple domains.

Our young must be able to learn more about the world around us, and all Singaporeans to learn for life, throughout our lifetimes. We should also keep Singapore a hub for global decision-makers to connect and discuss the ideas, big and small, that can make a difference.

Singapore's success has also offered this simple and profound truth: People matter, and how people interact with one another matters. At the national level, the government has had to adapt its strategies and policies to nudge and nurture industry as they strive to take full advantage of the new possibilities. At the societal level, institutions like the family, schools, public service, community, unions, civil society and others have played an important role in keeping our individual identities and passions steadfast even as external changes buffet us. I have no doubt that our future success will depend in no small part on the ability of our institutions to stay true and healthy, and the ability of our society to cohere and excel together as one community.

Values will determine not only the future of our economy, but also the fabric of our society. On the cusp of our golden jubilee, Singaporeans joined in a nationwide dialogue — Our Singapore Conversation — and, after thousands of hours of exchanges, agreed that we aspire to a shared future of Opportunities, Purpose, Assurance, Spirit, and Trust.

These must be built on values. Opportunities to achieve and succeed whatever our starting point, whatever our passion, are done justice to by hard work, perseverance and a commitment to excellence. Purposeful living is centred on the importance of contributing to the greater good. The call for Assurance is born of an innate sense of what is fair and just. A Spirited society is built out of individuals who are caring, responsible, resilient and who value harmony. And Trust will take all parts behaving with respect, integrity, and commitment to not plunder from the future in order to serve only the present.

For the future, will we have the wisdom to cooperate and expand our space, or will we, like the nutmeg traders of the 17th century, fight and kill one another over something whose value is finally perishable? Will we make the wise decision to develop free economies, with innovation powered by new ideas and new technologies? Will we have a growth mentality or a scarcity mentality? The questions, and the possibilities, are many and indeterminable.

One thing that is very probable is that the changes in the next 50 years will be greater, quicker, and ever more disruptive than those of the last 50. They will hold both threats and opportunities. Growth, equality, and harmony will depend on how well we work as one, and with others, to grow the pie for all. With timely ideas, and timeless values, we can expand our space for growth and share the fruits of growth with all.

For all of this is not about economic growth alone. Though we often speak in terms of growth numbers and productivity figures, these are all just means to an end. That end is a better life for all, a life where every Singaporean can fulfil his potential and realise his aspirations, all while keeping our Singapore character and values.

At the turn of the century, Singapore had made our rapid journey from Third World to First World. Our founding prime minister and then Senior Minister Lee Kuan Yew said, "There are two parts to Singapore's success: the hardware or the hard economic data that adds up to good gross domestic product figures; and the software that drives this hardware."

Just as we need economic success to improve the lives of Singaporeans, we must draw together as one caring, cohesive society if we hope to succeed. That is why Mr. Lee said, "Without a cohesive society, a people who care for each other, especially for the less successful, we cannot succeed."

As we look forward to the next 50 years, the goals of our founding leaders remain as current as ever. I have faith that we can achieve our goal, and that Singaporeans will be able to step forward and contribute good ideas to the world, in our own humble way.

A life of opportunities and purpose for every Singaporean, and a life of giving back to others each in our own small way. This is the real goal, and this will not change, whether it is 1965, 2015, 2065 or beyond.

The Next 50 Years of Singapore's Economy and Business

Ho Kwon Ping
CEO
Banyan Tree Holdings

Singapore is the only fully sovereign and independent nation with such disproportion between its land mass and population size. And yet, despite the absence of a hinterland, Singapore has chosen a path of economic development which is unprecedented elsewhere. What Singapore's leaders did immediately upon an independence more thrust upon them than actually desired, was to embark on what I will call the "Three Ls Strategy":

1. Location: Building upon Singapore's historic choke point between East Asia and Europe to ensure that it remained the maritime trading centre between these two worlds, and then leveraging on its location to be the regional aviation hub and financial centre.
2. Land: Intentional intervention against free-market principles for allocation of scarce land to achieve very purposeful and targeted national objectives, ranging from affordable public housing to industrial estates for foreign manufacturers.
3. Labour: Liberal policy towards foreign workers to keep costs low, while continually upgrading skills and productivity of Singaporeans to ensure competiveness against neighbouring countries.

In the next 50 years, what then are the threats to each of the 3 Ls of the strategy, and what are the possible responses?

Threats

Location

Is our hub status declining into irrelevance as global trends create new hubs or have those developments rendered the whole notion obsolete?

Climate change has opened a year-round, ice-free Artic passage between the massive economies of Northeast Asia and Europe which may eventually bypass Singapore. Massive investments in rail and road networks will allow every part of China to access ports in the Indian Ocean, or carry cargo across Russia and Central Asia to Europe directly, without passing through the Straits of Malacca. Changi Airport and Singapore Airlines are challenged by the rise of Middle Eastern airports and airlines. And the rise of numerous world-class airports in China has resulted in direct flights between the rest of the world and Chinese cities, bypassing Singapore.

Another hub-based business activity is financial services. The rise of China has created a strong East Asian financial cluster comprising Shanghai, Hong Kong, Tokyo and Seoul. Further westwards, Dubai, Doha, and Abu Dhabi effectively service South and Central Asia, and Africa. And with Sydney servicing Australasia, that leaves Singapore as the financial services centre for only Southeast Asia.

Land

Are we simply running out of it despite ceaseless reclamation? And is its high cost making manufacturing so unviable that we should simply get out of it? If we are running out of land, should we not focus on high value-added services and abandon a manufacturing strategy?

The other big issue involving land scarcity is its impact on the price of public housing. To the extent that worsening wealth inequality is a growing economic and social problem, is our land pricing policy serving the needs of our people? What indeed is the value of a rising per capita GDP if the cost of our homes per capita is rising even faster?

Labour

The same doubts plague this resource as with Land, but this is more intractable because it involves human lives. Whereas the dilemma of land scarcity is largely one of pricing and allocation priority, labour scarcity, cost, and productivity are related in complex and sometimes contradictory ways.

Response

Location

How do we maintain our competitiveness as Singapore's strategic location declines?

I believe that the answer is in creating several critical ecosystems of business activity which are so elaborately inter-related that they cannot be reconstructed by competitors, is the result of continual incremental improvements over decades, and can hold their own in global competitiveness regardless of geography.

Let me highlight an example of such ecosystems which we have been building over 20 years.

In aviation, Changi Airport and Singapore Airlines may decline in importance. But if we add to our early start as an aviation hub global capability in aviation leasing, financing and insurance; if we have the top engine repair and maintenance facilities here manned by very skilled technicians; if we attract the most sophisticated avionics and small precision components manufacturers here; if we create a support environment of local small and medium-sized enterprises (SMEs) which can service the outsourced work of the MNCs that are here; and cutting-edge research in our universities on the digital technologies related to aviation, I think there will be at most one or two other global competitors to Singapore in this domain.

The same is true in the life sciences, petroleum refining industry, financial services, and other knowledge-intensive industries such as information and communications technology.

This strategy is good for another 50 years, but the purposeful, deliberate selection of specific industries as the winners of tomorrow is itself risky. It requires a judicious balance between planning and market forces, and close collaboration between policymakers and industry. Another risk is the very expensive link between applied research and product development. Research funding cannot always have immediate commercial applications and yet funding cannot be open-ended; finding the right balance will again require clear, far-sighted but accurate judgement.

Finally, even if Singapore's geographic location becomes less strategic in a global context, the eventual creation of a genuine ASEAN Economic Community will finally create opportunities for our SMEs.

Land

I had identified two challenges: viability of manufacturing in the face of land shortages, and housing affordability.

On the first challenge, there is no evidence that the manufacturing of high value, sophisticated products requires more space or labour than services. In fact, it may be the other way round — the output per square metre of space or per worker is probably multiple times higher in a life-sciences production plant than in a food court. The choice really is a false dichotomy if one chooses between services and manufacturing. The choice is not between services and manufacturing. It is between low and high-valued activities of any kind.

The second challenge of housing affordability is more intractable and perhaps requires a more radical approach. First, that property prices should perhaps be more actively managed so that they match the growth rate of lifetime income or about 4–5% per year. And second, that in terms of pricing the tail should not wag the dog — public housing prices should perhaps determine private housing prices, not the other way round.

Both of these suggestions point to one possible idea: that of a national housing price regulator. One objective of a national housing price regulator would be to integrate and influence the pricing of the three housing markets — Housing and Development Board (HDB) entry level flats, HDB resale, and private housing, so that the whole market is not led by private housing, which in turn is led by foreign demand. Another goal would be to have prices strike a balance between housing as an utility — the goal of young, first time owners — and housing as a wealth asset, a store of value — the goal of older owners or investors.

It may be timely for HDB to consider a gradual and phased exit over the next decades, from its role as housing developer in order to focus on a new dual role: first, as master land developer for entire new towns or districts, and second, as the regulator of housing prices in these areas, and to get out of the developer business entirely.

Its most important and sensitive function could be the setting of residential product sale-price caps for each land parcel, which in turn would then be auctioned off to private developers. The competition by private developers on detailed design, quality, features and so forth would ensure that market forces dictate, but within residential price ranges set by HDB.

Labour

One reason for Singapore's high income inequality is the high wage differential between different job vocations. Among all the OECD economies, Singapore has the highest income differential between a doctor or lawyer on one hand, and a construction worker or retail assistant on the other.

There are two reasons for this. First, a large workforce of low-cost, low-skilled foreign workers depresses the wages of everyone in that wage band, regardless of nationality. Second, our educational system creates a large differential in starting salaries between the technical versus university graduates.

There are two possible ways to address these two causes of our problems.

First, we can perhaps devise a more innovative immigration programme where foreign workers are seen less as a necessary evil but more as one element, and a positive one, in an overall population strategy which does not distinguish so much between foreigner and Singaporean, but recognises their mutual dependency. Instead of just drastically curtailing their influx, the focus could be on finding ways to drastically increase their wages, skills and productivity. And very importantly, to provide economic incentives to create desired outcomes.

Current immigration policy with its punitive foreign worker levy may be simply counterproductive. It raises the cost of employing them but does not reduce the demand, and furthermore attracts lower-skilled workers because the better ones prefer to go to countries where the take-home pay is higher.

The levy could instead be converted into each worker's deferred savings account — similar to a CPF — to be withdrawn upon his permanent repatriation so as to ensure good behaviour whilst in Singapore. Immediately and without an increase in cost to employers, the quality of foreign workers will go up since the higher-skilled will be attracted here. The conversion of levies into a CPF lookalike for foreign workers is also the most effective way to ensure voluntary repatriation after the long-term residency has expired.

After each round of economic restructuring, the foreign worker community in our midst should correspondingly be more skilled — perhaps all will even have a minimum high school education and certified skills. When that happens, we can perhaps see foreign workers as a potential talent pool. We can sieve through this pool to find a small minority who are self-motivated to attain measurably higher skills through training programmes and employer certification, and we reward them by longer-stay residency permits. Those who aspire even further upwards to change their careers can perhaps even find a pathway towards permanent residency and for some, eventual citizenship.

Second, perhaps education pathways can be re-designed to help reduce income inequality. Although much admired for its rigour, Singapore's rigid, linear pathways reflect the university bias of the Anglo-Saxon model. The starting salary of a Singapore university graduate is about 30–35% higher than that of a polytechnic graduate, whilst in Europe the gap is only about 10–15%. The gap is much bigger for an ITE graduate.

There are possibly two things we can do to reduce the income gap between technical and university graduates. First, we can amend the technical school — meaning polytechnic — educational pathway so that their students graduate at the same age as university graduates, and have starting salaries closer to graduates. Second, we can increase the intersecting pathways by which early entrants into vocational training can cross back into polytechnic or university streams. Today, the rarity of an ITE graduate making it to university justifies a news headline; this should become normal in future.

"Soft" Suggestions

Finally, I would like to make two "soft" suggestions which would not normally be associated with "hard" economics.

My first suggestion is that Singapore can take the lead, again over the next 50 years, in defining new and more holistic indices for economic progress, which take into account factors such as human wellbeing, environmental sustainability, and sociocultural development. There is a need to counter the complacency of affluence with a compelling vision for our young to aspire towards, measured by more than per capita GDP growth or billionaires per square mile. In other words, even if others do not want to measure against us, we should measure ourselves against our own yardsticks of holistic progress.

My final suggestion is that inclusion, diversity and freedom of expression needs to be proactively cultivated if we want to attract the best global talent for innovation in knowledge-based, creative industries, from artificial intelligence to biomechanics. The point here is that whilst tourists may come to Singapore for our mega-attractions, whether car races, casinos, or massive plant conservatories, the people we really want — indeed, need — to attract to Singapore to spearhead entrepreneurial innovation, come for different reasons. Our clean, safe, physical environment is of course important. But beyond that, a culture of freedom, inclusion and diversity is very important — perhaps even more than tax incentives.

Whither Singapore's Unemployment Rate?

Hoon Hian Teck
Professor of Economics and Associate Dean
Singapore Management University

In the period 1990–1999, Singapore's average annual real GDP growth was 7.3% with a coefficient of variation, which is a measure of dispersion of growth around its mean, of 0.49.[1] The average annual total unemployment rate during this period was 1.9%.[2] In comparison, in the period 2000–2012, when the average annual real GDP growth was 5.6% with a coefficient of variation of 0.79, the average annual total unemployment rate was 2.8%. Looking into Singapore's next 50 years, if real GDP grows at 3% on average, what does it imply for the rate of unemployment? Will slower growth coincide with more variable growth? This essay explores these questions.

Before proceeding to explore what slower growth might mean for the unemployment rate, let us review why Singapore is expected to grow more slowly. It helps to begin with a simple accounting relationship: Growth rate of total real GDP is the sum of the growth rate of real GDP per worker and the growth rate of labour force. Real GDP per worker is a measure of average labour productivity so we can say that total GDP growth rate is the sum of the growth of labour productivity and labour force growth. The

[1] By real GDP growth, we refer to the value of gross domestic product measured at constant market prices. The calculation here is based on the time series on GDP at 2005 market prices available from Singapore Department of Statistics. Formally, the coefficient of variation is calculated as the standard deviation divided by the mean.

[2] The data on unemployment is available from the Singapore Ministry of Manpower.

first three decades or so of Singapore's growth is best described as catch-up growth when labour productivity grew by racing to catch up to the world technology frontier, a process facilitated by its business-friendly environment which attracted multinational corporations to base their manufacturing activities here to produce and sell into the world market. This process of convergence involved moving up the value chain in manufacturing. Available data show that in the past decade, the employment share of manufacturing has shrunk while the share in the services sector has expanded. While the current restructuring effort is aimed at boosting productivity across all enterprises in the services sector, the experience in the developed economies shows that the pace of productivity improvement is more muted in the services sector. A frequent reference is made to the fact that the rate of growth of real GDP per person in the United States, a world technology leader, has averaged 2% over the last century. Even so, many economists now believe that future labour productivity growth in the US will be less than 2%.[3] If Singapore can manage to achieve labour productivity growth of 2% per annum and the labour force grows at 1% on average over the next 50 years, total real GDP growth will average 3% per annum.

Will the total unemployment rate rise above 3%? The framework that economists use to think about the determinants of the unemployment rate is the search-and-matching model of the labour market.[4] At the heart of the model is the decision that firms make to create job vacancies and to recruit suitable workers to fill these vacancies. If firms are free to create job vacancies so long as they are willing to incur the necessary costs to recruit workers, then the equilibrium condition that determines the tightness of the labour market equates the expected cost of recruitment to the surplus that the firm expects to gain from employing another worker.[5] The surplus, in turn, is given by the excess of the present value of the worker's marginal labour productivity over the present value of the worker's wage.

---

3 See J. G. Fernald and C. I. Jones (2014), The Future of U.S. Economic Growth, *American Economic Review: Papers and Proceedings, 104*(5), 44–49 and the references cited therein.

4 The Nobel Prize in Economics in 2010 was awarded to three economists who developed the search-and-matching model: Peter Diamond, Dale Mortensen, and Christopher Pissarides.

5 Formally, the tightness of the labour market is given by the number of job vacancies for every unemployed worker. The tighter the labour market is, the lower the rate of unemployment.

Using this equilibrium condition, we can draw a few inferences about Singapore's future unemployment rate.

First, the adage that "wage increases need to be matched by productivity increases" holds in the model. The result of having wage increases that outrun productivity gains is that there is a rise in the rate of unemployment. The experience of Western Europe provides a cautionary tale. France, Germany and Italy all had low unemployment rates in the 1960s — about 2% to 3%. However, in the succeeding decades, the average unemployment rate in these economies steadily ratcheted up with France and Italy experiencing double-digit unemployment rates by the start of the new millennium. One explanation points to how the rapid growth due to the rebuilding of these economies after the Second World War was not recognised to be transitional so that when the process of convergence ended the economies would necessarily slow down. As a result, the high growth expectations led to wage increases that were ultimately not met by actual productivity gains. As a consequence, the unemployment rate began to rise in Western Europe.[6] One lesson for Singapore is that the workforce must adjust to an era of slower growth. On the other hand, if efforts continue apace to generate innovation and achieve 2% of labour productivity growth, workers can look forward to real wage increases of 2% without rising unemployment.

Second, successful matching of workers with the right skills to meet the needs of the new jobs in the next half century will enable the unemployment rate to stay low. The modern economy is fraught with fresh novelties thrown up by new technologies as well as ideas of business people.[7] In a sense, this means that the type of skills needed for jobs of the future cannot be accurately forecasted. Yet, our educational institutions can seek to teach people how to learn so that they thrive in an environment laden with such novelties. Additionally, while it is the private business enterprises that will

---

[6] One might ask why the unemployment rate remained stubbornly high in Western Europe since, with the passage of time, workers would come to recognise the growth slowdown. An explanation is that institutions that provided strong support to the unemployed interacted with the growth slowdown to keep the unemployment rate high. See O. J. Blanchard (2006), European Unemployment: Evolution of Facts and Ideas, *Economic Policy, 21*(45), 5–59.

[7] See E. S. Phelps (2013), *Mass Flourishing: How Grassroots Innovation Created Jobs, Challenge, and Change*, Princeton: Princeton University Press, for an emphasis on the ideas generated by people engaged in the world of business.

create most of the new jobs, the government can facilitate a close communication between businesses and training institutions so that supply can match the demand for new skills.

Third, it appears, judging from the experiences of today's developed economies, that the era of slower growth will be accompanied by increased volatility. Without strong growth to provide a buffer, negative external shocks could translate into more lost jobs. Recessions could become deeper. What tools should be used to fight recessions? Since 1981, the Monetary Authority of Singapore has adopted an exchange rate-based policy rule, adjusting the exchange rate according to how far the inflation rate deviates from an implicit inflation target and the output gap.[8] This has led to reduced volatility in inflation and output.[9] However, during major recessionary episodes such as the 1997–1998 shock from the Asian financial crisis and the 2008–2009 Lehman Brothers crisis, major cuts in wage costs were implemented to fight the recessions. In order to finance jobs credits during episodes of negative external shocks, the government would need to save during good times. Even though the phase of catch-up growth is over, mature economies sometimes face prolonged periods when economic activity picks up — such as the US Internet boom in the second half of 1990s — and tax revenues increase (at given tax rates). A fiscally prudent government will save up these additional fiscal resources in order to use them to hasten economic recoveries when negative shocks hit the economy.

Singapore's first 50 years saw the economy deliver economic growth that very likely exceeded the expectations of its workforce. As a result, productivity growth exceeded wage expectations thus leading to a steady decline in the unemployment rate. In the next 50 years, Singapore can avoid the way that the unemployment rate has ratcheted upwards in Western Europe since the 1960s. To do so, it must be innovative to deliver the needed 2% labour productivity growth so that real wages can increase at 2% per annum. Its ability to facilitate the matching of workers to jobs will also help to keep the unemployment rate low. Finally, running budgetary surpluses in good times will enable the government to have the fiscal resources to fund jobs credits to save jobs in leaner times.

---

[8] The output gap refers to the deviation of actual GDP from potential GDP.

[9] See I. Mihov (2013), The Exchange Rate as an Instrument of Monetary Policy, Special Feature A, *Macroeconomic Review, April 2013*, Monetary Authority of Singapore, pp. 74–81.

Speaking for the Trees — Defining Moments of Environment Advocacy in Singapore

Faizah Jamal
Nominated Member of Parliament February 2012–August 2014
(Civic and People Sector), Environment Educator

Pushing the Envelope

Singapore. Early 1990s. A proposed 18-hole golf course in Lower Peirce Nature Reserve. Members of the then Malayan Nature Society (Singapore Branch), now known as the Nature Society (Singapore), protested vehemently. To garner public support, they did something they have never done before. They organised a public petition campaign. They literally went door-to-door.

One of them was a young lawyer who went round, asking lawyer colleagues to sign, in the belief that that would add credence and credibility to the cause. This young lawyer then got a call from the big boss to see him at his office. He said, "I understand that you have been asking the lawyers to sign a petition." The boss then asked the young lawyer if the lawyer knew the party behind the proposal to build the golf course. The young lawyer confidently said, "Of course. It's PUB. Would you like to sign?"

The boss sighed, looked at the young lawyer and said, "You know, PUB is one of our biggest clients."

At that point, the young lawyer wished there was a hole in the ground that would swallow her up.

True story.

That young lawyer? That was me, more than 20 years ago.

Incidentally we were roundly scolded by the government for having the gall to organise a petition campaign. We were publicly told "You do not petition the Singapore Government!"

Lower Peirce Nature Reserve is still there. No golf course. The government did not say why. And the young lawyer lived to tell the tale!

Invoking the Power of a Sensorial Experience

Fast forward 10 years. Chek Jawa, more than 1,000 people, through word of mouth and public education, turned up one weekend to see for themselves our newly found marine treasures and to signal their disapproval of the government's reclamation plans. No "immediate plans" for the next 10 years, said the government in response, calling off reclamation works. The 10 years ended in 2012. So far no word has been mentioned about extending the grace period. Chek Jawa is still there. However as we will see below, the threat to its existence is not over.

The Continuing Story of Bukit Brown

2012. The government's plans to exhume part of Bukit Brown Cemetery — the final resting place for many of our pioneers and a place well known by members of the Nature Society since the 1980s for its rich birdlife and fauna — to build an eight-lane highway created an uproar.

Significantly, the unhappiness was felt beyond the nature groups. For the first time, there was an alliance between the Nature Society and non-environment groups like the Singapore Heritage Society to lend weight to the issue. Concerns were also raised in Parliament at the Budget Debate 2012 by no fewer than four MPs, two of whom were Nominated MPs, and only one (yours truly) framing it along environmental terms, seeking to find out if environmental impact assessment studies had been conducted.

Significantly also, this issue brought about several rounds of engagement between the (then) Minister of State for National Development Mr. Tan Chuan-Jin and nature and heritage groups. Nevertheless, the plans for the eight-lane highway are set to proceed. The heritage enthusiasts calling themselves "Brownies" continue with their public awareness walks every weekend without fail.

From Golf Courses to Train Lines

In the meantime, the environment and nature groups have another — and bigger — challenge to worry about — the contentious White Paper and Land Use Plan unveiled in Parliament in February 2013.

While the arguments both in Parliament and out, centred on "the 6.9 million people" issue, environmentalists became alarmed at the plan to build a train line, the Cross Island Line, that will cut through the Central Catchment Nature Reserve, an issue that seemed to have escaped the attention of most Singaporeans more worried about jobs and migrant workers than the value of the gazetted forest "reserve."

The Nature Society lost no time in presenting their own alternative proposal to the government which will leave the nature reserve intact. Many people outside the nature groups also voiced their unhappiness, in part because they have been watching with great dismay, the increasing disappearance of many of places that they grew up with and have come to love, to make way for "development."

Speaking for the Trees in the House

In Parliament only one person saw the White Paper and the Land Use Plan, in particular with its proposed "train-line-through-the-nature-reserve," and the massive reclamation plans that will swallow up, among other places, the very same Chek Jawa that thousands of Singaporeans and tourists have known and grown to love, not only as a serious environment issue, and with the added argument that the government seemed to have forgotten the simple foundation of which our lives are built upon, which is "no environment, no economy" but also seeing the White Paper as a moral issue based on a skewed and no longer tenable economic paradigm of "growth."

Calling strongly for a compulsory environment impact assessment that is transparent and open to public scrutiny, in the spirit of openness and accountability that the government has claimed it is interested in, I chose to exercise my right to say "No" to the White Paper.

In all my 30 years being involved with environment advocacy there has not been a more defining moment personally than that day, standing up when called upon by the Speaker of Parliament for Members of the House who agreed with the Workers' Party Secretary-General Low Thia Kiang's call for a division, and to see my name as among the 13 MPs who said "No" to the White Paper.

The Evolving Nature of the Discourse

The upshot of this and the strong opposition by nature groups and members of the public is an unprecedented process of engagement between the Land Transport Authority with nature groups, chaired by no less than the Senior Minister of State for Transport Mrs. Josephine Teo herself. This process included taking the Senior Minister of State on a walk to the areas that will be severely impacted by the plans, which started in mid-2013 and are still continuing at the point of writing, a good fifteen months since the White Paper and Land Use Plan Debate.

The issue of environmental impact assessment also took centre stage with LTA agreeing to make it a pre-condition of the proposed train construction in consultation with the nature groups.

To the credit of LTA, these consultations with nature groups are still continuing and the outcome remains to be seen.

Whither Environmental Advocacy? The Next 50 Years

Even before the Lower Peirce issue was settled I had left on a European Union-ASEAN scholarship to pursue a Master's in Environment Law in London. Back then in 1993, very few people at home even knew there was such a thing.

Fast forward to 30 years after Lower Peirce. There are more nature groups now apart from the Nature Society. More significantly, it is the young people who understand what is at stake and want to protect what is left of our wild spaces.

With social media, petitions are a dime a dozen. Contrast Lower Peirce.

Witness also a small group of 19-year-olds led by Wong Xinyuan, who had contacted me upon reading that I had voted against the White Paper, because they wanted to do more than express their unhappiness over the White Paper online and asked me what they can do about it. Before I knew it, they had started "Eco Youth" and even had a dialogue with the National Population and Talent Division, which agreed that there should be more engagement with young people over what, ultimately, would be their future.

Witness another young man, Tan Yi Han, who was so concerned with the recurring haze issue that he started the "People's Movement To Stop The Haze" with other young people, making representations to the relevant agencies as well as contacts with Indonesian NGOs in their bid to do more than complain.

More young people are taking up courses in Environment Studies and related subjects in universities. One young lady from the Eco Youth group has expressed her interest to specialise in Environment Law. Younger lawyers are keen to develop public interest litigation. Presumably that would include environment issues. In fact, a very recent symposium organised by law students at SMU on a possible manifestation of public interest litigation in Singapore was well attended by not only students but also members of civil society.

For many young people, there is more to life than GDP.

More and more people want to take ownership and power over their lives back. Not for them the notion that an authority will decide that what is good for the economy is also good for them. Not for them the old paradigm that they will have to be cheaper, better and faster than their neighbours in order to protect their rice bowl. Not for them the old paradigm of lack and fear.

Is this peculiar to Singapore? Hardly. It is an awakening, happening all over the world, a consciousness that we have done more than our share of damage to the planet, and now it is time to say "Stop. Live a life of 'Enough.'"

Singapore Economy: Strategies for the Next 50 Years

S. Iswaran
Minister, Prime Minister's Office and
Second Minister for Home Affairs and Trade and Industry, Singapore

> *Today the economy is in a strong position. This is because we in Singapore believe in hard work... We believe that we must adjust ourselves to changing situations. We believe in seizing economic opportunities and not let them go past us. Finally, we believe in self-reliance.*
>
> Dr. Goh Keng Swee, 1969

Singapore's economic story is marked by an unrelenting effort to stay competitive and remain relevant within a dynamic external environment. In 1965, with a GNP per capita of less than US$320, Singapore was a newly independent nation with poor infrastructure, limited capital and significant unemployment. We emerged from this third-world status through a series of industrial transformations over the decades — from labour intensive manufacturing and regionalisation, to a knowledge-based economy driven by innovation, high-tech manufacturing and high value services.

By strengthening our core capabilities, and staying nimble and responsive, we have fared well against the challenges of the last five decades. Today, Singapore stands as a leading business and financial hub in Asia. We have a diversified economy with both a vibrant internationalised services sector, and an advanced manufacturing sector with strengths in several key niches such as electronics, petrochemicals and biomedical manufacturing.

The next 50 years will bring new opportunities but will also be fraught with challenges. In navigating the uncertain terrain that lies ahead, it is essential that we adhere to the very fundamentals that have brought us thus far and served us well.

Trends Over the Next 50 Years Present Both Challenges and Opportunities

Changes in the global economic landscape

The centre of global economic gravity is shifting from the advanced economies to the emerging economies of Asia. This will benefit Singapore in two ways. The first stems from a geographic advantage. With economic integration, distributed manufacturing and the growing sophistication of supply chains, Singapore is well-positioned to benefit from hosting high value-added production activities such as design and R&D in Asia. The second is a demographic dividend. Rising demand from a growing and wealthier Asian middle class will create new markets for our businesses. Growth in China, India and ASEAN will boost demand not just for our goods exports, but also exportable services like clean technologies and urban solutions.

However, the rise of emerging economies in Asia also portends heightened competition. We have witnessed the rise of China, the remarkable transformation of its economy, and the growing international footprint of Chinese enterprises over the past three decades. In the next phase, China will also pose increasing competition in high-tech manufacturing sectors like the semiconductor industry. Similarly, India's newly elected government has announced "Make in India" and "Smart Cities" as two of its priorities, potentially creating a new manufacturing base in Asia. In ASEAN, the advent of the ASEAN Economic Community in 2015, with its market of 600 million, will give added impetus to the growth of its member states. In short, the emerging economies of Asia will usher in a period of tremendous opportunities, but also heightened competition for markets, resources and talent in the region.

Demographic shifts

The global population is ageing. By 2050, one in every five people globally will be at least 60 or older, effectively doubling the current ratio of old to young. Singapore is no exception; at current birth rates and without immigration, the ratio of citizens of working age to each elderly citizen is projected to fall from 5.9 in 2012 to 2.1 in 2030. Many Asian economies enjoy a relatively younger population profile. An ageing and shrinking workforce bears serious implications for our economy. If we do not succeed in raising labour force participation rates and increasing productivity, our economic growth will inevitably slow.

Disruptive technologies

The emergence of disruptive technologies like additive manufacturing and machine learning will increase the applications of automation, and profoundly reshape our industries. On the one hand, it provides a path for Singapore to forge new capabilities and strengthen our competitiveness. On the other, it could also pose a threat if our workers fail to keep up with technological changes while other economies leapfrog us by adopting the new technologies. We are not alone in being confronted by such a challenge. A 2013 study by Frey and Osborne noted that 47% of total US employment is at risk of being computerised, highlighting the severe threat posed by technological advancement if countries fail to adapt.[1]

Allocating Our Resources Efficiently, Developing Our People and Raising Our Competitiveness through Productivity are Our Key Guiding Principles

Singapore has always competed on the basis of being an open economy underpinned by skills and sustainability. At each stage of our economic development, our strategies have focused on optimising our domestic resources, developing our people, and enhancing our economic space through connectivity and integration. These fundamentals will continue to be our bulwark against a rising competitive challenge as we seek new opportunities and growth over the next 50 years.

Optimising our resources

For a small economy like Singapore, the perennial economic question of allocating limited resources to the most productive uses takes on particular

[1] Carl Benedikt Frey and Michael A. Osborne (2013), "The Future of Employment: How Susceptible are Jobs to Computerisation?", Oxford University Martin School.

significance. In securing Singapore's economic future, we must ensure that input factors like land and energy do not become a binding constraint. Hence, we must harness innovation to maximise our supply side options and ensure efficient utilisation on the demand side.

In the coming years, Singapore will pursue more innovative solutions as we seek to push the boundaries in our quest to overcome our scarce land resource. The Jurong Rock Caverns show us what is possible with ingenuity and effort. The development of an underground master plan, exploring alternative uses for subterranean space, and designing innovative factories with smaller footprints are some key initiatives. Equally, our industrial land policy will assign significant weight to land productivity when evaluating competing uses.

For energy, our opportunity is bounded by Singapore's lack of indigenous energy resources, as well as any international accord to reduce carbon emissions. Hence, we must persevere in our efforts to diversify our energy sources and keep our options open. Our LNG terminal has unlocked new supply options beyond our immediate neighbourhood with US shale gas being a significant new variable. We also seek economically viable renewable energy (RE) options, which can contribute to carbon mitigation, and develop our cleantech sector. Some initiatives include the test-bedding of floating solar photovoltaic systems on reservoirs to maximise our limited space, facilitating the integration of RE sources into our energy system, and taking the lead in the adoption of solar electricity through the SolarNova programme. We will also intensify efforts to promote energy efficiency at the level of the household and the firm. This will entail the use of technology as well as allowing energy prices to reflect the true cost by avoiding consumption subsidies.

Ultimately, our efforts to ensure the optimal and sustainable use of our resources will not only yield economic benefits but also enhance the liveability of our city.

Developing our people and productivity

Recognising our people as the core source of strength, we have always invested heavily in a comprehensive pre-employment and continuing education system. Our challenge is to equip Singaporean with deep multidisciplinary skills that can be updated periodically, so that our workforce can stay relevant in the face of change and competition.

The recommendations of the ASPIRE committee to strengthen applied education pathways, and the work of the SkillsFuture Council are important in this regard. By working closely with industry and our institutions of higher learning, it will help ensure that our students are endowed with work-relevant skills and competencies to succeed in a dynamic economic environment. In addition, we continue to invest significantly in Continuing Education and Training (CET) to give workers opportunities to upgrade their skills throughout their careers. As Singapore deepens its integration into the global economy, we will also equip Singaporeans with the differentiating skills and experience that will enable them to operate effectively in a multicultural environment. Programmes such as the Strategic Attachment and Training Programme (STRAT) will provide Singaporeans with opportunities for overseas training and attachments with leading global companies.

Education and training are integral to our efforts to sustain productivity growth in the long run. In complement, businesses will have to continually adjust and improve their work processes to increase efficiency and enhance their innovation capabilities. The Government will continue to support this through the Research, Innovation and Enterprise plan. In particular, we will continue to promote greater collaboration between industry and our research institutes, through the establishment of joint corporate laboratories as well as plug-and-play technology solutions for SMEs to adopt, to sharpen our competitive edge.

Staying open

Singapore's genesis as a trading port and subsequent evolution as an economy has rested heavily on our economic connectivity. As an open economy, we have been able to overcome the constraint of a small domestic market, selectively complement our domestic talent base, and seize opportunities for our people and businesses. Indeed, our deep and broad economic links have been central to our competitive advantage. As we look ahead, economic integration continues to gather pace. These include regional efforts like the Trans-Pacific Partnership and Regional Comprehensive Economic Partnership, as well as multilateral initiatives at the WTO. To secure Singapore's economic future, it is essential that we remain actively engaged in this evolving international trade architecture.

Conclusion

In a speech at the Chinese Chamber of Commerce in 1969, Dr. Goh Keng Swee said, "Today the economy is in a strong position. This is because we in Singapore believe in hard work ... We believe that we must adjust ourselves to changing situations. We believe in seizing economic opportunities and not let them go past us. Finally, we believe in self-reliance."

Dr. Goh's wise words remain as relevant — today and for the future. Singapore progress in the past 50 years has been underpinned by our willingness to adapt to a changing external environment and to seize new opportunities. To do so effectively, we must be prepared internally — by optimising the use of our limited domestic resources; endowing our people with broad and deep capabilities; and staying open and connected as an economy. If we abide by these key principles and remain open to change, I am confident that the Singapore of 2065 will be a thriving economy, one that creates interesting and exciting jobs for Singaporeans to realise their aspirations.

Singapore 2065 — Economics and Beyond

Basant K. Kapur
Department of Economics
National University of Singapore

This is a visionary book, and it requires a visionary individual to conceive it and see it through to completion. May I congratulate Professor Euston Quah for his boldness and insightfulness in launching this enterprise, and for encouraging varied perspectives on what the Singapore of 2065 will, or should, be like, and how we can best arrive there. I am sure that much stimulating, and indeed, fascinating, food for thought will be found in these pages.

There are many concerns which, as is well known, weigh upon us in the near future. National economies have yet to recover fully from the Great Recession of 2007–2009, and the tasks of financial, fiscal, structural, and economic reform more generally, are still uncompleted. Geopolitical tensions, regionally and globally, are severe causes of concern, as are environmental problems. Income gaps are stubbornly persistent. More can be added to this list. However, 50 years is a long time, and in this article I am taking an optimistic view, or rather examining the implications of an optimistic scenario which, in my view, has a reasonable likelihood, though not a certainty, of materialising. Suppose that short- and medium-term problems and difficulties can be satisfactorily resolved. What will Singapore, and the world (given that Singapore cannot be dissociated from the global economic environment) look like 50 years hence?

Technological Change

A key determinant in my view will be technological change, and the rapidity with which it is progressing. (Another key issue is how closely Singapore will become integrated with its neighbours in ASEAN, China, and India, but I will leave this to others more qualified than me to discuss.) By its inherent nature, it is impossible to predict with high accuracy what specific forms future technological changes will assume. However, some broad developments are evident, and I shall focus on a couple of these, and the implications they have for people and societies.

Two key areas of intense, active technological progress are the advent of 3-D printing, and robotics. *The Economist*, in a 19 January 2013 article on "Reshoring Manufacturing," succinctly describes these phenomena:

> 3-D printing, a process in which individual machines build products by depositing layer upon layer of material, is already being used in research departments and factories .... Additive manufacturing machines can be left alone to print day and night. For now they are used mainly for prototyping and for complex parts, but in future they will increasingly make final products too .... Robots are already making a difference to the share of labour in total costs. Cheaper, more user-friendly and more dextrous robots are currently spreading into factories around the world .... Relative to the cost of labour, average robot prices since 1990 have fallen by 40–50% in many advanced economies, according to McKinsey. Baxter, a new generation of robot made by Rethink Robotics, an American firm, costs $22,000 apiece and is so safe and simple that it can be taught by an unskilled worker and operate right next to real people.

The labour market implications of these and other similar developments are illuminatingly discussed in a 29 March 2014 Special Report on Robots, also in *The Economist*. While there are little grounds for a crude Luddite-like concern over large-scale job erosion (as in the past, one might expect new sectors and activities to arise and provide new, varied, job opportunities), major structural changes in labour markets are to be expected. The demand for unskilled labour will decline, and so will even the demand for moderately skilled labour. The latter decline, the article claims (citing a study by Erik Brynjolfsson and Andrew McAfee of MIT) would be due to factors such as "the exponential growth in computing power," and "the progressive digitisation of things that people work with, from maps to legal texts to spreadsheets." "(S)oftware will take over a lot of the tasks carried out by humans sitting in front of screens," and as "machine learning" intensifies and accelerates, one might expect even more activities currently carried out by human labour to be automated.

Challenges for Singapore

What, then, are the resulting challenges for Singapore, and indeed for all societies, over the next 50 years? In my view, there are three implications, two practical and the third more philosophical in nature. After describing them, I will argue that they are in fact related.

The first has been much discussed in recent years — the need for individuals to "think smart and act smart." They will need to be highly skilled, versatile, and creative. Educational systems will need to be transformed accordingly (more on this below). As an interesting article by Carl Benedikt Frey points out, the well-paying jobs of the future will be in occupations that have yet to emerge, or are only now beginning to emerge, such as "big-data architects and analysts, cloud services specialists, ... and digital marketing professionals," and, rather than training individuals for specific occupations, educational systems will have to endow them with the skills, versatility, and creativity to do well in the occupations of the future.[1] Frey adds that individuals will, evidently, have to be skilled and capable enough to work with, rather than compete against, computer-based technologies.

The second has to do with the distributional dimension. There will always be individuals who, through physical or other handicaps, will not be able to take advantage of the available educational opportunities to be well prepared for the high-paying occupations of the future. In the optimistic scenario I am postulating, most individuals, and society at large, will be much more productive and prosperous than they currently are, and

[1] C. B. Frey (2014, July 18), Surviving the Tech Upheavals Ahead, *The Straits Times*.

any civilised society will have to devise mechanisms to ensure that those who are less able, through no fault of their own, are well looked after.

The third takes off from my observation above that most individuals, and society at large, will likely become increasingly productive and prosperous as technology continues its multiple advances. Do individuals, in Singapore and elsewhere, still wish to preoccupy themselves with the rat race — with materialistic possessions and obsessions, and keeping up with the Joneses? I am reminded of the opening paragraph of John Kenneth Galbraith's *The Affluent Society* (1958, rev. 1984), written in his inimitably insightful and witty style:

> Wealth is not without its advantages and the case to the contrary, although it has often been made, has never proved widely persuasive. But, beyond doubt, wealth is the relentless enemy of understanding. The poor man has always a precise view of his problem and its remedy: he hasn't enough and he needs more. The rich man can assume or imagine a much greater variety of ills and he will be correspondingly less certain of their remedy. Also, until he learns to live with his wealth, he will have a well-observed tendency to put it to the wrong purpose or otherwise make himself foolish.

Non-instrumental Passions and Activities

A historian (I believe it was Christopher Dawson, although the exact details elude me currently) said, if I recall correctly, "When starving people alight on a feast, they are apt to gorge themselves. Such has been the case with the materialism of the 20th Century." 50 years hence, the vast majority of people in Singapore and elsewhere are likely to be materially far more comfortable than their predecessors are today. Societal value systems, and the social, political, and educational climate generally, will have to be reoriented to place a much greater emphasis on promoting and fostering individuals' cultural, social, creative, and spiritual awareness and pursuits. Only then can individuals, in my view, lead truly satisfying and fulfilling lives. With much higher productivity, individuals need not have to work as long hours as they do today, and will need to fill their lives with activities that are aesthetically, intellectually, socially, and spiritually satisfying and enlightening — activities, in short, which are conducive to their self-actualisation as individuals and members of society.

Ironically, such intrinsically "non-instrumental" passions and activities may also prove to be instrumentally beneficial, although the latter benefits should by no means be the motivation for the former, nor the measure by which they are to be evaluated. In his fine book *Passions within Reason: The Strategic Role of the Emotions* (1988, especially Chapter 4), economist Robert Frank adduces findings from experimental psychology to show that people generally have an innate pre-disposition towards "short-termism," or "time-inconsistent behaviour" (preferring immediate to delayed gratification in very near-term choices, even though they prefer the reverse when the same choices are presented to them at more distant horizons). People who are mainly concerned about material gain are thus likely to make ill-advised short-term choices, which, ironically, reduce their material gain from their pursuits and activities, while those who have an intrinsic passion for the activities they engage in are likely to "seek perfection" to the best of their ability, and hence end up being more successful — and more fulfilled. In short, the continued progress of Singapore and other societies, 50 years hence, in all fields — scientific, technological, cultural, social, political, and spiritual — will be a consequence of individuals' pursuits of their passions in all these areas, rather than of personal, material benefits.

Renewable Energy and Its Relevance for Singapore in 2065

Er. Edwin Khew Teck Fook
Chairman, Sustainable Energy Association of Singapore
and Managing Director, Anaergia Pte Ltd

"Can Singapore 'Electrify' the World?", asked Prof. Kishore Mahbubhani in his article in *The Straits Times* (12 December 2013). I would like to ask a similar question that goes further — "Can Singapore 'Electrify' the World with Renewable Energy?" Where Prof. Kishore is proposing "a 'bold' national project to 'electrify' all vehicles in Singapore and create a new chapter in world history by becoming the first country in the world not to have petrol driven vehicles on the road," I would like to suggest that 50 years on we can indeed have an all-electric mobility system in Singapore supported by a smart grid, with charging stations in all HDB estates, shopping malls, condominiums and public places like hospitals, schools, universities, etc. Moreover these e-vehicles will be charged by clean renewable energy supplied by solar photovoltaic (PV) systems, biomass, biogas, wind, marine, biofuel and other renewable energy systems which are being developed in our research centres like the Energy Research Institute at NTU (ERI@N), the Solar Energy Research Institute Singapore (SERIS) and our various Polytechnics (Polys). In this scenario Singapore will be a model urban city operating on mostly renewal energy for all its power needs and a centre for these technologies, supplying total solutions to all urban cities in the world that aspire to be totally sustainable.

In this chapter I will like to elaborate on why I feel the above scenario is possible and how we can get there and how it can economically contribute significantly to Singapore's GDP.

I was asked by the Straits Times in an article they wrote on the sustainability of solar PV (18 August 2014) and its use in Singapore in 2050 and whether it is realistic at that point of time to have solar energy contribute more than 30% of Singapore's power and energy needs. Without hesitation I said, "Yes," as I know that much is being done in Singapore today to develop, test and commercialise all forms of solar energy systems (PV as well as thermal solar systems) and their projected contributions to Singapore's power and energy needs will be much greater than the 30% which is based on conservative projections of the researchers at SERIS.[1]

The projected electricity consumption in year 2065, assuming a population of approximately 7 million, will be about 65 terawatt hours per year (TWh/year), assuming that we have reached the maximum energy efficiency levels for our industries and homes — these are estimates provided by population[2] and electricity consumption[3] data, from which I have made my own simple straight line projections. Based on this estimate I am looking at the following projections for electricity production using the following technologies which will provide the renewable energy (RE) content in the projected 65 TWh/year of electricity consumed in Singapore:

<u>Solar PV</u>: Based on a scenario of high efficiency PV systems with area factors of 0.30 kilowatt peak per square metre (kWp/m^2) and a maximum implementation of energy efficiency in industries and homes, PV solar if deployed in the 45 square kilometre (km^2) projected total effective area (as based on information in "Solar PV Roadmap for Singapore") will contribute 20 TWh/year or approximately 30% of the electricity demand in 2065.

<u>Bio-gas from Organics:</u> Based on all food wastes generated (approximately 2,500 tons per day (tpd)) and other organics (animal manure from

---

[1] See the Solar PV Road Map for Singapore (2013), prepared for the Economic Development Board (EDB) and the Energy Market Authority (EMA), Singapore.

[2] National Population and Talent Division (NPTD) (2013), *Population White Paper: A Sustainable Population for a Dynamic Singapore,* Singapore: Prime Minister's Office. Retrieved February 23, 2015 from http://population.sg/whitepaper/downloads/population-white-paper.pdf.

[3] World Bank (2015). Electric power consumption (kWh per capita). Retrieved February 23, 2015 from http://data.worldbank.org/indicator/EG.USE.ELEC.KH.PC.

chicken, horse, zoo animals, etc.) including sewage sludge, industrial sludges, fats, oil and grease (FOG) from grease traps (approximately another 10,000 tpd) bio-gas (65% methane/35% CO_2) can produce approximately 4.0 TWh/year or approximately 6% of demand.

Power from Biomass: Based on about 900,000 tons/year of recoverable wood and horticultural waste generated and about 8,000 tons of municipal solid waste generated per day that will be incinerated or gasified, the total electricity generated from these waste resources is approximated to be 900 gigawatt hours per year (GWhr/year) plus 2.0 TWhr/year from wood waste and MSW respectively. This should contribute approximately 3.0 TWhr/year or 4.7% of demand.

Power from Marine Energy: Experiments are being done on tapping tidal in-stream energy where energy may be extracted between 300–600 GWh/year without any significant environment impact. This translates to a peak capacity of 250 megawatt peak (MWp). There is also a potential of tapping wave energy up to 52.9 GWh/year and presently pilot studies are in progress at the Tanah Merah Ferry Terminal with ERI@N's prototype design.

Wind Energy: There are 2 types of wind turbines — horizontal axis (HAWT) and vertical axis (VAWT). In Singapore because of the low wind speeds (between 2–4 metres per second (m/sec) average speeds measured at a height of 90 m) it may be possible to apply wind turbines on roofs of high-rise buildings and on offshore locations in our Southern shores where water depths are less than 20 metres (shallow water) and unused by marine traffic. A potential of up to 370 MWp can be harnessed from offshore wind to support the remote islands of Singapore and approximately 130 MWp can be obtained from VAWT generation on buildings in Singapore providing a total of 500 MWp or about 4 TWh/year for wind or 6.15% of demand.

Biofuel from Algae: Singapore's tropical conditions experience enhanced algae and bio-organism growth compared to other parts of the world. We have complementary industries (petroleum and oleochemical refineries, biomedical). Thus we could explore the synthesis of biofuel from algae as a byproduct and ensure its application in the production of energy.

Co-generation: this technology can also be explored based on Salinity Gradient Energy principles which can be coupled to a desalination plant's brine yield (such as from NEWater Waste Brine Water and other desalination plants' brine output). An energy source of up to 100 GWh/yr can be recovered.

Onshore & Offshore Floating PVs: Floating PV test units are being test-bedded at our inland reservoirs and also shallow offshore water regions of Singapore not used for shipping but which experience high sunlight irradiance. Hence, inland and offshore floating PVs can be a potential alternative energy source when coupled with floating systems made from novel materials and coatings.

Energy storage: Transmission costs are huge barriers and very difficult to justify. Energy storage and distributed generation are very viable solutions and will have major applications in 2065. One of the many storage solutions available is to produce hydrogen and transport it for real time generation. Hydrogen can be used for utility scale electricity generation in power plants to mitigate emissions. There are two ways to generate hydrogen: (1) Existing gas pipelines can be used and storage could be in the power plants. (2) power plants can produce hydrogen during off peak periods. Presently ERI@N has a project with two European companies to address power to gas (P2G) processes. If the concept works the gravimetric energy density will be 2,000 watt-hours per kilogramme (Wh/kg) and volumetric energy density will be 1,570 watt-hours per litre (Wh/l). The research challenge will be in developing new catalyst technology. Similarly seawater electrolysis can be explored for energy storage.

I project a scenario that all these technologies will be commercially viable and operating in Singapore for commercial applications and the power generated by all these technologies will be measured, monitored and controlled by a smart grid with micro grids as subsidiary systems. Solar power will generate the bulk of the clean energy (approximately 30%) injected into the grid and the other renewable energy components can contribute about another 15–20% of the total requirement of the grid (65 TWh/year) contributing a total of about 50% of the grid.

This will make Singapore a sustainable green urban city utilising and showcasing how an urban city in the tropics can operate with 50% or more of its energy and power needs from renewable sources. When we add to this our offshore supply of solar PV and solar thermal power and nuclear and wind power from our neighbours (Indonesia/Malaysia) via subsea cables, Singapore could effectively run on 100% clean and renewal energy, which will give Singapore a zero carbon footprint.

The supply of renewable sources of energy from our neighbours is a distinct possibility as there are many large islands owned by Indonesia and Malaysia which can be developed into an integrated power island to supply power via the ASEAN grid (which may be a reality if politically, all governments begin exploring the possibility of developing such a facility. A number of these facilities can be built on islands that are currently uninhabited or have small populations).

The future of Singapore electrifying the world with renewable energy technologies to maximise local resources of renewables is a very real possibility, knowing that we are already developing these technologies today. Twenty years from now we would have fully commercialised these technologies and we will be using them in and around Singapore. In another 10–20 years, we would have made all these technologies economically viable and we should be able to supply totally integrated RE systems in urban cities all over the world, as we are doing with water recycling and treatment today — producing NEWater (recycled waste water that more than meets World Health Organization (WHO) drinking water standards), and applying the latest in membrane technologies to reduce its production costs.

So in 2065 I can see Singapore as an urban metropolis:

- Producing all its electricity from renewable and clean sources (solar PV & thermal, marine tidal systems, wind, biomass, biogas, co-gen, biofuels, nuclear, etc.);
- still manufacturing and producing a quarter of its GDP from high-tech manufacturing (from petrochemicals to pharmaceuticals to food products) but using clean renewable energy to do so;
- having a total transport system that is electrically driven, with driverless or driven e-vehicles;
- being the largest data centre in the world driven by clean renewable energy;
- having the lowest carbon footprint per capita globally, and;

- the cleanest, greenest, most sustainable urban city in the world (having the lowest PM2.5 reading in the world, with the cleanest drinking water in the world, and totally sustainable in terms of biodiversity in our forest reserves and marine ecosystems).

It can be done. We only need far-sighted planning and the political will to do so and we need to start planning today so that our future generations will continue to enjoy a cleaner and better Singapore.

Economically this will bring Singapore billions of dollars of projects ("Renewable energy's share of world electricity generation continued its steady climb and contributes US$214.4 billion in investments", UNEP News Centre Frankfurt/New York, 7 April 2014) in providing technical solutions and infrastructure for renewable energy systems throughout Asia and the world, as Singapore will have the know-how, the financial capabilities, the engineering and project management competence, as well as the operations and maintenance (O&M) capabilities to provide turnkey and O&M services and integrate all the technologies listed above.

The world needs renewable energy to combat and mitigate climate change. At the recent United Nations Climate Summit (23 September 2014), this point was stressed and the Summit ended with "an agreement to widen the use of renewable energy and that it will raise billions of dollars in aid of developing countries" (*The Straits Times*, 25 September 2014). Singapore can be one of the main suppliers of these technologies and systems.

This will also provide high-end employment for the technicians, engineers, and scientists that graduate from Singapore's ITEs, polytechnics and universities. We should continue to seek and attract the very best researchers from all over the world to keep Singapore at the cutting edge of these technologies so needed by the world to mitigate climate change. This will also ensure that we continue to live a sustainable life in an environment that can responsibly maintain the nexus of producing water, energy and food, essentials that we all need to live sustainably now and for our future generations.

The Impact of Technology on Singapore's Economy and Living Environment in 2065

Koh Boon Hwee
Chairman
Credence Partners Pte Ltd

By 2065, the digital revolution, currently in its infancy, would have matured. Like the Luddites who protested against industrialisation on the grounds that it would create massive permanent unemployment, early 21st century pessimists sounded the same alarm about technology and its impact on employment. They were wrong. Instead, the digital revolution eventually enhanced Singapore's economic competitiveness and the quality of life in 2065 Singapore had no match anywhere else.

The Singapore Economy in 2065

Technology and the digital revolution turned out to be a real blessing for Singapore. The cost of computers, robotics and sensors fell rapidly in the first two decades of the 21st century. As a result, labour cost became an increasingly small element in the cost of manufacturing. What became more important was stability in the economic ecosystem, a position along the global supply chain together with a network of suppliers, efficient logistics and transportation, a communication network that facilitated communications and distributed computing, and a seamless financial system to facilitate trade. All of these played to Singapore's strength. Together with an older and slower growing workforce, the digital revolution allowed

Singapore in 2065 to continue to be a major player in manufacturing, although it now employs less than a third of the number 50 years ago.

Building on Singapore's reputation for quality and safety, she is in 2065 a major food manufacturing location for both international and several large homegrown companies. Labour cost is insignificant in this business, and a reputation for quality and food safety commands a premium that easily absorbs Singapore's higher costs.

More surprisingly, in 2065 Singapore is more self-sufficient in food production than at any time in the past. Advances in LED lighting technology, innovations in vertical farming, a growing environment sealed off from the outside world and computerised digital control of water, nutrients, lighting and infrastructure turned Singapore fruits and vegetables into some of the most sought after organic brands in the world.

Fifty years ago it looked like the electronics and technology industry was another sunset business. China's abundance of inexpensive labour coupled with the lure of a large market led to an exodus of manufacturers from the region, including Singapore. Perhaps it was serendipity, but the rapid rise of robots and sensors, fuelled by rapidly dropping prices of the chips and processors that enable them, led to a major rethinking about where things were made. The US saw a major resurgence in manufacturing, but without creating industrial jobs. Similarly, Singapore saw a resurgence in advanced robotic manufacturing enterprises. In deciding where to locate these plants, political and economic stability was a key factor as labour cost was no longer significant. As part of the ecosystem, the advanced factories for making chips and sensors were also attracted here. As each of these involves an investment of several billion dollars, the criteria for the investment decision played to Singapore's strengths.

At the same time, Singapore in 2065 benefitted from being located in the centre of a thriving economic region. After many years of effort, most of ASEAN has been lifted out of poverty into the middle class, and a "common market" of 500 million consumers has made a big difference to the region. Regional headquarters of many companies worldwide are located in Singapore, but now each has thousands of employees, reflecting the overall size of the pan-ASEAN economy.

In spite of the phenomenal growth throughout Asia, Singapore hung on to its status as a major financial hub, principally due to a "best in class" regulatory and legal framework, as well as the most advanced communications network in the region.

But besides finance, in 2065 she is also a major centre for big data and analytics, and of genetic information. The sustained and major investments in life sciences research eventually resulted in almost all major players locating significant bioinformatics enterprises here, leveraging on not only the availability of research and trained people, but also Singapore's reputation for IP protection.

Quality of Life in Singapore in 2065

All these economic achievements would have amounted to naught if the quality of life of Singapore residents did not benefit from it. By 2065 Singapore is home to almost 10 million people, in spite of the fact that population growth had slowed to only 1.3% p.a. Yet she remains one of the cleanest and greenest spots in the world. Urban development and planning has been completely reimagined. Underground, she is home to the densest underground railway system, and using sensors and software advanced by the digital revolution, it is a fully automated, self-sensing and self-correcting system, capable of speeds that make no commute in Singapore longer than 30 minutes.

At ground level all vehicles are electromagnetic and fully automated. Fossil fuel burning vehicles are relics of the past. A single keystroke delivers a driverless cab within five minutes. All human traffic has been elevated one level higher, and it is at this elevated level that the greenery and plants that Singapore has become famous for are planted. Almost all structures are connected at that level, separating vehicular traffic from pedestrian traffic.

Intelligent buildings have gone beyond managing energy consumption or regulating cooling. Technologically advanced light pipes bring sunlight into the innermost parts of buildings, while the skins of the buildings themselves generate most of the energy required for operations. Gardens are interspersed throughout and interstitial floors dedicated to greenery are a common feature of many structures. Tenants and employees in the building are recognised by sensors and software and admitted expeditiously — receptionists issuing visit passes are an anachronism in 2065.

Singapore has progressed beyond measuring everything only in economic terms. It is in 2065 the centre for the arts, drawing performers and patrons from all over Asia in particular, much like the role London and Paris had in the late 20th century. Her museums have risen to the status of the Louvre and the Hermitage of the last century.

She has become renowned for her status as the medical hub for Asia. But it is not all business. She is highly respected for taking on some of the most complex medical cases in the world for those who are too poor to afford the care themselves. Partly as a result of this, she has become one of the world's foremost medical and life sciences research locations, and in its wake, many foundations and NGOs have located their operations here.

TV channels and newspapers have long since disappeared. Everyone customises what they want to watch, when they want to do it and the device they choose to do it with. And all are synced to work seamlessly so you can pick up where you left off on any of your devices and at any time. 50 years ago most students could type better than they could write, but in 2065 almost all commands are voice or gesture activated because of the phenomenal advances in speech and gesture recognition. And almost all machines talk back to you. So while the abilities to speak and listen are natural extensions of the technology-enabled environment, educators worry about the loss of ability to write by hand, and the ability to read.

The landscape in Singapore for education has also changed. The idea that learning is confined to the early years of our lives is a thing of the past. Technology means that people continue to learn at their own pace and on their own time. Accreditation and certification of what has been learned is the new mantra. Superstar professors are now like professional athletes, commanding incomes unheard of in academia compared to half a century earlier. There is furious debate about what all this means as the best education increasingly seems to favour those who are better off.

Conclusion

In spite of the challenges, the increasing momentum and impact of technology on all aspects of life, and the massive productivity that followed, allow most people to earn a middle-class wage for a 30-hour workweek that supports a comfortable life style in cosmopolitan Singapore. The debates of the past about the influx of foreigners in Singapore have disappeared. Of the 10 million in population, less than 3 million are third-generation Singaporeans — most are newly minted citizens.

Singapore 2065: A Leadership Role in Legal Education in Sustainable Development?

Koh Kheng-Lian
Emeritus Professor
Faculty of Law
National University of Singapore

Legal education for sustainable development (LESD) is critical as one of the disciplines in promoting sustainable development and improving the capacity of institutions and people to address the "triple bottom line" of environment, development and social equity issues. This is underlined in *Agenda 21*, the *Post-2015 UN Development Agenda* and many other environmental instruments. Singapore can take a leadership role in developing a regional hub for LESD.

In setting the stage for a leadership role in LESD, we need to understand the complexity and dynamism of environmental law now and into 2065 and beyond. Environmental law is wide ranging, covering the protection and conservation of the earth's natural resources, water and air — almost everything around us. There are unique features in environmental education including LESD. Environment is *sans frontières* as we share one atmosphere, one stratosphere, and one nature with its varied ecosystems. Hence, we are an interdependent and interconnected world and when an environmental disaster occurs in one part of the world, it can impact, directly or indirectly, somewhere miles away. The outbreaks of Avian Flu, Ebola and climate change disasters bear testimony.

Environmental law must be viewed from three main dimensions — global, regional and national. There is also an interconnectedness of various sectors such as water, food, energy, biodiversity and climate change, as are their impacts on the political, economic and sociocultural contexts. To ignore the linkages is to miss out on an integrated approach in sustainable development which provides challenges, as cross-cutting issues are being mainstreamed into policies.

Environmental law has a crucial role to play in developing environmental sustainability in regulating laws and in bringing about environmental justice. The world is undergoing tremendous environmental changes as never before, witnessed by climate change with intensified and frequency of typhoons, cyclones, torrential rains and droughts — causing widespread human, material, economic and environmental losses. UN Secretary-General Ban Ki Moon said at the opening of the Climate Summit in New York on 23 September 2014, "Climate Change is a defining issue of our age. It is defining our present; our response will define our future."

Many international environmental instruments such as the United Nations Framework Convention on Climate Change, the Convention on Biological Diversity are "framework conventions" which do not lay down rules but provide guidelines for implementation. Many of them are ongoing or "unfinished" business, and require further negotiations and constant updates. The ASEAN region and the world must constantly analyse and take into consideration the concerns not only of its member countries but the common interests of the region and beyond. And, as scientists continue to make new discoveries of things that impact on the environment, the law must keep pace.

The very nature of sustainable development must take the interests of future generations into account — the rights of generations still unborn were recognised in the ground-breaking decision of the Philippines Supreme Court in case of *Oposa* v. *Factoran*. While the question of the right to a sound environment and legal standing of future generations to sue have been settled in the Philippines, can the case be regarded "*ergo omnes*" under international law (obligations owed by states to the international community as a whole, intended to protect and promote the basic values and common interests of all)? Other new and emerging issues include "ecocide" where whole ecosystems are being destroyed by denudation of vast forests, or where illegal trade in endangered species threatens their extinction; the notion of "Responsibility to Protect" (R2P); the question of "human rights and the environment." What about " human rights and business" — a new phenomenon of "land grabbing" where investors are taking large swathes of land near watersheds and depriving local subsistence farmers of their land with little or no compensation? What about the current climate change negotiations on the Warsaw International Mechanism for "Loss and Damage associated with climate change impacts" that are being contested by developing countries? What about the plight of climatic migrants? What about the traditional principles of sovereignty and non-intervention — should they still have the heyday as in Westphalian times, oblivious of the responsibility of states under the Rio Declaration?

The list goes on. What do all these mean when translated or operationalised, so as not to disadvantage the poor and the marginalised communities? Otherwise, it would be a travesty of one of the aims of sustainable development.

There is much ahead of environmental law — with many uncertainties not only in terms of concepts, structures and governance but the very uncertainty of the things to come in the environmental world. What would be the state of the environment in 2065? There is a great potential for environmental law to expand to shape the future when new and emerging environmental challenges call for new legal frameworks or amendments of old, inadequate laws. Law can provide a network to have "a whole-of-the-world" cooperation to solving environmental problems where no one country or a region can do so, as in serious environmental disasters seen in super Typhoon Haiyan in the Philippines.

What then is the role of LESD?

LESD, including environmental legal education generally, should not be viewed solely as imparting knowledge of the legal frameworks relating to environment. The role of LESD (and education) as envisaged in *Agenda 21* calls for public awareness and training in all areas of the Agenda — ranging from conservation and management of natural resources to strengthening of the role of major groups. LESD should meet the wider objectives envisaged in building capacity in environmental law for policymakers, judges, administrators, and the private sector, NGOs, the civil societies — indeed, the whole of society, so as to bring about a sustainable planet Earth — we being stewards.

Is there then a hope that Singapore can aspire to be a centre of excellence as a regional hub in 2065 for LESD in the Asia-Pacific region, drawing expertise from not only Singapore, the region but the world, as environment is *sans frontières*? There is reason to believe that it can. There is the infrastructure in place — the Asia-Pacific Centre for Environmental Law (APCEL) was established in February 1996 by the Faculty of Law, National University of Singapore at the initiative of the Faculty and the then World Conservation Union's World Commission on Environmental Law (IUCN WCEL) in collaboration with the United Nations Environment Programme (UNEP). This was in response to the call in *Agenda 21* to build capacity in environmental law and to promote awareness of environmental issues. During its some 19 years of existence, it has conducted training courses, workshops and organised conferences. It has also conducted cutting-edge research into wide-ranging areas including climate change, biodiversity, transboundary illegal wildlife trade, transboundary pollution, zoonotic diseases, marine environment in coastal region, and ASEAN environmental law, policy and governance. Its members have been invited to serve as resource persons in conferences, workshops and seminars worldwide, covering a wide range of cutting-edge environmental issues. It networks with numerous environmental law centres and organisations in the world. The region and the world are experiencing many environmental disasters as never before. What will it be like in the years ahead? Climate change is having negative impacts on water, food, biodiversity and other sectors vital to human and its ecosystems. Societies must build resilience and find ways to adapt and mitigate the onslaught of environmental disasters.

Law can be one of the instruments for the transformation of society to meet the challenges of the negative impacts of the environment. We need to start now to train more environmental lawyers so that they can together with environmental experts from different disciplines find solutions through an integrated approach. Singapore can serve as a regional "hub" for LESD.

At present, environmental law is only an elective module in the Faculty of Law, National University of Singapore, and is not offered in the other universities in Singapore. Also, not many law schools in the ASEAN or Asia-Pacific region offer such a course. Environmental law should be a compulsory subject in the law curriculum. The Law Faculty could develop APCEL into a hub for environmental legal education and engage legal environmental experts from all over the world to teach and conduct research together with its locals. Symposia, workshops and seminars can be organised for environmental law teachers, judges, administrators and other stakeholders. It could also conduct environmental law courses for lawyers in Singapore and the region. This will contribute to developing a critical mass of environmental legal experts for the leadership role in the run up to 2065.

The Singapore regional hub can establish a network of scholars in the ASEAN region to encourage the teaching of a course on ASEAN environmental law, policy and governance in their law schools, as this course has been developed in the Faculty of Law. Also the teaching of comparative environmental law with an ASEAN focus, together with other comparative experiences would be crucial in exchanging experiences and in devising a methodology to equip the judiciary, policymakers, administrators and practitioners in the region.

The importance of building capacity in environmental law (among other disciplines) cannot be gainsaid, as the outcome of the Rio+20 Conference on Sustainable Development has initiated an inclusive intergovernmental process to prepare a global development agenda of Sustainable Development Goals beyond 2015 with sustainable development at its core. One of the dimensions is in the first report of the UN System Task Team, *Realizing the Future We Want for All*, published in May 2012. The Task Team outlined a vision for the *Post-2015 UN Development Agenda* and suggested four key dimensions, one of which is environmental sustainability. In the second report on "*A Renewed Global Partnership for Development* in March 2013, it:

> provided recommendations on key dimensions and a potential format for a global partnership in the post-2015 era. It advised that the partnership should include universal commitments calling for actions from all countries, according to their national capabilities. It should build on existing commitments such as those reflected in the Millennium Development Goals, the Monterrey Consensus and the Johannesburg Plan of Implementation, but must also be broadened and strengthened to address the large array of global challenges we face today.[1]

---

[1] Environment Statistics Section, United Nations Statistics Division (UNSD)/DESA (2013). *Envstats: News and Notes, 33*, p. 6. Retrieved February 25, 2015 from http://unstats.un.org/unsd/ENVIRONMENT/envpdf/Issue33.pdf?

The United Nations Development Group has organised a set of 11 thematic consultations on conflict and fragility; education; environmental sustainability; governance; growth and employment; health; hunger, food and nutrition; inequalities; population dynamics; energy; and water.

The vision for LESD post-2015 through to 2065 and beyond should include developing an effective methodology to build capacity in environment that can transform individuals, institutions, and society as a whole. It requires more than a knowledge of environmental law, which is constantly "'moving" and changing — it should also include how other disciplines such as economics, science, engineering and politics interface with one another.

Students who take environmental law as a subject at universities may do it to pass examinations, or others such as administrators may attend such courses for short-term purposes. As has been shown, it will all too soon be forgotten. There is no real commitment to follow up or to put into practice or to give it a multiplier effect. No fire in the belly, except for some who will continue a lifelong commitment! So we need to not only instruct but to inspire. A change in mindset is the most difficult to achieve. We must first create an environmental culture among the citizenry — we should start them from young — at home, in kindergartens, in schools, in institutions of higher learning — at every stage of life and let it be part of their DNA.

With the outcome of the Rio+20 Conference on Sustainable Development initiating an inclusive intergovernmental process to prepare a set of sustainable development goals (SDGs) post-2015 and also to accelerate the MDG (Millennium Development Goals) process, there is much work ahead from 2015 to 2065 and indeed beyond (the scope of *Agenda 21* covers the whole of the 21st century). Singapore, the region and the world are part of the global partnership in the post-2015 era. Singapore has a great opportunity to take the lead.

Our hope lies in the youths of today and the generations unborn in Singapore and the world over to keep the environmental light shining. They together with other stakeholders must see *Agenda 21*, the MDGs, the *Post-2015 UN Development Agenda*, and all environmental laws at the national, regional and global levels. LESD should move in tandem.

APCEL has been widely acclaimed as one of the most vibrant regional centres of excellence in environmental law. If given the support (financial and otherwise) by the university, the government and other entities, APCEL can develop into a beacon for the region for LESD and, I dare say, the world. Be prepared!

Singapore in 2065: A Shining City on the Sea

Tommy Koh
Ambassador-at-Large
Ministry of Foreign Affairs, Singapore

I have a vision of Singapore in 2065 when it will celebrate the 100th anniversary of its independence. My vision is that of a shining city by the sea and on the sea: liveable, sustainable, economically prosperous, socially cohesive and equitable, culturally vibrant and diverse, a wonderful home for its citizens and a delightful city for its visitors.

My vision is based on three concepts.

Energy Policy

First, I want to talk about Singapore's energy policy in 2065. At the moment, electricity in Singapore is generated by power plants which use the three fossil fuels: gas, oil and coal. Burning fossil fuels, however, generates carbon, which causes global warming. Global warming is real and it is largely caused by man's activities. Global warming has caused a systemic change in our climate. If we do not succeed in limiting the rise in temperature to 2°C, the consequences could be disastrous for many low-lying countries and cities. Going forward, one critical question is whether we can reduce or end our dependence on fossil fuels.

End Dependence on Fossil Fuels

The Secretary-General of the OECD, Angel Gurria, was in Singapore recently. He has said that, if we are to have any hope of limiting the rise of global temperature by 2°C, we must have zero emissions from the use of fossil fuels by 2050. Is this an achievable target? The conventional wisdom is that it is not achievable. The conventional wisdom is that energy from clean and renewable sources will never be enough to end our dependence on fossil fuels.

Denmark's Pledge

One country which has challenged that consensus is Denmark. The Danish Government has pledged that by 2050, it will derive its power entirely from solar, wind and biomass and dispense with fossil fuels. Denmark does not rely on nuclear power and has no hydro or thermal potential. Singapore is probably unable to tap into wind power because of the lack of strong and consistent winds and lack of space to emplace the wind turbines. However, the idea of building wind mills at sea should not be discounted. Singapore is, however, not short of solar power or biomass. My first concept is that by 2065, 15 years after Denmark, Singapore will end its dependence on fossil fuels for its energy needs. Instead, solar power and biomass will supply all our energy needs. If Denmark can do it by 2050, I am confident that Singapore can do the same 15 years later.

Emulate Germany's Green Economy

My confidence that it can be done is based on several factors. The first factor is technology. Solar power is progressing by leaps and bounds. With each passing year, solar power is cheaper and commercially more competitive. Norway has a major plant building solar panels in Singapore. According to the Norwegians, solar power will be commercially competitive within the next five years. I am confident that, in 50 years time, solar power will replace power from fossil fuels. The second factor is the knowledge that, even today, Germany derives more than 50% of its energy from solar. Germany produces five times as much power from solar energy than the United States. Germany receives less sunshine than Singapore. Germany has also stopped using nuclear power. Germany's "green" energy policy has not undermined Germany's economic competitiveness. On the contrary, Germany has one of the most competitive economies in the world. It is, for example, the world's second largest exporter, after China. The big lesson that the world can learn from Germany is that it is possible to make a successful transition to a low carbon economy without losing economic competitiveness.

Cities on the Sea

Second, I want to talk about the new towns of the future. Singapore has very limited land areas. In order to house a growing population and to provide for other needs, we have been expanding both horizontally and vertically. We have been expanding vertically by building taller and taller buildings. We have been expanding horizontally by reclaiming land from the sea. Land reclamation is, however, very expensive and due to the non-cooperation of our two neighbours, we have had to buy the sand from faraway places.

Waterbuurt in the Netherlands

Technology is now available for us to build homes, housing estates, communities on the sea. Waterbuurt in the Netherlands is such a community. The 1,000 residents of the community live on the water. The dream of a floating city has come true. The new technology means that we do not have to reclaim land from the sea. New towns and cities can be built on pontoons. In addition to the Netherlands, Israel is also planning to build new cities on the sea, using a similar technology invented and developed by a group of scholars at the Israeli Institute of Technology (Technion). One of them came to visit me in Singapore recently, to explain how it works, and to look for investors.

Living by the Sea for Everyone

It would be wonderful if the future new towns of Singapore were built on the sea and by the sea. As an island people, many of us dream of living by the sea. Until now that dream is only achievable if you are very rich and can afford to live in Sentosa Cove. In Singapore, in 2065, you do not have to be a millionaire in order to fulfil that dream. This is my second concept.

Transport Policy

Third, I want to talk about the important question of transportation. What kind of transport policy and system will we have in 2065? My vision is that it will be fast, efficient, affordable, seamless and environmentally friendly. Our mass rapid transit system is not perfect but it is better than those in New York and Washington, two cities in which I had spent many years of my life. Let us make our Mass Rapid Transit (MRT) system the best in the world.

Electric Buses and Taxis

Our bus system can be improved. First, we should switch progressively to electric buses and remove a major source of air pollution in Singapore. Second, the bus lanes should be made more prominent and cars should, by law, be required to give way to buses.

Abolish Surcharges for Taxis

Our taxi drivers are great but our taxi system is not. As in the case of the buses, I propose that our taxi fleet should progressively be replaced by electric vehicles. Second, I suggest that we abolish all the surcharges which are now levied by our taxis. Taxis should charge the same rates at any time of the day and night. The current system is very confusing. I observe that other leading cities of the world do not have a system of surcharges for their taxis. The absence of surcharges does not seem to have a negative impact on the availability of taxis, throughout the day and night, in those cities.

A City for People, Not Cars

We should encourage Singaporeans to walk and to cycle. This requires a mindset change on the part of the policymakers and citizens. At the present moment, the car is the king of the road. In future, the hierarchy should be reversed and we should make the pedestrian No. 1, followed by the cyclist, the bus, the taxi, with the privately driven car at the bottom of the pyramid. This means that more space on our roads should be given to cyclists, buses and taxis and less space for the cars. We should also design the city to encourage walking. The critical element is shade. Our urban designers should provide pedestrians with shaded walkways.

A Nation of Cyclists

On my visits to Denmark and the Netherlands, I am struck by the fact that the citizens of these two wealthy countries prefer to cycle than to drive. I was told that the Netherlands has more bicycles than people. Cycling is a way of life in those two countries. They cycle all year round, even in winter when the weather is cold. By comparison, the weather in Singapore is conducive to cycling all year round. Let us seek to become a nation of cyclists.

I expect that, in the next 50 years, revolutionary changes will take place in the field of urban transportation. For example, driverless vehicles are being put on trial in Singapore. If the trials succeed and driverless vehicles of different types and sizes are introduced, this could bring about a revolutionary change to our transport system.

Toby's World

I also expect that the trend to replace the conventional vehicle with the hybrid and electric vehicle will accelerate. I would not be surprised if, in 50 years from now, cars which run on petrol, diesel or gas will no longer be in production. In 50 years' time, my grandson Toby will be 53 years old. He may choose not to own and operate a private vehicle. However, if he does, it may well be a solar-powered vehicle with zero emissions.

Social Business and Inclusive Economy 2065

David Lee Kuo Chuen
Professor of Quantitative Finance (Practice)
Sim Kee Boon Institute for Financial Economics
Singapore Management University

Time compression, capital flow and complexity are concepts fundamental to economic management and the formulation of public policy.

Singapore has applied the concepts remarkably well, as evidenced by the economic miracle of the last 50 years. Beset with high unemployment, low foreign reserves and an unskilled workforce in the 1960s, Singapore with nary a natural resource was vulnerable to economic failure, and few were optimistic of its future. However, blessed with being in the right place at the right time, and above all having the right people at the helm with the right talents and chemistry, Singapore gradually found a firm footing in global trade, finance and manufacturing in the 1970s. Its geographical position as the centre of Asia and being in a favourable time zone with regard to other major financial centres helped give birth to the Asian Currency Units that led to the development of the Asian Dollar Market in 1968. In tandem with the expanding economic development of its neighbours in the 1980s and 1990s, Singapore steadfastly forged ahead in commerce, telecommunication, marine and shipping, tourism and manufacturing. The increasing demand for foreign currency financing together with the significant capital flows and tourist arrivals at the time provided the impetus to further grow the finance, legal and tourism sectors. Today the city-state is a leading international business and global financial centre underpinned by cutting-edge information technology and high-speed networks, such as SWIFT, MEPS and others.

While some may argue that productivity is the primary cause for the miraculous growth, the truth is, the real driver is innovation spearheaded by a daring and committed spirit coupled with ingenuity, foresight and planning! In reality, productivity is a consequence and not the cause. Innovations have been the cornerstone of Singapore's economic success and self-reliance. By tapping on technological innovation, it has largely solved the water-scarcity problem, which had been troubling the government since its independence in 1965. Mindful that the right talents are needed to help propel the economy forward, the policymakers and regulators have successfully innovated schemes to attract and retain such talents. Singapore has generally been quick to anticipate and preempt difficult issues that may affect the nation's survival, be it political, social, educational, or financial. At a time when many countries were trying to implement varying components of the Washington Consensus, Singapore actively pursued economic growth with commendable success through innovative strategies based on pragmatism and eclecticism. It is not surprising that the Singapore Model has been widely studied and emulated by many developing and transitional economies, including China, whose Premier Deng Xiaoping, not long after his return from a visit to Singapore in 1978, liberalised the Chinese economy, which has since become a global economic powerhouse, second only to the US in terms of GDP.

In recent years, however, the accelerated economic transformation in compressed time on the back of an increased influx of foreign workers and capital flows associated with the integrated resorts has strained the Singapore's social fabric somewhat, as such movements have a tendency to cause large fluctuations in asset prices and income inequality. That clearly underscores the complexity and difficulty of balancing economic efficiency and inclusiveness of a society.

What will the next 50 years be like for Singapore? One can almost confidently forecast that changes will continue to occur, at a super exponential rate not seen before. As technology advances to new frontiers, time will be further compressed. The next 50 years are likely to witness occurrences that would have taken 100 years or more today to unfold. With the change in perception of time, economic planning and forecasting would be a lot harder and complex than it used to be. No wonder econometric forecasting, which was fashionable in Singapore 15 years ago, has evolved into scenario planning, data mining and crowd forecasting with complex systems.

The future is all about paradigm, revolution and disruption. It is also about leadership in government who is adept at harnessing, innovating and executing revolutionary ideas and changes in a responsive manner, and able to mobilise and connect the private sector to work hand-in-glove with the public sector. Singapore has in place an astute and disciplined government that has a proven track record in ensuring national financial health and social stability through fiscal prudence and innovative social programmes. This is unlikely to be different in 2065, given the stringency and rigour of the leadership renewal process and an educated and discerning electorate.

What is also unlikely to change is the continual emergence of simpler, cheaper, initially-lower-profit-margin disruptive products that empower and allow consumers with low purchasing power and little skill access to a product that would be otherwise inaccessible to them. As people in general have a tendency to express and assert themselves, including their wants and preferences, disruptive products can provide them with a brand new user experience in this aspect through Personalised-Identification-Proximity (PIP) technology. Whether it is in finance, medicine, education, commerce, fashion, media entertainment, performing arts or tourism, the possible use of similar PIP technology and its potential growth are limited only by our imagination. Given the objectives of cost-down and lower profit margin, emerging markets with the lowest consumption power and maximum welfare improvement will offer the potential for highest growth. With economies of scale, the profit margin can increase over time as the product is adapted at a higher cost with more features; known as reverse innovation, to cater to the more developed markets. M-Pesa is perhaps one such invention, and another is AliPay.

Going forward, I believe the Singapore economy will be riding on a strategy that leverages on finance, innovation and scalability. While most would like to think that Singapore is hardly a destination for technological innovation, my earlier observations about its ingenuity and capability for innovations that had taken place in various areas, especially in policymaking and implementation, may well portend an unprecedented technological innovation in Singapore sooner than expected. What I see in Singapore in the next 50 years is that we will have all the prerequisites for a repeat of its success story based on a strategy that will synergise finance, innovation, scalability, and an inclusive economy and society. We will be moving from physical time and space to virtual time and space. As a leader in cyber security, information and communication, Singapore will be able to integrate various economic sectors via the cyber space, as well as integrate economic regions, especially finance and trade sectors, via decentralised peer-to-peer networks. We will also move from high productivity and high-margin businesses to low productivity and low-margin "social businesses" that will improve the overall welfare of the people, as well as from a mere hardworking, knowledgeable and skilled workforce to an intelligent, nimble and tech-savvy workforce.

Singapore will survive well by not looking solely for solutions to existing problems especially low productivity and fertility that have given rise to low growth and an ageing population, but more importantly for more innovative ideas for social businesses based on the Internet that will lead to an all-round inclusive economy and society. Such social businesses are distinct from other business or social enterprises as they seek to address and solve a social need while pursuing a return for their shareholders. In short, they strive for the common good by excelling in what they do. Businesses that do not contribute to societal welfare and wellbeing will find it increasingly difficult to sustain in the long run.

The social network has a tendency to reject the notion of charity as the only solution to poverty but drives the market to create financially profitable businesses, via the Internet, based on high-volume, low-margin products and services. The term "social business" as used here is different from that defined by Nobel Peace Prize laureate Prof. Muhammad Yunus's "Social Enterprise." Yunus's Social Enterprise is a company created with the "sole" purpose of solving a social problem in a financially "self-sustainable" way. However, the underlying principles remain fundamentally the same.

Both Social Business and Social Enterprise have an underlying focus on meeting social needs with entrepreneurial energy, market discipline, and great potential for replicating and scaling successful enterprises. The future trend and profit opportunities for social businesses are driven by the market and social media, rather than the notion of corporate social responsibility. Singapore is well positioned in the middle of Asia to take advantage of the trend and development.

No one, however, knows for certain what 50 years will hold in store for Singapore. We can try, however, to conjecture about the probable and possible future, and aspire and work towards a desired outcome. But I am confident that good working principles and governance, such as prudence, pragmatism, efficiency and eclecticism, which have been the main pillars of success for Singapore and its people up to now, will remain intact. The increasing demand for more Singaporeans and their expertise from international and business organisations in the like and scale of the IMF, Vatican, Facebook, Alibaba and yet-to-be-digitally-transformed institutions will only accelerate. The future will be better than what we can conceivably think in this one-to-one future where extreme trust of centralised providers (Peppers and Rogers, 2012) and trustless decentralised world are working side by side for the future growth of Singapore! The future will be about reproducing similar but better "experience" that we had in the last 50 years in a futuristic and virtual world: a time-tested reliable and capable government that will strengthen Singapore's survivability and liveability by ensuring an optimum level of foreign reserves, a caring retirement and medical benefits scheme that promotes an inclusive society, a dynamic "Wild Wild West/Silicon Valley" entrepreneurial environment that will improve income equality, and a committed, compassionate and joyful community that remains united to achieve happiness, prosperity and progress for the nation.

In 2065, when we look back, the key measure of success for Singapore is perhaps not about what we have achieved in GDP terms, but rather how well we have performed in improving societal wellbeing and inclusiveness. Singapore will survive well by not looking solely for solutions to existing problems, but more importantly for more innovative ideas for social enterprises that will lead to an all-round inclusive economy and society.

Acknowledgement

I express my appreciation to Philip Foo, Tsui Kai Chong and Phoon Kok Fai for their contribution in revising this article. Special thanks to Herman and Noreen Harrow for making time available for several useful discussions and allowing me to complete the article in full spectacular view of the Monterey Bay area.

Reference

Peppers, D., and Rogers, M. (2012). *Extreme Trust: Honesty as a Competitive Advantage*. New York: Portfolio.

Low Growth, High Prosperity

Laurence Lien
CEO
National Volunteer & Philanthropy Centre, Singapore

It is 2065. The economic model that dominated capitalism in 2015 has been turned upside down, in Singapore and in the world.

The old capitalist model that had dominated since the end of communism as a dominant force has had to be revamped. The drive for growth — fuelled by materialist wants and consumption, and measured narrowly by GDP — led not only to decades of jobless growth, but also societies with declining personal wellbeing and social progress. Globalisation and technological advancements, while promoting productivity and efficiency, forced redundancies, shrunk job creation and depressed local wages.

The model triumphed a winner-takes-all approach. Companies maximised shareholder value, which was narrowly defined as growing profits, often with a short-term focus, while contributing to negative externalities, particularly environmental degradation that everyone has to pay for collectively.

To achieve this, companies often overshot market needs with their products and focused on wealthier customer segments, in order to charge higher prices to maximise revenues. Masses of the lower and even middle income, previously considered unprofitable segments, remained underserved.

It has been hard to see how a world could be sustainable where 1% of the world's population owns nearly 50% of the world's wealth (Shorrocks, Davies, and Lluberas, 2014), while at the same time, more than 800 million people go hungry every day (FAO, IFAD, and WFP, 2014).

The resulting income and wealth divides has serious economic, political and moral consequences.

First, inequality has been bad for the economy. The marginal propensity to consume is higher for the poor than for the rich. Put simply, if a poor person earns an extra $1, he is likely to spend, say, $0.95 of it; a rich person earning the extra $1 is likely to spend less than, say, $0.50 of it, because he already has too many things. Lower consumption leads to lower economic growth.

Secondly, the income divide has manifested in growing political problems. Over the decades, the Occupy movements have grown. Political stratification in many countries, including countries close to us, has led to labour unrest, and political impasse between the elites and wealthy on one side, and low and middle income on the other. Singapore has not been spared the tensions either.

Thirdly, the extent of the income and wealth gap has become morally repugnant. The world has reached a turning point where the clarion call has become too loud not to deal squarely with the social issues, especially with a backlash against the blatant ostentatious consumption of a select few, while many others struggle to eke out an honest living.

2015 already saw some green shoots in the efforts to redefine capitalism to make economic and social progress more sustainable for all. This more inclusive capitalism model required that the dignity of the human person — whether at work, at home or in the community — is put at the centre.

In 2065, economics is clearly no longer the card that always trumps the social. They are both equally important, and are inextricably linked through a circular relationship. In the first place, the end of job and wealth creation is social — to meet the human needs and aspirations of individuals, and their families and communities.

Around the world, countries, particularly developed ones, now pursue a low-growth, high prosperity model. A high-growth model is not only socially divisive and ecologically unsustainable, but has also not produced the desired employment and economic stability.

The previous narrative was that without growth Singapore would have a high jobless rate, Singaporeans' quality of life would suffer and the government would not be able to afford more social programmes.

The new narrative is to set low growth more as a constraint than a target, and to maximise a holistic form of prosperity, measured not just narrowly in material terms, but also in terms of social, emotional and psychological wellbeing. As Professor Tim Jackson argues in *Prosperity Without Growth*, "an important component of prosperity is the ability to participate meaningfully in the life of society" (Jackson, 2009, p. 189). In this regard, nurturing loving relationships, building a sense of belonging and trust in the community, and ensuring work is purposeful and useful are critical for prosperity, even if they do not show up in GDP figures.

GDP is then not the predominant metric to measure a nation's success. Just as for for-profit enterprises, integrated accounting has become mainstream in 2065 — bringing together all aspects of societal and environmental value creation and destruction into a holistic approach — for nations, national accounting increasingly includes not just GDP but also a basket of indicators that together measure economic and social health in a rounded way.

Singapore Economy and Business

In 2065, the Singapore economy and business sectors have been transformed in line with this new, more inclusive vision. I will mention just three specific areas here.

First, business owners and management are consciously re-examining their conception of the good society, and their own role within it. Many have begun to see and practise the higher purpose of business, beyond merely making money, to building a better world. They regularly evaluate whether they are producing goods and delivering services that are genuinely useful to human kind and that improve their lives.

Businesses are creating shared value, as advanced eloquently by Michael Porter and Mark Kramer, in their 2011 thought piece, "Creating Shared Value": "The concept of shared value can be defined as policies and operating practices that enhance the competitiveness of a company while simultaneously advancing the economic and social conditions in the communities in which it operates" (Porter and Kramer, 2011).

In 2015, shared value was known by few in corporate Singapore. In 2065, it is mainstream. Businesses are creating economic value by addressing key social problems facing Singapore — whether in providing healthcare, eldercare or greater financial security, or in protecting the environment.

At the macroeconomic level, top-down industry development is complemented by the mobilisation and empowerment of entrepreneurs and social entrepreneurs to maximise social returns. Social problems are increasingly either addressed at their root through viable business models or through community problem solving, reducing the pressures on expanding government social expenditure.

New avenues of innovation have also significantly opened up opportunities not only to solve local issues, but also regional ones. Local industrial development has evolved from predominantly selling expensive, high end goods to the developed markets to serving the unmet needs of a vaster low and middle-income sector in Asia.

The next generation of leaders in family businesses are running their entities differently from their parents. For years, they had, as a group, been increasingly wanted to make a societal difference, beyond making profits. After taking over the company reins they have significantly reoriented their businesses to the pursuit of shared value.

Not content with just developing new business models that serve unmet social needs from the confines of their plush offices, they are active in the community, understanding unserved customers, convening multi-sectoral stakeholders to bust barriers to make supply viable and developing disruptive, innovative models to meet new demand.

Secondly, apart from businesses changing, non-profits have also transformed as the two worlds converge. The non-profit sector has flourished in the conditions made possible by a low-growth, high prosperity mindset, leading to rapid job creation and market penetration in non-traditional markets.

In 2012, charities in Singapore had income of S$12.6 billion in 2012, which was about 3% of GDP. The income of the charity sector grew by 12% per year in real terms from 2007 to 2012, far outstripping GDP growth of 5% per year over the same period.

The entire sector, including cooperatives, non-profit social enterprises and other non-charitable non-profits, is now at 10% of GDP. It has been active in maximising its potential to grow substantially, especially in complementing the work of businesses in addressing unmet social needs.

Large social enterprises dominate, not just in meeting the escalating needs of elderly care and healthcare, but also in traditional sectors previously dominated by the government or the private sector, like housing, education and financial services. With a steady flow of talent searching for meaning beyond pay, and with innovative and disruptive business models, these new-age non-profits have expanded fast.

Both profit and size have mattered for social enterprises to provide the capacity to constantly innovate, to invest in cross-sector collaborations and to proactively address market failures to create new markets. More than this, they are creating new social impact by doing the right thing for their customers — working continually to empower them to become more independent, to exercise self-determination and to demand fewer services eventually.

Thirdly, the health and eldercare industry has seen the fastest growth among all industries. National healthcare expenditure has doubled from 4% of GDP in 2015 to more than 8% of GDP. The OECD average was 9.4% in 2010, and continued to hover around these levels because of fiscal constraints.

As one of the fastest ageing populations in the world, Singapore has had to turn a significant weakness into a strength and an opportunity. Singapore is not just a healthcare hub for the region, continually attracting many patients to its shores, but is also innovating and disrupting the way that healthcare is delivered.

Healthcare is now much less transactional and standardised, but more relational and customised, focusing significantly more on self-management, independence and personal choice. The health ecosystem has concomitantly moved to a more collaborative, distributed and community-based system, and has become less centralised and professionalised.

Healthcare technology is the key enabler in allow this to happen — playing a mammoth role in all aspects of healthcare delivery — whether in diagnosis, monitoring, interventions and documentation, and whether in the primary or acute setting. Technology has also turned a domestic service into a global service, with significant degrees of specialisation across borders possible.

Conclusion

Together, a new social compact has been evolved. Everyone — citizens, families, communities, NPOs, companies and the government — is contributing meaningfully to the Singapore that is our home. The public, people and private sectors have all converged and become aligned to delivering one key primary goal — improving the wellbeing of all Singaporeans. Each plays its unique role in serving the common good and in creating the high prosperity platter of personal happiness, community togetherness, corporate success, economic stability, ecological sustainability and good governance.

References

FAO, IFAD, and WFP. (2014). *The State of Food Insecurity in the World.* Rome: FAO.

Jackson, T. (2009). *Prosperity Without Growth: Economics for a Finite Planet.* New York, NY: Earthscan/Routledge.

Porter, M. E., and Kramer, M. R. (2011, January). Creating Shared Value. *Harvard Business Review.*

Shorrocks, A., Davies, J., and Lluberas, R. (2014). *Global Wealth Report 2014.* Zurich: Credit Suisse Research Institute.

Singapore in the Year 2065: A Peep Ahead

Lim Chong Yah
Emeritus Professor of Economics
National University of Singapore; Nanyang Technological University

On what bases should we look into our future, especially in as far away as in 2065? I would use the following three bases for my "forecast": one, the strategic location of Singapore; two, the achievement orientation of Singaporeans; and three, the orientation and ability of the Singapore Government.

The Strategic Location of Singapore

Singapore exists, survives and prospers because of its location along the important sea-route between the Indian Ocean and beyond and the South China Sea and beyond. Singapore is located at the narrow Straits of Singapore, which is at the mouth of the Straits of Malacca. When global trade prospers, Singapore prospers. However, there is the assumption that the trade route is open. This assumption is true now, in the past as well as, I suppose, in the future.

On location, Singapore too occupies a central position in Southeast Asia. In colonial times, the British had her Commissioner-General in Singapore for British territories in Southeast Asia. During the Japanese Occupation in World War II, the Japanese made Singapore (which they called Syonan-to) their operational headquarters in Southeast Asia.

Added to the sea traffic arising from the location must include the air traffic in the modern globalised world. With strategic location as its foundation, over the decades, Singapore has successfully built itself up as the important economic hub of Southeast Asia. This economic hub has taken the integrated form of not just a shipping and aviation hub, but also a financial and banking centre, a healthcare centre, an educational centre, a tourism hub, a trading emporium, a centre for higher-value added manufactures as well as a centre for the headquarters of MNCs.

Singapore thus will have to maintain good relationships with all her numerous trading and economic partners, particularly with the riparian states of Malaysia and Indonesia. I do not see any problems, domestic Singaporean problems, on this count in the future. This locational comparative advantage is the "blue ocean" of Singapore. Conditions for the use of its seaport and airport, and as an economic hub, however, have to remain very favourable. These conditions, I presume, will prevail, despite some occasional hiccups, way into the future to the year 2065.

Love our neighbours, in the hope that they too would love us.

The Will to Progress of Singaporeans

Singapore had metamorphosed from a "basket case" to a showcase state in the last 50 years since Independence. Has the further achievement factor been blunted, especially for the future? Certain blunting in the will to further progress in the economic sphere is inevitable. There are already visible signs of this phenomenon. To those who have achieved so much economically as well as to those who have inherited so much wealth, the upper-end of the tapering effect of Lim's S-Curve Theory generally applies. Growth rates on the count of the already very high growth level will inevitably slow down. As long as they are not negative for long, the consequential problems can still be handled without despair or mass emigration. On balance, I am also not pessimistic on this will-to-progress factor, with serious decline in domestic population replacement rates notwithstanding, provided there continues to be a steady, reasonable and selective inflow of more hungry new immigrants to Singapore. The new mix will contribute to the new impetus for a brighter future. Singapore would then not deteriorate into a wasteland or become only a laidback township, not a vibrant, dynamic nation and an affluent society as we are today, and hopefully, also in the future.

However, the will to progress in future will take the form of human endeavours in all fields, not just economic achievements only. The signs of this happening are already there. There will be an attitudinal change in emphasis, but hopefully not in achievement orientation.

The Orientation and Ability of the Government

Like the earlier two co-determinants, government orientation is unlikely to vary much between now and 2065, oscillating between more state intervention and less state intervention in economic and social management in a predominantly market-oriented economy and society. The quality of intervention, however, can differ and differ widely, reflecting the ability of the government in power. Thus far, except for the transition year of 1959 when self-government was attained, the quality of state intervention in Singapore has been on the whole very high by global standards. Some foresee some deterioration of quality as we move further along, both in policy formulation and in policy implementation. I doubt the intervention quality in future would be so low as to result in serious deterioration in the balance of payments, unemployment rate, stability in the Singapore dollar, international fiscal indebtedness and serious fall in the rate of capital formation in the private sector. Should the serious secular deterioration in the macroeconomic factors, particularly in private sector investment, take place, Singapore would go to the dogs or would move dangerously towards that direction. I am fairly optimistic of the outcome though, based on the collective self-interest of Singaporeans, the successful and impressive investment in human capital in the past, the considerable investment in national service since independence, and in the expected maturity with time in the conduct of public affairs.

Deterioration in economic performance, it is much feared, will follow the probable emergence of an alternative government as we move towards 2065. The emergence of an alternative government, in the view of some Singaporeans, is likely to be sooner than later. They may add that the eventuality is not only inevitable but also desirable: the PAP being in the Government since 1959. However, conservative Singaporeans should be consoled that the incumbent Government would in turn become the next alternative government, should the first alternative government fail to deliver to the satisfaction of the electorate.

A 50-Year Forecast

With time, our average real GDP growth rate is likely to slow down. Not surprisingly, for the next 50 years, real GDP growth rate might average about one-third to half of the average growth rate in the last 50 years. With this assumption, the wide per capita income gap between us and our beloved neighbours, including China and India, would likely to shrink. That notwithstanding, our general standards of living would still be one of the highest in Asia. That is my prognostication.

Further, I would also prognosticate that the ups and downs in the Singapore economy, given increasing globalization, would be more pronounced, with severe external shocks more frequent in the next 50 years than in the last 50. Society should remain thankful that the reserves built up over the past 50 years would become useful in cushioning and overcoming the shocks. As the saying goes, 前人种树，后人乘凉 (*qian ren zhong shu, hou ren cheng liang*, "the earlier generation plants the trees, the next generation gets the shade"). Cheer up. Have confidence in our future as a society and as a nation, a city state in a more globalised 21st century.

Nonetheless, by 2065, for sure the writer, and together with all the other pioneer generation of Singaporeans, would not be around to celebrate the 100 years anniversary of our Independence. Some economic and social reforms are bound to take place in the interregnum, such as the introduction of a compulsory minimum wage and the inflation indexing of the annuities for the compulsory CPF minimum sum contributions.

Lastly, I hope and pray that the succeeding new generation of Singaporeans will continue to live in peace and harmony with one another, if not in prosperity as well, as we of the pioneer generation have done to the best of our ability, and very successfully. May you continue to sing our national anthem and recite our national pledge in 2065 and beyond, as we have done each year in the last 50 years of our independence. Happy 50th Year and Golden Anniversary. Merdeka, and Majulah Singapura!

Singapore's Next 50 Years: Singapore in the International Economy

Linda Y. C. Lim
Professor of Strategy
Stephen M. Ross School of Business
University of Michigan

The next half century will see Singapore as integrated into the international economy as it has been in the past. Modern Singapore was "born international" and to remain so is our destiny. But our role in the global economy will change as the world itself evolves, and the one thing we can be sure of is that the future will not be like the past. How exactly the world, and the world economy, evolves will have a major impact on Singapore, and on our economy.

For most of Singapore's history it has existed to serve the economies of the developed — mostly Western — world, largely as an intermediary with the rest of Asia in the exchange of first, raw or processed commodities, and then, manufactured goods, in addition to various commercial services. This more or less reflected the needs of distant rich countries, for which Singapore served as a useful Asian regional "outpost" or "hub" for global businesses, including as a sophisticated "node" in complex regionally dispersed value chains in manufacturing and services.

Changes in the affluent, mature domestic economies of Western countries and Japan are the first major change to which Singapore must and will adapt. These include their slower GDP growth, ageing populations, shrinking governments, and acceleration in reduced demand for manufactured goods (which can be mass produced in and transported from anywhere in the world) and increased demand for customised personal and social services (which by definition must be produced at the point of consumption). Given the slow but inexorable rise of new technologies like 3-D printing, manufactured goods will increasingly also be produced close to the point of consumption, saving on transport and inventory costs.

With the shortening of product and technology transfer cycles in an instantly connected world, many of these trends will also take over in the more advanced (and ageing) Asian economies — Japan, Korea, Taiwan, Hong Kong, Singapore, China and very quickly thereafter, our neighbours Thailand and Malaysia. We are likely to see the rise of increasingly localised economic zones centred on the most populous markets — what some have called an era of "de-globalisation," compared with the recent past. Goods, services and people will no longer need to travel long distances, and geographically dispersed value chains will be consolidated. At the same time, international trade rules under WTO and other agreements increasingly disallow and penalise state subsidies for foreign investment, which have been a major source of Singapore's manufacturing competitiveness.

For Singapore this means a continued decline in export manufacturing, which already employs ever fewer people per unit of output, given rising capital intensity; imports of energy to fuel highly automated manufacturing will also decline, as will the associated carbon emissions, chemical pollutants, and hopefully also the volatility that characterise such manufacturing. With a lower level of long-distance international trade in goods, including the imports and re-exports previously required by distributed manufacturing value chains, port and airport activity may also decline (all of these declines being in relative, not necessarily absolute, terms).

In response, the services sector will continue to increase its relative share of the economy, as scarce land and labour resources are reallocated away from manufacturing and manufacturing-related services such as transportation and utilities. Singapore, in short, will become more like cities in other affluent countries, which are service centres, rarely with large industrial sectors.

But exactly what services will Singapore provide to the changing world economy? Financial services for a global market — foreign exchange trading, wealth management and private banking, trade and investment intermediation — have been a forte so far. But this role may also decline (relatively) due to increased competition from other cities and nations as their financial sectors liberalise and mature, and the ongoing tightening of national and international regulation on global capital flows, including a crackdown on the tax avoidance strategies of multinationals and wealthy individuals who favour offshore tax domiciles. We also can no longer rely on being a "safe haven" for flight capital from less secure jurisdictions as the latter themselves evolve. It will take time for other countries to reach Singapore's level of institutional sophistication and integrity, but 50 years is a long time.

In both high-tech manufacturing and financial services, Singapore lacks not just market scale and supply-chain depth and diversity, but also a sizeable globally competitive labour and talent pool. So far it has succeeded by importing the narrowly specific skill sets that these sectors require — like electronics engineers from China and financial and IT experts from India — but this has already bumped up against physical-infrastructural costs-and-congestion and local social-cultural-political constraints. In the next 50 years it will also become more difficult to attract top talent from other Asian countries as their economies develop, giving their talented citizens better career opportunities and lifestyles at home.

Fortunately, Singapore's scale also confers certain advantages, in that it only needs to excel (on the supply side) in relatively fewer, smaller but higher-value, product niches in order to compete globally and provide sufficient employment opportunities for its resident population, with the help (on the demand side) of expanded domestic consumption by the local population, and demand from increasingly affluent regional neighbours. Looking forward 50 years, two major intrinsic assets that the country possesses are its geographical location in the centre of what will be the world's largest fast-growing middle-income regional market (the currently 600-plus million in Southeast Asia, together with the 1.5 billion-plus in South Asia), and its own population's cultural affinity with the populations in that market, which will be particularly important in various professional, personal and social services.

In financial services, for example, the principle of portfolio diversification alone will dictate that some segment of the burgeoning mass middle classes of Southeast Asia will place some portion of their savings in or with

Singapore-based financial institutions and finance professionals, just as high-net-worth individuals from the region and the world already do. In tourism, there is already a large and vibrant regional market, which will only grow as more families are able to afford short holidays in neighbouring countries. Health and educational services are already well-developed and have further room to grow, especially for average-income customers.

Thus the **second major change in the world economy** that will condition Singapore's economic future **is the shift in the locus of international trade and investment "from the West to the East,"** which is already under way, as part of a progressive **regionalisation of the world economy**. Related to this is the **democratisation of economic growth**, at least in this part of the world as domestic demand grows from hundreds of millions of lower- and middle-income consumers as happened in earlier eras of mass industrialisation, first in the Western world, and then in East Asia. As average incomes rise, so too does the share of income devoted to services (as opposed to food and manufactures), in which Singapore is more likely to have market-based comparative and competitive advantages.

The **third major change that these changes in the world economy will require of Singapore is internal — a necessary refocus of infrastructure, skills, customer orientation and general mindset away from the wealthy and the West toward the middle-income in our own Southeast Asian region**. Our focus in the last 50 years has resulted in the country climbing to the top of the ranks of the world's wealthy, but in the process we risk pricing ourselves out of the economic opportunities that will come with the next 50 years.

Focusing on employment and income creation for the average native Singaporean as opposed to income maximisation for footloose foreign corporations (which requires disproportionately employing foreigners in a process that cannot continue forever) requires a shift in economic policy and individual thinking from, among others, the global to regional, manufacturing to services, capital to labour and skills, high-end to middle, foreign to local, state to market, large to small, profits to wages, corporate to entrepreneurial, and so on.

In terms of a practical example, in the tourism sector, this might mean smaller entrepreneur- and family-owned 2- and 3-star hotels catering to near-regional visitors, rather than large 5-star foreign hotel chains catering to a "global elite": the former may take in less gross revenues (lower GDP) but yield higher net income that stays in the country, including higher wages for local hotel workers. This relative shift will also reduce inequality, since the purchasing power and consumption profile of the Southeast Asian middle class will more closely approximate that of lower-income Singaporeans: it would also provide a channel of upward mobility for hardworking and entrepreneurial locals who may not have the academic credentials and international experience to advance in global sectors. Given the demographics of the Asian (and Western) market, I see a particularly promising niche in elder services (including elder tourism, possibly related to health and education services, which is a thriving business in other developed and some developing countries).

Related to this, Singapore can carve out a unique niche in international traded services if it develops the cultural and linguistic capital and skills that both derive from our own history and identity and serve to help us relate to our Southeast Asian customers and clientele. It is strategic differentiation versus others who are bigger, cheaper, faster or more talented that will enable us to develop competitive advantages that are sustainable through the next half-century and beyond. What must people get from or come to Singapore for, that they cannot get elsewhere? It is not high-end hotels and restaurants, international branded-goods shops in luxury malls, packaged international entertainment (casinos and theme parks), even high-end medical services and MBA degrees, since these can be found in cities all over the world, and will be readily available throughout Asia in 50 years. Rather, it is our multicultural and hybrid food, history and culture, found nowhere else (except Malaysia), that are the rare and precious "uniquely Singapore" assets that we need to value, conserve and enhance as the Southeast Asian region comes into its own.

The good thing is that becoming truly ourselves, original and not imitative, will strengthen our nation as well as our economy. Here's to Singapore 2065!

Two Milestones for Singapore in the Next 50 Years

Selena Ling
Chief Economist
OCBC Bank

As an economist watching the Singapore economy for the last two decades, there were already a couple of big "game changer" steps in my view. These included the Workfare Scheme and the Pioneer Generation Schemes which illustrated that policymakers are not as averse to traditionally defined "social welfare" as typical official rhetoric would suggest. In addition, the quickstep of healthcare reform and other policy responses to improving longevity and tackling the challenges of an ageing population revealed that public policymakers were profoundly rethinking the socioeconomic goals and probably also acquiescing to the demands of an increasingly vocal populace.

The next 50 years will likely mark a great transformation of Singapore as we know it — not from a growth miracle to another economic miracle, but more likely the maturing of a still young and restless society in search of an identity anchor in an ever-changing global world. In particular, the incorporation of pressure release valves and the reassurance that civil society advocacy and political activism are not incompatible with economic success, may help to narrow the perceived distance between the man on the street and the ivory tower of policymakers amid the embrace of globalisation, technology, and the efficiency of markets.

It may be foolhardy, to say the least, to forecast what Singapore will look like in 2065, but there are two key milestones that I will be looking out for in the next 50 years.

Wealth and Income Inequality

First, tackling income inequality as a national priority. Recall that Singapore's deep-seated ambitions as a fledging nation and economy was to become the Switzerland of the East. While the original intention was noble and to achieve the economic wealth associated with Switzerland, will taking this ambition to its logical conclusion also mean the continued rationalisation of financial rewards over other less quantifiable goals like improving the lives of low-income workers and reducing the GINI coefficient? Will rising inequity, for instance, denoted by top corporate CEOs making more than 200 times the lowest paid worker like in some developed economies like Switzerland, be an inevitable outcome? "The market economy is very good at wealth creation but not perfect at all about wealth distribution," as Jonathan Sacks, Chief Rabbi of the UK, observed.

Note that as part of its own soul-searching, there was a proposal in Switzerland in late 2013 to introduce a basic income of 2,500 Swiss francs per month, which, in a departure from other welfare programmes, was unconditional and does not require beneficiaries to document that they are unable to work, but is aimed at providing a financial safety net for the population and eliminating poverty. While this may be the equivalent of building castles in the air, audacious (even if populist) proposals should be given some airtime and seriously consulted and studied rather than summarily dismissed as unworkable. The fact that Swiss law allows citizens to organise popular initiatives and hold referendums on such issues is not to be sneered at. Instead of a top-driven approach to tackle the issue of income inequality, it may be better to find a balance between ensuring economic growth and encouraging bottom-up conversations and consensus-building ideas on how to tackle the inequality gap. For instance, let the people decide if they want to have a higher tax regime or even to have mandatory contributions to a pool for this purpose to subsidise the poorest in the society. The trade-off should be among the various stakeholders in the Singapore economy, and not simply reduced to a fiscal responsibility of the state.

That said, it may be worthwhile thinking about setting a national KPI (Key Performance Indicator) for the GINI coefficient that is in line with the medium-term GDP growth targets to ensure that the policy mindset is correctly aligned with this thinking rather than subject to the whims and fancies of the electoral cycle. Having a social value revolving around the equity issue could soften the perception of an all-out materialistic society. Should Singapore target a levelling of the GINI coefficient back to around or even below the 0.40 handle or is the direction of change more important? Or is the relative standing of Singapore's GINI coefficient vis-à-vis our ASEAN neighbours the right yardstick? Or would the OECD average serve as a better benchmark? These are also important considerations to ponder on as we strive to avoid the over-stratification of Singaporean society.

Singapore and Ranking

Second, surrendering the "Singapore must be the best/first" mentality. Will Singapore continue to breeze ahead as the world's business-friendly bastion, a top investment destination, the most welcoming nation for foreign trade and investment, the easiest place to do business, the most competitive city, the least corrupt economy, the most transparent business regime, the best quality of life in Asia, producing the top PISA scores, so on and so forth, 50 years down the road. History generally counts against such a track record over an extended period of time. Any obsession with Singapore's competitiveness rankings or rankings of any sort, while useful and purposeful in the short term to building the economy and the nation, could be ultimately detrimental in the long run.

One example of this could be the current education system where Singapore has chalked up an impressive performance across a wide range of education league tables and is usually held up as an exceptional case study for the rest of the region, if not the rest of the world. It is admirable that the government walks the walk when it comes to education spending and the single-minded focus on achieving bold results in the drive for academic success whether in education or lifelong learning. But one unintended consequence is that young students and their parents are now embroiled in this high-stakes game called the Primary School Leaving Examination (PSLE), and the attendant flourishing private tuition industry that caters to the associated exam anxieties that arise from "kiasuism" (the fear of losing out).

While there have been policy efforts to ensure "true meritocracy" and "social mobility" over the last five decades, the complicated system of school affiliations, "through train" schooling, and the concentration of "good" schools in select neighbourhoods, contribute to many parents believing that paying for their child's education is the best investment they can make. The consequential result is excessive private tuition, and the "neurotic obsession" with exam results and paper qualifications as the key benchmark for "success." There must be something wrong with the psyche when private tuition is seen not as help for struggling students, but a must for top students to ace all subjects in top schools, and tuition centres see exponential growth in demand — the number of tuition centres registered with the Ministry of Education has surged from 700 in 2012 to 850 in 2014. There are currently 94 primary schools, but the competition to get onto the parent volunteer scheme of the more popular schools may seem absurd to an outsider.

The pre-school or early childhood education sector, on the other hand, was largely left to the private sector until recently, which seems to me such a wasted opportunity to ensure a level playing field for all Singaporean children to receive a head start in education regardless of their family background. Instead of disparate fees being charged by private providers and the current perceived "pay peanuts, get monkeys" mindset, mandating a free and high-quality pre-school education on a national scale, regulated by the Ministry of Education, could help uphold the ethos of being an open and inclusive society where every Singaporean child can begin their learning journey at the same starting line so that those from less advantaged backgrounds do not feel shortchanged later in life.

At the other end of the spectrum, the relentless pursuit of paper qualifications especially for higher education degrees also appears insatiable, despite the establishment of six universities providing 14,000 university places in 2014. Although the MOE's target is to offer publicly funded university spaces for 40% of every cohort by 2020 and there has been substantial policy efforts to open up additional education pathways through polytechnic and ITE options, parents still willingly fund private or even overseas university educations in the belief that it is critical for good job opportunities. Singapore should be careful not to go down the path of South Korea where there are more college graduates than available good jobs in the quest for tertiary education. While this is largely a generational shift in educational standards, creating sufficiently high-skilled and well-paying jobs to satisfy all the graduates will be an uphill task if the Singapore economy is not vibrant enough to attract investments and groom companies to create good jobs.

Education and the Future

Education Minister Heng Swee Keat had highlighted that in the next chapter of Singapore's education story, the challenge for teachers will be to help students develop values and strength of character amid the more volatile, uncertain, complex and ambiguous environment in the next 50 years. Like Martin Luther King Jr. once said, "Intelligence plus character — that is the goal of true education." To further advance along the educational continuum, a persistent meritocratic approach with liberal doses of creativity and innovation are critical.

Looking at the rise and fall of great nations, it would be presumptuous to proclaim with certainty that what worked well in the past, be it great infrastructure, a clean and efficient government, good corporate governance, and a well-educated workforce, will continue to be the success factors for the future. Future-proofing may seem like an exercise in futility, but preparing for a changing and uncertain world with tenacity and careful planning have underpinned Singapore's success story to date. Indeed, one key ingredient that is unlikely to diminish with time is the adaptability of the Singapore economy and Singaporean workers. To quote Napoleon Hill, "the strongest oak of the forest is not the one that is protected from the storm and hidden from the sun"; it is the one that stands in the open where it is compelled to struggle for its existence against the winds and rains and the scorching sun. Singapore, as a small, open and dynamic economy, continues to fit this bill well.

The End of the Singapore Consensus

Donald Low
Associate Dean
Lee Kuan Yew School of Public Policy

and Sudhir Thomas Vadaketh
Writer
Co-authors of *Hard Choices: Challenging the Singapore Consensus*

These are the best of times and the worst of times in Singapore, the world's only global city without a natural hinterland, whose prosperity and good governance are the envy of much of the world, and a model for others to follow. But while the city-state remains an alluring success story to much of the outside world, Singaporeans themselves are starting to question the long-term viability of their longstanding adherence to elite governance, meritocracy, the primacy of growth and state paternalism. The "Singapore consensus" that the People's Action Party (PAP) government constructed and maintained in the last five decades is fraying, partly because many citizens perceive it to be outdated.

The Singapore consensus has been underpinned by the idea of vulnerability — that because of its small size, lack of natural resources, ethnic and religious diversity, and geographic location in a potentially volatile region, the city-sized nation is inherently and immutably vulnerable. From this existentially anguished reality, a developmental belief system emerged. Its tenets include a strict academic meritocracy as the best way

---

This essay was adapted from an earlier piece written for the New American Foundation Weekly Wonk blog.

to sort talent; elite governance insulated from the short-termism and myopia of ordinary democratic pressures; the primacy of growth, delivered through export-led industrialisation and a heavy dependence on foreign capital and labour; an acceptance of the need to equalise opportunities but not outcomes; and an indifference to inequality, as reflected in the state's aversion to welfare.

The Singapore consensus made possible impressive socioeconomic development for much of the first 50 years, when demographic and domestic political conditions were far more favourable. Yet today, many Singaporeans are contesting the consensus. At first glance this might seem odd: Singapore has one of the highest per capita incomes in the world. But its economic success masks some uncomfortable truths about life in this city-state.

First World Problems

Income and wealth inequalities in Singapore are among the highest in the developed world. For many of its residents, the country's impressive material achievements have not translated into higher levels of happiness or well-being. In various surveys, Singaporeans are found to work some of the longest hours in the developed world and are described as one of the world's least happy peoples. Almost three-quarters are afraid to get sick because of perceived high healthcare costs while more than half indicate they would emigrate if given the chance.

In December 2013, Singapore had its first riot in 50 years — reflecting its inability (and possibly, unwillingness) to accommodate the more than one million low-skilled foreign workers in Singapore. Yet its economic model is still highly dependent on taking in increasing numbers of such workers as Singaporeans continue to shun and stigmatise menial jobs. In December 2012, low-wage mainland Chinese bus drivers, bereft of bargaining power, instigated Singapore's first labour strike in 26 years. Meanwhile, economic pressures coupled with the lack of efforts at fostering integration have led to an uptick in racism and xenophobia, tarnishing Singapore's reputation for openness and tolerance. A country long admired for its stability and openness to foreign nationals and ideas is now witnessing pent-up tensions bubbling over from time to time.

Domestically, the rapid ageing of the population is likely to put a number of cherished public policies and institutions to much higher levels of scrutiny. Already, Singaporeans are beginning to question the adequacy of the Central Provident Fund (CPF) — the country's 60-year retirement savings system that is usually lauded as being fully funded and sustainable in the face of demographic change. To the surprise and chagrin of Singapore's leaders, segments of the population even raised questions over the system's integrity.

Housing policy represents another area where changing demographics and socioeconomic realities demand not just policy tweaks, but quite a fundamental rethinking of the primary purpose of public policies.

Contending Visions and Contradictions

In many ways, Singapore is a victim of its own success. From the 1970s to 1990s, it developed from a trading and manufacturing hub to a highly globalised service and knowledge economy. In the process, a nascent, post-colonial city-state evolved into one of the world's most well-governed states and dynamic economies. This rapid transformation, largely driven and engineered by the state, outpaced the ability of entrenched ideologies, policies and institutions to keep up.

At the same time, contradictions in the Singapore story are beginning to emerge. For instance, the government's aspirations for Singapore to be an entrepreneurial and innovation-driven economy collide with the institutions, policies and practices that inhibit risk-taking, experimentation, collaboration, and egalitarian norms — all of which are critical for a creative economy.

Singapore's global city ambitions bump up against an emerging national identity. The nation also faces a quandary: Singaporeans question whether the country's strict academic meritocracy and the belief in the necessity of elite governance have also bred a narrow administrative and political elite that is increasingly out of touch with ordinary citizens. This has happened precisely as the electorate, increasingly weary of a sycophantic government-controlled national media, is seeking more mature engagement and debate about Singapore's future.

By failing to adapt to these new socioeconomic and political realities, Singapore has set the scene for a fierce clash between competing societal and political visions. The big question is how to forge a new consensus — which we believe will involve, among other things, greater welfare and lower immigration — without swinging too far in the other direction, and without undermining the very efficiency, market orientation and openness that made Singapore so successful in the first place. At the same time, an increasingly plural and contested political scene is likely to offer voters greater choice about the balance they want to strike.

Democratic Transitions

In this regard, a brief analysis of how South Korea and Taiwan democratised and developed more redistributive policies and institutions is instructive. In both countries, the transition to full democracy was, initially at least, wrenching, socially divisive and politically destabilising. But both countries managed eventually to amble towards stable, rule-based and competitive democratic systems. This, in turn, paved the way for the emergence of properly organised, collectively financed welfare states that enabled both countries to balance economic growth with social investments in areas such as healthcare, old age security and unemployment protection.

Singapore's transition is likely to be much less wrenching and destabilising. First, the city-state is nowhere near as repressive as the dictatorships in South Korea and Taiwan that ruled until the 1980s. Equally important is the fact that the vast majority of Singaporeans are homeowners. A home-owning society is far less likely to upset the apple cart of stability and prosperity.

For these and other reasons, we are sanguine about Singapore's transition to a liberal democracy with a far more redistributive state. Our optimism stands in stark contrast to the government's fears about how increased democratic pressures here will make Singapore less governable, impede quick and enlightened decision making by elites who know better, and increase the likelihood of policies being made for short-term or populist reasons.

We argue that such fears are mostly misplaced. The contest in Singapore is not primarily one over basic political rights and freedoms. But neither is it just over "bread and butter" issues. Rather, it is a debate over how a developmental state that has been so vital to Singapore's modernisation would have to adapt to a society that is becoming less compliant and conformist, less enamoured of the country's governing elite and its penchant for paternalism, and less willing to trust the government by default. It is also a debate over the people's ability to determine what constitutes success and wellbeing. While a narrow focus on GDP growth, academic achievement and material prosperity helped to raise living standards early on, they have also proven to be incomplete barometers of success for Singaporeans. For businesses and policymakers in Singapore, the days of easy political consensus, stability and insulation from short-term electoral demands are over. Having sacrificed two generations to attain modernity and prosperity, Singaporeans are now wrestling with a post-modern future.

Singapore and Nature in 2065 — Progressive or Pragmatic?

Shawn Lum
President
Nature Society (Singapore)

Predicting the future state of Nature in Singapore may make this one of the most straightforward of all essays in this collection. Almost everything we need to foresee the status of nature in Singapore in 2065 is in place: Singapore's biodiversity is well documented, land use plans are prepared and published decades in advance, we have a vibrant science and policy community with the capacity to predict trends, and our island's modest size leaves little ambiguity on likely changes to our physical environment.

There should not be major deviations from Singapore's commitment to a clean, comfortable, hygienic, and green home, for this formula has proven successful in creating a liveable, attractive home and a recognisable Singapore brand. Generally, with abundant and verdant greenery comes rich biodiversity. A near-certain forecast for Nature in Singapore would be to guess that 2065 will not be too different from 2015. A "more of the same" view, however likely, crucially misses a few elements that depend on the scale of Singapore's ambitions and the values of its people.

1965 to 2015: Gains and Losses

We marvel at the changes in the Singapore landscape since independence, but with regard to terrestrial nature and biodiversity the major changes took place over a century ago. Widespread land clearing reduced the amount of original vegetation covering the island to less than 10% by the late 1800s. The greatest species losses on land probably happened in the mid to late 19th century due to habitat loss and the reduction of Singapore's forests to scattered fragments. In 1965 the island's Central Catchment Area forests were in a slow recovery mode, as they are today.

By the early 1960s, large areas of formerly cleared land were regenerating. These include what is today the Western Catchment Area, along with parts of Yishun, Bukit Batok, the Southern Ridges, and Pulau Ubin. Moreover, the policy of relocating people from the many villages spread across the island added to a surge in the post-independence greening of Singapore, as many areas that were villages and orchards in 1965 reverted to forest. These young, fast growing forests are not rich in tree species. Some are dominated by non-native trees such as albizia (*Paraserianthes falcataria*), but they provide a good home for animals such as birds.

Habitat losses since 1965 occurred mainly along our coasts and in our waters. Species-rich intertidal zones were lost to land reclamation (East Coast) or to port and other coastal development (West Coast). Mangrove-lined estuaries that were the staging grounds for migratory shorebirds were reclaimed and/or converted into the numerous freshwater reservoirs that line our coasts. These include the Serangoon, Lower Seletar, Kranji, Jurong, and Pandan Reservoirs, and Marina Bay. Land reclamation also led to the direct loss of coral reefs from reclamation, or to substantial impacts on remaining reefs due to the siltation of coastal waters. Suspended silt impacts reefs by settling onto reef organisms as well as reducing water clarity, which lowers reef productivity and viability.

Nature, however, can be as surprisingly resilient in water as it is on land. Witness the reappearance of intertidal life on reclaimed land (e.g. Tanah Merah coast, Pulau Hantu, Tuas), or the return of coral reef communities (former Keppel Shipyard, reclaimed land on the Southern islands). The 2065 outlook needs to consider nature's resilience in addition to our commitment to look after natural habitats.

A Good but Blurry View

Current policies and science point to things we can be fairly sure about in the next 50 years. There will be as many if not more people in Singapore in 2065 than in 2015. Many areas that witnessed the return of forests in the past

50 years will once again be devoid of them by 2065, except that in place of the former villages and kampong orchards, there will mostly be concretised surfaces and buildings. Singapore will be warmer due to global change and to an increase in built-up areas. We will experience wetter wet periods and drier dry periods. A number of species that today have very small populations will have disappeared when Singapore celebrates its Centennial.

The general trend will be for a decrease in terrestrial species diversity. It will probably not be a dramatic downturn from 2015 levels, but habitat loss usually leads to species losses, and in 2065 we will have fewer natural green spaces than in 2015. Our forests will not die out, but there will be a shift in their species composition: plants that can better withstand drought should thrive at the expense of those that do not.

In our waters, on the other hand, recovery of reefs and coasts may carry on if water quality continues to improve, if port activities shift to Tuas as planned, and if future coastal development is more environmentally friendly than it is today. Today's incipient efforts at reef restoration will be a well-honed craft well before 2065, and there is a real possibility that our waters and marine life in 2065 will be closer to that of 1965 than in 2015. The principal danger to our reefs and coastal areas will be warming waters. Higher water temperatures can severely impact corals, as seen in 1998, when elevated water temperatures led to the death of 25% of our corals. Marine habitats exposed to prolonged surges in freshwater discharge during big storms will also suffer, as the intertidal habitat at Tanjung Chek Jawa on Pulau Ubin did in 2007 following precipitous increases in the flow of the Johor River. Fortunately the species rich southern shores of Singapore should be relatively free of these impacts.

The general prognosis: slightly lower biodiversity on land in 2065 compared to 2015, with slightly higher diversity in our waters. We will have less biodiversity in 2065 than today if development encroaches into Nature Reserves, if there is an increase in high-impact recreation in nature areas, and if there are insufficient green spaces outside protected areas. Few would bet on that happening, but it could if Singapore does not know about nor value biodiversity.

The Human Factor

While science gives us a decent, if indistinct, view of the future, the less predictable human factor will truly determine the state of nature and biodiversity in 2065. Policies, stewardship of wild places, consumer behaviour, and the collective will of Singapore will result in whether we remain a green city with an incidentally rich flora and fauna, or a progressive society that boldly and imaginatively looks after natural heritage; that we successfully learned to mainstream biodiversity, nature, and conservation into everything we do, and that we became a more vibrant and contented society as a result. The way forward could look something like the following.

Doing the Good Things Better

Singapore has in the past twenty years taken a more proactive approach to the management and protection of nature. This has been partly self-initiated, with the general acceptance that greenery is good for us (that biodiversity is a good thing is probably not as prevalent a view). Advances in nature conservation have also been due to Singapore being party to global biodiversity policies such as the Convention on Biodiversity.

The people who today manage nature in Singapore have an intuitive understanding of its ecosystems. Monitoring biodiversity is an integral part of its management. I expect this to continue, and if science is allowed more room to inform policy, we will see nature areas that are better protected and funded, more systematically studied and surveyed, better buffered, and better safeguarded against negative impacts. Our secondary forests will be actively returned to their richer, more complex original state. Should this transformation occur, we may find that many of the animal and plant species that were lost long before 1965 will be able to thrive in Singapore's forests in 2065.

Nature as Necessary

Dramatic gains in biodiversity conservation will happen when Singapore agencies and the general public see nature in Singapore as something more than just "good to have." If nature and biodiversity are deemed too valuable to lose, different sectors will begin working together not to minimise impacts, as is currently done, but to carefully avoid negative impacts and to coordinate across sectors to protect nature and ensure its recovery.

The loss of nature areas is generally seen today as an unfortunate but unavoidable consequence of development. Might we see the day when the loss of nature is considered intolerable? The former view helps keep Singapore green; the latter view will be transformational, with impacts far beyond Singapore.

Biodiversity Protection as Self-actualisation?

Singapore does not see its full potential as a leader in nature conservation and management. We have developed a Cities Biodiversity Index adopted by parties to the Convention on Biodiversity, but Singapore's role can be far greater. We just do not realise it yet.

Nature and biodiversity are of great concern only to an active minority. However, if enlightened environmental stewardship is considered inseparable from other strategic issues such as economic development and social stability, Singapore will become a driver for conservation action throughout the region. Treasured local nature will be seen part of a larger, interconnected continuum; the preservation of ecosystems in other countries will become imperative to us.

Singapore has considerable economic reach, enviable technological prowess, an impressive communications network, an influential diplomatic corps, a heralded education system, and extensive ties throughout Asia. When Singapore sees nature as critical to national and regional security, its capabilities will be ramped up in support of the many extensive but threatened ecosystems across the region: peat swamps, rainforests, rivers, reefs, and montane areas. We will begin to work with our partners to identify and strengthen the factors that are key to the survival of rich, intact, and life-giving natural ecosystems: thriving local communities, progressive local and international policies, sustainable fisheries, careful resource use, implementation of transnational conservation strategies and a regionally integrated protected areas system, and thoughtful and holistic regional development.

If nature and the environment become a part of mainstream Singapore thought and action in time for SG75, Singapore and the region will together reap the material and intangible rewards of inspired environmental management and protection well before SG100. If nature and the environment do not become integrated into our policymaking and everyday living, I worry for those who will be around to read this essay in 2065.

Singapore: A Zero Car Ownership City

Kishore Mahbubani
Dean
Lee Kuan Yew School of Public Policy
National University of Singapore

In 2065, the Singapore government finally abolishes private ownership of cars. It is one of the last major cities to do so, after New York and London, Shanghai and Tokyo had done so decades earlier.

Indeed, as early as 2015, on Singapore's 50th anniversary, it had become clear that modern technology could allow Singapore to be the first city in the world to abolish private car ownership. The development of driverless Google cars and the ability to book taxis on smartphones meant that the technology to deliver driverless taxis to the doorsteps of Singapore homes had already arrived. As the world's only truly independent city-state, and facing an incredible space crunch, it made both technological and economic sense for Singapore to be the first city to work towards abolishing private ownership of cars.

Initially, the Singapore government was very interested in exploring the idea as Singapore had an extraordinary record of being remarkably bold and imaginative in the formulation of its public policies in the first 50 years of modern Singapore. This is why land-scarce Singapore was the first city in the world to introduce Certificates of Entitlement (COEs) to regulate the supply of cars, and Electronic Road Pricing (ERP) to regulate the use of cars. Having watched how many of Singapore's neighbouring cities, including Bangkok and Jakarta, Kuala Lumpur and Manila, had choked themselves with traffic jams and slowed their economies, the Singapore government wisely took preemptive measures to control both the number and usage of cars in Singapore. The Singapore government took pride in the fact that it could look 10 to 20 years down the road and anticipate the future challenges coming Singapore's way.

This is why the Singapore government wisely decided to be among the first cities in the world to explore the possibility of abolishing private car ownership. The main reason for owning a car in Singapore is to go from point to point effortlessly without having to walk to Mass Rapid Transit (MRT) stations or wait for buses in hot and humid Singapore. Hence, travelling in air-conditioned cars from point to point was a perfectly understandable desire. By the 2020s it had become clear that the old policies, the COE and ERP, were not enough to prevent traffic jams in Singapore. The effectiveness of raising COE prices had reached a plateau, while public dissent was rising fast. Lack of information made it difficult for the government to change the ERP prices rapidly to match traffic flows. Hence, when a group of visionary Silicon Valley entrepreneurs approached the Singapore government to work together on a trial experiment to abolish private car ownership, the government readily agreed to do this pilot project.

The pilot project was a great success. Given the small size of Singapore, the ready availability of smartphone networks, and a highly educated population, Singapore citizens had no difficulty mastering the technology to call for driverless taxis to appear at their doorsteps. Having keyed in their destination, they would be driven there and step out without having to make any payment, as the payment would have already been made from the smartphone. More Singaporeans used these taxis to travel to the extensive MRT network, which had been streamlined to enable efficient and cheap transfers from road to rail.

To regulate demand, there was no fixed price. Sophisticated algorithms would instantly calculate demand and supply and ensure that the price would reflect demand minute by minute, if not second by second. And if at any minute, the supply of driverless taxis exceeded the demand in any area, the passengers would only be charged the marginal cost of the energy and capital for the use of these air-conditioned driverless taxis. This was an ingenious move by the Singapore government to gain political support for their move to get driverless taxis to replace private ownership of cars.

The success of this pilot project demonstrated that Singapore would gain enormous benefits from being the first city to abolish private cars and switch to a large and equivalent pool of driverless taxis which could provide transportation doorstep to doorstep. Firstly, as all these Google cars were battery-powered, the pollution from gasoline-driven cars would fall to zero. Singapore would then have the cleanest air of any modern city.

Secondly, as the total pool of cars in Singapore shrank steadily, the amount of land set aside for road usage and parking would gradually shrink. Fewer cars needed to go on the highways, especially as the government massively streamlined the entire public transport system. As high-speed trains now came reliably at pre-determined times, Singaporeans could also opt for road-to-rail options, which were often cheaper and quicker. Hence, instead of boasting that the government was on a project to "upsize the PIE," the government could launch a campaign to "downsize the PIE." Huge underground parking spaces were planned for this new fleet of driverless taxis. Most of the land freed from shrinking road and parking spaces could be allocated to planting trees and expanding parks. The larger space allocated to parks and green spaces also helped to reduce the city's temperature, which had been steadily rising due to global warming. All this led to energy saving as less energy was required to cool the city. The increased green spaces also helped to reduce flooding and improve water quality. Hence, Singapore could have an even cleaner and greener environment to boast about.

Thirdly, as Singapore demonstrated its vision by moving towards becoming the world's first zero car ownership city, it attracted some of the best talent in the world who were looking for the most environmentally responsible city in the world to bring up their children in. Singapore's goal of becoming the "brainiest" city in the world was thus boosted by its plans for a zero car ownership city.

Fourthly, the level of happiness of the Singapore population could also increase as the population no longer needed to see the car as a status symbol that defined their place and role in Singapore city. Instead, the car was seen as a purely utilitarian vehicle that was only necessary to go from point to point, not to make a point about one's social standing. Interestingly, the new sign of affluence became ownership or use of green technology. People raced to have the most environmentally friendly devices and habits. Nonetheless, in recognition of the fact that the very affluent, the billionaires, would still expect instant car service, the government set up a premium high-cost and super-comfortable driverless taxi service that was priced to be affordable only for a select few that wanted transport to be at their beck and call 24 hours a day. In short, abolishing private car ownership would not create any severe inconvenience to any citizen of Singapore.

As the pilot project proceeded, it became clear to the Singapore government that the project was producing even more benefits than it initially conceived. Since Google Maps could also provide information on which roads were less busy, the driverless taxis could incorporate this information when they calculated a route. This reduced costs and made traffic flows more efficient. Similarly, the electronic system could also calculate when exactly one should leave the house in order to catch the train on time. It could also ensure that another driverless taxi was ready and waiting to take the passenger from the destination train station to work. Hence, waiting times would be minimised, leaving more time for productive activity. At the same time, as the overall system was electronically managed, it was possible for it to arrange for carpooling for Singaporeans on a budget. Singaporeans needed only to input their schedules ahead of time, such as the time their children needed to be in school. Larger taxis or buses would then go around to the carpoolers' homes. The same electronic system could also be used to facilitate trips to Malaysia. Driverless taxis could also be used by Singaporeans to take them to the train station connected to Malaysia, similarly reducing Causeway jams.

One major unanticipated benefit was that fewer people were killed or hurt on roads. Overall road safety was improved due to automatic sensor systems. The driverless taxis were constantly remotely updated regarding traffic light statuses and other traffic safety information. At the same time, safety was improved for women and children taking taxis late at night — since taxis could be relied upon to appear at a specific time and place, and commuters did not have to wait by the road in the dark for one to come. The electronic system could also log which specific vehicle was used, improving information regarding lost and found items, young children's whereabouts, and so on. "Black box" information could also be provided in case of accidents (which became increasingly rare). Of course, there were fears that systemic failures in the electronic system could create a massive catastrophe. To circumvent these problems, the Singapore government hired the best experts to update the system's digital protections regularly. Failsafes were also installed in the cars so that they could be shut down remotely in case of an emergency. Since driverless taxis had released a significant pool of Singapore citizens from driving taxis, they were retrained to create large pools of emergency workers to handle disruptions.

Since the pilot project was clearly exceeding expectations, the Singapore government began to dream of even more radical approaches to make the driverless taxi system work even better. It began working on a plan to move most of the electric car system underground, thus saving a great deal of road and parking space. At the same time, the government worked on a plan to connect the entire city with bicycle and pedestrian routes, which would become even more enjoyable as the road and parking spaces began to shrink. The increasing shade from the trees made it more comfortable to walk or cycle in the heat of Singapore. In 2014, Hamburg had already been undertaking such a plan that Singapore could emulate. In 2015, Helsinki announced a plan to eliminate private car ownership by 2025.[1]

The success of the Singapore pilot project began to inspire and excite many of the leading cities in the world, including New York and London, Shanghai and Tokyo. They sent their urban planners to learn from the Singapore project and they began similar pilot projects. Given the success of the Singapore project, the whole world expected Singapore to become the first global city to abolish private car ownership as it clearly did not make economic or social sense for Singapore to adhere to the ancient 20th century notion that private car ownership provided the best means of transportation.

Sadly, politics intervened. The ruling party lost one more GRC in 2016 and went on to lose two more GRCs in 2021. As a result, the Singapore government pulled back from bold visionary public policy initiatives and

---

[1] Helsinki's New Plan To Eliminate Car Ownership. Co.Exist, July 18, 2014. Retrieved January 9, 2015 from http://www.fastcoexist.com/3033125/helsinkis-new-plan-to-eliminate-car-ownership.

decided to become more cautious. It realised that the culture of car ownership and car worship had become deeply ingrained in the Singapore psyche. Unlike the founding fathers of Singapore, who had never hesitated to change the social mores of Singapore society (like corruption, or public spitting, or burning firecrackers on Chinese New Year, or loudhailers from Singapore mosques), the Singapore leaders in the 2020s and 2030s moved towards a culture of caution. Hence, even though the defenders of the culture of car worship were clearly a small fringe group who were loud and noisy, they dominated the discourse on car ownership. As a result, instead of being the first city in the world to abolish private car ownership, Singapore became one of the last major cities to do so in 2065.

Budget 2065: Balancing Head and Heart for Inclusive and Sustainable Finance

Ravi Menon
Managing Director
Monetary Authority of Singapore

You see things and you say 'why'.
But I dream things that never were; and I say 'why not'?

George Bernard Shaw
Back to Methuselah

BUDGET STATEMENT 2065 DELIVERED BY DR. RAHIM IBRAHIM, DEPUTY PRIME MINISTER AND MINISTER FOR FINANCE, ON 21ST NOVEMBER 2064

Madam Speaker, I beg to move, that Parliament approves the financial policy of the Government for 1st January 2065 to 31st December 2065.

Economic Performance

Our economy has been doing well. Real-time estimates show that GNI has grown by 2.1% and GDP by 1.8% year-to-date. Our GNI is now 25% larger than our GDP. Unemployment is 0.5%, the lowest since the Global Cyber Crisis of 2052.

The exposition here is an entirely personal vision of what the future could be like and does not represent the views or projections of the Monetary Authority of Singapore (MAS). I am grateful for ideas and statistical support from my colleagues in the MAS, namely Edward Robinson, Celine Sia, Ng Bok Eng, Tu Suh Ping, and Jeslyn Tan.

The prognosis for 2065 is good, with both the offshore and territorial economies expected to do well and yield GNI growth of 1.8% and GDP growth of 1.6%, closer to underlying potential.

Demand in the US, India and China — our three largest markets — will help to sustain activity in the ASEAN Free Economic Zones (AFEZ), from which our corporations and citizens derive 40% of their incomes. The production of space vehicles and supersonic jet engines will continue to be the main sources of growth in the AFEZ. Additive manufacturing of components for electric cars and fusion reactors will do reasonably well despite stiffening competition from new plants in Mexico and Brazil. But the assembly of "*Nightingale Robots*" will continue to contract as Germany, France and the UK join Japan in banning their deployment pending further tests, following the Robot Riots in Tokyo's Central Hospital two years ago when hackers gained control of these robots.

Activity within the territorial economy will be underpinned by healthcare R&D, digital finance, and the smart industry. Genome sequencing for disease control, infrastructure financing of the Sino-Indian lunar complex, and global supply chain management are expected to be the main sources of domestic output growth next year.

Expenditure Highlights

Let me highlight the Government's expenditure priorities for the coming year.

- *Ministry of Wellbeing*. We will upgrade our retirement villages in Malaysia, Thailand, Indonesia, and Western Australia. We will step up investments in the tele-medicine infrastructure and mobile-nursing programme to enhance healthcare support for less mobile elderly Singaporeans. We will build another six nursing homes and Alzheimer's Centres over the next 10 years; Alzheimer's care has become the fastest growing expenditure item, with 1 in 12 Singaporeans affected by this condition. Subsidies for MediShield Life premiums will continue to increase in line with sustained improvements in life expectancy and high medical cost inflation.
- *Ministry of Lifelong Learning*. Over the last 25 years, we have been steadily shifting the weight of government spending from pre-employment

training (PET) in the formal school system towards continuing education and training (CET). We will increase the paid CET leave from four weeks to six weeks per year and increase the annual CET subsidy to 50%. The only portion of the PET budget that will continue growing is for special needs education, especially for early intervention treatments and training in life readiness skills for our autistic children.

- *Ministry of Infrastructure and Mobility*. Next year, we would have completed the third and final phase of the Dyke Construction Programme, which we began in 2045 as a defence against the rise in sea levels induced by climate change. The Escalator and Travelator Upgrading Programme will be completed next year, enhancing the urban mobility of elderly Singaporeans. We are also on track to reach our target of placing underground 90% of our urban retail space and 60% of our road network, as envisioned in the Underground City Master Plan of 2055.
- *Ministry of Environment and Energy Resources*. With the completion of our second offshore nuclear power plant, spending will begin to taper from next year. Expenditure related to climate change adaptation will stay elevated in view of the continuing adverse effects of global warming. With the depletion of tropical farms in the region, we will expand our footprint of organic food and fish farms in Australia. We will also upgrade the Jurong Island Recycling Complex to better utilise the defunct petrochemical facilities.
- *Ministry of Social Harmony and Connectivity*. We will enhance connectivity with the 3 million Singaporeans living and working in the AFEZ, China, and India by upgrading the video capabilities of the current digital networks. We will organise more programmes to better integrate the 2-million-strong expatriate community within Singapore. We will start preparations for the Olympic Games to be jointly hosted by Malaysia and Singapore in the Iskandar Economic Zone in 2068 — a fitting way to commemorate the 40th anniversary of Iskandar's "Two Country/One System" model. We will also increase outlays to support the growing number of Singaporeans volunteering to help teach poor children, promote health education, and build irrigation facilities, under the SingCare Programme for Sub-Saharan Africa.
- *Ministry of Economy*. Resources will continue to be focused on building infrastructure in our offshore satellite towns and industrial parks in the

AFEZ to cater to the needs of our multinational companies and overseas communities. We will also enhance the cross-border infrastructure to strengthen linkages between the territorial and offshore economies.

Revenue Highlights

Next year, we will reach the long-term targets set in the 2050 Report of the Sustainable and Equitable Taxation Commission (SETC), which called for Income and Consumption taxes accounting for 30% each of total revenues and Wealth taxes and Net Investment Income accounting for 20% each. As members would recall, the Constitutional Amendment of 2052 allowed for up to 75% of net government investment income to be used for the Budget.

- *Income Taxes.* The Corporate Income Tax rate will remain unchanged at 14%. The Personal Income Tax will also remain unchanged, with the top marginal rate at 20% and the minimum taxable income threshold set at the median income of the population and subject to a 3% rate.
- *Wealth Taxes.* Wealth inequality has become the key socioeconomic challenge facing us, compared to income inequality 30 to 50 years ago. We will increase further the progressivity of our wealth taxes, to help enhance social mobility. Properties with Annual Value exceeding $2 million will be subject to a higher Asset Tax rate of 30%. The Capital Gains Tax, currently at a flat rate of 10%, will now comprise two tiers: 10% for gains up to $1 million and a marginal rate of 15% for gains above this level. Finally, the top tier of the Inheritance Tax, applicable to bequests received in excess of $20 million, will be raised to 30%.
- *Consumption Taxes.* Twenty years ago, growing subsidies for MediShield Life premiums outstripped our ability to pay for them. The President turned down the Government's request to draw down the reserves and called for a sustainable financing plan for healthcare. This led to the Constitutional Amendment of 2046 that limited the budget of the Ministry of Wellbeing to receipts from the Goods and Services Tax (GST). This discipline has served us well. The last increase in the GST rate was five years ago. With Alzheimer's care and Medishield Life premium subsidies rising rapidly, I will increase the GST rate to 14% next year. The Carbon Tax will remain unchanged, at $140 per ton of

carbon. Since its introduction in 2030 following the Global Climate Change Mitigation Compact, it has helped to reduce greenhouse gas emissions. It also helped to replace revenues lost when we discontinued the old motor vehicle taxes and vehicle quota system with the advent of the centrally managed driverless car-pooling system in 2042.

Budget Position

Let me summarise the 2065 budget position.

With Total Expenditure at $208 billion (20.4% of GNI) and Total Non-Investment Revenue at $188 billion (18.4% of GNI), the Primary Budget Balance will be a deficit of $20 billion (2.0% of GNI). After factoring in General and Special Transfers of $24 billion (2.4% of GNI) and the Net Investment Returns Contribution of $47 billion (4.6% of GNI), the Overall Budget Balance is a surplus of $3 billion, or 0.2% of GNI. The financial position of the Government remains sound.

Conclusion

Madam Speaker, next year, Singapore marks 100 years as a sovereign country. We took birth in 1965 as an improbable nation, achieved First World status by the time we celebrated our Golden Jubilee in 2015, and are today one of the top five cities in the world. We have come this far because we worked hard, we worked together, and we worked for the future.

And we lived within our means. 50 years ago, our third Prime Minister, Mr. Lee Hsien Loong spoke about the need to balance a warm heart with a hard head. And that is generally what we have achieved, even if we have got the balance wrong at times along the way.

We have certainly not lacked heart. We have sought to give all Singaporeans the means to succeed through lifelong *education* and the peace of mind that they will be able to afford good *healthcare*. We have been making large transfers for GST vouchers and CPF top-ups for the lower income and less wealthy. And we have focused government support on helping the truly disadvantaged in our society — the aged destitute, the disabled poor, special needs children. Consequently, total government spending as a share of GNI has grown, from about 15% of GNI in 2015 to about 20% today.

Fortunately, we have also been hard of head. Our people understand that spending more than what we can afford will undermine our economic stability today and forfeit our children's future tomorrow. Balancing the budget while spending more on healthcare and safety nets meant that we had to cut back on general subsidies and cherished middle-class programmes. Over the last two decades, we have progressively reduced subsidies and grants for HDB housing, extended means-testing to all healthcare subsidies, and replaced tertiary education subsidies with means-tested vouchers.

And doing more for those who have less meant that those who had more had to contribute more. Wealth taxes constitute 20% of our total revenues today, compared to 12% fifty years ago. But to be sustainable, the revenue base must be broad. With the income tax base shrinking due to slower economic growth, we have doubled the GST rate in the last 50 years, with full offsets for the lower-income.

We are one of very few countries which have been able to forge this social compact based on a balance between heart and head. If we can maintain this balance, then our financial policies will remain inclusive and sustainable — giving all citizens the opportunity to succeed and providing a safety net for the vulnerable while balancing the budget. Our prospects for the next century will then be as bright as it has been for our first century.

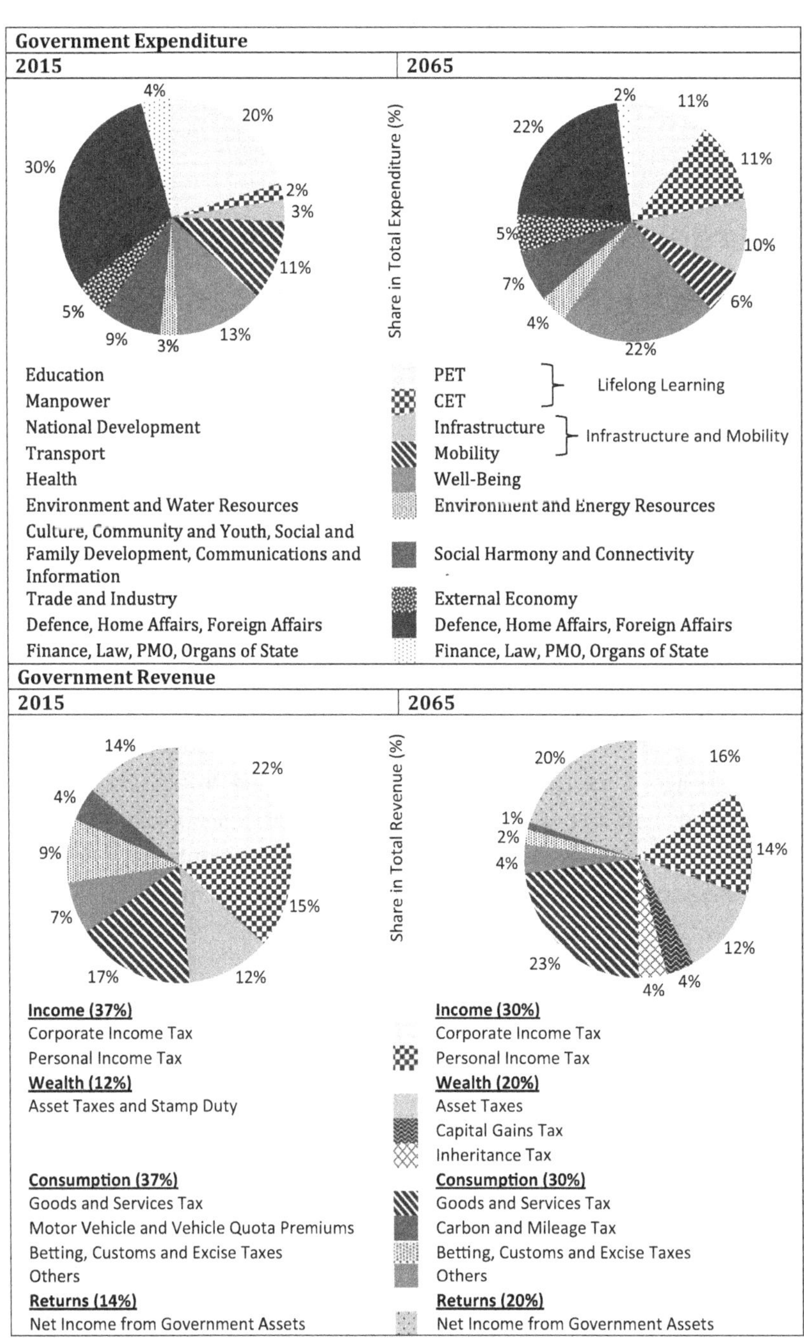
Government Expenditure
2015
2065
4%
20%
30%
2%
3%
11%
5%
9%
3%
13%
Share in Total Expenditure (%)
2%
11%
22%
11%
5%
10%
7%
6%
4%
22%
Education
Manpower
National Development
Transport
Health
Environment and Water Resources
Culture, Community and Youth, Social and Family Development, Communications and Information
Trade and Industry
Defence, Home Affairs, Foreign Affairs
Finance, Law, PMO, Organs of State
PET
CET
Lifelong Learning
Infrastructure
Mobility
Infrastructure and Mobility
Well-Being
Environment and Energy Resources
Social Harmony and Connectivity
External Economy
Defence, Home Affairs, Foreign Affairs
Finance, Law, PMO, Organs of State
Government Revenue
2015
2065
14%
22%
4%
9%
7%
15%
17%
12%
Share in Total Revenue (%)
20%
16%
1%
2%
4%
14%
12%
23%
4%
4%
Income (37%)
Corporate Income Tax
Personal Income Tax
Wealth (12%)
Asset Taxes and Stamp Duty
Consumption (37%)
Goods and Services Tax
Motor Vehicle and Vehicle Quota Premiums
Betting, Customs and Excise Taxes
Others
Returns (14%)
Net Income from Government Assets
Income (30%)
Corporate Income Tax
Personal Income Tax
Wealth (20%)
Asset Taxes
Capital Gains Tax
Inheritance Tax
Consumption (30%)
Goods and Services Tax
Carbon and Mileage Tax
Betting, Customs and Excise Taxes
Others
Returns (20%)
Net Income from Government Assets

A Larger Singapore Contributing to Human Welfare and Making Huge Money

Yew-Kwang Ng
Winsemius Professor, Division of Economics
Nanyang Technological University, Singapore

I was an undergraduate student at Nanyang University in Singapore around the time of its independence half a century ago (1962–1965). I returned in 2013 to take up the Winsemius chair in economics vacated by the eminent Prof. Lim Chong Yah. Comparing Singapore now to 50 years ago, I see tremendous progress on many fronts. Looking forward another half a century, I am confident that Singapore will become larger (slightly in land area but much more so in population), stronger, richer, and happier. I will not live to see 2065, but our children and grandchildren will.

A Larger Population is Good for Singaporeans

The population of Singapore will likely increase to about 5.56m by 2015. This is nearly 3 times its size of 1.887m in 1965 or an average annual compound growth rate of about 2.2%. The Population White Paper in 2013 projected an increase to between 6.5–6.9m in 2030, or an average annual rate of less than 1.3%. Allowing this rate to decrease further to 1% over 2030–2065, the population of Singapore will be about 9.5m in 2065. (Actually, my prediction is for over 10m in 2065, but I do not want to scare people.) Many people now may be astonished by this figure. Actually there is nothing to be alarmed at all. This is only an increase of about 70% over 50 years; we have tripled over the last 50 years and have done much better partly because of the increase!

True, the transportation, housing infrastructures, etc. have to catch up with the big population increases in the decades ahead. However, with a larger economy and more people paying taxes, the government will have more money to invest in these areas. When the population increased rapidly with investment in infrastructure lagging behind, essentially over the last decade or so, people experienced more congestion and put the blame on immigration and population increases. Actually, in the long run after investment in infrastructure has caught up, a larger population, within limits, usually leads to higher per capita income (due to economies of scale and specialisation more so than offsetting diminishing returns to land). In fact, even with decreasing per capita income with immigration, existing Singaporeans still benefit as immigrants bid for and push up prices of assets already owned by Singaporeans or their government. More importantly, Singaporeans will gain from having a larger population both through immigration and natural increase in the long run by having more people to share the costs of public goods, especially in defence and research. Without a large increase in population (almost trebling) over the last half a century, how could have our defence capabilities increased so remarkably?

Over my undergraduate years of 1962–1965, if we missed a bus from Nanyang University to the city, we had to wait for half an hour. Now, if we missed even two 179 buses in a row, the third one would typically come within 2–3 minutes. This is a benefit of a larger population that most people ignore. When travelling on a congested road or in a crowded train carriage, people wish that the number of people would be halved, ignoring that they each would have to pay twice the amount of taxes to have the same infrastructure with half the population! Holding the per capita tax unchanged, transportation will be enhanced, not worsened by a larger population. The densely populated London and Tokyo are much more convenient than the sparsely populated countryside! Given two jobs of similar pay, most people would choose the one in a larger city.

On efficiency in transportation, there is one thing that could be done well before 2065. Certificate of Entitlement (COE) prices for smaller cars could be reduced without causing too much congestion by taxing petrol much more heavily. After paying for the high COE and car prices, many drivers may drive more than absolutely necessary to justify the fixed costs. A high petrol price is needed to dissuade them from doing so. Moreover, petrol consumption is not only associated with congestion, but also with pollution, noise and accidents. Heavy taxes on petrol can be justified economically. I would also like to see more taxis made available, even at the cost of higher taxi fares. For those who can afford to take taxis, the convenience of readily available taxis is much more important than lower fares. The efficient public transport system plus the availability of taxis will convince most people of the non-necessity of owning cars in Singapore.

However, I would like to see the prices of owning luxury cars inclusive of COE to be raised very substantially. This is not so much as taxing the rich (which could be done by imposing higher income taxes on them, which I am also in favour of) than to achieve efficiency. Luxury cars and many other luxury items have conspicuous consumption (showing off wealth) effects and the related diamond effects (goods valued for their values than just for their intrinsic consumption effects). As I argued in *American Economic Review* in 1987, such goods should be taxed heavily just for efficiency. In extreme cases, taxes on such goods generate not only no excess burden (distortionary costs), there may be no burden at all. A tax of $10m does not generate costs of $13m, but no cost at all. It is even possible for consumers of such goods to be made better off from higher prices from taxation.

Joel Mokyr writes in *The Journal of Economic Literature* (2014, pp. 191–192): "...economic historians such as Lindert [and Solar, Greif and Iyigun] ... have shown the complex, but on the whole favourable, effect of the Welfare State on economic performance to the point where the full economic benefits and costs may have been roughly equal, making the Welfare State a "free lunch" ... the net effect of the Poor Law was probably to foster technological progress, because it weakened the resolve of the inevitable losers to resist it and thus reduced social unrest." This suggests that more equality-improving welfare spending may be welfare improving overall, provided that they are financed by taxation than by excessive debts. Thus, Singapore does not have to worry too much in its current slow shift towards more welfare spending. About four years ago, my predecessor Prof. Lim Chong Yah had the foresight of calling for more concerns with equality and the lower-income groups. The strong objection to his view then has now largely subsided.

Pleasure Machines for Brain Stimulation

I am confident, but by no means certain, that Singapore will remain largely very efficient, secure, safe, and clean. I am less confident and can only hope that the problems of haze from forest fires and hotter weather from global warming will be solved or significantly reduced by 2065. Speaking of hope, I hope Singapore can contribute hugely to the welfare of people in the future as well as making big economic gains at the same time, by pioneering research in stimulating the pleasure centres of the brain.

It has been known since 1954 that there are pleasure centres in our brain (and that of mice) the electrical stimulation of which generates intense pleasure, without the harmful health effects of addictive drugs. The normal stimulation through our five senses has rapidly diminishing marginal utility, e.g. each successive mouthful of ice cream becomes less and less tasty. This protects us from excessive eating. However, the direct stimulation of the pleasure centres produces intense pleasure with no diminishing marginal utility. Why has this not been developed into a reliable, safe, and convenient way of increasing our pleasure? Western countries have very stringent laws regarding animal experimentation, much less human experimentation. In my view, the relatively small pain inflicted on the experimental animals could be justified by the much greater gains of research results. Moreover, in developing the pleasure machine, the animals and humans experimented on would in fact enjoy themselves most of the time. I volunteer to be among the first human subjects for experimenting with pleasure machines.

Many people may find such stimulation unnatural and even revolting. By definition, all items of civilisation like chairs, fridges, stoves, books, computers, etc. are unnatural and did not exist in our natural living environment of the savannah. Being unnatural is not a reason for concern. If someone uses X to gain pleasure without harming anyone, finding that revolting is a very illiberal attitude that we should learn to get rid of, like we have largely done so regarding homosexuality. What about the danger of excessive indulgence in using the pleasure machine? If this is a problem, it could be easily solved by making the electricity for the stimulation available only between 7–11pm.

The availability of the pleasure machine will solve most social problems. If intense pleasure is available at the push of a button, why should we take the risk of using addictive hard drugs that are dangerous to our health and and may lead to increased crime?

If Singapore developed such pleasure machines, they could be sold both domestically and abroad at huge prices. I would certainly be willing to buy one using a large proportion of my total wealth and still would gain a huge consumer surplus. Thus, Singapore can contribute enormously to human welfare and make a lot of money at the same time!

A Place We Call Home — Growing and Maintaining Our Singapore Identity

Max Phua
Managing Director
World Scientific Publishing

Singapore in 2065 will be a very different country, demographically, from it was in 1965 (when it was separated from Malaysia) or even in 2015 (when it celebrates 50 years of nation building). Due to our low fertility rates, the rapid growth of immigrant population, globalisation and marriage trends, our social, cultural and racial composite will change drastically over the next couple of decades. We are absorbing 15,000 to 25,000 new citizens each year and around 40% of Singaporeans marry foreign spouses. For practical and economic reasons, this process seems unavoidable as we strive to maintain our status as a top global city and a prosperous country. It is therefore imperative that we define what "Singaporeness" is and maintain it or it will be diluted or lost in coming years. We have to promote this "Singapore identity" among Singaporeans living in Singapore and abroad, inculcate the idea in our new citizens and residents and continue to foster and grow it.

Our nation is young and its identity fragile. We have not had the chance to build a strong national identity as we were occupied with finding jobs for our people and raising our standard of living in the first couple of decades after independence in 1965. It was not until the early 1980s that the concept of a national identity started to emerge.

Compared to countries like China, Japan, France, and many European and Asian countries with thousands and hundreds of years of history, we are not even "teenagers" yet. These established cultures have the benefits of language, history and culture. Their museums are full of displays which carefully document their roots and history. They have countless folklore, art, music and literature to cement their national or cultural identity. They are proud of their heritage and traditions.

Relatively younger nations like the United States, Canada and Australia have forged strong bonds among its citizens through shared common values like liberty and democracy, and strong national pride through successes in important historical events like achievements in commerce, arts, music, science, sports, entertainment and even wars. They also have strong common interests and passion which help define their country. Americans love their automobiles and barbeques. Australians love sports and bushwalking. Canadians, among their other hobbies, are ardent fans of ice hockey.

The popular culture in the United States is so strong that most new citizens are automatically drawn to them. Many professors and graduate students from Asia or Eastern Europe whom I have met are very enthusiastic about the American way of life. They enjoy watching American football or basketball, attend musicals and plays put up by their new fellow countrymen and actively participate in political and social discussions. They feel proud to be part of their new country. American core values and way of life are consistently glorified in schools, popular media and books.

Defining "Our Singaporeness": Multiculturalism, Singlish and Singapore Food

Singapore needs to learn from these young countries which have been successful in creating their own unique national identities. For the last 50 years, we have inadvertently built some form of "Singaporeness." Multiculturalism, Singaporean Food and the use of Singlish in conversations are the foundation of our Singapore identity which I feel we should be proud of and continue to develop.

Our pioneer generation after the initial race riots has forged strong bonds with one another no matter what race or religion in the last few decades for the sake of economic survival. Over the past 50 years, we have learnt to live in harmony as one people treating one another with respect and showing appreciation for each other's culture, food and way of living. Along with various government policies to integrate our Chinese, Malay, Indian and Eurasian communities, we have created a unique multicultural society.

Having gone through the local school system, serving in national service and living in the same neighbourhoods, we have forged a strong Singapore identity regardless of our race or religion, all through our shared experiences. We identify ourselves first as Singaporean.

One of the quintessential of "Singaporeness" is our love for diversity. We should leverage on this platform and apply this to our arts, music, literature and popular culture. We have created a successful melting pot of cultures, something we call our own and not seen in many parts of the world. This multiculturalism should be treasured, protected and promoted and made fashionable and hip for the younger generation to embrace. We should write books, and produce TV series and movies on multiculturalism.

We should treasure Singlish and not try to change the way we speak. More TV shows and mass media should feature and celebrate Singlish. Its influence and contribution to our national identity is far reaching and bonds us deeply. I always love to hear Singlish spoken when I am travelling overseas. It never fails to evoke a sense of nostalgia in me. I always appreciate it when my friends and colleagues who have become new citizens try to speak some Singlish. Somehow, I feel satisfied when they start to pick up some Singlish through my tutorage!

We also identify with one another through our passion and love for our Singaporean food like laksa, chilli crab, nasi lemak, roti prata, bak chor mee, chicken chop, etc. Our food is a great symbolism of our multiculturalism. It is good to see we have started committees and programmes looking at preserving our hawker centres and coffee shops which play an important role in our social landscape. We should continue to explore various incentives and policies to conserve the quality of our Singaporean hawker food.

We should celebrate Multiculturalism, Singlish and Singaporean Food. Promote them to our new citizens. Educate them on why are they important to us and encourage them to appreciate these unique features.

Suggestions to Integrate New Citizens

We should offer new citizenships to mostly young married couples or families whose children are in pre-school or primary school. Children integrate much easier during early school years than at the tertiary level. Parents of these children are motivated to participate in activities in school and in informal "Whatsapp Chat groups" with fellow parents. This is a strong integration process which produces shared experiences with the new citizens. Also, once the children of new citizens are rooted in Singapore, the whole family will likely stay and not use Singapore as a stepping stone to other countries.

A Singapore community club should be set up in every neighbourhood and all new citizens encouraged to join. New citizens should not stay within their comfort zones in their own nucleus, clans, associations or clubs. These Singapore community clubs should be run by volunteers but funded by the government's National Integration Council. They should organise activities highlighting our "Singaporeness" and act as a platform for locals to bond with our new citizens to create mutual trust and establish friendships. Some form of National Education similar to those conducted in schools should be made available in these clubs.

We should also establish a systematic programme where new citizens learn English. Together with their active participation in their respective Singapore community clubs, they will have an environment to practice their English or Singlish.

We should encourage new citizens to work. Being in a workplace environment fosters the usage of English and creates strong social bonds. I have seen new citizens integrate very quickly under such circumstances whereas other new citizens struggle to identify themselves as Singaporeans due to a lack of interaction with locals.

As many Singaporeans are marrying foreign spouses, it is important for all Singaporean spouses to play a role in creating a strong social network for their foreign spouses. I have seen many cases of foreign spouses establishing strong relationships with their spouse's family and friends resulting in them feeling very much like home. On the other hand, some Singaporeans have to move to another country as their spouses were either homesick or could not adjust well to living here. Some national programmes should be set up to provide Singaporeans with foreign spouses assistance to help their spouses integrate. Of course, most of it has to be driven by individuals. I am sure the incentives are strong for Singaporeans to create a Singapore-loving culture at home and social network for their spouses.

Our Fellow Singaporeans Living Overseas

Besides the integration of new citizens, it is also crucial for Singapore to continue to establish close links with our citizens living abroad. It was reported by Channel NewsAsia in October 2014 that in a recent survey conducted by Friends Provident International, only 39% of respondents who lived overseas wanted to move back to Singapore when they retire.

The Netherlands and Israel, two relatively small countries, have done a good job in maintaining close ties with their citizens living overseas through their international schools, clubs and now through social media. Singapore Day, organised by the Overseas Singaporean Unit, has been a great initiative. Two key barriers which have always discouraged Singaporeans living overseas from returning are whether their children will be able to adjust to the local education system and the high cost of living in Singapore. More studies should be done to introduce new programmes and assistance to address these concerns. There are around 200,000 Singaporeans living abroad and they form an important part of our country.

Conclusion

If we do not manage the integration of new citizens well and encourage more Singaporeans living abroad to return, Singapore will become a hotel instead of being a home. We will not have a country but a transient global city. Our children deserve the right to be part of a country with shared values, experiences and vision with their neighbours and fellow citizens — fellow citizens with whom we relate to and feel a certain kinship. When travelling abroad, it is nice to bump into a fellow Singaporean who has a heart for Singapore and when you are back in Singapore, it is nice to feel like you are back home.

For the past 50 years, Singapore has been building a strong brand for investments and attracting foreign talent to contribute to our economy. Now is the time to put more effort in creating a strong Singapore identity in the interest of our children and future generations so that there is a place they can call home.

Care, Ownership and Responsibility

Jose Raymond
Chief Executive Officer
Singapore Environment Council

The First Fifty

Singapore's first 50 years of existence post-independence in 1965 has been nothing short of phenomenal. The transition from third world to first was swift, compared to many other developing economies. Singapore's size, a strong government and its sheer determination as a nation, helped to push through its economic and development agenda. The narrative was very clear; work hard, reap the benefits, have better lives.

Progress, though, has not come without its fair share of challenges, as in all other developing economies. Our spatial constraints and limitations in natural resources have always meant that Singapore needed to think outside of the box to ensure that we developed sustainably. From the greening of Singapore, to its tough stand on litterbugs, to its innovative offshore landfill and to the development of the water industry to ensure self-sustainability, Singapore has already been at the forefront of being clean and green, way before it was fashionable to do so.

As what Prime Minister Lee Hsien Loong said, "For Singapore, sustainability and reliability and liveability have always been important. We are a small country of 700 km^2; the city is nearly the whole country" (Lee, 2012).

The challenges have, and will become more acute because globally, more and more people are moving towards cities and urban areas. Today, already more than half the world's population are housed in cities and with another estimated 2.5 billion people expected to move towards cities in the first half of this century, primarily in Asia.

"The challenge is to ensure a high quality environment, a high quality of life for the city dwellers, where they can live, work and play," said Singapore's Prime Minister Lee Hsien Loong at the opening of the Singapore International Water Week in July 2012 (Lee, 2012).

Is it possible for economies to grow at a politically acceptable level that is also genuinely environmentally sustainable? The answer is yes. But it must be done carefully and sustainably, especially as Singapore's population continues to grow albeit at a slower pace (Department of Statistics, Singapore, 2014), and as space becomes more premium per capita. Population numbers are already hovering at about 5.46 million as of 2014 (National Environment Agency, 2013) and in keeping with global trends of migration towards cities, Singapore can expect that its population will continue to increase, which will mean that Singapore will have to deal with its urban issues. As Professor Tommy Koh, Singapore's Ambassador-at-Large once said, "Life in a city can be heaven on earth, or if mismanaged, it can be hell on earth."

The Next Fifty

As we move into the next 50 years of our existence as a nation, there will be more issues which we will have to grapple with and deal with together. More often than not, the conflict between preservation and progress will heighten. A one-size-fits-all approach will never be successful in dealing with issues which traverse across sectors, even across economics and the environment. Over the last few years, we have already seen that there are progressive issues of development which have brought about a difference in opinion. For example, when the Singapore government announced the Cross Island Line which was slated to be constructed below the MacRitchie Reservoir, there was a chorus of unhappiness from Singapore's green groups. So even though the line would have benefited Singaporeans, reduced our carbon footprint and made us more connected as a city, which would have helped us economically, there was opposition to the plan, in the name of environmental and biodiversity protection. The Land Transport Authority then worked with the green groups, and called for an Environmental Impact Assessment to be done before the green light was given to continue with the project.

Another major development which will also rally green groups and nature activists would be the redevelopment of Mandai and the Singapore Zoo, the Jurong Bird Park and its surroundings. So while the revamp will have immense economic impact for Singapore due to the expected influx of tourism dollars, the project will undoubtedly pit nature and economic development against each other.

There will be many more such difference in opinion as we move into the next 50 years of our independence, and it will become more critical for all parties, agencies and people to find ways to come to the table, exchange views, and to chart a way forward together.

Innovative Ideas and Collaborations

Currently, the purview of our green spaces and parks comes under the Ministry of National Development while that of our water bodies like our reservoirs comes under the Ministry of the Environment and Water Resources. The cleanliness of our seas come under the care of the National Environment Agency whereas the strategic growth of our seas for maritime purposes come under the ambit of the Maritime and Port Authority, which is a statutory board under the Ministry of Transport. The National Climate Change Secretariat is housed under the Prime Minister's Office and hence works like an aggregator of resources when necessary.

However, moving forward into the next 50 years, Singapore may need to bring as many of these agencies under one roof as possible. Similar to what the Government has done with the Department of Public Cleanliness, which was formed on 1 April 2012; and the Municipal Services Office, which will be opened on 1 October 2014 (Ministry of National Development, 2014), Singapore may need a Ministry or Department of Sustainability which oversees all aspects of our nation's sustainable development. It is no longer possible to work in isolation when dealing and in confronting global challenges of living in a city state like Singapore. And until there is a Ministry which oversees our sustainable development, it will be imperative that agencies, industries and all facets of society work together and to bring as many ideas of possible to the table as possible in dealing with issues of sustainability, climate change and environmental degradation. There can never be one agency which has a stranglehold on ideas. Collaboration will be critical.

Care for the City

So how can Singapore ensure continued economic progress while developing sustainably? As we continue to progress and as our economy remains vibrant, it is incumbent that every facet of society, from major industries to government agencies, from SMEs to MNCs, do their part to care for the city where they live, work and play. People must care for the city. And when there is care, there will be a sense of belonging. For businesses, relying on legislation before changing business processes must not be a business norm. Businesses must recognise that they must do their part to care for the city in which they do their business. By ensuring a caring culture within their respective organisations, the values will trickle down to their employees, who will then also drive the right behaviour. Caring for the city will mean that industries must step forward and be good stewards of the environment. So as they reap the financial returns from having their businesses based in Singapore, they must also demonstrate that they have done whatever it takes to protect the environment, and practice sustainable consumption business practices. Industries and businesses especially must think of a long-term perspective when conducting their business.

Ownership of the Community

Taking ownership will require everyone to play a part. In the first 50 years post-independence, there were many campaigns which brought people together to keep Singapore clean. There were many clean-up campaigns in the 1960s and 1970s. "Keep Your Beach Clean," "Big Sweep," "Keep Your Water Clean" and "Keep Your Factory Clean" were just some of the national campaigns which were started to keep the island as pollution free as possible. At the community level, Members of Parliament led in block washing and cleaning campaigns to bring out the "gotong royong" spirit of the community, and to instil a sense of ownership of our common spaces. It is rather strange that as we progress, this need for ownership has not been heightened. We will need to show more care for our common spaces and take a lot more ownership of the community spaces. Singapore must strive to remain clean and not cleaned. A dirty Singapore will not help our international reputation, and will only lead to a bad reputation in the international business community.

Responsibility for our Home

Singapore is currently ranked 16th in the Monocle's Quality of Life Survey and was also ranked 25th in the 2012 Mercer Quality of Living Survey in 2012 (International HR Adviser, 2012).

While we are among the top cities in the world in terms of liveability, we must strive to make Singapore a more lovable city. This can only come about if people feel a sense of responsibility for their home, which is Singapore. While Singapore continues to attract foreign immigrants and businesses to set up shop in the island city-state, they too must not treat the city like a transient home. It must be a home in which they care for and a home they would be willing to make sacrifices for. But this responsibility will not just lie on the shoulders of our foreign friends. Singaporeans, too, must feel a sense of responsibility for their country and their homes. It will be a collective responsibility of every individual to ensure that Singapore progresses at a sustainable pace.

References

International HR Adviser (2012). 2012 Quality of Living Worldwide City Rankings Survey. *International HR Adviser, 52*(Winter 2012), 33–36. Retrieved January 8, 2015 from http://www.internationalhradviser.co.uk/storage/downloads/2012%20Quality%20Of%20Living%20Worldwide%20City%20Rankings%20Survey.pdf.

Department of Statistics, Singapore. (2014). Population Trends 2014. Retrieved January 8, 2015 from http://www.singstat.gov.sg/docs/default-source/default-document-library/publications/publications_and_papers/population_and_population_structure/population2014.pdf.

Lee, H. L. (2012, July 1). Speech by Prime Minister Lee Hsien Loong at Opening of SIWW-WCS-CES. Retrieved January 8, 2015 from http://www.siww.com.sg/speech-prime-minister-lee-hsien-loong-opening-siww-wcs-ces.

Ministry of National Development. (2014, August 24). Municipal Services Office to Improve Service Delivery (Press Release). Retrieved February 25, 2015 from http://app.mnd.gov.sg/Newroom/NewsPage.aspx?ID=5553&category=Press%20Release&year=2014&RA1=&RA2=&RA3.

National Environment Agency. (2013). Cleaning of Public Areas. Retrieved February 25, 2015 from http://www.nea.gov.sg/public-health/public-cleanliness/cleaning-of-public-areas.

The Singapore Economy in 2065: Returning to Our Roots

Edward Robinson
Chief Economist
Monetary Authority of Singapore (MAS)

and Choy Keen Meng
Principal Economist
MAS

Anyone trying to describe the outlook for Singapore faces an immediate difficulty. And this is that the economy of Singapore is so unique ...

Dr. Goh Keng Swee
(1972)

Introduction

Singapore's GDP per capita in real terms (constant 2010 dollars) is estimated to have been US$3,919 in 1965. It reached US$51,213 by end-2014, implying a 13-fold improvement in living standards over the last half century. On a per worker basis, real output is estimated at US$77,298, placing Singapore at the 70th percentile of the US frontier level. These achievements of high and sustained growth since independence

---

This essay is submitted in the authors' personal capacities and none of the views here should be attributed to the MAS. The authors thank Celine Sia for her useful comments and suggestions.

have vaulted the country into a list of "13 Success Stories" as identified by the Commission on Growth and Development (2008).

Key Assumptions

The Commission had distilled five key factors that underpin sustainable growth: global integration, macroeconomic stability, high rates of savings and investment, market allocation of resources, and a committed and capable government. Assuming these policy and institutional prerequisites for success are retained, Singapore's economic performance in the next half century, as in the last, will be shaped by the external environment. Undoubtedly, there will be future crises and wars, yet it is likely that life will gradually get better for the vast majority of the global population on account of the steady catch-up of developing economies with the advanced world.

In developed countries, an important driver of long-term economic advancement according to neoclassical macroeconomic models is the rate of technical progress. And here, we are aligned to the "techno-optimist" camp, which holds that digitalisation, and information and communications technologies (ICT) more generally, form the basis of a meta-idea that supports the production and transmission of other ideas, in line with Paul Romer's knowledge-based endogenous growth theory. In our view, ICT may have reached a point where networked digital platforms will spawn further innovation, investment and efficiency gains.

Projections for Economic Growth and Structure

Accordingly, we predict that Singapore will experience further income gains, albeit at a slower pace, as its productivity level (beta-)converges to the US norm. Consistent with the role of ICT, Robert Lucas has characterised this convergence process as taking place through the diffusion of ideas originating in the leading economy. In his theory, the speed at which an economy closes the gap with the leader depends on their productivity differential, as well as a technology spillover parameter calibrated to the international growth experience over the four decades from 1960 to 2000. Applying Lucas' rule-of-thumb, we arrive at a future trend growth rate for

Singapore's per capita GDP of 2.5% per annum on average, over the period 2015–2065. This compares with the 5.5% rate in the past 50 years and implies that real incomes will more than triple again by 2065, which will place Singapore among the three richest countries in the world at that time, alongside Norway and Switzerland.

How would the economic tapestry of Singapore unfold along our projected growth path? Winston Churchill's dictum provides a useful point of reference for our narrative: "The further backward you can look, the farther forward you are likely to see." The archaeological evidence unearthed by John Miksic reveals a rich economic past, pre-dating Raffles' arrival in 1819, of Singapore's role as a regional and even global port during the 14th century. Looking back at the long sweep of Singapore's history, we put forth the view that the next 50 years for Singapore would represent continuity with its 700-year historical voyage from early emporium to world city. With China having become the biggest economy in the world and India in the top five, Singapore will return to its historical role as a key node along the "Silk Road of the Sea" linking the two continents.

Based on Simon Kuznets' and Barry Eichengreen's work on the relationship between economic development and structural change, the Singapore economy can be expected to become more servicised as income levels rise further. In the 21st century, the city-state's comparative advantage will lie in the supply of knowledge-intensive services to support catch-up economic growth in its Asian hinterland, and extend their reach to the rest of the world. As in earlier periods when Singapore acted as the *de facto* economic and financial capital of Southeast Asia, this advantage will rest in part on its superior physical infrastructure, cultural and geographical proximity to the region, as well as reputable legal and governance systems. But Singapore will also reinvent itself as a modern capital of the information age, connected to global networks of innovative ideas through state-of-the-art ICT infrastructure and an IT-savvy workforce.

In addition to the commercial, financial and transport services that underpin its traditional entrepôt role, Singapore is likely to specialise in providing "modern services" in the fields of management, consultancy, law, accounting, media and environmental planning, all of which are highly receptive to the application of ICT and increasingly tradable across borders. Along with rising affluence in the region, the income-elastic demand for Singapore's education, healthcare, recreation, wealth management and insurance services will also expand.

Implications for the Macroeconomy

Three further predictions for Singapore's macroeconomic profile arise from our futuristic scenario. The first is that, while shorter-term business cycles would certainly not disappear altogether, they are set to be less virulent than in the last 50 years and even during the colonial era. The taming of cycles stems from the lower sensitivity of service industries to cyclical gyrations, alongside reduced linkages between them, as compared to manufacturing. This dampening of output volatility will improve economic welfare and lead to more stable employment prospects, thus mitigating to some extent the need for activist counter-cyclical macroeconomic policies.

Our second prediction relates to the long-run evolution of the current account — the summary statement of Singapore's financial position vis-à-vis the rest of the world. We submit that the large surplus seen in the goods balance will reverse as the economy shifts to the export of services, while the deficit in services will eventually turn into a surplus. The current shortfall in the income balance, resulting from a net outflow of investment receipts, will similarly turn around as domestic corporates relocate to lower-cost locations abroad and repatriate a future stream of earnings, which will eventually accumulate to around 5–8% of GDP. Overall, we expect the current account surplus to shrink significantly, to about two-fifths of current levels (expressed as a proportion of GDP), consistent with the gradual slowing of GDP growth.

A review of saving and investment trajectories leads to essentially the same conclusion. From such an S-I perspective, the current account surplus has been the result of a high saving rate associated with a favourable demographic profile, sustained income increases as well as fiscal surpluses. Nonetheless, it is clear that the effects of these underlying factors will reverse alongside the ageing of the population and the secular moderation in income growth. In the public sector, the budget position will come under increasing strain as rising old age-related expenditure on healthcare and a more encompassing social transfer programme tax revenues, even though a higher proportion of the government's spending will be met by net investment income. Similarly, the private S-I balance will be driven by dissaving of older households which will not be totally offset by the savings of younger cohorts. Lastly, corporate investment needs are likely to diminish with the move to less physical capital-intensive services production.

The third point concerns Singapore's exchange rate framework. Taking a historical perspective of the international monetary system, we think that the breakdown of the Bretton Woods system will in time come to be seen as an anomaly, and that the inherent tendency towards stability and predictability in exchange rates will predominate over a longer span of time. Historically, a firm anchorage for the currency has formed the basis for the flourishing of international trade among open economies. Accordingly, Singapore's reversion to its roots as a key node in a vibrant global trading system will imply a high premium on stability and confidence in its currency, even as shocks that require a permanent change to the real exchange rate become increasingly rare. Hence, a gradual drift towards a tighter managed float is likely, in the context of stronger international coordination of exchange rates.

Conclusion

It is apt to conclude our essay by revisiting John Maynard Keynes' famous predictions made in 1930. Keynes foresaw that the standard of living in the rich countries would be significantly higher in a hundred years, and that would engender an ethical revolution in which humankind would resolve "to live wisely and agreeably and well." Like Keynes, we have a strong conviction that human welfare, broadly conceived to include leisure and happiness as normal goods, will continue on an upward trajectory along with the rise in material incomes. With the economic problem largely solved, we think that Singaporeans will strive for the higher ideals in life by orienting themselves to enhancing the welfare of their fellow citizens, as well as people in the neighbouring region. They will spend more time "living" and less "working," even as the nature of work itself will be transformed by new arrangements allowing people the flexibility to combine paid employment with leisure, study, and philanthropy. As individuals smooth work and leisure over a longer life-cycle, work will become humanising. The social value placed on different occupations will be harmonised, although the market will continue to price workers' contributions according to their marginal products. If the predictions outlined in this essay come to pass over the next 50 years, they will mark, in our assessment, the crowning achievement of a hundred years of remarkable economic development for a country which "should not have made it."

References

Brynjolfsson, E., and McAfee, A. (2014). *The Second Machine Age: Work, Progress, and Prosperity in a Time of Brilliant Technologies.* New York: WW Norton & Company.

Commission on Growth and Development. (2008). *The Growth Report: Strategies for Sustained Growth and Inclusive Development.* Washington, DC: The World Bank.

Eichengreen, B., and Gupta, P. (2013). The Two Waves of Service-Sector Growth. *Oxford Economic Papers, 65*(1), 96–123.

Goh, K. S. (1972). *The Economics of Modernization and Other Essays.* Singapore: Marshall Cavendish Academic.

Keynes, J. M. (1933). Economic Possibilities for Our Grandchildren [1930]. In *Essays in Persuasion* (pp. 358–373). New York: W. W. Norton & Company.

Kuznets, S. (1971). Modern Economic Growth: Findings and Reflections. *American Economic Review, 63*(3), 247–258.

Kwa C. G., Heng, D., and Tan, T. Y. (2009). *Singapore: A 700-Year History.* Singapore: National Archives of Singapore.

Lucas, R. E. (2009). Trade and the Diffusion of the Industrial Revolution. *American Economic Journal: Macroeconomics, 1*(1), 1–25.

Miksic, J. (2013). *Singapore and the Silk Road of the Sea, 1300–1800.* Singapore: NUS Press.

Romer, P. M. (1986). Endogenous Technological Change. *Journal of Political Economy, 98*(5), S71–S102.

Singapore as a Global Hub Port and International Maritime Centre

Andrew Tan
Chief Executive
Maritime and Port Authority of Singapore (MPA)

Strong Links to the Region and Rest of World

Historically, Singapore was a major trading centre for the region prior to the arrival of the British in the 19th century. Singapore was part of the ancient Maritime Silk Road that connected China to the East with India and beyond to the West from the 9th–14th centuries. From 1819 onwards, Singapore became the base of a new British settlement given its strategic location. The port grew as trade developed with the onset of steamships and the opening of the Suez Canal in 1869. From the mouth of the Singapore River, the port expanded to include Keppel Harbour, Telok Ayer Basin and eventually, Tanjong Pagar, where the first container berth began operations in 1972.

The decision to build the first container berth remains one of the defining moments in Singapore's maritime history. From the 1 million Twenty-Foot Equivalent Units (TEUs) of containers handled by the Port of Singapore in 1982 to the 33.9 million TEUs handled in 2014, Singapore today is among the world's largest and busiest ports, and is connected to more than 600 ports in over 120 countries. At any one time, there are more than 1,000 vessels present in the port. Singapore is also the world's largest bunkering port with more than 40 million tonnes of bunker fuel sold. The Singapore Registry of Ships is among the top 5 registries in the world with more than 4,000 registered vessels, totalling over 80 million gross tonnes.

Building on our port's success, Singapore has also established a growing and vibrant international maritime centre. There are now more than 130 shipping groups based in Singapore such as Pacific International Lines, Neptune Orient Lines, A.P. Møller-Mærsk Group, BW Group and IMC Shipping. This is supported by over 20 banks with shipping portfolios in Singapore such as DNB Bank, Standard Chartered Bank, DVB Bank and Oversea-Chinese Banking Corporation Limited, as well as over 20 leading ship-broking companies with significant operations in Singapore such as Clarksons, Simpson, Spence & Young, Braemar Seascope and Eastport Maritime. We also have 20 Lloyd's Syndicates and 7 International Group of Protection and Indemnity (P&I) Clubs, and more than 30 local and international law firms with maritime practice in Singapore.

Overall, Maritime Singapore — comprising our global hub port and international maritime centre — has become a key pillar of our national economy, contributing around 7% of Singapore's Gross Domestic Product and employing more than 170,000 people. The future growth of Maritime Singapore hinges on several key developments in the following decades.

Key Developments Shaping the Future of Maritime Singapore

The first is the rise of the regional economies of China, India and ASEAN. Given Singapore's geographic location and connectivity, we are well-situated to tap on the growth of China, India and ASEAN, which by 2060 will see combined populations of well over 3.7 billion people. This is significantly more than the projected combined populations of the European Union and the US, at over 910 million people.[1] With growing urbanisation and rising income levels, we can expect demand for goods and services to increase. While intermodal transport will open up new challenges and opportunities, growing connectivity in the Asia-Pacific region can be expected to spur intra-regional trade. For instance, trade among Asian

[1] UN Department of Economic and Social Affairs/Population Division (2013), World Population Prospects: The 2012 Revision.

economies is projected to increase from around 6% of global trade in 2012 to 16% by 2060.[2]

The second is natural resource constraints. Singapore faces rising costs for critical resources such as land and manpower, which are important elements of economic competitiveness. Maritime Singapore cannot compete on the basis of low-cost land and manpower but it can compete on the back of higher skills, efficiency and productivity, a pro-business environment, political stability, good governance and a non-corrupt system. Sound policies will be essential to maintaining our competitive advantage in these areas.

The third is the ever-present need to safeguard our strategic maritime interests. Singapore lies along the Straits of Malacca and Singapore (SOMS), which carries the lifeblood of trade through our port. The SOMS is one of the world's most heavily traversed shipping lanes, carrying half of global trade and about a third of global crude oil,[3] the latter supplying large economies such as China and Japan. Threats to the SOMS in the form of piracy, terrorist acts or environmental damage could undermine the safety and freedom of navigation. Tackling these challenges will require close cooperation between the littoral states, namely Singapore, Malaysia and Indonesia, as well as countries with an interest in keeping the SOMS open for trade.

The above developments pose both opportunities and challenges for Singapore. However, it is almost a given that opportunities for Singapore are opportunities for others too, while the challenges we face are in a way, unique. Hence, it is not inconceivable that Singapore may face greater competition from other maritime centres in the region which also seek to tap on Asia's growth. Alternate trade routes could also emerge in the region, such as the Isthmus of Kra, and elsewhere, such as the Arctic Sea Route, saving travelling time and costs, and reducing reliance on passage through the SOMS.

Given these developments, efforts to strengthen Maritime Singapore as a global hub port and international maritime centre must continue. By

---

[2] OECD (2014, July), Global Trade and Specialisation Patterns Over the Next 50 Years, OECD Economic Policy Paper No.10.

[3] US Energy Information Administration (EIA) (2013, April 4), The South China Sea is an Important World Energy Trade Route. Retrieved February 25, 2015 from http://www.eia.gov/todayinenergy/detail.cfm?id=10671.

2065, we envision that Maritime Singapore will have become a vibrant maritime ecosystem comprising the following:

Our Next Generation Port at Tuas

The Port of Singapore will continue to provide critical connectivity for our global city and be a global hub port for international shipping. Leveraging on the consolidation of the container terminals at Tuas, we will take the opportunity to develop a Next Generation Port (NGP) that will improve manpower productivity, enhance efficiency, safety and reliability, better integrate mission critical systems and intensify space usage to support the port and maritime sectors.

The NGP will encompass several key areas. The first of these is an efficient port where future container terminal operations will be automated with driver-less automatically guided vehicles and automated cranes. These operations will be managed by intelligent navigation, deployment and tracking systems from centralised control centres. When the entire Tuas Terminal is fully completed, it will probably be the largest container terminal at a single location in the world, handling container volumes of 65 million TEUs and doubling the current container handling capacity in Singapore. The automation of container operations in the future terminal will improve manpower productivity and raise the job levels and skill sets of port personnel. The air space above and the ground below the port land could also be stratified to create new useable spaces to house all these planned developments, maximising land use. Conveniently co-located near the port, the clustered communities in this hub and its surrounding developments will be able to conduct their businesses efficiently, cutting down travelling time. Some may even enjoy the convenience of being able to live, work and play within the maritime city itself.

The second key area of the NGP is an intelligent port capable of managing the future growth of marine traffic arrivals and departures from the Port of Singapore and the ever-increasing size of ships. The future port will be able to accommodate vessels that are even larger than the current Very Large Crude Carriers (VLCCs) or the largest container ship design that is known currently, which is of length 470 m and has a carrying capacity of 23,000 TEUs. A Next Generation Vessel Traffic Management System and new concept for the Port Operations Control Centre, integrated with smart sensor technologies, will be developed to meet future challenges. At the Next Generation Port Operations Control Centre, for example, any congestion hotspots within port waters will be detected early on and each ship's routing plan will be analysed to anticipate and avoid incidents by providing early warning of potential collisions in real time.

The third area of the NGP is to enhance a safe and secure environment to ensure that the Port of Singapore remains a trusted and reliable partner for companies whose vessels call at our port or pass through our waters. Some measures include sharing real-time information between different security agencies, facilitated by a common operational picture of the port and supporting facilities, and timely inter-agency communication and coordination of action. The shared system will integrate multiple sources of information, display results on a satellite image to give real-time security view of port facilities, thereby enhancing situational awareness.

The fourth aspect of the NGP will be a clean and green port, with green solutions and policies in place to reduce the environmental impact of our port operations and shipping activity. Alternative energy sources such as liquefied natural gas (LNG) or renewable energy sources like solar power, or even conversion of waste to energy resources, could be adopted to power the NGP and the vessels that call at the port, ensuring the sustainability of the future port. All these green solutions and policies will be incorporated into the master plan and new port systems. This will allow us to meet rising global environmental standards and higher local expectations for cleaner air and water and sustainable management of scarce resources in the NGP. We envisage our future port to coexist harmoniously with other commercial and residential developments in the area.

A Dynamic and Vibrant International Maritime Centre

Maritime Singapore will be home to a large core group of international ship owners and operators serving shipping interests in this region and globally. By 2065, Maritime Singapore will also be the world's premier centre for both commercial and technical maritime services, providing an international clientele with a full range of service offerings in areas such as insurance, ship-broking, ship finance, marine surveying and maritime arbitration. The Singapore Registry of Ships will remain a quality registry on the international arena, setting service standards which others hope to emulate, with vessels that are not only efficient and well built, but also compliant with international maritime regulations. Maritime Singapore will also remain a pinnacle hub for offshore and marine engineering.

Maritime Singapore will be Asia's leading centre for maritime research and development (R&D), driving the development of core areas of expertise in Maritime Singapore. This would include the emerging field of green shipping technologies in areas such as emission abatement, renewable energies, and ballast water treatment. In the marine and offshore sector, we will see improved designs for offshore platforms and vessels, as well as technologies that will bolster the productivity of our shipyards. There will be greater deployment of intelligent technologies such as data analytics as a force multiplier, with the potential to cut across various sectors. Our strong maritime R&D capabilities will be a source of growth for the industry and will enhance Maritime Singapore's attractiveness to maritime enterprises. In addition, maritime enterprises will be able to move up the value chain and find synergies in harnessing new technologies for their maritime operations. Together with our efforts to encourage more Singapore-developed technologies and increase cross-sector joint collaborations among the Institutes of Higher Learning (IHLs), maritime companies and technology providers, we envision a vibrant maritime technological landscape and a strong R&D ecosystem in Maritime Singapore.

A Key Maritime Player on the Global Stage

Maritime Singapore will be viewed as a pacesetter on maritime issues within the international maritime community. Our leadership and know-how will mean that we will participate in many key decisions on global maritime conventions, standards and practices at international fora that concern efficient shipping, navigational safety and environmental protection. These include the International Maritime Organisation, International Hydrographic Organisation, Regional Cooperation Agreement on Combating Piracy and Armed Robbery against Ships in Asia (ReCAAP), and ASEAN.

As long as the SOMS remains an important trade route for the shipping community, Singapore will continue to play an instrumental role in bringing together key user states of the SOMS to ensure that it remains a safe, open and secure international waterway for navigation, while protecting the environment.

Good Talent to Sustain Maritime Singapore

By 2065, Maritime Singapore could establish itself as a global maritime knowledge hub and a centre for maritime education and training. Singapore's IHLs offer globally renowned programmes in various areas such as maritime strategy, business, research and technology as well as technical training, attracting local talent as well as foreign maritime leaders and management personnel. The success of our efforts to develop and attract talent at all levels in the maritime sector will facilitate the growth of a quality maritime talent pool, catalysing the growth of Maritime Singapore in knowledge-driven sectors.

Ensuring a steady pipeline of passionate, dynamic and well-skilled professionals into the maritime sector will be a key challenge, and in the years to come, we will step up efforts to up-skill our maritime workforce with knowledge skills and enhance its productivity. We will continue to work actively with the industry and IHLs to enhance our maritime education and training programmes to ensure quality and industry relevance. These programmes will sustain our joint efforts with the industry to groom a local pool of skilled maritime professionals and researchers for subsequent generations. We will complement these efforts with outreach programmes and manpower development schemes to raise awareness of maritime careers and to encourage maritime sector employers to invest in human capital. We must also stay open to good talent from around the world in a sector that is essentially global in nature.

Maritime Singapore as a Vibrant Maritime Ecosystem

Maritime Singapore's position today as a global hub port and international maritime centre is not merely a result of chance or luck; foresight, forward planning and the courage to make bold decisions are what have always propelled our island nation forward. There is no assurance that Singapore's role as a maritime and trading hub will remain relevant in 2065. We will need to stay nimble, adaptable, and change as the world changes. However, the same values that have guided us before remain pertinent today and will continue to in future. Taking a long-term perspective, we must prepare ourselves now by investing in our infrastructure, systems and people. And when the time calls upon us to do so, we must be able to make the tough decisions that have defined our nation's development. If we can do this, we stand a good chance to tap on the growth potential of Asia and bring Maritime Singapore to greater heights, to create a vibrant maritime eco-system we can be proud of.[4]

[4] I wish to thank my colleagues in MPA for providing the relevant information for this article.

Economic Prospects of Singapore

Augustine H. H. Tan
Professor of Economics (Practice)
Singapore Management University

For Singapore's economic future, I assume that all Singaporeans want to ensure that our current standard of living is at least maintained, if not improved upon. Like most economists, I do not assume that material prosperity equals happiness. There exists, however, a minimum growth rate that is needed to maintain full employment for Singaporeans, especially young Singaporeans, and which will avoid graduate unemployment. Unfortunately, what that necessary minimum growth rate is, is absent from the national conversation. Nevertheless, that minimum growth rate should allow for the median wage to rise or at least, not fall as has happened in industrial countries. Can Singapore avoid the secular stagnation currently being experienced in industrial countries? For example, since the onset of Financial Crisis in 2007, the US trend growth rate has fallen from about 3% to about 1.8%, resulting in prolonged unemployment, stagnation of real wages, lower participation rates, not to mention homelessness, greater dependence on food stamps and other forms of welfare.

Jobless growth has been a feature of the industrial countries since the 2007 Crisis. Various explanations have been offered for the phenomena. The first is de-industrialisation, which shifted the economy towards services, resulting in low-wage and low-productivity jobs like personal and social services. Proponents of the virtues of a service economy were banking on the creation of well-paid jobs in IT, finance, etc. However, such jobs were too few to benefit most workers who lost manufacturing jobs that paid more, on the average, than personal and social services. De-industrialisation advocates also failed to foresee the important linkages between manufacturing jobs and related services. According to various estimates, each manufacturing job created 2–4 service jobs.[1] If this is so, the loss of jobs in manufacturing had a multiplier effect on job losses in the service sectors, particularly high end types. Moreover, typical new jobs created in America since 2007 involved poorly paid personal and social services, particularly healthcare.

Mismatch of skills has also been blamed for the jobless growth phenomenon. Graduates with the wrong skills do not find jobs or end up with low-wage ones. More people ended up with temporary jobs. Indeed, increasing graduate unemployment has been shown over the decades since the bursting of the property bubble in Japan and elsewhere.[2] I suspect outsourcing and offshoring have something to do, not only with the disappearance of jobs, but also with the rise of temporary ones. Typically, subcontractors do not maintain a core of many permanent workers but, rather, maintain a list of part-time workers who are relied upon when contracts are available. This surely means that productivity suffers because of poor worker morale and because employers will not bother to invest in training. Ten years ago, massive recalls of Japanese and American cars were rare, but it has become more common today. This may have something to do with poor attitudes of temporary workers who may not bother to report defects.

American students appear to have avoided the hard educational tracks in science, engineering, technology and mathematics, (otherwise known as STEM skills) in favour of soft subjects. Paradoxically, in the midst of heavy unemployment, employers in the US, UK and EU complained of short-

[1] H. L. Sirkin, M. Zinser, and J. Rose (2014), The Shifting Economics of Global Manufacturing: How Cost Competitiveness Is Changing Worldwide, Boston Consulting Group, puts the multiplier at 4.

[2] Manpower Group (2013), 2013 Talent Shortage Survey: Research Results, found acute problems in recruiting talent in many Asian countries but particularly in Japan and India. Retrieved February 24, 2015 from http://www.manpowergroup.com/wps/wcm/connect/587d2b45-c47a-4647-a7c1-e7a74f68fb85/2013_Talent_Shortage_Survey_Results_US_high+res.pdf?MOD=AJPERES.

ages of workers, particularly those with STEM skills. Political opposition to immigration at times of high unemployment means that critical skills are lacking, thereby preventing firms from expanding or even continuing operations.

Poor productivity performance lowers the potential GDP and largely explains the secular stagnation of the West. Typically, industrial countries economic policies focus on demand management as a counter-cyclical tool. J. M. Keynes, father of so-called Keynesian economics taught us that, when faced with a recession (i.e. negative GDP growth), the government is the main agent capable of jump-starting the economy via deficit spending. His teaching has been corrupted to become pump-priming to preempt recession or to jazz up economic growth for politicians to win a few more votes. Keynes' theory was that the offsetting deficit spending debt would be repaid when recovery occurred. Corrupted Keynesianism resulted in ever-increasing public debt. Indeed, mainstream economic thinking in the West was that public debt of about 60% was safe — this was the very benchmark entrenched in the Maastricht Treaty which set out the criteria for entry into the Eurozone. Indeed, shortly after the Financial Crisis erupted in 2007, the IMF, on its website, stated that most industrial countries still had the capacity to borrow! Nobody foresaw that, on the heels of the Crisis, private debt became public debt, which easily escalated to 100% or more.

It may also be noted that the common prescriptions of fiscal and monetary stimulus adopted to overcome the Financial Crisis, the subsequent Great Recession, and the Eurozone sovereign debt crisis, resulted in even more public debt rising to dangerous levels. Currently the common dilemma for the industrial countries is to balance the need for more stimulus with the need to contain dangerous debt levels. Unfortunately, the debate between the austerity and stimulus advocates continues without satisfactory resolution. Meanwhile, their economies, perhaps with the exception of the US (which is showing some signs of life), continue to languish.

The unfortunate consequence of huge budget deficits and unsustainable debt means that urgently needed money for infrastructure, education and R&D have not been there. Typically, these are the items that suffer the most cuts. Decaying infrastructure,[3] insufficient funds for education and R&D are surely behind the anaemic productivity performance of the West. American railroads badly need upgrading, not to mention dams, highways, airports, etc.

Rapidly ageing populations compound the problem. The combination of fertility rates well below replacement level of 2.1 and increasing longevity is resulting in age pyramids that are top heavy: with increasingly fewer individuals from the working-age population supporting retirees. The combination of exploding costs of social and health services for the aged plus inadequate pension funds means rising taxes for the young who already have to pay for the profligate ways of their forefathers for decades to come.

What can and should Singapore do to avoid secular stagnation, jobless growth, mismatch of skills, and a rapidly ageing population? Bear in mind that we are in the midst of a tectonic shift in the economic, political and strategic landscape. China is forging ahead into high-tech industries, investing heavily in infrastructure, education and R&D. It is also positioning the RMB to be a global reserve currency to eventually supplant the US dollar. India under new Prime Minister Modi is likely to be transformed into the next global manufacturing hub and possibly the No. 1 economic power after China's turn. America's comparative advantage is changing on account of cheaper shale oil and gas, cuts in wages, and pursuit of sensible industrial policy under President Obama. This has already resulted in the re-shoring of American manufacturing. Moreover, the secular stagnation of industrial countries may translate into trade protectionism and more serious competitive devaluations. The signs are already ominous.

New trade routes are emerging: the Artic zone is warming, allowing for the passage of ships, saving thousands of kilometres from their journeys. Thailand is planning to set up two ports in the south to allow shipments of goods arriving on the west and transported overland to the east, bypassing the Straits of Malacca. These developments will surely affect our port activities.

New planes capable of flying non-stop between London and Sydney will one day bypass Singapore. Already the burgeoning Middle Eastern hubs of Qatar and Dubai have taken away some of our business.

---

[3] 70,000 bridges of the sort that have already fallen down urgently need replacement in America!

New technologies are already transforming industries, particularly the so-called new manufacturing.[4] Such industries require highly skilled personnel (e.g. STEM skills) and will employ fewer people.

The challenges to Singapore and our future are manifold. Clearly our comparative advantage will change rapidly. We have already experienced the rapid decline of disk drive production and we are in the midst of a closure of electronic plants and relocation of factories elsewhere. Singapore's role in the value chain is becoming obsolete. Can we continue to produce and export semi-industrial products, i.e. parts and components which are nameless and brandless? Such products are easily produced elsewhere. Moreover, they face given world prices. When the latter rise, we do very well and vice versa. Export demand depends upon world demand, particularly in industrial countries. The only way forward is to produce goods that are branded, with the quality for us to dictate selling prices. Think of expensive Swiss watches, BMWs, expensive precision German machine tools. What are the niche areas that we can get into?

In the service arena, we also need to upgrade urgently. Can we continue to prosper with taxi drivers and shopkeepers who try to gouge tourists and provide poor service to boot? Can our ageing and high-cost private hospitals and clinics with indifferent service attitudes compete with resort-like facilities in other countries?

We are also rapidly ageing. Shifts of voting power plus one/two-child families will mean increasing dependency on the State to provide social and health services to the aged. Already, because of increasing longevity, there is concern about the adequacy of the Central Provident Fund (CPF) and other savings.

Another implication of rapid ageing is, naturally, the shortage of workers and skills to sustain a vibrant economy. Recent political trends have exposed the fear of congestion and the related dislike of having too many foreigners and fear of competition for jobs and promotion. Such fears may produce weak governments in future which will be populist and nationalistic. Singapore may no longer have a vibrant economy. Future deficit spending on burgeoning welfare, cheap healthcare, free education and cheap housing demands will gobble up our reserves. The Singapore dollar

[4] E. Brynjolfsson and A. McAfee (2014), *The Second Machine Age*, New York: W. W. Norton.

will sink, leading to rapid exodus of foreign and local capital, compounding the decline. Unemployment will rise, especially for the young and especially for graduates.

We need bold and sane policies. We need to increase fertility rates and productivity. Failure to do so will mean increasing reliance on foreign workers. Fear of congestion and fear of foreigners will restrain the influx of such workers, robbing us of needed skills and cheap help for the aged. Instead of excellence we shall be reduced to mediocrity.

We need to change our mindset about ageing. Too often the aged are described with words like "problem," "dependent" and "burden." Policies for the aged involve postponing the retirement age, one or two years at a time. Wages are cut for senior workers, etc. People who reach 50 are denied scholarships and entry into institutions of learning. If life expectancy keeps on extending, we should plan for re-education and re-skilling people upon reaching 50. Having a future and having opportunities to retrain to be relevant will surely have a tonic effect on attitudes and morale for senior workers. Mental and physical health will also benefit, reducing the need for costly healthcare.

Finally, what is our future as a financial centre? Competition from Shanghai will surely increase significantly, even as China opens up its capital market. Moreover, recent American concerns about tax evasion/avoidance by its citizens, residents and corporations portend trouble for us as a low-tax country, manufacturing base, and as a wealth management centre. We should also rethink the Government's active promotion of the financial sector. Remember, three island economies have already sunk under the weight of a disproportionately sized financial sector: Iceland, Ireland and Cyprus. Our Prime Minister acknowledged that Singapore is like a sampan, albeit bigger than before. Nevertheless a sampan, even if high-tech and well captained, can easily capsize in the Pacific Ocean. This is even more likely as the sail we have erected is six times the size of the sampan. The others which sank, of course, had sails eight times or more the size. We should be aware of an outsized financial sector which could compromise our reserves overnight and which would also distort the wage structure, enticing engineers, doctors, lawyers, etc. away from their trades.

Balancing the *Yin* and the *Yang*: In Search of the Art of Not Making Trade-offs

Eugene K. B. Tan
Associate Professor of Law and Co-Director
SMU Centre for Scholars' Development
Singapore Management University

I recall how awestruck I was by the stunning offerings of nature when I camped in Kandersteg in the Swiss Alps in 1992 with scouts from around the world. It left a very strong impression on me of how human beings are emotionally connected with nature. While we have fairly significant biodiversity on our small, urbanised island, we are not privileged to have a vast natural landscape in our backyard. Hence, our conception of the environment is very much influenced and limited by the clean and green definition and the instrumental trade-offs that we are familiar with in this "city in a garden" of Singapore.

Singapore in 2015 is a living example of how we have transformed the environment in the perpetual endeavour to overcome the constraints imposed by nature and by geopolitics. The physical landscape continues to change with predictable mundaneness even after half a century of rapid development and unrelenting change to various aspects of our lives. This will continue with the controversial population roadmap to year 2030 embodied in the *A Sustainable Population for a Dynamic Singapore* White Paper. In 2065, in 50 years' time, the abiding concerns of the economy and the environment will probably grow in intensity. Furthermore, climate change will pose greater challenges more than ever not just for Singapore but the whole of mankind.

"Bending" the environment to our will is an integral, if somewhat neglected, part of the Singapore story. But it is a powerful story that deserves a wider audience. The story is powerful because it is emblematic of our exceptionalism and the Singapore Spirit. It is also a grand narrative of our refusing to accept the geographical fate imposed upon us. So we reclaim land to meet our terrestrial needs and aspirations, harvest "NEWater" out of sewage and waste water to overcome our dependence on imported water, offshored our landfill to create a new environment with rich, vibrant biodiversity, and, now, exploiting the underground granite caverns for a variety of uses to overcome the limits to building sideways and upwards. We have made virtues out of our limitations!

These inspiring examples demonstrate the vision and power of political will, the harnessing of our ingenuity and creativity, and faith in deploying cutting-edge technology. And, to be sure, these apparent defiant acts against nature are enabled by our economic progress and prowess. Without the sustained financial sinews, such seemingly far-fetched environmental audacity would not have been possible. In a sense, our continued economic development has facilitated our creating these realities that, in turn, strengthen our security, wellbeing, and confidence as a sovereign nation. Furthermore, the economic prosperity has allowed Singapore to have the state of the art infrastructure, technology, and services that have facilitated our larger efforts in preserving and enhancing our limited natural and man-made habitats and heritage. Clearly, the economy and the environment are not antithetical to each other.

Perhaps we can square the circle after all? That while the tension between the economy and the environment, broadly construed, will persist as an immutable fact of our existence, we can and have and vividly demonstrated that a symbiotic relationship between the economy and the environment is necessary for our overall wellbeing. Like *yin* and *yang* in Chinese philosophy, too much of one and too little of the other will adversely affect our overall wellbeing and quality of life.

Put another way, we should see the economy and the environment, at this stage of our state- and nation-building, as conjoined twins: intimately connected, with the fate of one being dependent on the other. This is crucial as grounding the story of Singapore's progress requires that intimate and nuanced understanding of how the environment matters in how we see and define ourselves. We do not appreciate this enough. In turn, and more importantly, this mindset can open new pathways to a dynamic future in which our progress and prosperity are in sync with our environment and our heritage. It will also help the present connect with the past and the future as well in more ways than the economic dimension can.

Partly socialised by the change as modernisation paradigm, Singaporeans have come to expect rapid changes in our lives even as we yearn for constancy and familiarity in our surroundings and lament our disappearing heritage — both natural and man-made. The controversies over the demolition of the old National Library, Bukit Brown cemetery making way for new roads, or even our angst and anger with the overall population policy with rapid immigration and how it affects our national identity continue to remind us if we have got the balance of continuity amid change right.

Coexistence of the economy and environment is not enough in the next chapter of our history. Coexistence signals living together despite fundamental disagreements. Embedded in coexistence is the language of trade-offs. And in our context, it is very often the economy that takes precedence. The environment seemingly exists at the behest of the economic imperatives. However, there is no denying that we did not completely sacrifice the environment at the altar of progress and development.

In our next stage of nation-building, we need to have the economy and environment go beyond mere coexistence so that both dimensions are in harmony and aligned with each other. To see the economy and the environment as two separate spheres or as two distinct set of rights, interests, and power is a false dichotomy. Given the mantra of economic growth, the environment will be subordinated to the economy. In this scenario, trade-offs are portrayed as inevitable and necessary for our survival. But must it be so? If we see the economy and the environment as two sides of the same coin, then trade-offs will be seen as poor choices. The fact of the matter is that if we look for trade-offs, we will find them.

In short, a significant challenge facing Singapore in this regard is to develop the art of not making trade-offs, and that means striving to align the interests and needs of the economy and the environment in a holistic manner. This does not take away the necessity of making policy choices. But what it does is to avoid the propensity of looking at policy options in binary terms. By doing so, we can prevent adverse impacts on the environment in the quest for economic growth, such as reducing our biodiversity and/or giving up our natural or cultural heritage.

The language of trade-offs can straitjacket our thinking of what needs to be done to attain the ideals of economic growth and environmental sustainability. Such a language contains the grammar of domination (where one prevails over the other) and compromise (where both give in to maintain harmony). But this means tension will be inherent in such a system. Perhaps in governing development, could we instead look at the economy and the environment as checks and balances of each other? Must nature always be contained? Or should the economic aspirations be contained recognising the inevitability of limits to growth?

At the same time, the search here, where the economy and the environment is concerned, is for balance — not a perfect equilibrium, it must be said. Otherwise, we would have replaced one dogma with another. A balanced development recognises that the economy and the environment is not a zero-sum proposition. More than that, it recognises that the imperatives of the economy and the environment may shift according to needs. It can prevent extreme pendulum swings in how we approach development and growth. Such a dynamic equilibrium and perspective of development encourages systemic resilience, adaptive capability, and societal responsiveness. This will heighten the quest for holistic solutions that will exercise our resourcefulness, creativity, and innovation while avoiding the mutually exclusive boundaries of what is economic and what is environmental.

Much as we have the repute of being a society and government of *homo economicus* (economic human — rational and governed by self-interest towards subjectively defined and narrow ends), should the economy dominate every time, a larger motion vis-à-vis our societal values is also set in place by looking at the economy and the environment in Manichean terms. If the economy trumps the environment more often than not, then policies, including strategies and interventions, will also likely ignore the troubling questions of unequal access to finance, land, and other resources. It also signals that the appropriate balance between the societal, community, and individual needs and concerns is not attained since a sticker price is attached to most things. So we may put a price tag to a good, a service, or a person's worth to a company but we may fail miserably to recognise the value of nature and our heritage where there may be no price tag or valuation in terms we are familiar with. Such negative knock-on effects will result in further entrenchment of inequality, a deeper divide between the haves and the have-nots, while pandering to and reinforcing unsustainable patterns of resource use and consumption.

At this stage of our nation-building, having had the benefit of rising incomes combined with sound environmental policies and institutions, we are well positioned to tackle both economic environmental and environmental challenges in an integrated manner. It is also clear that we cannot segment our policy considerations into water-tight compartments of the economy and the environment. In this connection, we need to adhere more to the precautionary principle, which nudges us to respond to identified threats of serious or irreversible damage to the environment or human health, even with the lack of full scientific certainty, by not postponing cost-effective measures that can help prevent or reduce environmental degradation or damage to human health.

We have been enamoured with how Singapore has transformed the lives of Singaporeans past and present in one generation. Such an economic uplifting of the life chances of at least three generations of Singaporeans is not to be trifled with. It has given us a strong identity and pride in the community of nation-states despite our small size and the lack of any natural resources. We have made tremendous progress and it is time to urgently consider what would be the legacy unborn Singaporeans would inherit from us. We are not anywhere near an environmental collapse. But the natural and man-made heritage, replete with diversity, memories, and life are things which no amount of economic progress and wealth can buy once they are consigned to the museums.

We live amid tremendous depth of biodiversity and cultural heritage that we are not even aware of. Reflective of our own experience on this city-state, the artificial and natural environments have to live cheek by jowl. We owe it to ourselves and future generations of Singaporeans to right-size and re-balance the economic and the environmental. Otherwise, we would leave them with nothing more than imposing edifices of progress and deficit accounts of our natural and cultural heritage. And they might just rhetorically ask of us, "Was it worth it ultimately?"

Singapore in 2065: Sustaining a City-State Amidst Global Uncertainties

Tan Kong Yam
Co-Director, Asia Competitiveness Institute
Lee Kuan Yew School of Public Policy
National University of Singapore

Turbulence and Uncertainties

It is extremely difficult to look 50 years ahead. We need a heavy dose of humility in this exercise.

In 1965, China was in the midst of turbulent Cultural Revolution that was tearing the country apart. There were dead bodies of refugees who never made it to Hong Kong. Who would have foreseen that 50 years later, Deng's pragmatic reform would have catapulted China to the second largest economy in the world. In my years of working at the World Bank in Beijing from 2002–2005, I have often had opportunities to meet with senior leaders who participated in the reforms directly. None admitted that they would have foreseen the dramatic changes unleashed by Deng. Even Deng's daughter Deng Rong remarked that her father was surprised by the dramatic changes when they took him around Beijing and the country.

In 1985, Japan was riding high and spoke arrogantly about overtaking the US. When I was invited by the Ministry of Finance of Japan to visit Tokyo in 1990, the huge banner that greeted me at the Tokyo Stock Exchange proudly proclaimed: "the largest stock market in the world."

Less than 30 years later, Japan lay prostrate after 25 years of sustained decline and crushing debt burden. A senior corporate executive told me he is worried that the Japanese government might go bankrupt.

In 1956, the former Soviet Union looked formidable and Nikita Khrushchev threatened to bury the West. A year later, it launched Sputnik I into space. Less than 40 years later in 1991, the Soviet Union collapsed and disappeared from the surface of the earth. When I visited the Kremlin compound in 2013, the giant hall that used to serve as the assembly hall of the Soviet Communist Party was converted to serve occasional private functions to generate some revenue for maintenance.

In 1989, Francis Fukuyama triumphantly published an essay, "The End of History," proposing that the advent of Western liberal democracy represented the endpoint of humanity's sociocultural evolution and the final form of human government. In early 1990s, the indispensable US spoke about its "unipolar" moment. Less than 25 years later, the US is mired in political dysfunction and quagmire in the Middle East with two out of every three Americans saying that the country is heading in the wrong direction.

Over the next 50 years, it is even more foolhardy to predict the direction of major countries and their effect on Singapore. Will China continue to march ahead and eventually become a dominant modern day Tang dynasty or would its challenging social and political transition into the information age lead to serious national crisis, social polarisation and political instability? Would Indonesia's fragile democracy gradually mature and the economy be propelled forward by a rising middle class amidst sustained growth or the fragile institutions and religious conflict amidst global uncertainties and contagions undermine growth and development leading to fragmentation and instability?

Further afield, it is even more uncertain how Putin's Russia will turn out over the next 50 years, whether the EU will remain a liberal and prosperous entity for its members or the US will manage its conflicts with jihadists, increasingly protracted political dysfunction and an emasculated middle class amidst rising national debt and an isolationist tendency, without triggering domestic and global instability.

Given these formidable uncertainties in the external environment, the key for Singapore in looking forward 50 years to ensure national survival and sustainability is to distil certain fundamental principles that are critical for long-term survival and ensure that the nation adheres to them.

Like a cat that is unable to anticipate how external turbulence will throw it into the sky, the only way to sustain itself and land safely is to ensure that it is nimble and alert and its muscles fine-tuned so that it will be able to land softly on its paws rather than flat on its stomach with a thud.

Fundamental Principles for Long-term Sustenance

Several key fundamental principles could help Singapore navigate through the increasingly treacherous and turbulent waters over the next 50 years.

Firstly the Singapore brand needs to be continuously nurtured and well managed. This would include sustaining the key competitive strength of our key infrastructures, governance, quality of life, industrial relations and global trust and confidence in the Singapore system.

With the Singapore brand sustained, global talents and capital will continue to gravitate to Singapore to supplement domestic talents and capital to propel Singapore forward as a leading global city. No matter how other nations thrive or decline, how industries shift, new technologies evolve and patterns of consumption change, Singapore will always be there to capture the new emerging value creation and ride the next wave to reach greater heights. An alert and skilled surfer would always be able to catch the next wave while a sleepy sunbather would be swept out and swallowed by the rising waves.

The top 30% of local Singaporeans can ride this continuous wave of development and transformation with the inflow of global talents to sustain Singapore's competitive strengths. They will be the locomotive of sustained development. The next 40% of Singaporeans can also thrive in the supporting services, the wagons that are pulled along by the locomotives. However, it is likely that the lowest 30% of the population will be partly squeezed by the continuous inflows for they will be stressed by the resulting rising costs of land, housing, transport, healthcare and food. They will also confront the unrelenting forces of globalisation and technology that would undermine their rate of return to labour. They might not be able to hitch the ride unless efforts are made to hook their carriages to the locomotives and wagons.

Winners Compensating Losers of Globalisation

Singapore is a city-state. Within a continental economy like the US or China, the ambitious, driven and capable people move from all over the country to competitive key cities like New York and Shanghai. The less ambitious and capable born in these competitive cities eventually might move to less stressful and competitive smaller cities and states like Colorado or Hunan. So there is a natural flow of the population across the generations to maintain dynamic equilibrium.

In Singapore, in order to sustain our position as a major global city, we mimic the inflow into New York and Shanghai through the foreign talents policy. However, the less capable and ambitious are not able to migrate easily to other less stressful and less competitive cities and are trapped into permanently more stressful and competitive conditions. They could become a permanent underclass. Their carriages could be permanently unhooked from the other locomotives and wagons.

To maintain social cohesion and political stability, it is in the interest of Singapore to ensure that the lowest 30% of income earners can have decent housing, job prospects as well as an income that ensures a reasonable and dignified standard of living, after taking into account government support and subsidies.

Consequently, for this model of continuous sustenance of global competitiveness and vibrancy to work in a city-state without hinterland and out-migration options for the lowest 30% of income earners, a sustained compensation scheme will need to be worked out to maintain social and political stability.

The recent events of Occupy Central in Hong Kong reveal the stress points. Young people see no future being trapped in a globalising city with the fruits of prosperity monopolised by an increasingly narrower segment of elites while they face stagnating wages, rising costs and escalating housing prices. Scotland was on the verge of breaking away from the United Kingdom because all the fruits of prosperity seem to have gone to the city of London and very few crumbs of wealth are filtering down to Scotland.

Singapore's Hougang might not be able to break free from Shenton Way but the grievances must be addressed before the tension becomes destabilising. The winners need to compensate the losers of globalisation to maintain social cohesion and political stability.

To maintain this model of sustained competiveness and prosperity, the global talents and capital that come to Singapore's shores and benefit from the painstakingly built up Singapore brand will need to be taxed to compensate the lowest 30% of Singaporeans. Subsidies can be distributed in housing, healthcare, transport and utilities. This designated revenue can be from their car purchase, housing spending, as well as income and wealth tax. Presently they might be lumped together with different sources of revenue and different forms of subsidies. Given the modest amount of revenue involved, the tax can be light and not onerous enough to drive away talents and capital and can be calibrated according to evolving global conditions.

Conclusions

With greater global volatility and shocks, management and diversification of risks become critical. We are a small open economy subjected to almost instantaneous global shocks. We have no hinterland and limited strategic depth in economic defence. We are not an aircraft carrier able to weather drunken captains. The law of small numbers ensures that key events, specific groups of people or even individuals, would have a disproportionate effect on economic and political outcome. This could be our karma. However, a complex dynamic system that is prone to frequent instability could be stabilised through adjusting some key controlled parameters.

Each individual household in Singapore is more like a sampan in a turbulent ocean. However, rafting the sampans together will provide a greater sense of stability against the turbulent seas. The rafting comes from key institutions like policies to promote inclusive growth, the CPF scheme, housing grants scheme, workforce income supplementary scheme, MediShield subsidies and GIC investments for global risks diversification. Consequently, as a collective, we need not be seasick because of the turbulence.

In the 50-year journey as an independent nation, we have always been able to rise up and overcome new challenges, thanks to a resilient people, strong nimble leadership and robust institutions.

Some Singaporeans and foreign analysts have all along expressed concern about the long-term sustainability of a tiny island nation. It might be worthwhile to examine the long-term evolution and survival of various animal species. As every schoolchild knows, about 65 million years ago, an asteroid struck the earth, leading to catastrophic climatic change. The large dinosaurs were not able to adapt and perished, partly due to shortage of food. On the other hand, the humble sparrow was able to survive on crumbs. Today we only see dinosaur remains in the museum while the humble little sparrow is still chirping around the tress. The lesson is that it is the nimble and adaptable that survive, not necessarily the large and powerful. It is a very uplifting message for a small open economy cast in the turbulent sea in the next 50 years.

If the Haze Lasts 50 Years

Simon Tay
Chairman
Singapore Institute of International Affairs;
Associate Professor
Faculty of Law
National University of Singapore

Singapore enjoys, by many measures, a good environmental record. From the Republic's very start, the aim was to be a "clean and green" city and the government gave attention to environmental protection. The first pollution control unit reported directly to the Prime Minister's Office and the Ministry for the Environment was established back in 1972, when few other governments in the world thought the issue worthy of a full ministry.

Even as the economy boomed and the city grew, Singapore has managed its urban environment and pollution control credibly. We can and should hope that the next 50 years match and even surpass this achievement.

One critical area of weakness for Singapore is, however, the external environment. What happens regionally and globally matters greatly to Singapore and yet there is only so much that this small country can do to influence the outcomes. In this context, the haze is a signal event.

The haze is a recurring disaster not only for Singapore and other neighbouring states in ASEAN; the release of climate change gases and loss of biodiversity and forests make this a truly global challenge. The proximate and chief causes are clear: the haze stems from the use of fire to clear land for plantations, mainly in the Indonesian provinces of Riau and Kalimantan, by larger companies as well as small-scale farmers (Sizer et al., 2013).

Solutions have however been elusive. In Indonesia, there are questions of capacity and political will in addressing not only the fires but underlying issues that relate to land management and the sustainable development of major plantation industries, like palm oil and pulp and paper.

For Singapore and other neighbours who suffer the consequences, there is a limit to what they can do, given the respect for Indonesia's sovereignty. ASEAN has taken steps on the issue, moving from an Action Plan in 1994 to a full-fledged and legally binding Treaty on Transboundary Haze in 2004 (Tay, 2009).

These efforts have emphasised cooperation, rather than blame, and there are reasons for optimism that this is gaining traction as the Indonesian government increasingly recognises the economic and human costs of the problem. In 2014, the Indonesia administration of then President Susilo Bambang Yudhoyono declared an emergency in response to the worsening situation in the Riau Province and, on their part, the Indonesian Parliament agreed to ratify the ASEAN Agreement, after holding it in abeyance for a decade.

Also in 2014, Singapore enacted laws that will allow those entities that cause haze in Singapore to be punished, under civilian and criminal law, no matter where their actions took place. Even if it remains too early to say for certain, incoming President Jokowo Widodo has recognised the problem and promised an active response. Signs are more positive that action will be taken.

Yet the haze could persist. What if this is not only an immediate problem, but continues or even worsens into the longer term future? What if the haze lasts 50 years and we face a future of haze?

A Future of Haze

We should hope not. But this is not outside the realm of possibilities. Historical record shows that the practice of using fires to clear land has been extant in the region for over 100 years. It is only the scale of fires that has increased in recent decades. Moreover, if we mark the larger scale fires and haze from the worst episode of 1997–1998, the problem has been with us for more than 15 years and others, remembering the problem from 1994, would count a full two decades have past.

Nor can we assume that time alone will lessen the problem. After years of relatively low levels and contained episodes, primarily in the September–October period, the haze and underlying fires in 2013 and 2014 have returned with a vengeance. In 2013, Singapore suffered a record high of over 400PSI, far in excess of any other incident. In 2014, the haze was evident over prolonged periods and even from early in the year and other months, when the skies were normally clear.

There would be considerable impacts if the haze would persist, without solution, over the next decades, and perhaps worsen. This is true not only for Singapore, but for Indonesia, the region and the world.

For Singapore, if the haze persists and worsens, this would diminish the liveability of the city. Many Asian cities suffer from air pollution and, in China, awareness of the problem has spiked. By comparison, Singapore at present enjoys a better reputation. Its liveability, including clean air, has been a noted factor in the decision some companies and individuals have made to locate themselves in Singapore.

For Singaporeans too, clean air has become an expectation. Lifestyles — such as outdoor activities and al fresco dining — have evolved in the city around this expectation. In 2013, when the PSI spiked, masks were out of stock and there was some panic and recrimination. In other cities that suffer air problems, residents do express concern and anger and vote politically for change, or else vote with their feet by leaving. This could happen to Singapore in the event that the haze continues and worsens.

It is worse still for Indonesia, and I would have mentioned this first except that this collection of essays is focused on Singapore. The Indonesians are the first victims of the haze. This is not only about the direct impact on the land and nature. There are health, economic and political issues at stake for Indonesia.

When it is 400PSI in Singapore, conditions in the provinces are far worse. Residents there, moreover, may not have the masks and other facilities (like indoor air purifiers). Studies also show that the economic impacts on Indonesia are outsized. For the 1997–1998 fires, the Asian Development Bank estimated that the country suffered economic losses of about US$8–9 billion. In contrast, the estimated economic damage to Singapore for the same haze episode was only some US$3 million (Quah, 2002).

Politically, the haze is a tense issue not only between the neighbouring states but also among different segments of Indonesian society. There are centre-periphery tensions; local residents suffer, while policymakers and office holders in Jakarta seldom if ever see the haze (in 2014, there were brief episodes when haze from Kalimantan were swept by winds to Jakarta). There are also rich-poor issues and land management issues as the larger plantations often blame smallholders for setting the fires, and yet it is the large corporations that reap the lion's share of the benefits from the agro-forestry plantations and industries that are the site of the problem.

Thirdly, a long term continuation of the haze would impact ASEAN, the regional organization. Treaties are rare in ASEAN yet part of the new approaches to helping integrate the diverse member states into an ASEAN Community, with a greater emphasis on rule-based decision-making. If, despite the Treaty on the haze, and other efforts, there is no progress, this would dent ASEAN credibility.

A fourth impact of the haze would be at the global level. The fires and haze are more than local pollution and represent a large and sudden release of CO_2, a climate change driver. It is estimated that Indonesia is now one of the world's larger emitters of climate change gases and, moreover, that most of Indonesia's emissions result from the destruction of forest and peatlands by logging and burning. In 2011, President Susilo Bambang Yudoyono declared a two-year moratorium on forest clearing concessions. This was triggered by Norway's promise to grant up to US$1 billion on the condition that Indonesia undertake a verified programme on Reducing Emissions from Deforestation and forest Degradation-Plus (REDD+) ("Logging the Good News", 2013).

A fifth impact of the haze would be on industry. Given the growing global concerns with sustainable development and climate change, companies have come under increased scrutiny about their environmental impact and corporate social responsibility. In the case of the haze, there has been increasing pressure on companies in palm oil, pulp and paper, and other industries connected to the use of fires that cause the haze. Some companies like Unilever have taken steps to buy only certified palm oil, despite higher costs. Some financial institutions, like Standard Chartered Bank, now screen their corporate borrowers on environmental parameters, on top of credit and reputational risks. If the haze persists into the longer term, we must expect that calls to discipline the relevant industries or else to boycott them and their products would grow (Tay and Chua, 2013). There are, after all, alternative products and producers.

What Can Be Done?

I share the belief that the future is not pre-determined and that we can make a difference. By that "we," I mean not only the governments and our leaders, but also the private sector and opinion leaders in our civil society. We are not doomed to a negative outcome and a future of haze.

The factors that can drive our action to prevent that negative future can be found in the impacts that we will suffer if that should eventuate.

There are things that Singapore can and should do. One is to hold companies responsible for the haze if they are based in our country or finance and trade through Singapore. There are things that Indonesia can, do the sake of its own people, economy and ecology. There are ways that government in Jakarta and at the provincial level can act to regulate the agro-forestry sector with the aim to twin growth and sustainability. There are ways in which people can cooperate across borders, as citizens and consumers, and in collectives like non-governmental organisations and grass root, community groups. There are links to the global issues that can be developed so that the issue of the haze is better recognised and dealt with in tandem with the international efforts to address climate change and biodiversity.

These actions need not mean an end to the agro-forestry sector. But it does mean that steps must be taken to make these industries sustainable and many of those steps will deliver benefits in terms of innovation and productivity, and companies that are not only profitable, but also better managed and responsible for the longer term future. These efforts, taken together and taken now and into the near term, can prevent that terrible scenario of a future of haze.

References

Logging the Good News. (2013, May 25). *The Economist.* Retrieved November 27, 2013 from http://www.economist.com/news/asia/21578441-president-has-helped-transform-debate-about-forest- conservation-logging-good-news.

Quah, E. T. E. (2002). Transboundary Pollution in Southeast Asia: The Indonesian Fires, *World Development (United States), 30*(3), 429–441.

Sizer, N. et al. (2013, June 21). Peering through the Haze: What Data Can Tell Us About the Fires in Indonesia," World Resources Institute blog. Retrieved November 27, 2013 from http://insights.wri.org/news/2013/06/peering-through-haze-what-data-can-tell-us-about-fires-indonesia.

Tay, S. (2009). Blowing Smoke: Regional Cooperation, Indonesian Democracy, and the Haze. In D. K. Emmerson (ed.), *Hard Choices: Security, Democracy and Regionalism in Southeast Asia*, Singapore: ISEAS, 229.

Tay, S., and Chua, C. W. (2013, September 23). The Haze: What Governments Must Do, and What They Can't. *TODAY Newspaper*.

SG50: Letter to a Young Singaporean

Josephine Teo
Senior Minister of State
Ministry of Finance and Ministry of Transport, Singapore

There are two countries I consider myself very lucky to have visited 20, 30 years ago. They allowed me to see and experience for myself what the passage of time can mean for people and societies.

Let me start with Egypt.

My first visit was in December 1991, as a student backpacker. My companions and I took a bus from the seaside town of Eilat in Israel to the border at Rafa, walked 1 km in no man's land, and then took another bus to the Mount Sinai region.

If you are thinking of air-conditioned buses like what we have on our roads, I will have to tell you the buses we took were quite different. They were at least 20 years old and completely weather-worn. Road and weather conditions in these parts can be rough, and one could not expect anything less than a bumpy ride for hours and frequent breakdowns.

But the scenery was out of this world, and I was absolutely intoxicated by the Arabic pop songs that played endlessly in the background. We learnt to recognise Arabic numerals so we knew how much to pay for stuff. We certainly could not afford to get fleeced.

Against this backdrop, we began to learn more about the region's explosive historical conflicts. However, there was never any trouble and beyond aggressive souvenir salesmen, we never felt unsafe as tourists, even when we were the only non-Egyptians around.

As it turns out, the cheapest hotel I have ever stayed in my entire life was in Luxor, for 80 p a night or the equivalent of S$2.40 then. It actually came with an attached toilet, but the less remembered about that, the better.

As much as I was enjoying Egypt's enormous charms, I could not help but feel perturbed. For a country so endowed with great ancient monuments and historical artefacts, why was tourism rather poorly organised, with so many illegal touts? How was it possible that the Egyptian Museum did not even put the extremely valuable mummies and statue of King Tut's head in glass enclosures?

Why was public hygiene so lacking and traffic congestion in Cairo so overwhelming? Why were the homes so haphazardly constructed (the top is almost always unfinished), and why did so many people stick out their hands to ask for "baksheesh" (a tip or small reward), for providing no service? Why were there so many children who appeared to be working rather than studying?

My second visit was 20 years later in 2011. This time round, we could afford to stay in better hotels and hired a private van to take us round. While still excited by the sights and sounds, a number of things saddened me.

First, we were greeted on the first day by violent clashes among protesters at Tahrir Square. At one point, they were running at or away from one another, barely 50 m from our van. Our driver told us the protesters were not to be taken seriously — they were likely unemployed people with very little to lose. Ordinary people were tired of the drawn-out conflicts and wanted life to just go back to normal. But it seemed that this simple objective could not be met.

Second, the cities not only did not look better, they were more run down and some prominent buildings including the Egyptian Museum were visibly damaged by fire and explosives.

Most unhappy of all was seeing how sparse work and business was for Egyptians. Tourism was down drastically; there were far fewer people competing to take photos at attractions, but that was not good news actually. Many hotel rooms and river boats were empty, restaurants and souvenir shops closing or closed. Our knowledgeable tour guide, Mohamad Badawi, who had just had a baby girl, was worried if he could get regular work.

It has been nearly four years since then. I had thought in 2011 that when a democratically elected government was in place, Egypt would get back on its feet and I would encourage my friends to visit this fascinating country. But that was not to be and Egyptians continue to face significant uncertainty about the future.

Let me talk next about China. My first visit was as a 15-year-old in 1983, just over 30 years ago, and my second visit in 1992, also as a student backpacker.

One way to appreciate the impact of China's transformation is through the stories of some friends.* George Cheng, Amelia Zhou and Lai Hongjun were my colleagues when I was working in Suzhou in the mid-1990s, in the joint venture company that was developing the Suzhou Industrial Park.

As young university graduates then in a competitive job market, each saw an opportunity to distinguish himself. George and Hongjun learnt German and Amelia learnt Japanese. It was hard work because they came from working class families and the language courses were not cheap, but they became valuable staff for dealing with foreign investors.

Not long after working for the joint venture company, Hongjun left China to work in Denmark, eventually settling down and taking up Danish citizenship. George and Amelia got married. Soon after their daughter Xuan was born, George set up a manufacturing business dealing with German automotive components. To hedge their bets, Amelia went to work for the local government, earning considerably less than if she took the plunge to join the private sector.

As China developed and Suzhou boomed, however, both grew in their careers. Last winter, when I visited their home in Suzhou, I realised that they had moved from the two-bedroom apartment built by the local government into a bespoke house in a private gated compound by the lake. Each of them has their own car; Xuan is already in secondary school and an accomplished calligrapher.

Whereas their parents could hardly imagine seeing the Great Wall in Beijing, George, Amelia and their daughter are seasoned travellers having been to exotic locations like the Maldives.

That evening in George and Amelia's home, we reminisced about the old days. Hongjun left at a time when the standard of living in China was still far from that of Denmark. It was hard to believe then that China could close the gap with the Western world, and many who had the opportunity to, decided to build their lives elsewhere. But in hindsight, they might have done even better if they stayed in China.

---

* Names and details modified for privacy.

To be clear, the point of the story is not that many Chinese have grown rich. It is that their circumstances are dramatically different from just a generation ago, because the country has prospered and they themselves have worked hard to seize opportunities.

Not everyone is China has emerged from poverty. In rural areas, the standard of living is much lower than in the coastal cities. But the overall story is the last 30 years has been largely about the positive transformation of China and the lives of its people.

There are problems of course:

- Pollution has reached unacceptable levels and food safety troubles everyone, from young parents buying milk powder to people who grab a quick bite at fast-food joints.
- China produces 7.5 million university graduates each year — that is more than the population of Singapore or Switzerland — and many of them are underemployed in jobs that do not require graduate qualifications and do not pay graduate salaries.
- The one-child policy which was introduced in the 1990s to curb population growth is now being reversed because the population of China will soon age rapidly.

In spite of the problems, it is unlikely that any Chinese citizen would wish to return to the China of 30 years ago.

How might these two tales — of Egypt and China — help us think about Singapore on the eve of the SG50 celebrations? I have three reflections.

The first is that no country can hope to run out of problems to solve.

However, the problems differ in terms of severity, and countries differ in their abilities to solve them._

The problems in Egypt and the Middle East may seem far away but it was not so longer ago that Singapore had racial riots and was officially at war with Indonesia.

On the eve of Singapore's independence, my father who was then 26 years old could not have imagined his life that was to follow. The yet-to-be-married eldest son of a widow, he pondered the few job options available that would help put enough food on the table for the entire brood of 10.

In 1968, when the British troops announced their full withdrawal from Singapore, our fledging nation was staring at the loss of one quarter of its economy. If a fortune teller had told my father he would one day own his home, live well beyond 70 and his children would all have respectable jobs, he would have laughed off the predictions as nothing but a pipe dream.

Just as it was hard for my father's generation to imagine the developmental progress that Singapore would make in the 50 post-independence years, the present generation of young Singaporeans may wonder whether our nation's second half-century will bring about improvements in their lives.

There are new problems, some seemingly intractable. But in truth, they pale in comparison to the dire straits we found ourselves in 50 years ago, when our abilities to tackle problems were still untested.

The second reflection is that very few citizens can hope to succeed unless their countries are also successful.

Think about this: in 1992, Egypt's GDP per capita was twice that of China's; fast forward 20 years to 2012, China's GDP per capita had become twice that of Egypt's.

Mohamad Badawi, the Egyptian tour guide I told you about, is no less intelligent, earnest and hardworking than my Chinese friends. And yet, the hope of him achieving more for himself and his family is considerably less, unless he leaves Egypt for a place with brighter prospects. But not everyone has that option, so what happens to people who are unable to do so?

Today, in Singapore, the idea of GDP growth is sometimes talked about in slightly disdainful term, as though we are embarrassed to want it. And yet without the growth, how possible or likely is it for people to achieve more for themselves and their families, or to reverse their fortunes? Without growth, how likely is it for a country to have resources to support its citizens in healthcare, education, to attain new highs in arts and sports?

The third reflection is that quality of leadership matters and is the critical difference.

Here I want to say something that we do not think much about nowadays, and that is how miserably unlucky Singapore was at birth.

When we look around Singapore these days, it is easy to forget what was quite clear to our pioneer generation of citizens — a place with no natural resources (not even water) and not much inherited human capital (having been poorer immigrants mainly). You could not grow enough food or depend on agriculture, and tried as you might to dig, you would not find anything underground of value like oil, gas, copper or diamonds. You even had a potent mix of multiple races, religions and culture to deal with. It was quite a "basket case."

Egypt's "inheritance" is far better than Singapore, and better than perhaps even China. But inheritance is no guarantee of success and Singapore today is a far cry from that hopeless country of the 1960s, not by chance but through a combination of hard work, determination and leadership.

As a country, we have created opportunity where there was none and supported our people to go much farther than their original immigrant ancestors dared to hope. That alone is remarkable.

We are by no means perfect. But our problems are not insurmountable and there is room to make Singapore a better home for all. The question is whether we allow opposing views and voices to tear down what has been painstakingly built up or do we find common ground afresh to move forward together.

In 2065, will a young backpacker to Singapore today, on revisiting Singapore, see a country that has regressed, stagnated, or moved forward?

That answer depends very much on my generation and yours.

It depends on my generation, how well we anticipate problems and address them. If we pretended the problems did not exist or did not have the courage or to address the problems, or could not persuade fellow Singaporeans to move in the same direction, then those problems will be left to your generation to solve.

In 20, 30 years, you will be in the prime of your lives and will, in many ways, take charge of Singapore. You will not have run out of problems to solve. And leadership will still be the critical difference.

You and your peers will certainly have a say in the kinds of leaders that are installed then, because no one who seeks to be elected in our system can afford to ignore your preferences. In exercising your choices, I would like to suggest that you take into consideration the fact that Singapore is still very much a work-in-progress. Even as we grapple with important domestic concerns, the winds of global change do not stop blowing. For SG100 to be better than SG50, our best bet is a leadership that unifies our citizenry to grasp the implications of these changes and helps our country make adequate adjustments. It is a simple enough goal which, sadly, eludes so many countries.

Take good care of our country, because it really is a most unusual and precious little red dot. Leave it an even brighter red dot than the one we will be leaving you.

Succeeding in an Uncertain World

Leslie Teo
Chief Economist and Director, Economics and Investment Strategy GIC, Singapore

Introduction

Singapore has come far in the last 50 years. Our strong work ethic, good government, and first rate infrastructure has enabled our city state to benefit from the great post-World War II expansion in global trade and finance, economic development, and technological progress. For instance, over the past 50 years, Singapore's per capita income has expanded by nearly 13 times. Life expectancy at birth has risen from about 66 to slightly above 80. Infant mortality has fallen from 26 per 1,000 live births to about 2 per 1,000, among the lowest in the world. In 1965, 2% of the labour force had tertiary education while today nearly 50% have some form of tertiary education.[1] And we are now one of the richest nations in the world.

But just like 50 years ago, the future remains uncertain. In the short term, we still face the lingering effects of the global financial crisis. The global recovery remains weak, while policy responses are near their limits. Technological change and globalisation are putting pressure on jobs and income distribution. In the longer term, ageing populations, the shift in economic power to Asia, climate change and resource constraints, the unpredictable consequences of technological progress, and rising geopolitical

[1] Data from www.singsat.gov.sg, data.worldbank.org and esa.un.org.

stresses are the key trends which will shape the broad contours of our outlook over the next 50 years.

In this note, we will explore how these long-term trends could evolve and their potential impact on Singapore. While the outlook for Singapore is uncertain, we are well placed to deal with any problems that may crop up.

Key Trends

Ageing populations

In line with global trends, we are likely to see a dramatic change in the composition and character of Singapore's population. Due to a combination of increasing lifespans and declining birth rates, the defining characteristic of the next 50 years will be rapidly ageing populations, both in Singapore and many other developed countries.

For Singapore, net immigration could mitigate ageing, although the proportion of those above 65 is still expected to rise from about 10% of total population today to 15–20% by 2065.[2] Without immigration, Singapore's population will not only age more rapidly but will shrink over the next 50 years.[3]

Ageing societies are likely to bring challenges associated with lower economic growth and increasing demands for healthcare and other retirement needs. For instance, we would expect potential GDP growth rates in countries with rapidly ageing countries to decline. For Singapore, GDP growth will slow down to something around 2% or even lower if productivity growth is weaker than expected.

Shift in economic power to Asia

Second, we will see a continuation of the shift in economic power from today's developed countries — the US, Europe, and Japan — to tomorrow's growth engines, i.e. developing countries in Asia, in particular China and

---

[2] This proportion is very sensitive to the level of net immigration. Without net immigration, the portion could rise more than threefold, to nearly 30%.

[3] With some modest immigration, Singapore's total population could increase from today's 5 million to 6–7 million by the middle of this century. These estimates are based on scenarios done for the Population Outcomes: Singapore 2050 Project (Revised, 30 September 2014), Yap M. T. and C. Gee (Eds.), Singapore: Institute of Policy Studies.

India. To be sure, the US, Europe, and Japan will remain rich, especially in per capita terms, but today's developing countries will become tomorrow's centres of economic activity. For instance, the list of the world's largest economies in 2065 would include China and India as the largest and third-largest economies, respectively. In fact, it is likely that today's low- to middle-income developing countries will constitute the majority of the world's largest economies in 2065.[4]

The rise of the developing countries will have positive consequences. It will mitigate the declining contribution from older developed countries to global economic growth. It will also usher an estimated 3 billion people into the global middle class[5] who will increasingly live in cities: by 2065 the number of mega-cities could exceed 41, up from today's 28, with many of these great urban centres lying in Asia.[6]

The rise of the middle class in the developing world and increasing urbanisation will boost demand for more sophisticated goods and services, including healthcare, education, financial services, and tourism.

All this looks good for Singapore. We are well placed to take advantage of this shift in economic power, the rise of the middle class, urbanisation, and the need for more sophisticated goods and services. However, these positive developments have to be weighed against the problems raised by the other key trends.

Climate change and resource constraints

Our current carbon-intensive model of economic growth is not sustainable as the cost to the environment, via an increase in the average global temperature, is real and increasing. Even if we manage to stabilise greenhouse emissions at present day levels, the stock of CO_2 already in the atmosphere will still cause global temperatures to increase. Our current levels of energy and water usage, as well as pressures on natural resources and the environment, also cannot be sustained over the long term.

---

4 K. Ward, The World in 2050: From the Top 30 to the Top 100, *HSBC Global Economics, January* (London: HSBC Global Research, 2012).

5 K. Ward, The Consumer in 2050: The Rise of the EM Middle Class, *HSBC Global Economics, October* (London: HSBC Global Research, 2012).

6 United Nations, Department of Economic and Social Affairs, Population Division (2014), *World Urbanization Prospects: The 2014 Revision, Highlights.* Retrieved February 25, 2015 from http://esa.un.org/unpd/wup/Highlights/WUP2014-Highlights.pdf.

Unfortunately, given the uncertainties over climate change and the long-term nature of this challenge, along with the clear short-term economic costs of reducing greenhouse emissions, we should not expect preemptive and resolute global responses to reduce greenhouse gas emissions. The same is true of our overuse of limited natural resources: environmental degradation, crises, and supply disruptions may need to become more acute before action is taken. This means that we in Singapore should be prepared for some of the effects of climate change such as extreme weather events, higher rainfall, and, especially, rising sea levels. We will also have to work out other ways to deal with resource constraints, such as greater reliance on renewable resources like solar energy.

Technological change

Over the next 50 years, the pace of technological change will continue to accelerate. A major paradigm change is possible: if history serves as a guide, we are likely to experience a major technological revolution within the next 10–20 years. The most likely areas for such a breakthrough would be the biological sciences and information technology, complementing the advances in physics and chemistry made during the last century. These breakthroughs could include advances in artificial intelligence, big data, human performance enhancement, medical sciences, molecular biology, renewable energy, and robotics. Singapore is well placed to be a hub for research and innovation in and dissemination of these ideas.

Technological advances also hold the key to future productivity improvements, and ultimately a sustainable pace of economic development in the long term. Technology narrows the gap between countries by enabling developing countries to catch up to developed countries. However, it is not clear if technological progress will create more jobs than it displaces. Techno-optimists argue that technology will lead to a productivity boom and eventually create jobs. More skeptical observers find little evidence that technology has led to productivity improvements, even as middle class jobs are being destroyed.[7]

---

[7] See for instance E. Brynjolfsson and A. McAfee (2014), *The Second Machine Age: Work, Progress, and Prosperity in a Time of Brilliant Technologies* (1st edition) and R. Gordon, (2014) *The Demise of US Economic Growth: Restatement, Rebuttal, and Reflections*, NBER Working Paper No. 19895.

The more pertinent challenge is for society, including Singapore, to embrace technology and to use it to bring positive change to all of its people. If not, stresses are likely to grow between those who are able to use technology and those who are left behind.

Continued political stresses

Geopolitical stresses will rise and, along with them, domestic social tensions. The shift in economic power from Europe to Asia will cause a realignment in the international balance of power. Another likely source of geopolitical tension will be conflict over limited natural resources, especially with the growth of developing countries like China and India and their resultant need for increased natural resources, compounded by the negative results of climate change. Finally, while globalisation and technological change have generally brought benefits to society, not all benefits have been equally shared, nor have all aspects of change and development been positive. And the resulting social discontent, as indicated by various forms of fundamentalism and extremism, has been ironically facilitated by the very same technological innovation that helped trigger it.

For Singapore, a key external uncertainty will be how the China-US relationship evolves in the light of these rising geopolitical tensions and stresses. A peaceful return of Chinese influence over the Asian region would underpin the continued expansion of trade, capital and people movements across the region. An increase in tension between the two global powers, however, could lead to balkanisation along regional lines, if not outright conflict at some point.

Building Our Future

We are living at the crossroads of economic, environmental, technological, and political change. The external environment could be supportive or challenging. We could see a repeat of the last 50 years where global trade and finance expanded rapidly, underpinned by globalisation and technological revolutions. Or we could be in for rougher times given ageing populations, weaker growth, climate change, and geopolitical and social tensions.

However, this is in essence no different than in 1965 when Singapore was a nascent city-state facing equally, if not more, daunting challenges.

Singapore's strategy of openness, self-reliance, hard work, meritocracy, good governance, and investment in key infrastructure and education[8] created a perfect environment for the free exchange of capital, labour and technology. With this strategy, Singapore's pioneer generation managed to transform a colonial entrepôt with high unemployment into a thriving, sophisticated and diverse economy with virtually no unemployment. And today, our citizens are educated and global, our institutions are strong, and our resources ample. We are thus now even better equipped to deal with the vagaries of the global economy.

Thus, regardless of the future, if we remember what made Singapore today, we cannot only take but make the best out of what the future will throw at us.

---

[8] See for example, Dr. Goh Keng Swee's speech to the Chinese Chamber of Commerce at the swearing-in committee of the new committee that explained Singapore's economic strategy on 15 March 1969. Ministry of Culture, Microfilm No. NA 1250. Retrieved January 13, 2015 from http://www.nas.gov.sg/archivesonline/data/pdfdoc/PressR19690314a.pdf.

Inventing Governance to be the Best Country and City in the World

Thia Jang Ping
Director (Security & Resilience Programme/Transformation Office)
Ministry of Finance, Singapore
and
Director (Social and Economics)
Civil Service College

A Preamble

Fresh from the Cuban missile crisis and going into the Vietnam War, the world would not have imagined that the collapse of communism was just slightly more than two decades away. On science and technology, very few would have imagined the pervasive use of personal computers and smartphones, the World Wide Web or air travel for the masses. Few planners would have foreseen China embarking on its economic reforms, and eventually overtaking the United States as the world's largest economy. In 1965, who could have imagined Singapore 2015 as a leading global city?

Five decades, less than the lifespan of most people, is long enough for a complete remaking of societies, transformation of economies, and reordering of geopolitics. Prediction of the future is always difficult. I find it useful firstly to rule out any obviously unsustainable paths (or wishful thinking), and leave only the most plausible scenarios for consideration. Secondly, I find it instructive to review the state of the most advanced countries of 1965, and how they have progressed since then. The changes between now and 2065 will likely be more rather than less of what developed countries experienced in the past 50 years. Finally, I find it helpful to dream a little on what a good outcome for Singapore might be, if only to allow us some vague vision to work towards.

The Unsustainable

Unfortunately, it is necessary to point out the obviously unsustainable demographics. Singapore has a fertility rate hovering around 1.2 to 1.3 today, even lower than Japan, and one-third below the sustainable rate of 2.1. For four out of five decades of Singapore as an independent state, its birth rate has been below replacement. No developed country has successfully raised its replacement rate back to 2.1 after experiencing such low levels. City demographics do not stand a chance.

Particularly difficult for policy makers is also the fact that Singapore's low fertility is in part driven by high singlehood rates (below Japan, but higher than Korea, see Exhibit 1).[1] Child-bearing incentives may not be able to resolve this.

Leaving the impact on ageing aside, the projection clearly points to a lower number of local-born citizens. If this fertility rate persists, live births

Exhibit 1: Total Fertility Rate and Female Singlehood (age 35–39).

	Japan		Korea		Singapore	
	TFR	Female Singlehood Rate	TFR	Female Singlehood Rate	TFR	Female Singlehood Rate
1980	1.75	5.5	2.82	1.0	1.82	8.5
1985	1.76	6.6	1.66	1.6	1.61	11.5
1990	1.54	7.5	1.57	2.4	1.83	14.8
1995	1.42	10.0	1.63	3.3	1.67	14.9
2000	1.36	13.8	1.47	4.3	1.60	15.1
2005	1.26	18.4	1.08	7.6	1.26	15.0
2010	1.39	22.7	1.23	12.6	1.15	17.1
2012	1.41	n.a.	1.30	n.a.	1.29	16.6
2013	n.a.	n.a.	n.a.	n.a.	1.19	17.3

[1] Singlehood rates refer to those never married. It is important to note that Singapore also has high male singlehood rates. Female singlehood rates are cited here as it is more proximate to fertility.

could be less than 20,000 per year in 2065, compared to around 56,000 in 1965 and 40,000 in 2015. The cohort size two generations later (roughly 50 years) will only be 50% of what it is today for such is the tyranny of the geometric process. Added to this, there will also be more Singaporeans living overseas.[2]

TFR may rebound with greater policy actions, but a sustained rate of immigration cannot be avoided; it is Singapore's existential challenge. Singapore will have to manage this fundamental social change. We should see this as an opportunity — to take in talent, to connect with the world, and to shape society towards one with more diversity and strength. This should be a cause for celebration.

Singapore the Developed Country

Whether it is Germany's "Wirtschaftswunder" or France's "Les Trente Glorieuses," growth always follows the same pattern which is to reach a slow but unspectacular rate once the catch-up phase is over. Likewise, Singapore's economy will likely grow around 2–3% per annum over the long run. There will no doubt be a few economic crises along the way; there may even be a feeling of stagnation in some years.

We will also face the same rich world problems and politics in the coming decades. An older population will demand increased public healthcare expenditure, together with demands for greater social security. A large swath of infrastructure, from stadiums to expressways, from trains to drains, will age. The HDB heartlands will have to be completely remade. Rebuilding these in a dense urban environment will be far more costly compared to when Singapore was a green-field country.

With slower economic growth, there will be greater pressure on the national economy (and public finances) in the coming decades to find the resources to consume and invest. Singapore's current account surplus will decline; taxes and size of government will increase. The Deputy Prime Minister and Minister for Finance Mr. Tharman Shanmugaratnam outlined these challenges and made significant moves to prepare the country for the

[2] More than 210,000 Singapore citizens are residing overseas (see NPTD, 2014). Taking the UK experience as a baseline, an estimated 1 in 10 citizens may live overseas (see Finch, Andrew, and Latorre, 2010). Singapore could also experience this ratio of overseas citizens going forward.

future in the Jubilee year budget of 2015 "Building our Future, Strengthening Social Security."[3] More will have to be done in the coming years.

The point here is not about painting a pessimistic picture of Singapore's future decades, but to provide a sense how normal it will feel and more importantly, how there will be real progress. Between 1965 and 2015, per capita income in the United States grew at 1.9% per annum, and it is now 2.5 times the level in 1965, which represents a major transformation. Television box sets had black and white images in the 1960s, but people today watch programmes on smart-phones on the move.

A similar path is likely for Singapore, a much slower rate of growth than before, with ups and downs, but with an accumulation of progress that allows us to maintain our position in the leading pack of nations. With hard work, normal is within reach, and this too is worthy of celebration.

Inventing Global-City-Nation-State Governance

Singapore is a rarity in history, a global-city and a nation-state. Many commentators have observed the tension here — policies that advance Singapore's position as a global city do not always add to its sense of nationhood. While there is no denying the policy tension between the two, this view nonetheless overstates Singapore's constraints and underplays its unique proposition.

Global cities are in fact highly constrained by the politics of their domestic hinterlands. For example, the interests between London and the rest of UK do not always align. London effectively has to subsidise the rest of the UK;[4] and if the rest of UK still decides to curb immigration, London's competitiveness will be affected.

Singapore, being small, compact and with the sovereign right to chart its own course, is in fact uniquely advantaged in this regard. No other city sits in the United Nations or signs its own Free Trade Agreements. It has the opportunity to build a set of governance structures to function

---

[3] These included a programme to equip Singaporeans with skills (under SkillsFuture), increasing revenues to strengthen social security and for infrastructure development, and strengthening social security provisions through the introduction of the Silver Support Scheme.

[4] Tax receipts in London amounted to around 45% of its GDP, while public expenditure in London accounted only around 35% of GDP (estimates by CEBR, 2012).

effectively both as an international city and as a state. Beyond capital accumulation, beyond human capital development, the set of institutions Singapore builds for the globalised age will become a key competitive advantage. What needs to be done?

First, we will have to think of how to integrate the large number of non-citizens into our larger society, and not just having policies that deal with them as transient workers. As their numbers can only grow, it is highly important that we have deeper engagements with them, in order to transform the economy and maintain overall social cohesiveness.

Second, we will have to creatively maintain links with many Singaporeans overseas, even into the second or third generations.

Third, we will have to reorganise the way we share responsibilities like National Service, taxes and social security between citizens and non-citizens here, as well as with citizens overseas.

Fourth, given that rights go in hand with responsibilities, we also have to rework our model of representation to fit the cosmopolitan reality.

Fifth, for many of the above to happen, we will have to pursue a deeper level of integration perhaps with a small set of likeminded nations to secure a joint economic space for the greater freedom of our citizens.

There is no model in the world to copy. We will have to literally invent the governance structure of a global-city-nation-state. It will require a huge amount of political imagination and leadership.

A Bigger and Better Singapore

An ideal scenario will see a relatively stable global geopolitical environment, with Asia continuing to develop; historic animosities fade into the background; globalisation is entrenched in a large part of the world. Physical constraints will become less binding as Singapore will be more connected to the rest of the world than ever before.

In 2065, Singapore becomes a globally connected nation of 10 million citizens. There will be many Singaporeans and companies located beyond city limits, even as Singapore takes in many new residents. There will be many little red dots elsewhere; some cities in Asia could have quarters that feel like Singaporean suburbs. Likewise, Singapore will feel like the world-in-one place, there will be many little some-other-countries springing up in Singapore, even in the traditional HDB heartlands, infused with Singaporean traditions and characteristics.

This is the good scenario, and a plausible one. With good fortune and hard work, Singapore can become the best city and country in the world.

References

Centre of Economics and Business Research (CEBR). (2012). *One Pound in Five Earned in London Subsidises the Rest of the UK.* Retrieved February 25, 2015 from http://www.cebr.com/reports/how-money-in-some-regions-subsidises-others/.

Finch, T., with Andrew, H., and Latorre, M. (2010). *Global Brits: Making the Most of the British Diaspora.* London: Institute for Public Policy Research. Retrieved February 25, 2015 from http://www.ippr.org/assets/media/ecomm/files/Global%20Brit%20summary.pdf.

National Population and Talent Development, Singapore (NPTD). (2014), Population in Brief.

Shaping Graduates: Head, Heart and Habit

Tsui Kai Chong
Provost and Professor of Finance
SIM University, Singapore

SIM University (UniSIM) is a private university for working adults. It offers more than 50 programmes to meet the skills and knowledge updating and upgrading needs of our workforce. In 2012, the university was asked to offer selected programmes to full-time students as well. This paper summarises the issues that we considered and the requirements we introduced to our full-time, and later to our part-time, programmes to address the current and future needs of our graduates.[1] We trust that our graduates will be prepared for 2065.

The shift from an industrial to a service economy, technological advancements, the Internet, information explosion and social-economic-political events shape the world we live in. Given current trends, the world of the future favours "learners" over "knowers." There is a shelf life to work skills and competencies. The emergence of new technologies, organisations and markets suggests that having an educational foundation for individuals to begin their careers with is no longer sufficient. There must be opportunities for these individuals to update their skills or retrain for new jobs throughout their working lives. Continuing education is the key to sustaining a dynamic, vibrant, competent and knowledgeable workforce.

---

[1] This paper summarises the work of UniSIM College team. It has also benefitted from the helpful comments provided by Prof. Koh Hian Chye.

The transition from an agricultural to an industrial economy has been characterised by some as a revolution. Likewise, the shift from an industrial to a service economy, which is evident in all developed economies — while it has proceeded more quietly — has similar revolutionary implications.[2] By 2000, the majority of the workforce in developed economies are already employed in services.[3] With manufacturing slipping to less than 20% of GDP and services rising to more than 70% in some OECD countries, services are the key drivers in these economies.[4] Furthermore, job creation has taken place almost exclusively in the services sector.[5] We are certain that Singapore is not immune to such trends.[6]

Wages are highly correlated with skill levels. Higher paying service jobs require better trained people, and higher paid employees tend to have better working conditions. The skill premium in wages persists despite the increase in the supply of high-skilled workers.[7] Skilled employees continue to be valued because they are in demand, whereas the unskilled ones are easily replaced or outsourced. Thus, skilled employees must keep their expertise current so as to keep themselves in demand throughout their careers. Customer-centric jobs in the service industry require certain skill sets. These include: listening, communicating, adapting, problem solving, anticipating the next thing, building relationships and getting the job done.

Technology transforms and extends our capabilities. In the past, we are assigned a desk, a landline telephone and a desktop computer connected to an in-house server and supported by an in-house IT department. These required us to be in our office to perform our work. Today, those bonds are replaced by smart phones, the Internet and social media. We can build our

---

2 V. R. Fuchs (1968), *The Service Economy*, New York and London: Colombia University Press.

3 74% of the US workforce, 72% in Holland, 71% in the UK, 71% in France, 63% in Spain, and 62% in Germany. Organisation for Economic Co-operation and Development (OECD) (2000), *Employment Outlook*, Paris: OECD.

4 OECD (2000), The Service Economy. Business and Industry Policy Forum Series.

5 A. D'Agostino, R. Serafini and M. War-Wamerdinger (May 2006), Sectoral Explanations of Employment in Europe: The Role of Services, European Central Bank, Working Paper Series, No. 625.

6 In 2011, services account for 65% of Singapore's GDP. In contrast, it is 54% (2007) for India and 41% (2004) for China.

7 F. J. Buera and J. P. Kaboski (2012), The Rise of the Service Economy, *American Economic Review, 102*(6), 2504–2569.

networks online. Today's employees are capable of doing much more in their technology-assisted roles.

Likewise, technology is transforming education. Lectures, course materials and assessments are going online. Educational technology companies, like Coursera, offer courses from many top universities to millions of students online. Technology changes faster than culture. Entire product lines or companies or markets can be obliterated.[8] Despite this, we need trained and talented people to invent new technology and make it work in organisations.

Globalisation has increased the movement of people, culture, goods and services, and capital and investments, as well as information and technology, across countries. Technology has enabled small and medium-sized companies around the globe to connect to each other and to their customers.[9] With Asia's billions marching towards modernity, the economic centre will shift from the West to the East.[10] One view is that China will lead this march.[11] Multinationals are also moving their core decision-making units to Asia[12].

Unfortunately, human activities and technology have significant environmental impacts and they impose economic, social and ecological costs. These heighten our concerns for sustainability. Let us also remind ourselves of issues faced by the Singapore community. The National Volunteer & Philanthropy Centre provided 10 such issues in no particular order, and mentioned that they are not exhaustive.[13] These range from ageing population

---

[8] L. Downes and P. F. Nunes (2013, March), Big-Bang Disruption, *Harvard Business Review*. Retrieved January 14, 2015 from https://hbr.org/2013/03/big-bang-disruption.

[9] O. Ralph (2011, October 10), All Change: Long-term Success Requires Flexibility and Co-operation, *Financial Times*; and also observe Alibaba.

[10] K. Mahbubani (2008), *The New Asian Hemisphere: The Irresistible Shift of Global Power to the East*, New York: Public Affairs.

[11] M. Jacques (2009), *When China Rules the World: The End of the Western World and the Birth of a New Global Order*, London: Allen Lane.

[12] S. Wagstyl (2011, October 10), Global Competition Drives Change, *Financial Times*. Retrieved January 14, 2015 from http://www.ft.com/intl/cms/s/2/7df0e59c-f31b-11e0-8383-00144feab49a.html#axzz3OmpHt13H.

[13] National Volunteer & Philanthropy Centre (NVPC) (2010, February), Issues Faced by the Singapore Community. Retrieved January 14, 2015 from https://www.sggives.org/CheckAccess.aspx?url=/imagerepository/01_top_menu/news/2.%20issues%20faced%20by%20the%20singapore%20community.pdf.

to family/youth at risk, and from healthcare to Singaporeans without relevant job skills.

Our graduates must be prepared for a global, demanding and changing work environment. Technology has made information available at our fingertips, so knowledge acquisition alone is insufficient. To be effective, we need to challenge our students to assess and acquire, as well as apply, knowledge to solve real problems. We believe that education needs to be life and work relevant as well as values-driven. At UniSIM, we tap technology to optimise the proficiency of our students, who are digital natives. Our programmes and their learning environment must be aligned with lifelong learning, which not only serves the students' formal education years but also other spheres of their lives. Further, a graduate is not just a contributor to the economy; he/she should also be a contributor to the community. We must bring out the best in our students by inculcating in them a sense of community.

The traditional university lecture-tutorial model is a thing of the past. In UniSIM, we require pre-class preparation, in-class activity and post-class reflection. Lectures and learning materials are placed online, enabling students to take charge of their pre-class learning. Classroom engagements are activity-based. They require students to exchange views and decisions. Reflective processes, including e-Portfolio and online group discussions, consolidate what they have learnt. By so re-configuring learning responsibilities and sharpening higher order thinking, formative habits can develop into lifelong practices. In addition, our full-time students attend some evening classes with working adult students; this enables them to appreciate the need to re-tool and re-skill; as well as balance between work, family and studies.

In addition, we have introduced a set of common courses to provide a common intellectual experience for all our full-time undergraduates regardless of their major; it also serves as a bond among students at the start of their academic journey. It instils openness to diverse realities and modes of inquiry, and cultivates other attitudes necessary to examine world trends and issues, including the looming problems of our community and our world. Students learn that issues are interconnected and they often do not neatly fall into one domain or discipline. Hence, there is a need for a holistic and systems approach to problem solving and that solutions may, or must, be drawn from different academic disciplines.[14]

Each course requires students to listen, read, discuss, write and present. Listening, as opposed to merely hearing, require students to make sense of and understand what another person is saying. Reading introduces new and great ideas, illustrates good writing and hopefully inspires. It would improve the students' ability to think critically and analytically. Discussion requires students to prepare by reading and listening; then, articulating their ideas. Writing requires students to record their ideas into a structured, meticulous and concise form. Presentation requires students to work in teams to formally and succinctly communicate their ideas to an audience. These presentations are pre-recorded and limited in length.

In addition to self-study and classroom activities, we require a 24-week Work Attachment as well as a Service Learning experience to have students put their learning and knowledge to action. The Overseas Experience requirement, preferably in an Asian country, adds an overseas dimension to their education. An Applied Project requires students to identify and provide solutions to an issue in an organisation or the community. Academic and practical work-relevant skills are distilled in a reflective process through the students' e-Portfolio, which is a dynamic résumé that enables students to document their reflections, share their experiences, monitor their personal growth and showcase their achievements.

In short, to better prepare our students for the challenges in the future we groom them to have a head to apply what they have learnt, a heart to help others and a habit of self-directed lifelong learning. By 2065, we envisage that the pace and depth of change will be faster and more disruptive. Thus, "head" and "habit" will be crucial for individuals to function in that world. Unavoidably, there will be some who are unable to keep pace with the changes. Consequently, "heart" is crucial for us to retain "humanness" in our community. While "head, heart and habit" are important now, they will become even more important in 2065.

[14] Students have a tendency to treat knowledge as discrete and pre-determined. Thus, one of the essential qualities they have to cultivate is preparedness for contextualisation of knowledge and a general pre-disposition towards cross-disciplinary study and questioning.

Singapore 2065: Is Demography Destiny?

Aline Wong
Academic Advisor
SIM University

In January 2013, the Government published a Population White Paper, entitled "A Sustainable Population for a Dynamic Singapore" that sought to address the issues arising from the declining fertility trends that we have been experiencing for several decades past. Based on various assumptions, the White Paper projected that Singapore's population size might range between 6.5 and 6.9 million by the year 2030. This raised a huge public outcry, and the subsequent open debate became fixated on this figure, irrespective of what the Government proposed to do further to boost fertility through enhanced marriage and parenthood packages, slow down the growth of immigration, restructure the economy and raise productivity, as well as invest in infrastructure and social services to meet the needs of a larger and older population within a quality living environment.

One of the objections raised to the Paper was that: "Why do we need to think so far ahead towards 2030? Is it possible to plan for 2030 — while we have burning issues to resolve right now: the rising costs of living, the large number of foreigners working and living in our midst, the squeeze on public services such as housing, medical facilities and public transport?"

Against this background, it may seem foolhardy to talk about population issues again and plan towards the year 2065. But it will be a grave mistake if thinkers, policymakers and planners avoid the exercise of imagining the long-term future.

To guide our thinking on the future, we can start with several long-term trends. Barring certain extreme changes to Singapore's external environment (such as war, terrorist attacks, pandemics, natural and man-made disasters such as rising sea levels and nuclear power plant meltdowns), and assuming Singapore still remains a sovereign country 50 years down the road, there are certain social economic trends that will "work themselves out" in due course. I will briefly outline five such trends: the changing social-demographic structure, generational changes in values and lifestyles, evolution of civic community and political culture, globalisation and the drive for a quality living environment.

Trend Number One: Population Ageing

As we approach 2065, the proportions of the population who are over 65, 75 and 85 years of age are going to be higher and higher. Even way before that, we will have become an aged society. Our resident population structure will be very much skewed and will resemble an inverted pyramid in shape. There will be several times more women among the elderly and aged, as compared to men. This dimension alone has tremendous implications on income security, types of health and social services, eldercare, etc. in future. Gender-specific policies must be put in place.

At the same time, the total citizen population size will decline. In fact, at current birth rates and without immigration, the citizen population will shrink from 2025 onwards. And even before that, the number of working-age citizens (20–64 years of age) will start to decline from 2020 onwards. No matter how we raise productivity in the labour force, the gains are unlikely to offset the effects of the declining population, resulting in slower economic growth. As Singapore's economy is also entering a mature, lower growth stage, we can expect a slower income growth, lower tax revenues (in spite of rises in the tax rates) and a lower standard of living, particularly for the elderly.

It is clear that we continually need immigrants to replenish the energy, creativity and size of our labour force. For our working adults, we would still be able to make a good living through a good education and lifelong learning.

By 2065, I hope our degree or certification mindset about education will have changed thoroughly, and lifelong learning will have become entrenched in our education landscape. By then, I hope we will also have become a post-materialist society, where people find satisfaction in a better quality of life which is not equated with a higher standard of living.

Trend Number Two: Generational Shifts in Values and Lifestyles

Looking at the future older generation, these are the current Generation Y young adults (born between 1980 and 1995). They are now in their twenties and early thirties. They will enter their seventies and eighties by 2065.

Generation Y has grown up during the time Singapore enters the global arena, becomes a world city and develops a knowledge economy. They are living in a digital age, and the Internet and social media offer them endless possibilities to be connected with the world for learning, working, doing business, social networking and joining diverse interest groups. They have higher education, are trained to believe in creativity and entrepreneurship. They are adventuresome, they work hard, play hard, and lives life in the fast lane (24/7 on the go at work, always connected, and globetrotting on job assignments). They enjoy life to the fullest — fine dining, wine-clubbing, enjoying arts and sports, holidaying in off-the-beaten-track locations, taking sabbaticals from studies or from work in order to find their own "self." Increasing numbers of young adults will remain single for life. Life is good in spite of a lack of job stability; and in spite of — or because of — late marriage and parenthood. Divorce is on the rise, single parenting is commonly accepted. This is the generation that faces the challenges of global competition, and finds affinity in global causes such as environmentalism, social entrepreneurship, conservation, gay rights and animal rights.

As Generation Y journeys through their long lifespan, how would they think, live and express themselves, say, 25 years down the road when they are middle-aged? Will they form the solid middle-class, middle-aged electorate that will vote for stability, prosperity and an inclusive, socially just society? Will they have the sustained economic earning ability to pay the higher taxes, accumulate sizeable savings for their old age? Or would they be somewhat like their counterparts in the West — who, having lived a good life, have scant savings except for their CPF and HDB flat as assets, and they will look towards the government to provide extra social security for them? Will income inequality be a great concern among the future middle-aged group?

We do not know how the above scenario will pan out for Generation Y in their middle age. But it can be foreseen that, among the old population in 2065, Gen Y will become a vociferous retirees' lobby group.

Trend Number Three: Rise of Civil Society and Normalisation of Opposition Politics

As Generation Y is highly educated, and as the participation rate for university education is being expanded by a wide margin for the upcoming generation within the next few years, there will be more and more citizens who will be knowledgeable, professionally competent, confident and articulate in their views on various issues. They will want more space for civil society, and join diverse groups and associations catering to the needs and interests of different communities. The Internet and social media will make it much easier for them to disseminate views, get organised and rally around causes. They will be better positioned to challenge the government inside or outside Parliament. They will have serious alternative ideas to offer to shape the future of Singapore. There will be more substantive contestation of political party platforms at future general elections.

By 2065, the PAP will be over 110 years old. It will have evolved from its current structure and ideology. It will need to evolve in order to stay relevant to Generation Y and younger generations. This will involve, among other things, a realignment of the party's structure and processes in accordance with the expectations of the party's members and cadres for greater participation in decision making. The activists will also want their imprint on party policies that will translate into national policies. This is in accordance with the spirit of the times, and applies equally to one single dominant party, or split factions within the single party, or between ruling and opposition parties.

Trend Number Four: "Extreme Futures"

As James Canton (CEO and Chairman, Global Futures) put it, we are now living in a highly complex, multi-dimensional world where the key to survival lies in our capacity to anticipate, adapt, innovate and evolve. The future that Canton described in the early years of the millennium has already come about. This future is marked by fast innovations, global connectivity, hyper-competition, real-time transactions and digital lifestyles. Human performance is enhanced by IT, gene therapy, and nanotechnology. As Singapore is a developed economy, we are no less blessed by such advances. Equally we will be subject to new stresses and strains in "extreme futures" coming from climate change, "weird science," destructive innovations, and the pervasiveness of global trends and forces beyond our control.

How can we make sure Singapore will remain a welcoming place to foreign talents and an endearing home for our citizens even as we are buffeted by "extreme factors" and global forces?

Trend Number Five: Towards a Liveable Environment and a City for All Ages

During the first 50 years of our independence as a nation, we have wrought an economic miracle that has uplifted our standard of living and propelled us into the First World. The next 50 years will see us striving to maintain a quality of life high enough to continually attract talents and capital, and to satisfy the aspirations of our own citizens who would have gone beyond the needs of the consumption lifestyle, to the post-materialist need for a quality living environment which is healthy, sustainable and ultimately fulfilling.

With an ageing population, we would require more resource inputs into providing a quality living environment for the old. Whether it is in terms of innovative designs in public and private housing, retirement communities, provisions for mobility and access in the city, a clean and green environment, or social and recreational services at the doorstep of the elderly, we require more space, possibly land, and more manpower and other expenditures to meet their aspirations. At the same time, we must pay due attention to intergenerational bonding. We will need to refresh the social compact which will redefine the responsibilities of the state vis-à-vis the older citizens, where the family and traditional social networks will have lost significant ability to care for them.

Strong Society for a Sustainable Economy

Lawrence Wong
Minister for Culture, Community and Youth, Singapore

A Fair and Just Society

The story of Singapore's economic miracle is well known. Our transformation over the last 50 years from a small trading port in the Malayan archipelago to a cosmopolitan, globally competitive economy was made possible through the grit and determination of our pioneer generation, on whose shoulders we stand today.

How will Singapore evolve in the next 50 years? In the coming decades, I believe our economic progress can be sustained only if we also progress socially. So while we continue to keep an eye on the economy, we need to strengthen the processes and institutions to build our society at an equal pace.

The principles are different. In building the economy, the principle of the market rules supreme. The economy runs on Adam Smith's principle of the "invisible hand," that everyone working to maximise his own benefit makes the marketplace work. But society cannot be structured as a winner-takes-all contest fought in the marketplace. If everyone looks out only for his own interest and champions ideas that only benefit himself or his interest group, then we will have no common ground on which to build our society.

The irony is that Adam Smith himself was vitally concerned with the moral underpinnings of society. His concept of rational self-centredness was only a small part of his broader belief system, as reflected in his own writings. As he put it, "no society can surely be flourishing and happy, of which the far greater part of the members are poor and miserable. It is but equity, besides, that they who feed, cloath and lodge the whole body of the people, should have such a share of the produce of their own labour as to be themselves tolerably well fed, cloathed and lodged."

At the heart of it all, I believe that fairness is the indispensable value that underpins a good economy and society. This concept of fairness is not one that simplistically assumes equal outcomes for everyone. Instead, it is about the principle of "just desserts." In other words, wealth has to be earned and rewards have to be commensurate with the discretionary effort. Holding people to account for the degree to which they make an effort is also a sign of our respect for their dignity and autonomy as human beings.

At the same time, we recognise that luck plays a part in any individual's fortunes. Because outcomes are uncertain, the collective purchase of reasonable levels of social insurance will enhance the overall welfare of society. This is especially so at a time when individuals are facing growing uncertainties and pressures brought about by rapid globalisation and the IT revolution.

In this regard, the government has made major shifts in policy to strengthen social safety nets and enhance social mobility. We have increased our investments in pre-school education to give every child an equal chance to excel and lead a full life. We have rolled out initiatives like the universal MediShield Life to pool individual risks and strengthen our healthcare system.

But government policies are only part of the solution. A fair and just society cannot be conceived only in transactional terms, or in terms of income redistribution. It must involve the community — to engage the human spirit, to provide personal fulfilment and to strengthen collective wellbeing. It must strengthen the culture of responsibility for one another, so that we all feel a duty to one another and not just a right to the benefits of citizenship.

Philanthropy as an Integral Part of the Solution

Philanthropy must therefore be an integral part of the solution in strengthening our economic model for the next 50 years.

Philanthropy has the potential to mitigate inequality, and soften the hard edges of the free market. It provides a mechanism to dismantle the accumulated wealth tied to the past, and reinvest it to strengthen the entrepreneurial potential of the future. Through this recycling of wealth, philanthropy creates social stability and opportunity for those who have to be helped to the starting line. This is an important part of the implicit social contract that continuously nurtures and revitalises our society. In other words, individuals are free to generate and accumulate wealth; but that wealth must be recycled and invested back into society to expand opportunity for others.

The US has a long tradition of philanthropy, which counts capitalist giants like Andrew Mellon and J. Paul Getty among its ranks. These people had vast bank accounts, matched only by the generosity with which they gave. The fruits of their philanthropy can be seen all across the country, from hospitals and universities to a range of cultural institutions.

Some of the wealthiest people today have continued this proud tradition of philanthropy. The difference is that they have taken a more focused approach in their philanthropic giving to create bigger impact. They go beyond writing cheques and providing financial support. Instead they are more akin to social entrepreneurs and investors, looking to where society is most in need and helping to create new, innovative solutions. A good example of this is the Gates Foundation, which operates very much as a hands-on "venture philanthropist," seeking to make the greatest possible impact to social problems, or to maximise their "social return."

In Singapore, we are seeing a rising trend of philanthropic giving. Our philanthropic tradition started with our early immigrants. Those who made it good in Singapore felt the compunction to give back to the community that had so richly supported them. It is to these pioneer philanthropists that we owe some of our first schools, hospitals and religious organisations like St. Andrew's School, Tan Tock Seng Hospital and Ngee Ann Kongsi.

This sense of strong mutual support remains today. Philanthropists stand behind new institutions like the Khoo Teck Puat and Ng Teng Fong Hospitals, as well as the Lee Kong Chian School of Business in the Singapore Management University. But more than just big ticket donations, we have also seen strong support from the public towards worthy causes. For example, the Community Chest and the President's Charity raise tens of millions every year, contributed by a wide range of donors, from the man in the street to foundations and businesses. In 2012, charitable giving to Institutions of a Public Character or IPCs hit a record high of over S$1 billion.

So we have made progress towards becoming a nation of givers, but more still needs to be done. The culture of philanthropy has yet to sink deep roots in our national psyche. There is potential for everyone to contribute to society, including local businesses. This is critical in an age of widening gaps between the haves and have-nots. When those with the most resources choose to help those with the least, we will open the doors to a society that stands together in its compassion.

Volunteerism

Besides philanthropy, another key plank of a culture of giving is volunteer service. Volunteering can have a profound effect on our lives. It teaches us to care for the wellbeing of others, especially those in need. When we serve, we meet people in circumstances different from our own; we develop greater empathy and learn what it means to walk in the shoes of others; and we have a stronger sense of duty and responsibility for our fellow citizens. This binds us. This makes us a community.

Indeed, surveys have shown that positive volunteer experiences in youth tend to lead to generous giving and volunteering later in life. To instil the right habits from a young age, the Ministry of Culture, Community & Youth and the Ministry of Education are working on several joint efforts. For example, we have introduced Community Youth Leadership initiatives in certain schools to complement the broader "Values in Action" programme that has been rolled out across the school system. In 2014, we also started a new Youth Corps programme to match youth volunteers with critical community needs, and help them make sustained and meaningful contributions to society.

Singapore in 2065

No one can predict what the future will hold in 5 or 10 years, much less 50 years' time. But I believe we are taking the right steps today to strengthen our social foundations for sustained progress into the future.

Competitiveness, flexibility and market dynamism have long been hallmarks of Singapore's economy. In our next phase of development, we must build a stronger nation that successfully embraces both flexibility and security, both competition and social justice.

These goals can only happen with active citizens, who are willing to step forward and do their part to help their fellow Singaporeans. This is very much what one of our founding fathers Mr. S. Rajaratnam had envisioned when he called for Singapore to be a "democracy of deeds," and for citizenship participation "to solve practical problems in a practical way."

This is why it is important for us to focus on strengthening our social institutions, especially in areas like philanthropy and volunteerism. We must find different mechanisms and platforms to encourage all Singaporeans, including our businesses, to get involved in building a better society. For while the Government can and will do more, it is ultimately this spirit of fellowship and mutual support that is crucial in taking our nation forward.

Singapore's Social Compact Trilemma — The Dynamics of a Critically Uncertain National Future

Yeoh Lam Keong
Vice-President
Economic Society of Singapore (ESS)

The political problem of mankind is to combine three things: economic efficiency, social justice and individual liberty.

John Maynard Keynes

The last 50 years of nation building has firmly established Singapore as a globally competitive, highly successful economy and city-state with strong fundamental foundations of prosperity and potential undreamt of by its frugal and visionary founders with one of the highest per capita incomes in the world.

The next 50 years will determine how much of his hard-earned, miraculous potential is actually realised for her people and whether the shining city-state that she now is can also become a nation-state; a "true home" where all citizens live securely and free of want, with the wellbeing, sense of community, participation and opportunity that would make them proud to be Singaporean and happy that their children remain so.

As a pragmatic economic and social analyst schooled in studying global long-term trends, I am optimistic we can get there. But a happy ending is by no means certain. Globalisation and technological innovation have generated a distressingly extreme income and wealth inequality in the developed world economy of which now we are an inextricable part, an inequality also often marked by stagnation and increased economic uncertainty for the majority. This makes the new globalised inequality both a political as well as an economic problem; a crisis of the social compact, not just socioeconomic policy.

In Singapore these distressing trends have been exacerbated by a misguided labour-intensive growth model over the last two decades, which has raised the population from 3 to 5.5 million, depressed wages and productivity and led to a potentially acute overcrowding problem that is already damaging to citizen wellbeing and the social fabric. Key social services like public housing, healthcare, transportation, education and social security have also lagged behind the social dislocation caused by globalisation, poor policy and demographic ageing. This has markedly strained our social compact and trust in public policy.

Without a healthy and stable social compact, the social cohesion needed for national identity and belonging is precarious. Political legitimacy and its vital twin, trust in governance institutions and policy, likewise tends to become weak and dysfunctional. A healthy social compact is therefore fundamentally necessary if we are to make a successful transition from being merely a successful city-state to a viable, resilient and cohesive nation.

In the long term, there are three key requirements for a stable and successful social compact — market competitiveness, adequate social protection and sufficient democratic development. A study of long-term trends suggests these are three unavoidable and irresistible social demands for both political legitimacy and stable governance. They constitute an essential foundational trinity for a healthy economy, polity and society. Governments that can provide these three requirements in balance will tend to have a relatively healthy social compact, those that fall short will tend to have their social compacts undermined by the very area they fail to develop.

The demand for social protection is inherently driven by the need for market competitiveness in a globalised economy. Globalisation and the inevitable competition with the huge cheap workforces of the emerging world plus the exponential rise of labour displacing and outsourcing info-comms and artificial intelligence-based technologies mean the middle and working classes of the developed world will increasingly face poor income and employment prospects generated by global free markets without sufficient social protection. This is exacerbated by demographics and the need for adequate social security for rapidly ageing populations. Providing the social protection that insulates citizens from the worst risks and stresses of an unavoidable engagement with globalisation is one of the major tasks of good government.

The demand for democratic development is driven by an increasingly large proportion of politically active, well-educated younger cohorts, informed and connected by social networking technology as never before in history. This is immeasurably strengthening and qualitatively transforming the very nature of democratic accountability. It enables an increasingly activist public to intervene, check, make accountable and influence both major and minor policies on an almost real-time basis. The main message of the recent book pulping drama at NLB[1] is not just the need for an improved, more inclusive and transparent process of book classification; it also means that policymaking at a micro level and by extension politics at a macro level will never be free from an unprecedented level of public scrutiny and influence again.

Lest you think that having a good balance of market competitiveness, social protection and democratic governance is Utopian, many Northern European and Nordic states as well as some Anglo Saxon states provide all three requirements quite well and are as a result among the most stable, most cohesive and happiest nations in the new globalised world. Even our developed Asian neighbours, e.g. Japan, Korea, or Taiwan seem to have achieved a better balance between these three requirements — and as a result have less fundamental social compact problems stemming from inadequate social protection or democratic development that Singapore seems to chronically suffer from.

Singapore's essential social compact trilemma is a highly developed economic competitiveness but underdeveloped social protection and relatively

[1] For an overview of the incident, please refer to Tan Dawn Wei (2014, July 18), NLB Saga: Two Removed Children's Books Will Go into Adult Section at Library, *The Straits Times*. Retrieved February 25, 2015 http://www.straitstimes.com/news/singapore/more-singapore-stories/story/nlb-saga-two-removed-childrens-books-will-go-adult-secti.

undeveloped democratic development. Our polity therefore tends towards social compact crisis centred around social protection and democratic development issues. The most likely political expression of this is a gradual loss of political legitimacy and policy credibility, a cumulative loss of social cohesion and social capital as well as creeping policy paralysis, populism and a politics of petty recrimination rather than constructive debate.

The only stable positive long-term solution to breaking out of this vicious circle is to broaden governance priorities to seriously develop both adequate social protection and working democratic institutions.

Adequate social protection in Singapore needs major social policy reform in six key areas: social security, healthcare, public housing, education, public transport and population/immigration policy.

To be fair, the government has woken up to the importance of social protection in "inclusive growth." There have been major recent reforms including moving towards universal healthcare in hospitalisation. The price of new public housing has been delinked from market determined resale prices and a serious effort has been made to make first time flats more affordable. A pioneer generation package has been introduced mainly to reduce the medical expenses of the elderly and major reforms in non-graduate education and training are planned. A basic pension supplement for the elderly poor has been introduced. This is commendable and is moving social protection policy significantly in the right direction.

However, legitimate concerns remain that such efforts are piecemeal and insufficiently bold and transformative. Public rental housing is still not sufficiently available as an option to meet low income housing needs. Long-term chronic primary care and long-term care are still sadly inadequate for middle- and low-income citizens. Both the working poor and the unemployed and elderly poor are not getting the full state help they can or need to get and which the government can well afford to give. Retirement adequacy for the poor is still lacking. The education system remains far too reliant on unnecessary streaming and mass testing, hampering social mobility owing to the better access of the better-off to the massive shadow education system of private tuition. Public transport in a country where few can afford cars still markedly lags public transport systems in Hong Kong or Taipei. While excessive immigration has significantly lessened, we could still easily be on trajectory for a terminal population much above, not significantly below 6.9 million by 2065. All this represents outstanding unreformed social protection policy that is still undermining vital policy credibility and ultimately political legitimacy.

Democratic reforms in Singapore will be even more difficult, requiring the development of a wider range of democratic institutions and practices from even lower starting levels. This requires major political reform in five key areas: free media and speech, guaranteed access to public information, stronger rights of association and organisation in civil society, a non-partisan civil service and stronger and more supportive government-civil society links.

In my view over next two decades the good news for Singapore is that we could well look back on an unprecedented period of reform in these two major currently underdeveloped and undeveloped areas — social protection and democratic development. And well before 2065 it is quite likely we will have much fuller range of both social policy and political reform driven by the irresistible demands for social protection and democratic development demanded by an increasingly informed and organised electorate. Lest this seems implausible, keep in mind that this means we would merely be converging towards developed country political and social policy norms from a highly exceptional and probably unsustainable current position. However, this could also happily result, as it did following the political liberalisations in Japan, Korea and Taiwan, in a much more mature and vibrant society, as well as a level of social and cultural wellbeing and richness well beyond our current norms or imagination.

The critical uncertainty is how smooth and successful or fractious, disruptive and contentious this journey will be. The more the current government leads genuine, transformative reform in both these areas, the smoother and more successful this process will be. The more the government resists or only carries out merely piecemeal reforms, the more potentially disruptive the process, with greater public loss of trust, less social capital, greater policy paralysis and more suboptimal populist policy outcomes that could be difficult to reverse. Our national identity itself may be the ultimate casualty.

Government in Singapore is institutionally strong partly because of the civil service's excellent policy formulation and execution capability, but this is not enough. While it needs to be responsive to elected political direction, the civil service also needs to be above and independent of partisan politics for the long-term public good. Key areas of social policy like healthcare, education or immigration policy for example, need to be planned and executed over a decade or longer. Political parties have shorter term, sometimes populist horizons that may or may not coincide with the common long-term good. This means that top civil service appointments need to be independent of partisan political influence. Government also needs go to beyond its traditional role as director, producer and regulator and move towards roles as facilitator, coordinator and co-creator. To do this effectively it needs open and supportive partnerships with strong, well-researched and responsible civic society groups which share and can help anchor and guide its long-term social vision for the common good, insulating long-term policy from the finicky ebb and often unsound flow of populist political dynamics.

The current government has seen the need to strengthen safety nets and social protection and are moving in the right direction, arguably in too piecemeal a fashion. Can they continue to do so transformatively, coherently and boldly enough? As importantly, does a deeply held elite governance philosophy prevent government from adequately leading political reform and development of democratic institutions? If so, this could pose difficult times for Singapore's successful future development from city-state to nation as Singapore's key social compact trilemma remains painfully unresolved.

Beyond 50: Journalists

Silver Roadmap and Golden Gates: A Portrait of Ageing in Singapore in 2065

Fiona Chan
Deputy Political Editor
The Straits Times

On New Year's Day in 2065, Mr. Tan awakens before 6 am, as he has done every day since he turned 65 a decade earlier. Detecting wakefulness from his movements and respiratory patterns, his SmartBed triggers soft room lights that will automatically fade away as daylight intensifies through the window. The lights have helped Mr. Tan navigate more than one midnight trip to the bathroom; he has not fallen yet, but if he does and cannot get up, motion sensors embedded in the ceilings, walls and floors of his apartment will sound an alarm. Mr. Tan's mattress also logs his sleep data and vital statistics such as weight and heart rate, and transmits them to the National Authority for Ageing (NAA) — the government agency charged with ageing issues. Set up in the 2040s, the NAA aims to, among other things, improve the efficiency and efficacy of medical care for the elderly by compiling the health records of all Singapore residents and monitoring their health conditions around the clock. This passive surveillance allows it to alert family members or caregivers about abnormal readings, or to dispatch paramedics or ambulances swiftly in the event of an emergency.

While SmartBeds have become commonplace in recent decades, not all Singaporeans have the budget or inclination for one. Mr. Tan's SmartBed comes courtesy of the Golden Gates (GG) Paya Lebar development, into which he and his wife moved five years ago after he had a mild heart attack. Located in established neighbourhoods across Singapore, the GGs are among the country's premier multi-stage retirement villages: sprawling integrated developments that cater to the continuum of housing and elder-care needs of Singapore residents in their golden years. Resembling mini townships for senior citizens, such villages host a variety of properties including high-rise apartment blocks, assisted living centres, aged care facilities, hospitals, pharmaceutical dispensaries, recreation venues and shops. The large tracts of land they require were freed up by the government, which in the 2040s started relocating the residents of HDB estates that were nearing the end of their 99-year leases.

The retirement villages, along with the NAA, are part of the Silver Roadmap for an ageing population that Singapore started devising in 2025, the year its citizen population started shrinking.[1] Even back in 2013, the Republic was among Asia's fastest ageing countries with one of the world's highest life expectancies,[2] a trend accelcrated by its historically low birth rate and restraints on immigration starting in the 2010s. It was little surprise when the island nation became one of the first to join the world's "super-aged" group of societies, where elderly folk make up more than 20% of the population, by 2030.[3] Technological breakthroughs such as driverless cars and medical advances that can stave off physical degeneration have further increased longevity. In 2030, there were just two working-age citizens (aged 20 to 64) for each citizen aged 65 and above, down from about five in 2015.[4] Thirty-five years later, despite successive increases to the retirement age, the ratio of working-age adults to retirement-age ones — also known as the old-age support ratio — has continued to slide. The

---

[1] National Population and Talent Division, Prime Minister's Office (2012), Citizen Population Scenarios. Retrieved from http://www.nptd.gov.sg/content/dam/nptd/Occasional%20Paper%20-%20Citizen%20 Population%20Scenarios.pdf.

[2] Department of Economic and Social Affairs and Population Division, United Nations (2013,), World Population Ageing 2013.

[3] Lim Y. H. (2014, February 26), S'pore on Its Way to 'Super-Ageing'. *MyPaper*. Retrieved February 24, 2015 from http://mypaper.sg/top-stories/spore-its-way-super-ageing-20140226.

[4] National Population and Talent Division, Prime Minister's Office (2015), Our Demographic Challenges and What These Mean to Us, *Our Population, Our Future: Public Engagement on Population Challenges*. Retrieved February 24, 2015 from http://population.sg/key-challenges/#.VCNyepSSySp.

largest age group in the nation is now the one Mr. Tan belongs to: those between the ages of 65 and 75.[5]

As expected, this "silver tsunami" has rippled through every part of economy and society. Economic growth moderated across the globe as projections that ageing workforces would lead to lower productivity and innovation materialised, albeit more slowly in economies with highly educated senior citizen populations. The shrinking sizes of families and family homes, along with greater female participation in the contracting workforce, have led to the diminished importance of family as the primary provider of shelter and care for the elderly. Much of this responsibility has been shifted onto the elderly themselves, with a larger share also borne by the state.

Singapore's Silver Roadmap, building on work done previously by the Committee on Ageing Issues and similar national workgroups, aimed to tackle some of the challenges of increasing longevity. It identified four main areas of concern: (a) retirement financing, particularly the public-private split of the cost of housing and medical care for seniors; (b) provision of high-quality services for the elderly, ranging from healthcare to companionship; (c) social support, such as dealing with changing family dynamics and ensuring the continued integration of the elderly into society; and (d) economic vitality, including creating more employment opportunities for older workers. Addressing these issues would require some game-changing initiatives — which was where the GGs and other retirement villages came in.

Features vary for each retirement village, but the GG complexes are relatively cookie-cutter. Most individuals gain lifelong membership into a GG by buying a strata-titled apartment in their choice of GG development when they turn 70.[6] The apartments are manageably sized studios ranging from 300 to 500 sq ft, and some have connecting doors that can turn two adjoining studios into a larger unit for an elderly couple, as Mr. Tan and his wife have done. The units are thoughtfully designed with SmartBeds,

[5] UN Department of Economic and Social Affairs, Population Division, World Population Prospects: The 2012 Revision (Medium variant), Singapore, as cited by M. De Wulf, Population Pyramid: Projecting Singapore's Population Characteristics in 2065. Retrieved February 24, 2015 from http://populationpyramid.net/singapore/2065/.

[6] This rule was implemented by the Singapore authorities when younger buyers snapped up units in the first "retirement resort" in Singapore, The Hillford, back in 2014.

motion sensors, remote-controlled appliances and bed-to-bathroom handrails. Some of the higher-end GG apartments are outfitted like luxurious condominiums, complete with automated bathing machines and household and companion robots. Residents live independently until their physical or mental health deteriorates, at which point they vacate their apartment and shift to one of the GG's other accommodation facilities: assisted living centres for seniors who are still relatively mobile, or aged care facilities that are equipped to house the incapacitated. At any stage in their stay at the GG, residents can make free use of the communal properties, and receive priority admission to the GG's hospitals.

GGs and most similar integrated retirement communities are built by property developers, owned by developers or real estate investment trusts, and run by private corporate operators who specialise in elderly care — a system not unlike that in the hospitality industry. The comprehensive end-of-life ecosystem these retirement villages provide, which builds on a concept first introduced in countries like Japan and Australia in the early 21st century, has several advantages.

First, it provides certainty as to the cost of retirement. All expenses for accommodation, daily meal and caregiving services for the rest of a resident's life are included in the price of a retirement village apartment. The cost of medical treatment is not, but MediShield Life — Singapore's 50-year-old universal healthcare plan — covers the bulk of this for most residents. A GG apartment is affordable for most owners of five-room HDB flats and private properties, while other retirement complexes cater to four-room flat owners — in other words, some three-quarters of Singapore's seniors can theoretically afford to join the system. GG apartments, in particular, come with a partial money-back guarantee: Should a resident die within 15 years of buying the unit, a pro-rated portion of the purchase price will be returned to his or her beneficiaries. Singaporeans can also be admitted to a retirement complex's later-stage facilities without first buying an apartment, but they have to pay a one-time membership fee and a recurring monthly charge. Those who cannot afford entrance into a privately run retirement village often opt for heavily subsidised nursing communities run by government agencies like the NAA or non-government organisations. At the other end of the spectrum, the wealthiest seniors generally age in place, cared for in their own well-appointed homes by expensive but highly skilled stay-in caregivers.

Since retirement village apartments must be paid for in full, many senior citizens — such as Mr. Tan and his wife, who have no children — finance them by selling their own homes, which they have saved up their whole lives to buy. Others budget for two homes from the start: one they can leave to the next generation, and an investment property that can be cashed in to buy a retirement residence for themselves. Jumping on the bandwagon, banks and insurers have started offering savings plans that allow people to put aside money for a retirement home once they start working. This use of residential assets and private savings to finance end-of-life needs continues Singapore's historical maxim of financial self-reliance, and helps to ease the burden on state finances that a higher dependency ratio poses. However, the government has also had to step up its own spending. For the poorest 20% of the elderly, the government subsidises nearly all nursing community expenses; for four-room flat owners, it tops up most of the gap between the flat's sale proceeds and the lowest price of retirement village admission. These assistance measures have been funded mainly through higher taxes and exceptional drawdowns of its bounteous past reserves.

A second advantage that integrated retirement villages offer is the ability to raise the standards of eldercare. Residents seamlessly transition between accommodation and healthcare facilities, allowing for better tracking of their lifestyle habits and medical history, and giving them the opportunity to form relationships of trust with the village's caregivers. Most retirement village owners and operators are large corporations that benefit from economies of scale in their offerings, ranging from recreational venues to capital-intensive robotic care. Some, like the GGs, have built their brand name on the basis of their skilled staff — after all, the human touch remains essential even in a digitised world. Like the investment banks and law firms of the past, eldercare providers now draw top talent by offering exhaustive training programmes, steady career progression and the job security of a growing and evergreen industry. Retirement villages also tap on the talent pool available within their gates. Energetic seniors perform part-time jobs — Mr. Tan's wife, for instance, prepares food in the retirement village's central kitchen — while most residents serve as willing subjects for surveys on elderly behaviour and research on senior-friendly technologies, helping to refine the quality and efficiency of eldercare.

These self-sustaining retirement villages thrive because GGs offer not just rest-of-life security for the elderly but a desirable environment in which to live — a third advantage of the integrated system. They go beyond meeting basic needs to cater to other critical aspirations, such as frequent social and physical activity, a sense of belonging and community, and respectful surroundings in which the elderly can age with dignity. Some retirement complexes also host childcare centres, facilitating interaction across generations and making it more convenient for working adults with young children and ageing parents. Performing this hybrid function has also enabled these retirement villages to integrate more closely into their respective neighbourhoods, removing the once-held stigma of senior citizen homes nestled within residential estates and encouraging greater social support for the elderly within the wider community.

The retirement complexes, of course, are just one element of how Singapore has adapted to its ageing population. The country has also made its urban infrastructure more elderly-friendly and expanded public transport; as a result, more people have switched from driving to walking and cycling, improving their fitness and health levels. Big data has made it easier to track the daily wellbeing of the first generation of senior citizens to have grown up in the digital age, many of whom still prefer to live out their golden years at home despite the growing popularity of retirement villages. Home-based monitoring systems — comprising motion sensors, appliance use trackers and medicine reminders — help by noting unusual situations and triggering calls to an elderly person's primary caregiver.[7] Mobile applications have also been developed to enable elderly people to interact more frequently with one another and with their families, to track seniors via GPS if they get lost, and to use small samples of blood, saliva or tissue to identify early warning signs of health problems such as Parkinson's disease, heart disease, diabetes and even some forms of cancer.

Technologies such as these are among the booming elderly-centred industries that have risen in economic importance in the wake of global ageing. The growth of the silver dollar cannot quite make up for the dwindling vibrancy of a maturing workforce, and the frenzied pace of economic expansion that Singapore enjoyed in the 20th century has mellowed into

[7] Some ideas inspired by The Design Incubation Centre, *Big Data for the Elderly: Using Digital Data to Enhance the Well-being of the Elderly*, Retrieved February 24, 2015 from http://www.designincubationcentre.com/bigdataelderly/wp-content/uploads/2012/12/BigDataElderly-DIC.pdf.

barely noticeable annual growth. Still, the country's standard of living remains high, and inflation is no longer quickening as aggregate demand stabilises and slowly contracts. The silver tsunami has swept through Singapore, but is far from drowning it. As the country prepares to celebrate its 100th year of nationhood in 2065, what is more important than the daunting economic and social challenges that still lie in Singapore's path is the nimbleness it continues to display, even as a centenarian itself, in dealing with them.

The End of Singapore's Golden Age?

Robin Chan
Manager
Media Strategy and Analytics Division
Singapore Press Holdings

As Singapore turns 50, are the best years already behind us?

The country's incredible third world to first world story has been well documented: rapid economic growth and wealth creation on a foundation of sound, long-term policies and predictable politics, powering the Singapore miracle.

Since independence, Singapore has developed relentlessly, but it is in the last decade that Singapore has truly made its mark as a global city to be reckoned with. Former Prime Minister Lee Kuan Yew suggested in 2007 that Singapore was entering its golden period, marked by vibrant economic and social development.[1] Yet in the years since, with concerns over the income gap, a shock riot in Little India, and tensions over immigrants, some may well point to those events and say Singapore has already peaked.

There are three broad trends that will impact Singapore in the next 50 years, and how policies and our people respond to these will be key in determining the country's trajectory.

The first is economic. Our position in the region will face increased competition from fast-emerging countries and cities for investments and talent in the global market place. The time of rapid economic growth has

---

[1] *The Sunday Times*, July 8, 2007.

passed. Indeed, in each decade, Singapore's economic growth has slowed. From double-digit Gross Domestic Product (GDP) growth in the eighties, potential growth is projected optimistically at 3% to 5% for the rest of this decade. It will be even tougher to grow over the decades after that.[2] There will be more competition in the region, with countries such as China, India and Indonesia, and the ascent of cities like Shanghai, Mumbai, Jakarta, and more, are likely to diminish the role of Singapore as an international centre, whether for business, finance, trade or transit. They will provide greater competition for the investments of global companies, who are looking to place a factory, research and development centre, or international headquarters. While Singapore has done well to constantly adapt and move up the value chain to provide a strong proposition to such companies, to continue to lean heavily on the foreign investment development model, which requires making the right bets, is a risky one. As the investment disclaimer goes: past performance is no guarantee of future success.

How Singapore grows will therefore have to change. A more sustainable approach is to put greater emphasis on developing homegrown, global companies, and to innovate, in order to push growth far beyond what its actual physical limits will allow. But this requires a system that encourages individual risk-taking, and big, bold ideas, for talent and capital to flow into entrepreneurship, creating a vibrant, self-sustaining ecosystem. The economy must continue to provide meaningful and decent-paying jobs to a larger number of educated graduates across a variety of fields, making economic planning all the more complex.

How income and wealth inequality is managed will also be key. The perceived fairness of the system in how it rewards, taxes and redistributes will come under more scrutiny, given global and domestic developments that have served to widen the gap between rich and poor. It will require deft skill to strike the balance between being competitive yet compassionate, and business-friendly yet citizen-friendly.

The second trend is demographic. Singapore has a small and ageing population. Even if the population were to increase to as much as 10 million,

---

[2] In the Population White Paper the Government estimated average GDP growth of 3–5% until 2020 based on 2–3% productivity growth per year. Beyond 2020, it said that average GDP growth of 2–3% a year from 2020 to 2030 might be possible.

Singapore would still be far smaller than its neighbours.[3] How the population size and mix are managed will be critical to Singapore's long-term prosperity and stability. A population that grows too large, too quickly, will have its attendant problems of crowding and social unease. We have already seen the effects in recent years.

Yet unless the low total fertility rate[4] were to go drastically against the trend, without allowing for the population to grow in other ways, Singapore's population will age faster, putting a greater burden on future generations. It will impede the competitiveness of Singapore companies, which do not have the benefit of a large domestic market to give them the resources and capital to compete regionally or globally. A greying population will also have implications for the long-term dynamism of the economy and its ability to attract young talent.

The third trend is political. The most crucial factor undergirding Singapore's success has been the sociopolitical stability over the last 50 years, in contrast to more unpredictable developments elsewhere in the region.

But it is looking more likely that one-party rule has been an exception that cannot be sustained. A normalisation process is now taking place in the political landscape. A greater variety of communication platforms is fuelling more debate, and increased education and wealth have created a diversity of demands and needs. They are adding to the general restlessness for change to one-party dominance. It is difficult to see this trend reversing.

Within this more competitive political climate, can there still be stable, long-sighted governance? Or will politics succumb to short-termism and populism? With issues of cultural values gaining prominence, will politics become a contest of ideology and values, pitting conservatives against liberals, and deepening social divides?

Given these trends, growing up in Singapore in the next 50 years promises to be a much more challenging prospect than it is today. But this future need not necessarily be bleak.

---

[3] Dr. Liu Thai Ker, Singapore's former chief planner, has argued that Singapore should plan for a population of as many as 10 million in the long term.

[4] The TFR for Singapore rose to 1.25 in 2014, up from 1.19 in 2013, but is still below the replacement rate of 2.1.

Any "decline" will, after all, be relative. It is relative to Singapore's past performance, but also relative to the region in which Singapore is located, which will be subject to geopolitical tensions, black swan events, and each country, its own share of domestic concerns. Technological progress, which is disrupting our lives at a faster pace, will change how we age, live and work, and the need for economic scale, and could well help overcome Singapore's economic and demographic constraints.

But while it is certainly fathomable to envision "more of the same" over the next 50 years — that is continued economic growth, prosperity and stability — a more realistic forecast is for economic growth to indeed slowdown, and for there to be greater social and political instability. But does that mean Singapore's golden age has come and passed?

I disagree. I posit that the best days are still ahead, that Singapore's real pinnacle as a society has yet to arrive. Crucially, beyond policy, it is our society's culture and values that will guide how we as a people respond to these challenges. I hope that over the next 50 years there will be a moderation of economic preeminence in national strategy and an opportunity to focus on the nurturing of arts, culture, and philanthropy. That there will be more opportunities to understand Singapore's shared history and values, which are fundamental to the development of national identity. This requires greater citizen activism, tolerance, and the open sharing of ideas, anchored by a collective desire to keep Singapore exceptional through openness, diversity, and human endeavour.

These may seem incongruous with the coming economic, social and political challenges. But they are not. As economic growth becomes harder to come by, and as differences are highlighted and tensions rise, it is these underlying values and spirit that will keep Singapore united, a country to be proud of, and truly a nation worth fighting for. The future is uncertain, but I hope that rather than tear us apart, it will bring us closer together, making us a more confident, more vibrant nation. That would be the true mark of Singapore's golden age.

Singapore may never reach the heights of growth and stability again, but the next 50 years could give rise to a much more meaningful period in our history. That is a future not to be feared, but to be embraced.

Where the Wild Things Are

Chua Mui Hoong
Opinion Editor
The Straits Times

Every few months or so, I go in search of my wildlife fix.

I go somewhere quiet and green, armed with a camera phone, sometimes a pair of binoculars, and always with a sense of anticipation. Will I be lucky enough to spot wild creatures as they go about their daily life? To be in the right place at the right time, to witness a white-bellied sea eagle swoop on its prey, or to see the moment when two damselflies perform their courtship dance?

Will I have my National Geographic moment?

This morning was one of those days. The haze that had hung like a pall over Singapore for a week, courtesy of forest burning to clear land in Indonesia, had lifted. It was the annual migratory season for birds, so I decided to make a trip to the Sungei Buloh Wetland Reserve with a friend. The first hour was thin on sightings. Even the large colonies of monitor lizards had chosen to stay away that morning, and nary a one was in sight. We reconciled ourselves to zilch sightings. It was in that poverty of spirit, and just when I decided to give up and just enjoy the walk, that we began to spot wild creatures. A white-breasted kingfisher sang on a branch. A school of archer fish glided in the sun-dappled riverine water, its neon tip glittering. Up ahead, a monitor lizard slithered out of our path.

As we rounded a corner, a heron on a branch greeted us — a distinctive squat silhouette that called to mind a creature we had seen before, on one outing to Pulau Ubin, its crown and back dark, and its breast pale. I checked the list of birds at the main hide, and narrowed down its identity to a little heron or a dark-crowned night heron. Back home, I looked up my *New Holland Field Guide to the Birds of South-East Asia* and confirmed it was the latter. The night heron is active in the day but hunts at night. The desire to identify a bird I had spotted, and to get its species just right, remains strong. The human need to name, categorise and understand wild creatures, and ultimately to retain a sense of control, is hard to put away.

The heron opened our eyes to more. The mudflats were grey and sandy. A first glance yielded little. But as we slowed down and looked more intently, we saw dozens, then hundreds of migratory birds. Sandpipers, redshanks, whimbrels, and on the far shore, herons and egrets. In the waters, jumping fish kept flashing in the sun. Wildlife rewards those who take time to slow down and look, not those who hurry through a reserve.

And then came a special moment for me. On the far bank of the river, my partner spotted a large grey heron on the water's edge. It was standing ankle deep in water, eyes intent on the flowing river. As I watched through the binoculars, it craned its neck and its leg started to move half a step, and then it paused. I continued my gaze. And in that flash of a moment, a fish chose to jump out of the water. The fish in mid-air was framed perfectly in the small round of my binocular's field of vision, with the grey heron picturesque beyond it. I could see water droplets spray, and the flat face of the fish and its pale eye gleaming at me in the sun. And then the fish plunged back into the water and was gone.

It lasted barely a second but I had my National Geographic moment. The mosquito bites, the sun, the long drive to Kranji fighting tipper trucks, were all worth it.

What is it about wildlife encounters that lift the soul? For me, they represent an encounter with serendipity, that intersection of my here and now, with that of the creature I am seeing. It reminds me that the chance encounter wrought by a synchronicity of time and space can bring moments of beauty and awareness that no amount of planned experience can replicate.

Those moments speak to my soul, reminding me that sometimes, the best approach to life is to let go, and let things happen. I have often felt that wildlife spotting is good discipline and therapy for a Type A, highly strung individual. Out of the urban landscape, in the forest, or on the wetland reserve, we are brought out of our need to control the environment, and brought face to face with our sense of powerlessness. No human, no matter how powerful, can command the presence of wildlife. A wild bird appears at its will, not ours. When we understand this, we also understand something else: that humans may name, categorise, study and otherwise manipulate wildlife, but they remain wild creatures fundamentally beyond our control. Then we will learn to see beyond our anthropocentric perspective.

Seeing wildlife in their habitats remind us that this world is not ours alone, and that we share it with myriad other creatures. When we enter a nature reserve, we are guests in wild creatures' homes and must accord them the respect due to hosts.

As I write this in October 2014, it is my fervent wish that Singaporeans in the year 2065 will continue to be able to find pockets of nature where they can have encounters with wildlife, and learn all that such experiences can teach.

This is no easy endeavour, in a city of just 710 square kilometres. The Urban Redevelopment Authority's 2013 Master Plan says that 9% of the planned land area in 2030 will be set aside for parks and nature reserves. That sounds like quite a lot — but the Nature Society of Singapore points out that only 4.4% of land in 2030 is committed to preserving flora and fauna. The rest is made up of parks, and "nature areas" which are vacant land which lie fallow until the government has development plans. They are not areas which are safe from development.

To be fair to the Singapore government, it has done a good job to preserve the country's natural heritage. According to the 2009 Sustainable Singapore blueprint, "A Lively and Liveable Singapore: Strategies for Sustainable Growth," "Between 1986 and 2007, the green cover in Singapore grew from 36% to 47% despite a 68% growth in population." It notes that 10% of Singapore's land is committed as green space, of which about half are gazetted nature reserves. It has expanded on the park connector network; preserved the rail corridor; and conserved Chek Jawa in Pulau Ubin. It set aside Sungei Buloh as a bird sanctuary. The latter is an accredited member of the East Asian-Australasian Flyway for migratory birds, a network of over 113 sites in 16 countries that allow about 50 million migratory birds to rest and recharge during their annual marathon flights to avoid harsh winters in their homelands.

Will these efforts be enough? And will future citizens learn to appreciate, and conserve Singapore's tremendous biodiversity? It is home to 2900 species of plants, 360 species of birds and 250 species of hard coral. With a land mass equal to just 0.2% the size of the United Kingdom, it has 60% of the number of species found in the UK.

My concern is twofold. One: Whether our resident and migrant wildlife can adapt, and still find spaces and the ecosystem to support their habitats, so they can grow and breed, generation after generation.

There is some hope yet, that local creatures are as adept as our citizens, in adapting to rapid urbanisation. The vivid blue flash of the collared kingfisher is a common sight in nature areas, and in parks and even in Housing Board estates, testament to its hardiness. After a successful conservation project, the hornbill is thriving, and can even be spotted sometimes sitting on lamp posts in Seletar. Wild otters have been spotted around the northern shoreline, and even as far south as the Marina Bay area.

But when natural habitats shrink, wildlife starts to encroach into human habitats. And when wildlife and humans interact, it is often to the detriment of the former. This leads to my second concern: Can we humans adapt to the close proximity of wildlife?

When we come across wild creatures in our daily lives, when they encroach into our residential and recreational areas, how do we react? To be sure, human safety remains a key priority. So when a wild boar ambled across Upper Thomson Road, from Peirce Reservoir to Bishan Park, and a boy was hurt, the authorities started a campaign to cull the numbers to keep the population in check. But if safety were not an issue, could we learn to live and let live? And when we encounter wild creatures in their habitats, can we understand that we are the interlopers in their natural habitats, and accord them the respect due to any resident in their own homes? Can we leave the wild otters to frolic in the waters unmolested? And teach our children the right response to wild creatures is not to throw stones at them, chase them, or frighten them away, but to give them space and leave them be?

In the past, at Sungei Buloh, visitors have seen many lizards draped across the walkway, right in the path of human visitors. They splay and sun themselves as though it was their grandfathers' land — as indeed it is. But this morning, we spotted just three reptiles. Two were in the water, and one was clambering away as we approached. When we asked one staff why there were fewer lizards, he told us: "There have been many groups of schoolchildren coming in the mornings, and the lizards have learnt to hide from them. The kids take selfies with them and frighten them away."

Two generations ago, kampong boys may run after monitor lizards, wanting to catch and cook them for food. A generation ago, the instinct might be to shun them. Today's generation brought up in an era where everything is under control may have little fear of wildlife, and seek to tame wild animals with a selfie. What of tomorrow's young? Will they learn to put some distance between themselves and wild creatures, and give them the space they need, to thrive? If wildlife adapt to humans, by thriving in human built environments, could we humans also learn to adapt, and keep our instinct to control and tame wild creatures, and give them sufficient berth to remain wild?

Zero Waste Nation?

Feng Zengkun
Environment Correspondent
The Straits Times

In 2065, every household and business in Singapore will be less than 300 m from a recycling bin or chute.

After the recyclables are deposited in the bins and chutes, they will be whisked by collectors to a large centralised plant that uses advanced machinery to sort out the different waste types with minimal manpower.

The overall recycling rate will have exceeded the old 2030 target of 70% by some measure, reducing the amount of waste that needs to be burned and the ashes buried in the expanded landfill on the nearby Pulau Semakau island.

A fantasy? Yes, but not one that is completely out of reach.

In the past year, Singapore has made giant strides towards this once-unlikely future.

In October last year (2014), for the first time, every single public housing block of flats had a recycling bin for residents, compared to one bin for every five blocks previously.

The same year, the Government announced that every new block of flats would also have chutes for recyclables on every floor, further reducing the excuses for not doing the right thing.

For its part, the National Environment Agency (NEA) launched three big projects, including one that may turn out to be pivotal to the 2065 vision.

The agency outlined plans for a new type of multi-storeyed recycling plant that could vastly improve the city-state's capacity to deal with mountains of plastics, paper, metals, glass and other recyclable waste.

The plant, slated to be built on a plot of land in Lim Chu Kang or within the Sarimbun Recycling Park in the area, will also be designed to be generic and adaptable enough for other sites and future expansion.

A second piece of the waste management solution was the NEA's proposal for a new mega waste treatment plant.

By "mega," I mean the integrated facility will be able to deal with half of Singapore's waste when it begins operations in 2024.

The Tuas plant will be able to handle solid waste, food waste, recyclables and, in a first, even sewage sludge from water treatment plants.

It will also extract resources like biogas and energy from the rubbish, joining four existing waste-to-energy incineration plants in Tuas and Senoko and a fifth to be completed by 2018.

Taken together, all of the developments and projects represent a single, multi-pronged attempt to plug gaps in, expand and refine the island's ability to cope with its trash.

But it is NEA's third project, a table-top exercise, which may turn out to be the most important one of all.

In July last year (2014), the agency uploaded a set of documents on government procurement website GeBIZ, to ask for proposals to review how the country collects, sorts, separates, recycles and treats its rubbish.

The project was expected to provide "a clear and realistic" vision for the country's waste management future up to 2030, and a more "ambitious" one for 2050.

The documents outlined in detail an internal review the agency had done, and the areas that it had found lacking.

In waste collection, for example, it noted that "most of the current waste collection equipment and facilities, such as the single steam chute system in most high-rise flats, do not allow for separate storage and collection of waste streams."

This makes it more inconvenient for people to separate their dry and wet waste, for example paper and plastics from food waste, to recycle more of both types.

It added that Singapore uses both indirect and direct collection methods, but the direct version, which involves a refuse truck with two crew members going door-to-door to collect the rubbish, is labour-intensive and time-consuming.

Since it is difficult to find and retain people to do such jobs, "improvements are needed to at least double the manpower productivity to meet the waste management demand in 2030," the NEA said.

The same problem exists in the sorting of the recyclables. Currently, mixed recyclables collected from homes, offices, and companies are sent to different firms for sorting. But most of these firms are small-scale operations that employ people to do the separation.

"Manual sorting is considered both expensive and time-consuming when handling large volumes of materials," the NEA said.

The potential cracks and leaks in the system would be worrying in any circumstance. But the NEA had, in earlier projections, estimated a 57% increase in rubbish between 2013 and 2030.

In 2030, Singapore would generate 12.3 million tonnes of trash, or 12,300,000,000 kg of it. This is equivalent to 400 kg of waste created per second that year, up from about 250 kg per second in 2013. The 2065 figure will most certainly be even higher.

While the agency has successfully pushed the overall recycling rate over the years from 40% in 2000 to 61% in 2013, the achievement masks several sobering trends.

The overall 61% recycling rate was achieved because almost all of the construction debris, used slag, ferrous metal and scrap tyres were recycled, with the rates at 99%, 97%, 97% and 88% respectively.

But other types of rubbish that are more associated with households had dismal recycling rates. The rates for paper, glass, food and plastics were as low as 54%, 20%, 13% and 11% respectively.

In fact, the non-domestic recycling rate for 2013 was 77%, while the domestic or household recycling rate was far below that at just 20%.

This chasm is why, in 2014, the Ministry for the Environment and Water Resources took the unprecedented step of setting separate recycling targets for the household and industrial sectors.

Instead of just aiming to recycle 70% of all rubbish by 2030, it specified that households should aim to recycle 30% of their rubbish by then, while industries should aim for a rate of 81%.

Boosting the household recycling rates is also likely to be an uphill task. The rates for glass and food grew by just 11 and 6 percentage points respectively between 2001 and 2013, while the rate for plastics rose by a single, embarrassing percentage point.

The new projects, including the provision of recycling bins across all housing blocks, will go a long way towards plugging the infrastructural gaps. Other solutions suggested by experts, such as the importing of advanced, automated waste-sorting machines from overseas, can fix man-power problems.

But more direct ways of influencing people's behaviour may be needed, if the passive supply of infrastructure does not work effectively enough.

While the government's recycling goal of 70% of waste by 2030 may seem an environmental good, it is in fact also an imperative for Singapore.

The Semakau landfill is only expected to be filled up by 2035, although the authorities hope it will last longer. In its review of the waste situation, the NEA stressed that "land is extremely scarce and only one offshore landfill is available."

What will Singapore do once that option is literally closed off? Will the tiny city-state-country have to ship the burnt ashes of its waste overseas, or find ways to use it in, say, construction at a premium, as it has tried before?

To head off and minimise the potential dilemmas, "it is critical to reduce, reuse and recycle waste more effectively and improve our waste-to-resource management system," the NEA said, adding that failure to do so would affect Singapore's vaunted clean and sustainable living environment and business competitiveness.

To nudge Singaporeans into action, some changes may be needed.

Between 2012 and earlier this year (2015), the NEA progressively introduced a uniform fee for waste collection for all HDB households, and another uniform fee for landed property households, in order to aid in the consolidation of the nine public waste collection sectors into six sectors.

This was intended to help the waste collectors gain economies of scale, to mitigate the rising costs of labour and fuel. The savings would in turn moderate residents' waste collection fees against the industry's growing costs.

But a flat fee does not give households any incentive to recycle or cut back on their waste. A "pay as you throw" system on the other hand would encourage people to recycle more and dump less.

Taipei began such a system in 2000, with residents being required to buy government trash bags to throw away their household rubbish. The amount of waste dumped at the Shanchuku landfill in the Nangang District plummeted from 2,501 tonnes per day in 1994 to just 59 tonnes a day in 2009.

Greater partnerships with firms or even laws will also be needed to tackle specific waste types like plastics and electronics waste, which is on the rise.

A partnership between telecommunications firm StarHub, DHL Express and homegrown recycling firm TES-AMM, supported by the NEA, aims to put hundreds of bins around the island in the next few years to collect people's unwanted mobile phones, laptops, lithium-ion batteries, set-top boxes and other electronics.

The Singapore Packaging Agreement between the NEA, companies and non-government groups to reduce packaging waste from consumer products and their supply chains, also resulted in 20,000 fewer tonnes of packaging waste between 2007 and 2014. The agreement has been extended to 2020.

These are all examples that should be replicated and expanded.

In Sweden, companies are required by law to handle all costs related to the collection, recycling or appropriate disposal of their products. So if a beverage is sold in bottles, the financial responsibility is on the producer of the product to pay for all costs related to recycling or bottle disposal.

In Singapore, people are not required by law to recycle bottles, cans and food waste, which make up significant amounts of trash in the country. In 2013, the Republic generated 796,000 tonnes of food waste alone, an increase of 13% from the 703,200 tonnes in 2012.

While Singapore may not need or want to go as far legislatively as Sweden, more needs to be done to tackle the types of waste that are persistently and largely thrown away and not recycled. This includes plastics as well as electrical and electronic equipment such as home appliances.

But the most crucial change that is needed is intangible — it is in people's mindset towards re-using and reducing, two of the three Rs that have been Singapore's mantra for decades. While Singapore and Singaporeans have made great progress in achieving and maintaining its clean and green reputation through the final R, recycling, the best way to prevent the country from having to deal with more waste is to not have that much of it in the first place.

If the utopian view of 2065 is to be achieved, a master plan for the country's future and futuristic waste management systems will help, but it is not ideal. People can make it happen by taking advantage of the new infrastructure to recycle their waste, but they can also lessen the country's burden and worries in a simpler way — by creating less of it.

Vintage Years

Salma Khalik
Senior Health Correspondent
The Straits Times

Grey will be a common colour.

Although many seniors may dye their hair as they age, most men would welcome the dignity of a silver crop, especially as they approach their century mark.

There would be no avoiding the pervasive presence of seniors at public spaces as most elderly folk will be out and about, unlike today.

Indeed, by 2065, Singapore can expect its people's average life expectancy to be in the high 90s, given that the average lifespan has been rising by three years every 10 years, since the country's independence.

In 1965, it was 65 years. This year, the average hovers around 84 years with about 1,000 people above age 100.

As the trend has remained consistent, a lifespan of more than 100 years in Singapore in 50 years' time is not far-fetched.

Both Japan and the United States already have more than 50,000 centenarians each today, with figures in both countries projected to grow as their populations continue to age.

Like the elderly of today, they too will fear ill health, not having enough money and loneliness in their twilight years, especially for the many singles who will grow old with no children or grandchildren to care for them.

But they will be much more fortunate, for advances in healthcare and technology will make their lives a far more fulfilling one.

So what kind of life will the hundreds of thousands of octo- and nonagenarians in Singapore be leading in 2065?

Certainly, they will not be lying in bed, waiting for the Grim Reaper.

Health and Mobility

Most will be striding out with artificial knees and hips, feeling energised by vitamins and living a life less fearful as pills keep their blood pressure, cholesterol and blood sugar levels in check.

A major focus of medical research today is in diseases and disabilities of ageing, such as dementia, osteoporosis, cardiovascular diseases and cancers.

Already, there are vaccines against certain cancers, such as cervical, liver and certain prostate cancers. According to the United States' National Cancer Institute, there is active current research into 14 more anti-cancer vaccines, including those for breast, lung and blood cancers.

There is also a host of vaccines against various infectious diseases, with many more being developed, that will protect people against dengue, the flu, pneumonia, herpes and HIV/Aids.

Developments in medicine have already resulted in the possible reversal of weakened heart tissue, so that heart failure patients can actually grow stronger and do far more than they could before.

For countries like Singapore with its high rate of diabetes (9% of adults here have diabetes), research into a cure is terribly exciting. One of the most promising is the transplanting of insulin-producing cells into the pancreas to reverse the body's inability to deal with blood sugar.

If successful, it holds the promise of repairing the ravages on the body by diabetes, including kidney failure — doing away with the need for dialysis and transplants.

Nevertheless, as lives get longer, some will eventually become frail. But mechanical aids will ensure they do not live a sedentary life unless they choose to.

In short, these better-educated elderly of the future will be in control and more determined to stay in touch with the world about them.

Today, hundreds of older people are already zipping about their neighbourhoods in motorised wheelchairs and scooters designed for the elderly.

They retain their independence with these electric mobiles that let them do their own marketing, go out for lunch or a show with friends, or simply to the nearby park for exercise.

By 2065, such mobiles will be a common sight and the physical landscape will need to change to cater to their proliferation.

Most notably, pathways have to be widened, and the MRT will have to provide them space as will restaurants and cinemas.

As more seniors take to them, scooter lanes will have to be built across Singapore, much like the walking and cycling paths that thread through housing estates nowadays.

HDB flats will also need to be modified to accommodate them: lifts have to be bigger or perhaps parking and recharging bays in the void decks have to be built. Parking bays for these scooters could well replace the potted plants that dot today's HDB corridors.

In spite of the best medical care, frailty will set in for most.

But even severe frailty can be overcome for seniors bent on remaining independent but no longer able to handle a motorised wheelchair or scooter.

Both Japan and South Korea are working on nerve stimulated arms and legs that can enable a paralysed person to move around.

This is how it works: Light titanium rods are attached to the arms and legs when the senior wakes up. These can be controlled with minimum movement. A squeeze of the bum muscles will move him from a sitting to a standing position. A slight twitch in the leg muscle will result in the foot taking a step forward. A shrug of the shoulder will lift the arm.

Even a person suffering severe paralysis from a major stroke may be able to care for himself with minimal help.

All he needs is for a carer to help him put on the robotic limbs in the morning and to remove them at night.

The prototype costs about $1 million. But as production ramps up, fuelled by demand, the price will inevitably fall.

In fact, as robotics and information technology become more prevalent, today's frail, elderly person who is dependent on others for every need may, on his own, be able to sit on the living room sofa and remotely clean the house, do the washing and shop for groceries.

While nursing homes will continue to be in demand for the very frail or those with severe dementia, most dementia patients will be able to continue staying at home, with electronic "pets" safeguarding them.

These "pets" will read the person's mood and initiate action to protect the patient. When he gets agitated, it will make soothing purring sounds and distract the person. When the person goes out, it follows and shows him the way home.

Studies in Japan shows the frail elderly would cling to these pets for emotional support and listen to what they say rather than the words of even the closest of relatives.

Doctors believe it is because they perceive no threat from a "pet."

These pets will be multifunctional, taking regular health readings and transmitting them to a healthcare provider, reminding the patient to take their medicine and alerting emergency medical staff if a dangerous medical situation is imminent.

But such quality comfort comes at a price. How will the majority manage to pay for it all?

Financial Security

Some things, such as major health procedures, would be taken care of largely with MediShield Life, the national insurance scheme that will cover everyone for life. But even so, there are premiums to pay, as well as co-payment for large hospital bills.

Collecting CPF monies at age 55 and retiring at age 62 could well become a memory of less hectic and demanding times.

By 2065, Singaporeans can expect to remain in the workforce for at least another 15 to 20 years, because they will not only be able to, but because they would also need the income to stretch their savings for their elongated lifespan.

It will no longer be feasible for most people to use savings accumulated from working for 40 years to live in retirement for another 40 years.

People have to work for many more years than they do today to afford these comforts of life as they age.

Regardless of whether they work full-time or part-time, get paid the same or less than they did when younger, the majority will remain in the workforce because not doing so will no longer be an option for the majority.

However, continuing to work has benefits other than financial independence.

Medical benefits, for one, will still be available for the seniors to keep chronic diseases at bay. They will have the mental stimulation from interacting with colleagues and clients. And for the single elderly, it staves off loneliness as they will continue to be surrounded by people they know.

Loneliness in Twilight Years

One of the greatest fears of the elderly is being lonely in their twilight years. But these Internet-savvy seniors will have social media to keep them plugged into the community.

Catering to seniors will be big business with every neighbourhood having their seniors clubs that organise activities for them. In the United States, Australia and some European countries, these are fast becoming popular.

These clubs provide seniors with a one-stop service for all their home needs, such as plumbing, repairs and even grocery shopping — at discounted members' prices.

They also organise games days, such as bridge with super large cards for easy reading and mahjong; talks on subjects of interest to the elderly, such as where to get things — like can openers that do not require two hands to operate — that will make their lives easier; visits to restaurants that cater especially to seniors.

Restaurants that offer healthier options or food that is easier to chew with dentures and digest would draw a long line of these silver-haired diners.

Slogans like "Tasty, nutritious with no need for Nexium to prevent heartburn," or "Meat so tender, you won't need your dentures" may well be the standard banner at eateries.

Advancing age is unlikely to stop future seniors from travelling. As most would be seasoned travellers, their preference will be for more leisurely quality holidays over the hectic six-cities-in-eight-days trips for newbies.

Cruises will be a top draw as it obviates the need to pack and unpack at each new city.

And a conducted tour would have to extend such standard offerings as porter service for luggage, frequent toilet breaks, and perhaps even a nurse or doctor to attend to illnesses that typically afflict the old, such as diarrhoea or heartburn from eating unfamiliar food, aches and pains from too much walking while sightseeing, or even the occasional heart attack.

It will be a rich life for seniors in 2065. Few will have time to be lonely or depressed, with activities to keep them busy, and the health and money to enjoy them.

Singapore 2015–2065: 50 Years of Adaptive Innovation

Vikram Khanna
Associate Editor
The Business Times

As we celebrate National Day 2065, it is instructive to reflect on how we have evolved over this century. We have faced many challenges, but we can take some pride in our achievements, as a city, society and nation. We have weathered health pandemics, a major terrorist attack, six recessions, sea storms and flooding. Our society has aged — our median age is now approaching 50 and we have more than 10,000 centenarians in our midst.

We have changed governments, endured disputes with our neighbours and adapted to a rapidly changing world. Our economy has created and absorbed innovations that would have been considered science fiction fifty years ago. Despite changes in our demographics and our ethnic and social mix, we have remained cohesive as a society. At independence a century ago, it was still an open question whether Singapore would retain its sovereignty a hundred years later. We have transformed, in many ways beyond recognition, but we are still here as a nation.

Many of the past debates on Singapore's nationhood, identity as well as population and urban environment have, in retrospect, become moot — a reminder of how easily we are influenced by immediate circumstances and how much we underestimate our capacity to innovate and change.

The issue of population is a case in point. Back in 2013, the Government released a landmark White Paper on Population which projected that Singapore's population would grow to 6.9 million by 2030. While that was a projection and not a target, the public reaction at the time was overwhelmingly negative. People and even some academics pointed out that there was no way Singapore could absorb such a large number of people, particularly in terms of housing and infrastructure.

According to the census of 2064, Singapore's population has grown to 12.1 million. While statistically we are the 10th most densely populated city in the world, we still win accolades for being one of the most liveable of urban environments. Almost 30% of land space is allocated for recreational use. More than 80% of people live within a 10-minute walk from a public park as well as a metro; there are 125 km of waterways, many of them navigable.

For all this and more, we must credit some of the innovations we have made over the last half century in urban planning, transportation and connectivity, and our continued ability to harness cutting edge technologies.

Energy use is one area where innovation has served us particularly well. It has been a challenge because the explosive growth of urbanisation over the last half century has created enormous demand for energy.

Fossil fuel technologies are still the most important source. But the reserves of some fossil fuels are fast depleting. There was panic in the industry in 2021 after the discovery that Saudi Arabia's oil reserves had been overstated by three times — although natural gas production from Russia, the United States, the Middle East and Australia have grown substantially and explorations elsewhere are continuing. Liquefied natural gas technologies became ubiquitous over the last twenty years.

But other technologies have also advanced. By 2030, there was a marked shift to relying on more diverse energy sources — especially among high energy importing countries such as China and India. Wind, solar and fuel-cell technologies began to proliferate. This has helped to prevent the rise of pollution which, given the degree of urbanisation and concomitant energy demand, would have been exponential.

In most urban areas across Asia, including Singapore, vehicular pollution has been dramatically reduced. From about 2025 to 2050, first petrol-electric hybrids, and then plug-in electric vehicles were the most common form of urban transportation, as mileage rates from electric cars increased and charging times were progressively reduced. But from 2050 onward, driverless hydrogen fuel-cell cars began to take their place as the associated infrastructure expanded and manufacturing costs came down.

While gas-based power stations are still the mainstay of Singapore's electricity generation, alternative energy sources are also tapped. After initial attempts, wind energy did not prove viable due to Singapore's low wind velocities, but tidal energy — based on highly predictable tidal movements came on stream in 2040 with the construction of two tidal lagoons.

About 20% of the energy for domestic and industrial use comes from concentrated solar thermal power which uses specialised mirrors and lenses to concentrate solar rays. Giant mirrors atop hundreds of rooftops reflect and concentrate solar rays on four energy towers, which convert them to energy. These towers are spread across the island and are connected to the power grid.

A few buildings have their own captive power from photovoltaic paint — a thin-film form of photovoltaic like a second skin, which emits solar energy sufficient to power the building. This is common in the buildings on the four floating islands off the southern coast.

We have also innovated in the development of our urban environment.

During the first 50 years of nationhood, land reclamation from the sea was the key means by which we were able to create space for new urban development Changi Airport, Marina Bay and parts of Tuas were built on such land. But reclaiming land from the sea proved unsustainable for two reasons. One was that repeated reclamations created frictions with our neighbours, Malaysia and Indonesia, which we resolved peacefully but not without difficulty. The second was the continued rise of sea levels in the wake of climate change and the melting of glaciers. Global sea levels have risen about 15 centimetres over the last 50 years, which has raised the risks of sinking land and sea storms — which we have experienced sporadically, and which are now recurrent problems in especially delta cities such as Kolkata, Shanghai and Guangzhou.

Thus over the last 50 years, more usable land area has been added by the re-routing of roads, the expansion of underground highways and commercial space, and the creative reclamation of airspace. For instance, the road to the airport that used to go along the old East Coast Parkway (ECP) now runs above the sea off the coast, thus freeing up the entire stretch of the old ECP for housing and recreational development. Much of the Ayer Rajah Expressway (AYE) runs underground all the way from the city centre to the border with Malaysia, which has likewise freed up a huge swathe of land for urban development and helped transform the one-time swamp of Jurong into a thriving mini-metropolis in its own right.

In public housing developments built after 2025, 50 storey structures have been the norm. Half a century ago, there was only one such development, The Pinnacle at Duxton; the typical public housing block was 20 storeys high. Many of our buildings are now fabricated by 3-D printers, using cement, sand and steel reinforcements. Building times have been reduced to two weeks and construction costs are 70% lower than 50 years ago — although land prices have gone up sevenfold on average.

Architectural and structural innovations have also enabled new forms of building that can create more usable space without encroaching on vital city infrastructure. Some of these innovations were, in fact, first aired as long ago as 2014, when architects such as Tan Cheng Siong and Liu Thai Ker were already thinking of designing for a population of over 10 million.

Tan's vision of "Skyland" was a compelling inspiration for later architects. New structures such as inverted pyramid-shaped buildings provided additional living space without interfering with the functionality of inner-city and highways.

Taller buildings, more creative residential architecture and the shifting of not only artery roads but also substantial commercial and retail activity underground — where close to 2 million square feet of usable space has been added over the last 25 years — has enabled the construction of more than 1 million new housing units during that period. Underground space is also used for warehousing and chemical storage.

The transport infrastructure has been massively expanded. The rail network which covered only about 180 km in 2014 more than doubled to almost 400 km in 2030. Since then it has grown to more than 600 km. Water taxis and hydrofoils ply the waterways. There are travellators along key shopping districts like Orchard Road, Jurong East and Marina Bay, which obviate the need for cars in these areas. Buses still ply the roads, but the old fixed-route systems have been replaced by ones in which buses fitted with on-board computers can respond dynamically to demand and traffic situations in real time, thus reducing waiting times and easing traffic congestion. Trials have begun for Airpods — aerial personal transporters with fly-by-wire technology that will enable licensed individuals to fly to designated spots across the island, which will open up airspace for personal travel within Singapore.

Skyrise greenery was mentioned in early master plans this century, but work on this began in earnest only in 2025, with the launch of the Skyfarm Movement. Hundreds of apartment blocks were built with multi-level cascading gardens, and by 2060, there was a total of almost 100 hectares of greenery in high-rise buildings alone. The growing popularity of urban gardening and farming over the last 30 years has been striking. Indeed, farming has become a viable profession in its own right, employing close to 20,000 people. High-quality home grown organic vegetables, which are now available in abundance, are even exported and new varieties of rice have been pioneered by some of Singapore's urban farmers, who also create new genetically modified foods.

While the expansion of housing through the reclamation of airspace, new architectural designs and smart urban planning have contributed to Singapore's ability to accommodate an increased population, Singapore's expanded connectivity with neighbouring regions has played a major role.

Last year, we celebrated the 40th anniversary of the Singapore-Kuala Lumpur high-speed rail link, which was upgraded a decade ago to the latest generation post-Maglev rail system, which can achieve speeds of 450 km per hour — or as fast as many planes. The travel time to Kuala Lumpur, including 5 stops, is less than one hour, which has created new synergies and narrowed the property price gap between the two cities.

But the biggest transformation has been the development of much of the area between Singapore and Kuala Lumpur into a vast urban agglomeration with a total population of 22 million. Johore's population alone has gone up past 10 million, compared to just under 4 million in 2014. The Iskandar Development Zone which was launched early this century has become economically contiguous and integrated with Singapore. In its early years, its economy was driven by construction, manufacturing and healthcare services. From 2010 to 2020 there was a property boom and bust cycle, but that has since stabilised as more economic activities relocated to the area, both from Singapore and other parts of Asia. Tourism facilities and other specialised services also multiplied. With three land links and two sea-links, plus the high-speed rail, there is a seamless flow of workers and travellers between Singapore and Johore. Earlier in the century, there were political difficulties especially relating to worker flows — Singapore was concerned about overcrowding — but as the economy of Johore took off after 2025, these concerns dissipated. The development of Johore helped to decongest Singapore as well as add another engine of growth.

Another stellar achievement was the construction of the bridge to Batam, which was completed in 2030. Called the Singapore Straits Crossing, the idea to thus link Singapore by road to Indonesia was raised as far back as 2010 by Indonesian legislator Harry Azhar Azis. But it was only 15 years later, during the second term of President Joko Widodo, that the joint Indonesia-Singapore project was finalised. The 18 km long, eight-lane bridge, which starts at Sentosa and ends at the northern tip of Batam with exits at St. John's Island and Tanjung Sari, is a marvel of engineering. It has more than 5,000 pilings using pre-cast concrete-filled piles composed of fibre-reinforced polymers — a 30-year-old technology that has been progressively refined.

The road link has enabled more activities to relocate from Singapore — particularly manufacturing, but also some services. Since 2035, Batam has grown into a "retirement hub" with several retirement villages established, which have proved popular with older Singaporeans. The availability of relatively low-cost labour, together with well-developed leisure facilities and the easy connectivity with Singapore has made this industry viable. The accelerated development of Batam has also provided a boost to Singapore's construction industry.

Our economy continues to be vibrant. Our GNH (Gross National Happiness) and QOL (quality of life) indices have been on an upward trend over the last 20 years, with only three dips during the recessions of 2046, 2052 and 2059 which were caused by waves of economic activities relocating out of Singapore.

However, we have continued to attract niche, high-technology firms from around the world. Singapore can be proud of some of the innovations created here, including in recent years, the 3-D printing of entire human organs, the swallow-a-surgeon technologies that enable internal operations to be performed with ingestible drugs, new forms of additive manufacturing, image-recognition technologies, and nutrition-rich genetically modified foods.

We have also become a centre for the manufacture of service robots, personal flying machines and high-power solar reflectors. With urbanisation having spread across Asia and Africa over the last 50 years, our urban planners have drawn up master plans for more than 80 cities across these regions and are even working in Latin America. Some of our urban solutions are also in high global demand. Personal and entertainment services have also grown rapidly, especially after the shift to the 4-day work week in 2050.

Despite the many disruptive innovations in finance over recent decades, our stability, infrastructure and trusted legal system have enabled us to retain our position as the region's financial hub, now serving a larger hinterland, the whole of the ASEAN Economic Community (AEC) as well as the economies of China and India. Our attractiveness as a convention centre has also grown, including in the area of remote conventions, which enable viewers from around the world to participate virtually in meetings organised here.

We have faced our share of problems. The terrorist attack on Jurong Island in 2047 was the worst we had experienced, but we were able to contain the damage which otherwise would have been severe.

The global MEDS pandemic of 2051 also hit our shores and contributed to the recession in the following year, but our social and health systems were robust enough to deal with the crisis.

Sea storms have also become more common since 2040 in the wake of the rise of sea levels, but we have built strategic sea walls around some of our shore and established effective early warning systems.

Our society has continued to face problems with inequalities in wealth and incomes, but we have used our strong public finances to aggressively redress this issue. New economic opportunities — including within the AEC — and greater cross-border mobility have also helped to mitigate the problem.

We have done this while still remaining an outward-looking society with a global mindset. Earlier in this century, there were some misgivings about this. Between 2010 and 2020, we had turned more nationalistic and inward. In response to political pressures at the time, we tried to develop a Singaporean variant of Malaysia's "bumiputra" policy, purportedly to rely less on foreign workers and more on productivity. But this mistaken policy was subsequently relaxed and then reversed as it hurt our companies, created inefficiencies, discouraged investment, cut our growth, constrained our innovative capacity and did little to boost productivity. Over time, and with the help of innovation and with a greater hinterland, we successfully accommodated to a rising population.

As has always been the case throughout our history, our people have been our most valuable asset. New generations of Singaporeans have kept building on the solid foundations laid down by our founding fathers. We can look forward with confidence to the next 50 years.

Beyond 50: Foreign Contributors

Singapore in 50 Years from Now

Parkash Chander
Professor and Executive Director
Center for Environmental Economics and Climate Change
Jindal School of Government and Public Policy

What will Singapore be like 50 years from now? It is not too difficult to predict what it will likely be in the next 10, 15, or even 20 years. But 50 years is a different guessing game. As Donald Rumsfeld said, there are known unknowns and unknown unknowns. One can at best make an educated guess along with a fair dose of daydreaming and crystal gazing to predict what it will be like. Given the fast pace of technological advances, the world itself will be then very different and so will be Singapore.

One issue on which everyone seems to agree is that income inequality will increase. But I think it will increase in a far more dramatic fashion than has been hitherto thought. First, all low-skill jobs will be done by robots and computers and therefore workers with low skills will be either unemployed or command very low wages, if at all. Second, the ever increasing investments in education will eventually lead to oversupply of workers with middle-level skills. Therefore, workers with middle-level skills too will have difficulty finding jobs and will certainly have to work for low wages. Their status will be similar to those of low-skilled workers of today. Only a few workers with exceptional skills bordering genius will be in high demand. In fact, competition for hiring them will be fierce and they will command very high wages. Their status will be similar to those of rock stars of today. These labour market conditions will be further compounded by the fact that people will have longer life spans and easily live up to 120 years. They will be healthy and fit to work until the age of 80 years or more. Therefore, to maintain social harmony and keep tensions in check, all countries, including Singapore, irrespective of their economic or political ideology will have to have comprehensive welfare programmes. These welfare programmes may consist of either direct income transfers or indirect income transfers through massive government support for art and culture, sports, and community services among others. These activities will employ a large number of the less-skilled workers who will otherwise be unemployed. Most people will have plenty of time to relax, read and reflect. They will have more time to spend with family and friends. People will be more religious and spiritual. Many of them would have experienced space travel by then.

The welfare programmes will be financed by ever increasing taxes on industry and businesses which will generate most revenues, but employ few workers except those with exceptional skills and talents. The heavy taxes, however, will not make countries like Singapore less competitive as all countries will have to similarly impose taxes to finance their welfare programmes. Smaller countries like Singapore, which presently have to spend disproportionately more on defence of the country, will benefit relatively more as the world order will have evolved mechanisms that guarantee the sovereignty and independence of each country. As a result there will be no need to maintain disproportionately large armies and equipment.

To guess further what Singapore will be like in 2065, let us take stock of some of its weaknesses and strengths and how they may play out over the next 50 years.

Weaknesses

1. Shortage of land and labour
2. Lack of natural resources such as minerals, oil and gas
3. Small population
4. Dependence on foreign workers

Strengths

1. Rule of law
2. An educated and disciplined work force

3. A proactive leadership in government
4. A modern working infrastructure
5. A world-class airport and airline
6. A strong and growing financial and banking sector
7. A seaport with an advantageous geographical location
8. A modern healthcare and medicine sector
9. Two world-class universities

Let us also take note of some facts which cannot be classified either as strengths or as weaknesses. Only time will tell what they are.

A Strength or Weakness

1. No agriculture sector and hinterland
2. No experience of change in political power
3. Controlled media

Let us first take a look at how the current weaknesses of Singapore may play out over the next 50 years. Shortage of land will continue to be a problem, but will not be as serious a problem as it appears to be now. Technological advance will allow construction of high rise buildings with 400–500 stories, all surface transport will shift underground, shopping malls will no longer be necessary as all shopping will be done online. The land in Singapore will be highly valued and it will become home to a population of at least 10 million. People will work mostly from home and travel to work only twice a week. The need for travel will be minimal as most work will be done electronically from home. The land size of a country will become less important as the world will be then well connected and integrated. Communication and exchange of data will be instant.

Singapore's dependence on foreign workers will end much before 2065 as most routine jobs will be taken over by robots and computers. There will be no shortage of unskilled and semi-skilled workers. But rather than waiting for the robots to take over, the sooner the dependence on foreign workers is ended, the better it will be for Singapore. Meeting labour shortages by instantly hiring foreign workers may lead to faster economic growth but it disincentivises businesses and the government itself from making sufficient efforts to meet the shortages on their own. It discourages skill enhancement and upgrading. Growing one's own timber takes time and effort, but importing it is instant. However, as far as workers with exceptional skills and talents are concerned, Singapore will have to compete globally which it should be able to do if it continues to be an attractive place to work and live.

By 2065 the world would have exhausted most of its natural resources. It will become more dependent on recycling and renewables. Thus, Singapore will not be particularly disadvantaged. In fact, with its educated and disciplined population it will excel in recycling. In keeping with the global trends, Singapore will harness solar and wind energy. Hybrid nuclear power (generated by a combination of nuclear fusion and fission processes) will become cheaper and completely safe and clean. Thus, Singapore in all likelihood would have built at least a couple of hybrid nuclear power plants and electricity will be cheaper and available in abundance in 2065 than it is today. All rainwater will be automatically harvested, purified, stored, and made available for consumption. Desalination plants powered by hybrid nuclear energy will be common place and Singapore will be no exception.

Though a population of 10 million would still be small by global standards, it is significantly more than the 5–6 million today. What will matter more is the quality of the population. Even a population of just 10 million talented and active people can significantly influence world affairs and economy. Globalisation will continue. It will no longer be possible to control the media. People will look to the social media for news and analysis. Governments across the globe will be active on social media and many government policies and programmes will be shaped by discussions on the social media. Thus, like many other countries Singapore will become a more vibrant democracy and a more open society.

So much for Singapore's weaknesses! Coming to its strengths, the question is whether Singapore would continue to maintain those strengths and should it make efforts to maintain those strengths. The first four in the list seem non-negotiable as they are a necessary condition for Singapore to continue to attract capital, business and talent. Political changes cannot be ruled out as fifty years is a long time in the political life of any country. Though it is hard to imagine that the same political party will continue to govern Singapore in the next 50 years, Singaporeans having experienced good governance by the PAP governments will fall back upon it if their experiments with alternatives fail. The governing philosophy of PAP is an idea that will survive.

The Singapore seaport, because of its geographical location, will continue to play an important role in the economy. Though transporting goods by air will become increasingly popular, transporting bulk of goods by ships, which will be faster and larger in size, will still be the most economical. The Singapore airline will cease to be as profitable as it is now because of ever increasing competition in aviation. The financial and banking sector will continue to grow and become the main driver for Singapore's growth. Healthcare is yet another sector that will keep growing and become more profitable. Data analytics is a potentially new sector. Singapore will more likely be a knowledge-based economy than a manufacturing hub.

All in all, Singapore will continue to be a success story. The technological developments will eliminate mindless chores of housekeeping. The advances in medical science will make childbearing unnecessary and fathers will be equally responsible for bringing up children. Both these developments will further unleash women's power and creativity. Children, though not necessarily born from a womb, will be well taken care of and well educated. This will lead to a more prosperous, loving and caring Singapore. Women have come a long way in the last 50 years. This process will continue and the women in Singapore and the world will have an equal, if not dominant, role in society, politics, and economy. Singapore in 2065 will most likely have a woman as prime minister.

A Visitor Since Near the Beginning: Some Notes and Speculations

Jack L. Knetsch
Professor Emeritus
Simon Fraser University, Canada

There would have been few indeed who, at the time of my first visit in 1971, would have predicted the growth and the changes we see in Singapore at 50. From dealers and shippers of rubber, tin, and other local commodities, a dominance of low value-added and low paying activities, and a population that was largely ill-housed and lacking the education and organisation to take part in the gains available to others, the rule now is quite the opposite in nearly all dimensions.[1]

Rather than spending much time and effort on the largely pointless exercise of trying to predict the future and asserting their role in leading it, which seems a chief preoccupation of so many governments, Singapore's counterparts more usefully employed themselves in working out and implementing things that would lead to improvements. They largely avoided the temptations of quick fixes that drain resources and squander opportunities in providing only low-everything jobs, and concentrated instead on efforts to increase returns to labour and other factors and investments, while creating and taking advantage of complementarities to improve other aspects of people's lives — the latter perhaps exemplified by

[1] For a particularly well-informed review, see Lim (2007).

Singapore's early massive improvements in housing. Other examples of important policies and programmes that have led to the Singapore of today, and have, for the most part rightfully, been the subject of much comment and praise, include savings policies that have led to sustained high rates; education programmes that while sometimes leading to perpetuations of inequalities, and most certainly to an increase in traffic congestion as children are ferried over long distances at peak hours to "insure" their later success, have doubtless created a more productive workforce and a more engaged and probably happy and contented population; heavy reliance on merit in the granting of rewards, though the excesses of competition and the sometimes narrowness in the determination of merit may cut into their net benefits; trade and investment policies that, for the most part, have helped attract higher valued and higher paying activity; and a legal system and effective anti-corruption measures that have not only been an important attraction for investment but have contributed much to people's confidence in the fairness of how things are done.

Policies and programmes have focused, and continue to focus, largely on material income and wealth, in part due to the bias in economic accountings of gross domestic product (GDP) and the like that look almost exclusively at economic values that are registered in market exchanges, and exclude many other things that people are willing to sacrifice for, and thus have economic value as well, such as family wellbeing, environmental quality, personal safety and security, and savings in the time taken to commute to work or school, but also in part due to a high felt need to provide housing, higher paying jobs, higher incomes, and other things that by their nature are "material," and counted in the GDP figures. But it has not been entirely so. An interesting example of providing a non-material benefit, that is now almost entirely uncommented upon because of its long-standing familiarity and acceptance, is the almost total ban on outdoor advertising (and "billboards"), that so ruthlessly appropriate the aesthetic landscapes of so many developing and developed countries for the narrow mercenary benefit of a small group of predatory interests.

Another characteristic of Singapore policy design and implementation, that is perhaps of even more interest to a non-Singaporean, like myself, is the quickness in making changes in the face, and on the basis, of evidence of its impact or lack thereof. An outstanding example is how the growing numbers of motor vehicles might be controlled. The initial attempt was to follow the dictates of economics, and therefore the usual advice of economists, that if an activity is to be discouraged, it can usually be done most efficiently and effectively by raising its price. Consequently, in the interest of keeping the number of vehicles on the roads down, very large purchase taxes and charges were imposed that made the final price often three or more times larger than the before tax price. For some, usually less affluent potential buyers, the high purchase taxes had the desired effect of discouraging purchases. But for many, and rapidly growing numbers of others, the taxes had little impact — the response function was nearly vertical, suggesting that the main outcome was a fairly massive transfer of wealth from vehicle buyers to the Singapore Treasury. When this failure of the policy to so dramatically not meet its intended goal of reducing the numbers of vehicles on the roads was observed and understood, a dramatic change was implemented. Instead of setting the purchase price by the imposition of taxes, and hope that potential buyers would adjust to the extent needed to meet the total vehicle count goal of the policy, the change insured that this goal would be met by requiring a "certificate of entitlement" (COE) to purchase a vehicle, and then distributing only the exact number needed to meet the policy goal and awarding them to the highest bidders in an open auction. Instead of allowing the "market" to determine the number in response to a set price, a public agency now sets the number and allows the "market" to set the price. This degree of policy nimbleness is, unfortunately, rare elsewhere in the world of government and public policy.

The high buyer prices of vehicles, whether a function of high purchase taxes or high auction prices of COEs, raises another interesting aspect of policy design and implementation. Standard economics, and the usual policy advice based on it, suggests that fixed costs such as the purchase price of a vehicle, are "sunk" and of no matter in terms of whether the vehicle is used or not. That is supposedly dependent only on the added cost of using it and the benefit from its use. But, of course, as most people realise, and the empirical evidence is now confirming, people do not regard such fixed costs as irrelevant. They instead feel that they must use the vehicle ever more to "justify" paying the high purchase price — no doubt a major factor in making the average distance driven per year one of the very highest in the world, in spite of Singapore's small size. Whether from an explicit recognition of this "fixed cost effect" or not, the policy in Singapore is changing to reduce the fixed costs and raise the variable costs of using the vehicle — a change likely to have a far more socially useful impact on use decisions.

In part because of deliberate intent, and in part due to the ease of implementing policy in a small urban city relative to the difficulty of doing so in a large diverse country, Singapore has in its years accumulated a likely unmatched collection of experienced policy experiments and adjustments that is of great value for the country as it moves forward. But this experience would also be of perhaps even greater value to countries throughout the world which could benefit from it in dealing with their own problems and opportunities. Yet, there has been, again especially to an outside observer, a puzzling degree of reticence to both make these results and experiences more widely available in the professional and academic literature, and to use the resulting data in analyses of, for example, factors leading to more success and those that appear to cause detriment. There are many exceptions to this pattern, and more so in more recent times, but a pattern of using datasets from elsewhere, and thereby passing up opportunities to provide valued findings from local experience in favour of those from distant sources that is widely believed to raise fewer questions appears to persist. Part of the hesitation may be due to earlier cases of alleged questioning and intervention by administrative overseers, but whatever impacts — real or imagined — remain, would seem at odds with the widely proclaimed desires to attain internationally recognised standings for research and analysis.

In part due to the successes of the past, and in part due to a changing world and changing tastes and preferences of Singaporeans, many things will continue in the future in at least recognisable ways, but others will need major adjustment or to be started anew.[2] While it is largely, again, pointless to attempt predictions of specifics, it seems, based on all present

[2] An excellent review of issues and possible responses is provided in the variously written chapters of Low and Vadaketh (2014).

evidence, that there are two areas which will most likely present problems and opportunities in the years ahead. One is the growing disparities in income, wealth and opportunities in the Singapore population. The other is the mounting concerns over healthcare. Neither is at all unique to Singapore. But both are sources of major concern and likely to quickly become more so as differences in wealth become even more apparent and thereby further erode people's feelings of fairness and community, and as the demands for healthcare, and the attendant costs, increase with an ageing population.

These two major areas of concern may, however, with imagination and inventiveness, here too offer opportunities to take advantage of complementarities between them. Singapore's present array of differing programmes and health policies, and seemingly endless adjustments and tinkering among them to accommodate growing demands and worries of overuse, intentionally leave essentially all Singaporeans with financial responsibilities for their use of health services. This is clearly a greater burden on those with less wealth than those with more — with the difference in worrying over their ability to bear such costs (not a minor concern) likely to be even much larger between them. Thus, given the importance of healthcare to all and the disproportionate ability to pay for it between income groups, any further measures to reduce the burden of healthcare for poorer Singaporeans is likely to also mitigate problems associated with income inequality — the more that such financial worries are removed, the greater this mitigation is likely to be. All Singaporeans will have an interest in the extent to which this is done, with the poor having here again the greatest stake.

That three of the five universities in Singapore have "Technology" as part of their name may well signal a justified faith in Singapore's comparative advantage in reaping rewards from efforts in these directions. However, this is unlikely to diminish the benefits of good research and analysis in other areas that can lead to better policy and institutional design that can improve things not only in Singapore but well beyond its borders — which, I suspect, most Singaporeans would consider a good thing, and many others of us would regard as a very good thing.

References

Lim C. Y. (2007, April). The Singapore Economy: The Right Options. Lecture given at the Singapore Soka Association Youth Peace Lecture.

Low, D., and Thomas, V. S., with contributions from Lim, L. and Thum, P. J. (2014). *Hard Choices: Challenging the Singapore Consensus*. Singapore: National University of Singapore Press.

The Scarcity Model — No Waste, Total Recycling

Joergen Oerstroem Moeller
Visiting Senior Research Fellow, ISEAS;
Adjunct Professor, Singapore Management University &
Copenhagen Business School;
Senior Fellow, MFA Diplomatic Academy

Until around 10 years ago Asia prospered with a global environment facilitating its economic rise. Global growth was high, resources were available at comparatively low prices, the US was maintaining security and order, the global labour force was growing, the global supply chain favoured production in Asia, and the environment was not regarded as a genuinely serious/threatening issue. Political leaders in Asia could concentrate on how to manage economic growth. In 2014 very little of this is still at work. Global growth is low, weighed down by debt, resources are becoming scarce and prices are going up, the labour force in China is starting to fall, the global supply chain no longer coruscates, global and local environmental issues are asking for solutions, and the US is in decline. Political leaders face the challenge of having to create the conditions for growth — a totally different and much more intricate problem sometimes harbouring great political risks.

Unfortunately economic models are still driving in the lane chosen in the industrial age which say that growth is what we need to look at and the distribution of growth suffuses the agenda underpinning whatever advice governments seek and receive from economists.

This is bad because it is overwhelmingly likely that the world over the next 50 years will shift from plenty and abundance to scarcity and shortages. Distribution of benefits will be replaced by burden sharing.

Such prognoses have been heard before. About 200 years ago the English scholar Thomas Malthus predicted that population growth would outstrip food production, eventually leading to global famine. Events proved him wrong. In reality he was right! Technological breakthroughs combined with a transport revolution made it possible to open up North America, Latin America, and Australia along with New Zealand as food producers. Looking at the world today we may hope for technological breakthroughs, but there is no evidence of progress comparable to what we have seen over the preceding 200 years and even the most optimistic analyst would find it difficult to spot a new North America + Latin America + Oceania. Africa and parts of Russia plus Ukraine are mentioned, but how can we expect production increases to be sufficient to feed a rapidly growing global population asking for more sophisticated and processed food. The same daily intake of calories for an individual through chicken, pork or beef rather than grain or vegetables requires more resources while at the same time resulting in a much greater carbon footprint (carbon dioxide equivalent emissions pound for pound: beef versus chicken: 13 times; and beef versus potatoes: 57 times).

Real non-oil commodity prices fell from the first decade of the 20th century to 1990–1995 from an index of close to 200 to 60, but have more than doubled over the last twenty years — the first sustained rise seen since the middle of the 19th century if periods of war are excluded. This cannot be neglected or sidestepped as an ephemeral incident. It is a new trend.

The oil price has for a long time been manipulated by the major powers and producers, but compared to the middle of the 20th century we find also in this case a sustained and strong rise.

Water is economically or physically scarce for almost half of the global population. All of South Asia, half of China, all of the Middle East and large areas of the southern part of the US and northern part of Mexico suffer.

A clean environment is fast becoming a scarce good in the sense that pollution over many decades has contaminated soil and water subsequently killing people, with air pollution doing the same in many geographical areas even in 2014.

All societies and all countries will have to tune into this new paradigm and acknowledge the need to change economic models. The sooner the better as the first movers gain a competitive advantage by adjusting first. For a small country like Singapore with limited space this constitutes a major challenge, but also a splendid opportunity to preserve Singapore as a country that is able to identify new trends and make the best use of them.

The new economic model or paradigm focus on a number of behavioural patterns different from what we have seen over the last 50–60 years.

Traditional theory says that economics is about consumption. In reality economics is about human wellbeing and happiness. It was a mistake to link this exclusively to materialistic consumption. Gradually it will sink in what other social sciences have detected long ago: the feeling of happiness is deeper and lasts longer if born out of doing something for others and/or with others; human interaction is key. The plinth of economics — the utility theory — cannot survive this cognition. Communication takes over from consumption — mass communication instead of mass consumption. The role of society will then be to provide an infrastructure securing the network making people feel at ease using it without fearing surveillance from the authorities and penetration of their privacy engineered by criminals or hackers finding it fun to put a spoke in the wheel for fellow citizens.

Production will be geared to use fewer resources. Over the industrial age, technology, innovation and invention have focused on saving manpower regardless of the side effect of achieving this through increasing the use of resources. This was logical because wage costs were high and on the rise while resource prices were low and going down. Now the opposite is happening. Presuming economic rationality, innovation will aim at reducing the use of resources and increasing the use of manpower. In fact we move towards a more labour-intensive and less resource-intensive production process. It will take time, but the underlying relative factor prices (manpower/resources) will make this unavoidable.

Production will reorientate — as will consumption — highlighting durability. Now a considerable part of goods labelled durable are nothing of the sort. They are in reality produced and programmed to last for a limited time period after which they would be replaced by new versions of the same good — upgrading. One of the fastest declining industries in the US is the repair industry, reflecting the fact that people no longer repair or replace the small gadget or whatever that has broken down, but buy a totally new product. This was rational when wage costs were high and resource prices were cheap, but not when the reverse takes over. A much longer life-cycle for goods will be the norm. It may even turn out to be the norm that the hardware, so to speak, of a good is constantly being opened up to replace the software inside with newer models. The military has been doing this for decades; maintaining the frame — the ship or airplane or armoured vehicle — while upgrading the weapon systems the platform is carrying.

The next major behavioural change is product cycles, meaning that a product is not thrown away after use, but is recycled or regenerated or undergoes remanufacturing processes. Most of us have read about 3-D assembling, which has earned the nickname "the third Industrial Revolution". It is doubtful whether it can live up to this expectation, but it certainly changes the manufacturing process. Even more important is what is labelled as 3-D disassembling. After end use a product is neither repaired nor thrown away, but disassembled by reversing 3-D assembling after which its components are used in other products — the product is not recycled, its components are.

The genuine breakthrough is a dawning understanding of waste as a resource to be used instead of being seen as garbage. The rising resource prices automatically make waste precious. Multinational companies have already detected this and are rapidly implementing programmes to recycle waste reaping large economic benefits. Countries are slower on the uptake, but will sooner or later get the point. Various estimates point to a potential gain from a coherent recycling plan for waste running into several percentage points of the Gross Domestic Product (it has been calculated that waste amounts to 7% of GDP in France).

Global warming has introduced the notion of carbon neutrality. Around the world cities and corporations have entered a race to become the first major economic zone to earn this label.

The next major change is the endeavour and ambition to be resource neutral; a city or a corporation or a region or even a country without any use of new resources — total recycling, no waste. Sooner or later we will get there, depending on how fast resource prices will rise, but through integrating the positive side effects such as innovation and healthcare plus less use of foreign currencies, and 2050 would be a good guess.

Maybe in 2065 celebrating its 100th birthday, Singapore will be the most competitive economy while at the same time the first country to breach the barrier to become resource neutral — no waste, total recycling. These two achievements reinforce each other inside a new economic paradigm where happiness and wellbeing have less to do with materialistic consumption than interaction and communication among human beings. Maybe we will even get to a stage in civilisation with a widespread acknowledgement that resource neutrality signifies a respect for nature and sustainability without which no civilisation can survive in the long run.

Singapore — The Next 50 Years: Opportunities in the Convergence of Environment and Finance[1]

Richard L. Sandor, Ph.D., Dr. Sc.h.c.
Chairman and Chief Executive Officer
Environmental Financial Products LLC and
Aaron Director Lecturer in Law and Economics
University of Chicago Law School

Markets in emissions and "rights-to-use" have solved environmental problems and are creating enormous investment opportunities. They achieved this by commoditising and pricing "externalities," with the same concept being applied to weather-driven events and catastrophes. The convergence of the environment and finance is here to stay, and the market-based applications in sulphur dioxide and carbon emissions are only the beginning.

This new asset class holds enormous promise in fields such as water quality and quantity and for countries like Singapore. Given Singapore's unique combination of strong financial institutions, human capital excellence and geographic advantage, it can position itself as an unequalled centre of environmental finance for the next 50 years.

[1] This chapter is derived from material previously published in R. Sandor, M. Kanakasabai, R. Marques, and N. Clark, *Sustainable Investing and Environmental Markets: Opportunities in a New Asset Class*, Singapore: World Scientific, 2014.

Value Creation: A New Paradigm

We are witnessing a major systemic transformation on how wealth is created. Wealth creation in the United States has changed dramatically since 1970. After World War II, from 1945 to 1970, wealth creation in the United States was largely driven by manufacturing, and US manufacturing strength helped the country lead the world in value creation.

The decade of the 1970s was different. Inflation was high, the world experienced two oil embargoes and commodity prices rose sharply. Wealth creation in the 1970s was driven by commodities and other sectors that benefited from inflation. Agricultural concerns, energy companies, and storied commodity trading firms were the major wealth creators of the decade.

This situation changed once more in the 1980s. In that decade came the full development of the financial futures markets, where interest rates and money became commoditised. This phenomenon was punctuated with the creation of interest rate swaps. The commoditisation of corporate debt via high-yield bonds led to further wealth creation by giving entrepreneurs access to traditional capital markets.

The drivers of wealth creation changed again in the 1990s. This decade was driven by innovations in technology — personal computers, telecommunications, and software. These developments enabled the commoditisation of data, communications, and information.

The past shows that wealth creation is guided by fundamental structural and technological changes in the economy. This lesson from history leads us to believe that the next macro trend will be the commoditisation of air and water. Environmental and economic shifts, policy changes, technology improvements, and other innovations will trigger this transformation.

Environment: A New Asset Class

Population growth, industrialisation, and urbanisation in the past 200 years have resulted in local, national, and global pollution of our environment. Fossil-fuel combustion has resulted in rising levels of pollutants that cause smog, acid rain, and climate changes. Entire populations are faced with inadequate access to clean air and water, including China, India, Africa, and large areas elsewhere in the world.

The lack of ownership of air and water is the cause of the problem. The profit maximisation model for a firm takes into account only the direct costs incurred by the firm, not the spillover costs, such as the negative effects associated with the pollution of air and water. Therefore, more goods and services are produced than would be if pollution were either controlled by fiat or internally priced (a condition in which the social, or external, cost of the pollution is figured into the decision about how much of the good or service to produce).

These spillover costs, called "negative externalities," can be dealt with by mandating limits on pollutants, i.e. a cap, or requiring specific modifications in the production of goods and services. Spillover costs or benefits can also be mitigated by taxes and/or subsidies designed to drive down the level of pollution. In addition, externalities can be mitigated when public or private entities create a limited number of pollution or use rights corresponding to the environmentally acceptable cap on the pollutant. These property rights, called "allowances," can be purchased by companies for the purpose of compliance with environmental laws if they exceed their individual caps. Companies that reduce emissions in excess of their targeted caps can sell their allowances. The creation of a limited number (a cap) of property rights and their transferability (trade) has come to be known as "cap-and-trade." The transferability of allowances results in the market putting a price on the right to pollute. The price discovery allows companies flexibility to choose the efficient way to reduce pollution. When the price is higher than the technology required to reduce or eliminate the pollution, companies will install the technology. If the opposite is the case, they will buy allowances. The price signals and flexibility enabled by a cap-and-trade programme result in a least-cost solution to environmental problems.

Early programme outcomes, such as the phasing out of leaded gasoline and the virtual elimination of acid rain in the United States, led to widespread adoption of cap-and-trade throughout the world. The result has been creation of a new asset class — the environment — to join the traditional asset classes of stocks, bonds, real estate, foreign exchange, and tangible commodities.

Markets, when designed properly, can be a powerful agent for social and environmental transformation. These markets also act as economic drivers, generating jobs and improving the overall quality of life while acting as catalysts for innovation.

Opportunities for Singapore

The speed and breadth of development of the global environmental markets has the potential to mimic the rapid transformation that Singapore has experienced in its modern economic development. This new asset category promises to continue to grow and expand dramatically and, just like Singapore has taken advantage of changes in world economy and trade in the last 50 years, it can do the same for the next 50 in the environmental space.

One example of this new asset class is water, and water resources are critical for the country. Singapore does not have enough water to meet its needs. Singapore has to import several millions of litres of fresh water from neighbouring Malaysia via pipelines. The UN's Food and Agricultural Organization (FAO) has officially classified the country as "water poor" (FAO, 2003). The water Singapore imports from Malaysia represents roughly 30% of its total supply. Due to its size, there are natural constraints on the availability of rivers and lakes as sources of fresh water and a limit on the amount of reservoirs that can be built to store it. The country has experience with the desalination of sea water and it has become a world leader in recycling and turning waste water into highly purified water, providing a more cost-efficient and eco-friendly solution. Using markets as a potential tool to deal with water scarcity can maximise innovation and entrepreneurship in these nascent technologies.

Singapore can take advantage and benefit from the expansion of this asset class by building on its already world-class market infrastructure, respect for property rights, technological advancements and human capital base. Turning Singapore into an environmental finance centre will allow for major new business opportunities while advancing environmental progress. Its existing financial markets and world-class universities can serve the Southeast Asian market (Thailand, Malaysia, Indonesia, the Philippines, Vietnam, Cambodia, Laos and Myanmar) and become an international centre of commercial and technical excellence in energy and emissions markets.

Establishing Singapore as a leading-edge centre of trade in environmental markets will also help to enhance its economic diversification. The human capital developed through environmental finance represent a talent pool that complements and enhances the technical and financial skills that Singapore's will need to optimise the value and use of its water resources.

Environmental asset classes are not a hope for tomorrow but a reality today. As Louis Pasteur said, "chance favors the prepared mind." Those corporations and countries that do not embrace it, will be left behind. But those that do will have the opportunity to have a cleaner environment and create value at the same time — a combination of being able to "do well and do good" at the same time. Singapore is well positioned to do both.

Reference

United Nations Food and Agricultural Organization (FAO). (2003). Review of World Water Resources by Country.

Beyond 50: Associates

Singapore's Future in Our Hands

Chan Pei Lin
Student (Economics)
Nanyang Technological University, Singapore

Singapore takes pride in being a renowned garden city and such an achievement is not an easy feat. It is attained through far-sighted planning by our forefathers and till this day, is still executed with utmost dedication. Over the years, Singapore has made good progress in adhering to being a green city. This can be seen through efforts made by the Ministry of the Environment and Water Resources (MEWR), which has taken steps in creating a national framework to guide Singapore in achieving sustainable development. The Sustainable Singapore Blueprint aims to guide Singapore to grow in a way that is efficient, clean and green. Involving five different ministries, Singapore is geared towards pursuing environmentally friendly economic growth.

Continued efforts are required as concerns over global environmental issues gain precedence. While such issues could be brushed aside in the past, it is increasingly difficult and dangerous to neglect environmental issues when planning for the future as the problems of melting glaciers and natural disasters are now real threats. I have faith that the government and the involved ministries are well prepared to combat environmental issues in the next 50 years.

While Singapore has made consistent efforts in environmental issues, the fact remains that Singapore is lagging behind fellow developed Asian countries in terms of civic consciousness displayed by citizens. There is a disparity between what the city aspires to be and what Singaporeans are causing it to become. Despite various movements to encourage Singaporeans in going green, they have been met with short-lived enthusiasm. This makes us question if we are lacking the right infrastructure to inspire Singaporeans to go green and whether the various movements in the past have led to public fatigue.

The sad truth is that people often do not care about issues that have no real impact on them and hence this could explain the lack of consciousness about environmental issues in Singaporeans. While governmental agencies and environmental organisations are actively doing their parts for their environment, the nation can only be truly considered a green city when its people have the corresponding amount of environmental consciousness.

In my opinion, civic consciousness has to be inculcated as a habit and this will require time for such efforts to be seen. Habits that permeate daily actions of people are not a result of any framework but come about due to repetitive actions. For Singaporeans to be able to embrace a green lifestyle, they must be able to come to the realisation that the environment needs protection and that they can do so through simple daily actions. Over time, daily routines will become habitual and civic consciousness will no longer be a term that environmental agencies have to preach about. In my opinion, we can view civic consciousness as a merit good, where it is underutilised as people underestimate the benefits from it. This can be due to a lack of information regarding its benefits. Hence, constant environmental movements encouraging Singaporeans to care for the environment are still necessary even if past movements were met with short-lived enthusiasm. This is because such movements act as channels through which Singaporeans are educated on the importance of civic consciousness. With time, when people understand that simple acts can help to protect the environment, civic consciousness will come about naturally.

Environmental protection will not stagnate but will only become increasingly important. In the next 50 years, I envision Singapore to be a city where citizens embrace environmental consciousness. We are already seeing more people who are aware about the environmental consequences behind their personal choices and hence, alter their daily routines in ways that are more environmentally friendly.

Singapore has also been doing well in the economic landscape. For four consecutive years (as of 2014), Singapore has been ranked second in the Global Competitiveness Index and such economic success can be attributed to strategic planning. Since independence, Singapore has been actively seeking opportunities and tapping on its strengths so that the small island can thrive economically despite its size. This is evident from the numerous structural changes we have had in our economy.

When Singapore was pursuing industrialisation, emphasis was placed on the manufacturing sector to boost economic growth. Since then, Singapore's economy has undergone restructuring and focus has shifted to the services sector, anchoring Singapore in providing intermediate services for further production of services, especially evident in financial and banking services. With significant advances in today's technology, Singapore's Economic Development Board (EDB) recognised the importance of creating opportunities in areas of science and technology. As such, investments are pumped into research and development, higher education and continuing education today, so as to prepare Singapore in creating its own comparative advantage in innovation-driven and higher value-added industries. The industries of biotechnology and pharmaceuticals are prime examples of such efforts.

Trade and investment has been a major pillar of support in Singapore's economy and I believe will continue to be so in the next 50 years. Education Minister, Mr. Heng Swee Keat has pointed out that regional integration efforts within ASEAN will boost intraregional trade and investment and Singapore should aim to position itself as the "Global-Asia node."

While Singapore is currently geared towards productivity-driven growth, the question for economists and policymakers in the next 50 years is to consider which areas to create windows of opportunities for economic growth. There is no formula in guiding economic restructuring and efforts in doing so may be shot down when slowdowns in Singapore's economic growth are observed. Nevertheless, Singapore has to constantly seek out new paths of specialisations and be ready to create and seize opportunities.

I envision Singapore to be at the frontline of research in the next 50 years, particularly in the areas of medicine, science and technology. With increased investments in research and development as well as in higher education, I believe that Singaporeans will be able to achieve research results that serve to better the lives of people. We can then position Singapore as a research hub, leading the ASEAN region in the aspect of research and development.

Singapore has come a long way for the past 50 years. As a Singaporean and a youth myself, I have not witnessed how Singapore has grown and progressed in the past but I am definitely grateful and appreciative of the stability and prosperity we enjoy in our home country. While celebrating Singapore's 50 years, it is a good time to reflect on how we want our next 50 years to be.

I believe the youths and young adults of today bear the responsibility in shaping Singapore to be the nation they envision it to be. The specifics of how we want Singapore to be like in the future will vary from person to person. However in my opinion, three ideals capture the essence of how I hope Singapore will be like in the future. These ideals are found in the national pledge that all Singaporeans are familiar with, namely happiness, progress and prosperity. By adhering to these ideals, I believe that the next 50 years for Singapore will be equally fruitful.

Energy in Singapore: The Engine of Economic Growth from 1965 to 2065

Chang Youngho
Assistant Professor
Division of Economics, School of Humanities and Social Sciences
Nanyang Technological University, Singapore

The economic growth in Singapore cannot be explained without mentioning how energy had helped Singapore move forward and transform her economy from a first industry-based economy to a second and third industry-based one. Singapore is a regional hub for energy as well as financial services. The process of transforming an ancient fishing town and port city into a regional hub for trading energy and providing financial services started from utilising the comparative advantage of geographical location (Huff, 1994) and human ingenuity by people in Singapore. What Singapore has worked as the hub for energy trading and financial services for the past 50 years will continue for another 50 years. This chapter presents a brief description of how the energy industry had started and flourished in Singapore and questions if the success story will continue in the future and if yes, how long it will be. Specifically, it revisits to how Singapore was in 1965 when it became independent, reviews what efforts she put and how to transform her economy after her independence and examines whether Singapore will flourish for the next 50 years or so.

When Singapore became independent in 1965, she did not have much industrial infrastructure. How Singapore has successfully transformed her economic status and achieved economic wellbeing is summarised as the outcome of the positive synergy among the government, the market and people.

First, Singapore has planned and executed her development strategies utilising the best of what she had at the time and the vision of industrial development. Singapore was a port city located at the southern end of the Peninsular of Malaysia. It had been developed as an entrepôt as it is in the maritime route between the East and the West. Noticing the geographical advantage of Singapore, Standard Oil had developed Singapore as their oil storage facility and added oil blending infrastructure to the existing storage facility (Horsnell, 1997).

In 1965, Singapore, a newly independent nation at the heart of Southeast Asia, offered favourable investment conditions for those who build refineries in her soil and secured to build five refineries within 12 years including her own refinery, Singapore Petroleum Company in 1973. The energy sector had contributed significantly to her economic growth in the late 1960s, 1970s and early 1980s. Energy was considered one of the five engines of economic growth during those periods — the US economy, worldwide semiconductor sales, ASEAN-2 countries (combined GDP of Indonesia and Malaysia) and domestic construction works. The energy sector has contributed 1.1 percentage points to economic growth and 50% of domestic export by commodity during the first decade from the independence (MTI, 2002). After two oil shocks, Singapore had lost her competitive edge in refining. At the time, however, she successfully transformed her economy into a manufacturing and financial service-based one. The energy sector is still contributing about 20% of domestic export by commodity and about 1% of employment (Department of Statistics, 2013).

The establishment of the hub for trading energy and transformation of her economy into a second and third industry-based one has been attributed by the concerted efforts of the government and people of Singapore. The Singapore government has implemented its plans for economic development with the vision of being a developed economy and transformed her economy to a highly value-added one following the vision through investment and education.

Second, Singapore keeps reforming her energy sector and tested her industry with new and innovative ideas. Singapore has successfully established a physical centre for refining oil in the region but two oil shocks and ensuing heightened concerns of energy security affected the status of Singapore as a regional oil refining centre. Facing an external threat, Singapore introduced the Approved Oil Trader (AOT) scheme in 1989 to revive her status as the hub for energy trading. The AOT scheme was merged with the Approved International Trader (AIT) in 2001 and the Global Trader Programme (GTP) replaced the two schemes in the same year (Chang, 2014). This is one of the key efforts Singapore has made to revive her energy industry and sustain the hub for energy trading. How the government refocused its efforts on reviving the energy sector as the engine of economic growth in the 2000s can be well explained by her efforts of diversifying her energy sources by building a liquefied natural gas (LNG) terminal and launching LNG trading in the near future.

Another key effort of reforming her energy sector came from the electricity market. The movement of deregulating or liberalising the electricity sector was sweeping the electricity market across the world in the 1980s and 1990s. After about 10 years of careful and well-managed preparation, Singapore gradually introduced the market mechanism and competition into her electricity market but put a check and balance system in place to minimise the possible negative consequences of deregulation. The efforts of reforming her energy industry continued. The deregulation of the electricity market in Singapore is on the right track and the government intends to complete its reform process by introducing demand bidding, electricity futures trading and importing electricity from neighbouring countries. This is a well-timed effort and movement considering the launch of the ASEAN Economic Community (AEC) in December 2015 that allows free flow of goods and services in the AEC.

Singapore revived one of her old growth themes — Energy for Growth by publishing the National Energy Policy Report (NEPR) in 2007. This emphasised the importance of energy in economic growth and put an innovative energy sector as a driver for economic growth again. NEPR specified three policy objectives and translated the objectives into six strategies (MTI, 2007).[1] Among others, it put institutional efforts to

[1] The three main policy objectives are economic competitiveness, energy security and environmental sustainability. The six strategies are to promote competitive markets; to diversify energy supplies; to improve energy efficiency; to build the energy industry, and invest in energy research and development; to step up international cooperation and to develop a whole-of government approach.

strengthen the roles of the existing statutory boards and establish new offices and a research institute to develop clean energy technologies, improve energy efficiency and carry out energy-related research. Singapore uses her soil as test hubs to develop new energy technologies and disseminate them across the world.

Along with institutional efforts of reforming the energy sector, Singapore launched the Singapore International Energy Week (SIEW) in 2008. At the SIEW global leaders of the energy sector and energy researchers and practitioners gather and explore the future paths in the energy sector. It has become one of the key international podiums where energy-related government officials, industry people and academics exchange innovative views and ideas on energy and share experiences of implementing energy policies and developing new technologies. Through organising such international energy conferences Singapore presents her experiences of the implementation of energy policies to the audience in the world, shares her knowledge of developing energy technologies with global experts and assimilates new trends and movements in making her energy sector more productive and sustainable.

Third, Singapore thinks and acts globally but does not forget her base in ASEAN and Asia. She connects the East and the West in many aspects from trade and business to culture and ideas. Singapore organises several summits on various key global issues that the world is facing now such as Liveable Cities. People come to Singapore and get insights and the feeling of a global citizen. Singapore has tested conventional and creative energy-related ideas in her soil. For instance, transportation and energy is fused as a future modality as well as a mode for energy storage. A hydrogen fuel cell vehicle was tested and a cost-benefit analysis of adopting electric vehicles was carried out. Singapore will continue to sustain such a competitive edge in incubating and testing new technologies for the global community.

Apart from thinking and acting globally, Singapore has implemented all policies and strategies based on long-term perspectives but with a regular fine-tuning on the way. The society moves to the direction she has envisaged out of the maximum support from diverse and in-depth discussions among people.

Planning with strategies, reforming with innovation and thinking and acting globally with the consideration of locality are expected to continue.

Along with this, well designed and managed economic, cultural, societal and strategic plans will be germinated. These would help Singapore excel in every aspect even in 2065. Singapore is a good and interesting example, which might shed light on how to develop an economy out of virtually no resource endowment other than people and bring it to the top of the world economy. The energy sector has contributed to economic growth in Singapore and this success story can be replicated in other developing economies with necessary modifications.

Energy is the key factor that makes an economy to function properly, prosper and be sustainable in the future. Singapore's energy endeavour will continue, which will help not only Singapore but the world flourish. Even in 2065, Singapore will still stand as an energy hub for not only energy trading but an incubator for developing new energy technologies and testing them. The accrued benefits from Singapore will spread across the world.

References

Chang, Y. (2014). Energy Commodity Trading in Singapore. In Han, P. and F. Kimura (eds.), *Energy Market Integration in East Asia: Energy Trade, Cross Border Electricity, and Price Mechanism* (pp. 13–26), ERIA Research Project Report FY2013, No 29. Jakarta: ERIA.

Department of Statistics, Singapore. (2013). *Yearbook of Statistics, Singapore 2013*.

Horsnell, P. (1997). *Oil in Asia: Markets, Trading, Refining and Deregulation*. Oxford, UK: Oxford University Press.

Huff, W. G. (1994). *The Economic Growth of Singapore: Trade and Development in the Twentieth Century*. Cambridge, UK: Cambridge University Press.

Ministry of Trade and Industry, Singapore (MTI). (2002). Singapore's Engines of Growth: A Demand-side Perspective, *Economic Survey of Singapore*, February, 83–98.

MTI. (2007). *Energy for Growth: National Energy Policy Report*.

Welcome to Singapore Inc.

Roland Cheo
Associate Professor
Centre for Economic Research
Shandong University, China

Imagine the year 2065 when you mention "Singapore," you no longer refer to an island but a Corporation. Singapore Incorporated runs several suburbs in northern India and China populated by a diaspora that had abandoned the island founded by Raffles. With the rising sea level and temperatures bearing down at almost 40 degrees due to climate change, the island is now 202 square kilometres, whose reclaimed land has long been swallowed by the sea and is often buffeted by tsunami-like waves. What was once a bustling city with towering skyscrapers now stands empty as a testimony of a bygone era, while the majority of the mobile labour force have since abandoned the city and moved to satellite towns operated by Singapore Inc. in the more temperate countries. Those who could not leave the island to better climes had retreated underground.

Only 30% of the population of Singaporeans still live on the island, albeit underground. These are the ones without the resources to relocate to better suburbs of Singapore Inc. in the more temperate countries. Subsidised air-conditioned housing board flats dominate the landscape of quarried pits under central Singapore island, illuminated by industrial strength LED lights leaving residents to view a perpetual night silhouette of the city. Manufacturing and service industries in Singapore are kept to a bare minimum since the now defunct Copenhagen Agreement and then the new Melbourne Initiative has cut global emissions by almost five times the levels that they were in 2010. Not many residents of the island actually live topside, exposed to the natural elements. In fact, hardly anyone actually ventures above ground. The heat is unbearable and only a small pocket of residents collectively known as Faith Spacers willing live in areas around Seletar Reservoir occupying what was once the Teachers' Quarters at Seletar Airbase.

Besides the poor, of those who have chosen to remain on the island are the intelligentsia who reside in the research institutions, primarily, in the National University of Singapore and Nanyang Technological University. The other private institutions have moved away to other more landlocked locales. These institutions are no longer comprehensive universities but are instead part of a larger network of schools that have pooled resources across the world in order to conduct online courses. Since no one attends lectures anymore, everything is experienced virtually in one's own home.

70% of the population live in satellite towns in India and China where the climate is relatively comfortable. The Singapore government wisely leased several large pockets of lands in relatively colder areas away from the main cities in India and China in the 2030s. These areas were relatively undeveloped at the time and the Chinese and Indian governments were more than happy to lease the areas to be developed by Singapore Inc. By the time, temperatures started to soar in the 2020s, many of these satellite towns had already developed the infrastructure that allowed Singaporeans and later foreign talent to live in a temperate and efficiently run suburb of Singapore Inc. Jurong Town Corporation (JTC) developed the land while the Immigration Authority managed the inflows and outflows of migrants in order to maintain the growth rates of the cities.

The global repercussions of climate change have also been felt all over the world. The driver of the world economy is no longer the US, whose unbearable temperatures have seen many migrate over to Canada, leaving the balance of power to reside more and more in the hands of northern territories. The northern part of China and Russia as well as Nordic countries now supply the world with most of the world's needed agricultural products while countries in the tropics such as Southeast Asia as well as India and Africa are the world's suppliers of solar energy. These countries are tapped into a worldwide grid which sells its energy supply to a central depository which in turns resells them to the rest of the world. Imagine that the United Nations is now headquartered in Iceland.

The knowledge economy has fizzled away like discarded old oyster sauce, fermented by its own infertile imagination clinging to the past: a focus on mobile devices or the push towards more computing power. In its wake came the virtual economy. In the early 2000s, Singapore had opened its doors to animation companies, especially companies working on 3-D technologies with the goal of supplying the movie industry. However in the 2020s, with the rising temperatures, also came the emergence of new strains of viruses in the vein of Ebola and SARS which created widespread pandemics. Policymakers around the world closed their borders to travellers, concerned with the spread of these deadly diseases. In fact even within local populations, new laws were enacted to enable one to minimise contact with fellow human beings. Social laws were passed which made gatherings of more than 10 people in one room illegal. Soon the closed door policy resulted in the movie industry collapsing. In today's world one has to go through a complicated set of protocols in order to organise a gathering. This includes a quarantine period to ensure no strains of viruses over the incubation period of one week, as well as to complete many forms which waives the right of the individual and cedes these rights to the authorities. Thus the authorities have the right to forcibly incarcerate anyone suspected of harbouring a deadly disease. Those suspected of being bioterrorists are cryogenically incarcerated before they are shipped to holding tanks on prison ships which are fully automatised and run remotely by human operators in Singapore Inc.'s headquarters in Gansu, China. Singapore Inc. runs some of the world's largest ship prisons.

Technology companies then scrambled to meet a new demand: the demand for social interactions without needing face to face interaction. Temasek Holdings rushed into the forefront, relocating promising tech companies to the island of Singapore where they provided these companies, state of the art facilities in underground caverns which were modelled after the New York skyline. Artificial lighting and green spaces using lichens and mosses were expertly interwoven into the very fabric of underground living. With full artistic license given to these companies, Singapore then became the leading nation to export liveable realities. Singaporeans went online in 2045, becoming the source of informational content to 2 billion users in all countries where pandemics were rife but dormant. Part of the liveable reality infrastructure included the buyout of major movie companies to allow content to be directly utilised in the virtual setting. This meant that one could potential live out one's movie fantasies. This mass commercialisation of exported experiences resulted in Singapore coming to the forefront of the global demand for entertainment. Singapore levied a high corporate tax rate in particular to this industry in exchange for maintaining the underground city and providing 24/7 services to the tech companies.

Singapore Inc. boasts five boroughs in India and China which have made it to the annual 20 most liveable cities in the world rankings. Where other cities have faltered because of their dying infrastructure and their exposure to the effects of climate change, Singapore Inc. has been able to use its collective reserves to revitalise the city landscape by starting everything from scratch. In light of social laws, public spaces have been reinvented such that no more than 10 people are allowed to enter light rail transporters which traverse the entire borough at designated pickup spots. Sensors pick out body heat and blood pressure in order to alert one to potential viral threats. Public spaces are no longer frequented by the public in high numbers and those wanting to do so need to participate in a lottery system which allocates the right to a time slot. Migratory birds have since made permanent residence in the many urban parks and nature reserves constructed in the early 2030s. Nature lovers are able to view monitors which channel live feeds to the population via wearable technologies. In this way, many people do not actually need to go out in order to experience the comfort of nature.

In spite of these social improvements, Faith Spacers choose to disregard the safety protocols. They have chosen to remain on the main island where they meet in groups beyond the stipulated ten. They refuse all contact with wearable technology but instead actively seek outdoor activities in teams. They restore antiquated bicycles and use it to traverse the island, establishing new outposts called Faith Spaces, which they encourage face-to-face contact. They describe it as a religious experience: the personal connection with people, without the use of technology. They advertise their activities and rely on personal trust to promote their cause. This counterculture is currently an annoyance to the safety of the majority of the populace; however, since they have chosen to bypass the general public, the authorities have closed a blind eye, as they continue to remain a small minority.

Making the Impossible Possible: Singapore as a Provider of Solutions to the Water Industry

Chia Wai Mun
Associate Professor
Division of Economics
Nanyang Technological University, Singapore

The Singaporean government faced some major challenges when the country was separated from the Malaysian Federation and obtained independence in 1965. Among them included limited natural resources, very low defensive capabilities and lack of water supply. While Singapore receives about 2400 mm of rainfall annually, more than twice of that of the global average of 1050 mm, with rainy days accounting for about 50% of a calendar year, the constraint is basically limited by the small land area of 710 square kilometres to catch and store rainwater.

Initially, water supply in Singapore was derived primarily from the Malaysian state of Johore. There were in total three water agreements between Singapore and Malaysia. The first agreement was signed in 1927 and had long expired. The second agreement was signed in 1961. It was effective for 50 years. This contract allowed Singapore to draw up to 86 million imperial gallons of water per day and expired in 2011. The third contract was a 100-year agreement signed in 1962 with effect through 2061. This contract which is still in force gives Singapore the right to draw up to 250 million imperial gallons per day. The price of raw water for the last two contracts was set at US$0.01 per 1,000 imperial gallons. Water was transported through a close to 1-km-long water pipe that runs along the Johor-Singapore Causeway. The water pipe was inaugurated in 1932.

Two episodes had subsequently led Singapore into enhancing self-sufficiency in water. First was due to the explosion of the Johor-Singapore Causeway in 1942 by retreating British troops. Singapore's water reserves then could only last the country for two weeks. Second was the threat of then Malaysian Prime Minister Tunku Abdul Rahman to cut off the water supply to Singapore when Singapore's foreign policy was deemed prejudicial to Malaysia's interests.

In 1963, the Public Utilities Board (PUB) was set up under the Ministry of Trade and Industry (MTI) with a mission to oversee and coordinate the three public utilities in the country including the supply of electricity, piped gas and water. In 2001, the PUB was reconstituted to overseeing the entire water loop in Singapore including the country's water catchment and supply systems, drainage systems, water reclamation plants and sewerage systems. A new statutory board, the Energy Market Authority (EMA), was formed separately to focus on the regulation of electricity and gas industries.

PUB's integrated and holistic water management emphasises on both supply and demand sides. The supply side focuses on catchment management, and protection and expansion of water sources. The country adopts a robust and diversified four-tap strategy which combines imports of water and land reclamation with rainfall storage, desalination and very sophisticated technology for recycling used water. The last two sources augment Singapore's water supply, allowing the country to be more resilient to weather variability. As for the demand side, PUB has put in place a comprehensive demand management policy to look more into water pricing and water conservation through public education programmes. An effective water pricing mechanism, consisting of a water tariff, water conservation tax, sanitary appliance fee and waterborne fee, is designed to encourage users to conserve water. Potable water is priced to recover the full costs of producing and supplying it. A water tariff which reflects the true cost of water production is reinvested back into research and development on water. Other measures include imposing mandatory requirements to install water-saving devices and limit the maximum allowable flow rate at water fittings. Public education and other water conservation programmes are also implemented. So far, the practices seem to have notable results. Singapore's per capita domestic water consumption declined steadily from its highest level of 175 litres per day in 1994 to 156 litres per day in 2008. The country has also targeted to further reduce this to 147 litres per day by 2020 and 140 litres per day by 2030.

In 2006, Singapore government committed to invest S$330 million over the following five years in water research and development. In 2011, an additional S$110 million was allocated. The Environment and Water Industry Development Council (EWI) was established to support research programmes on clean water. More importantly, more water companies were attracted to establish their business activities in Singapore. Today, Singapore has about 130 water companies and 28 research centres in this industry working on converting innovative ideas to make a difference to the water world.

What is the future? The answers lie in examining the current demand and supply pressures and looking at the trends of each. On the demand side, with the population continuing to increase dramatically with an expanding appetite for water-intensive products, water needs in the country are expected to double from close to 400 million gallons per day now to perhaps 800 million gallons per day 50 years later. The increase is expected to come primarily from non-domestic water use, which accounts for around half of the water demand now to more than two-thirds of the demand in 2065. On the supply side, by that time, given today's approach to water management, it is not surprising to forecast its capability to meet close to half of the water demand in the future, with the remaining 30% supported by desalination and 20% by internal catchments. Taken together, it is then pretty much safe to forecast that by 2065, the necessity to import water will be significantly reduced, if not eliminated completely. This forecast is however made with the assumption that climate change does not radically transform the amount of rainfall in the country annually.

The world is witnessing how Singapore, being one of the world's most densely populated countries, is transforming its vulnerability in water into self-sufficiency and strength in the industry. Can we take one more giant step forward? Imagine one day, when we travel around and find out that in a foreign country, the bottled water in our hands actually has a label that says "Product of Singapore"!

Singapore, 50 Years Old, and Still Growing (Reflections on Economic Growth and Sustainable Development)

William Henry Clune
Policy Director, Sustainable Earth Office
Faculty Associate, Division of Economics
Nanyang Technological University, Singapore

First things first, congratulations to Singapore on the auspicious occasion of its 50 year celebration! To be sure, my essay's focus on growth, specifically the relationship between growth and sustainable economic development, is intended to celebrate the opportunities 50 years of growth and development have created for the nation and the world, at the same time it discusses some of the challenges and opportunities related to growth for the next 50 years.

From a human and humane perspective, only the most cynical among us would deny the enormous benefits that economic development brings to the lives of so many people. I have seen pictures of Singapore in the 1960s and 1970s, and the changes are as remarkable as they are swift. We can acknowledge that these changes and benefits are not always evenly distributed (within one country or between nations), but remain confident that our predecessors have done the right thing, both within Singapore and globally: in lifting populations from poverty to allow people to live in dignity; to give people work and life opportunities to achieve their human potential; by providing education to girls, boys, men, and women; by improving medical care, nutrition, and health outcomes. In these important ways, just to name a few, we live together in a wondrous time, and the rise of China, as well as economic development in places like India and Brazil, must be seen for what they are: opportunities that should not be missed to raise billions of people from poverty or subsistence to a much better life.

Now here comes the catch. And it is a particularly sticky wicket for those of us living together in the economically connected world of today. Our global development and economic growth are not sustainable; our growth and consumption trajectories have exceeded the planet's ecological capacity to sustain us. While there is little immediate threat to our standards of living or even business as usual, our natural and ecological deficit spending has been clearly identified, and quantified, and tallied; and sooner or later, and in one way or another, the debts will be paid. If we were to say that this is a foolish position in which to deliberately put ourselves (and our children), we would be on solid ground in connecting more sustainable economic development with a desire to preserve and extend the positive opportunity we now have to create better lives for everyone.

Ironically, the challenge of sustainable development, in a modern city-state like Singapore and elsewhere in the world, does not primarily reside with a lack of technological, or even innovative, capacity. From cleantech for industrial operations, to industrial ecology approaches that close input and output loops for resources and pollution, to proven renewable energy sources, to government planning and long traditions of urban design, to effective environmental management systems and corporate responsibility policies, the world, our governments, and our major economic actors have more than enough know-how at their disposal. In fact, Singapore, in step with its good governance, excellent universities, and engineering expertise, has excelled at creating and applying innovative solutions, effective management systems, and new technologies.

While I am at it, another (often unfair) irony is laying the primary blame for unsustainable global development on rapid population growth. The world's most populous regions are singled out, and we lament our inability to stop ourselves (or, perhaps, mostly others) from reproducing so quickly. Global population, like population and demographic pressures in

Singapore, is certainly a stressor and will continue to play an important role in defining growth and development strategies. However, of the world's approximately 8 billion human residents, it is important to note that only about 2 billion of us are living beyond our ecological means or on more than our fair share of planetary resources. This statement is not an acceptance or endorsement of poverty, but simply a fact, to say that approximately 6 billion people on the planet are already living rather sustainably, if we focus on per capita resource and energy consumption.

This brings our economic growth and development challenges into clear focus. In fact, all of our biggest environmental impact challenges are related to economic development, consumption, and growth. On one hand, we have agreed that development and lifting people out of poverty are global priorities. On the other hand, if two billion of us are already living beyond our ecological means, how will the planet cope when successful economic development brings another one or two billion consumers on-line? This is the crux of our sustainable development challenge. And as Singapore contemplates, for example, a large scale coastal protection plan as a coping and survival adaptation to rising sea levels caused by global warming, it is also part of Singapore's sustainable development challenge.

One part of the answer, and one that in many ways is already happening in Singapore and other countries, is in a more effective integration and combination of the different parts of sustainable development: technology and innovation; economics and financial incentives; governance and legal frameworks. In order to address the complex challenge of sustainable development, the approach should be viewed as multidisciplinary, multiministry, and multi-sector. Further, an increased focus on regional integration, connections, and economic development is often necessary, to create systemic resilience, robustness to shocks, and a greater understanding of ecological stress points. In fact, as a densely populated city-state, Singapore relies heavily upon its neighbours for key resources, is vulnerable to environmental decline in surrounding areas, and is inextricably tied to the political, economic and security dynamics that define the Southeast Asian region.

The Indonesian haze problem in Singapore is a good example of a regional pollution problem driven by an integrated economic system. But let me ask first if you think characterising this as the Indonesian haze problem is completely fair? Farmers, small stakeholders or those working for larger corporations, are burning forests in Sumatra to inexpensively clear land for palm oil plantations. Who uses this palm oil for cooking or as inputs for other products, it is not primarily the Indonesians who clear the land or cultivate the crops, is it? Who profits from these palm oil sales, and the sales of products that incorporate inexpensively produced palm oil, is it not mainly corporations and consumers located in Indonesia, Singapore, and throughout the world? How many of us have seen our personal investments or pension funds increase by holding stocks in our portfolios in the profitable palm oil or related sectors? And if the farmers and residents of Sumatra are actually the least wealthy stakeholders involved in this haze controversy, is there not also some question of equity in asking the poorest participants to take on most of the financial burden? We truly now live in an economically and regionally integrated world, in respect to our biggest environmental challenges and the sustainability solutions we require.

Singapore is in many respects ideally situated to lead, develop, and share sustainability solutions with the world. For starters, Singapore is committed to finding workable sustainability solutions; integrated national frameworks and strategies are being developed here in the context of emerging domestic and global challenges. Sustainable development for Singapore is defined as growing the city-state in a way that is resource-efficient, prevents pollution of the environment, and preserves greenery, waterways and the natural heritage; sustainability must also be liveable, and in a manner that accounts for the vital connections between people, economic opportunity, and culture. Important questions are already being asked here and elsewhere about economic and growth goals, about defining economic success in terms of wellbeing and opportunity, not only in terms of production or GDP. The fact that there are significant economic opportunities to be had in becoming a global sustainability leader supports Singapore's overall growth objectives, by building an economy that grows with productivity increases (rather than increases in people and infrastructure), on its innovation and information capacity (rather than production and manufacturing), and in exporting beneficial sustainability solutions to growing international markets.

Urban centres like Singapore will continue to be the economic and innovation drivers of our future, especially given increasing urbanisation which will see, by 2050, around 70% of the world's population living in urban areas. This also presents exciting opportunities, because cities are the most diverse, dynamic, and economically efficient places on the planet. Global cities will be the places where economic, social, and environmental conflicts are increasingly mediated, whether they are local, regional, or have their origins far away. And, while many of our most pressing sustainability challenges are created by growing cities and their growing economies, it will be the global cities, like Singapore, that continue to develop our most promising, and fully integrated, sustainable development solutions.

Singapore 2065: The Great, The Challenges and The People

Dannon Hong
Student (Economics)
Nanyang Technological University, Singapore

First and foremost, congratulations are in order as Singapore celebrates her 50th year of independence. The road to independence has not been easy and many difficult decisions had to be made along the way. Through the years, Singapore has progressed from a colonialised city-state, to being a part of Malaysia and finally as an independent multiracial city-state country with a GDP per capita of US$55,182.48 (World Bank, 2013). This is an amazing feat, comparing GDP per capita with the United States (US$53,143) and the United Kingdom (US$39,337). Undeniably, Singapore has done outstandingly in the previous 50 years of independence, but will it continue to thrive in the next 50 years' time? Faced with challenges such as an ageing population, more competitive neighbours and a seemingly growing unhappiness among its people, will the growth of the Singapore economy continue to be stable? In light of these challenges, we shall examine a few significant problems that Singapore faces.

1. Will Singapore lose its economic competitiveness with growing competition from her neighbours?
2. Foreign talents or ageing population?
3. Tough decisions vs. happiness

Will Singapore Lose Its Economic Competitiveness with Growing Competition from Her Neighbours?

50 years into the future is a long time, and neighbouring countries will certainly develop alongside with Singapore. In the past 50 years, Singapore has thrived to be one of the top seaports and investment countries in Southeast Asia but her position will most likely be challenged in the future. Malaysia, Indonesia, the Philippines and many other Southeast Asian countries have already developed themselves to be substantially attractive locations for investments and economic activities. With more land, more favourable labour rates and an abundance of natural resources, the odds seemed to be stacked against Singapore in the years to come. The abundant land space and population that our neighbouring countries have will result in a much larger domestic market and lower cost of rent. Moreover, neighbouring countries have been advancing their talent pools for the last 50 years as well. With more universities, specialised vocational schools for skills and higher literacy rates, they will have more skilled labour at a more affordable rate than Singapore. In terms of natural resources, oil and tin are some of the many natural resources that our neighbouring countries are well endowed in. These resources create great incentives for foreign investors as they will not need to import resources and thus, are notably encouraged to invest in these neighbouring countries rather than Singapore. Without foreign investment and with a small domestic market for consumption, Singapore's economic growth seems heavily challenged in 50 years' time.

However, in the past 50 years, Singapore has continued to attract foreign investment even without abundant land, natural resources or lower labour rates as compared to her neighbours. This is due to its stable political situation, multiracial society and its secure business environment. Throughout the past, Singapore's political leaders have always maintained a welcoming attitude towards foreign investments. This is especially important in Southeast Asia as political turmoil and changes will render the economic situation unstable and foreign investment regulations may change abruptly. Multinational firms will not be greatly encouraged to invest millions in a factory, only to realise that they are unable to own any assets due to changes in investment regulations. Moreover, a multiracial society provides good opportunities for a firm to reach out to different cultures and races. For example, by having locating a headquarters in Singapore, firms are able to send Indian managers to India, Chinese managers to China, Malay managers to Malaysia and so on. With a relatively weaker labour union presence and laws to ban riots and mass gatherings without appropriate reasons, Singapore provides a safe and secure business environment for foreign investments. I strongly believe that these reasons will continue to attract multinational firms to invest in Singapore. Nonetheless, it is with little doubt that the type of investments may change, less investments from the lower value chains of labour-intensive industries and more from service, research and development industries.

Hence, we must ensure that Singapore remains a politically stable country with a vibrant multiracial society, without which we will lose our competitive edge. While some may argue that neighbouring countries will reach a similar point of stability as Singapore, with recent riots in Thailand, Vietnam and election changes in Indonesia, it suggests that stability will take some time. Thus, in the next 50 years, I foresee that Singapore will still be competitive in attracting investments and economic activities.

Foreign Talents or Ageing Population?

In the next 50 years, it is reasonable to assume that countries such as Bangladesh will become more urbanised and there will be more job opportunities, and China, with her western development plans, will create more employment alongside the urbanisation of some rural cities. With more opportunities in their home countries, there will be fewer foreign talents coming to Singapore to seek employment. The number of Bangladeshis, Chinese, Malaysians, Filipinos and other foreign talents will be reduced. Developing countries will require top-notch foreign talents to help plan and grow their economies and hence, will offer attractive incentives to foreign talents. The pool of foreign talents in Singapore will inevitably decrease regardless of higher skilled or lower skilled individuals. While some Singaporeans may rejoice now and encourage the decrease in foreign talents, this will cause more harm than benefit to the Singapore economy.

Singapore's fertility rate of 1.19 (Singapore Statistics, 2013) is under the replacement fertility rate and this will result in an ageing population. The solutions proposed by the government has two goals. Firstly, to encourage birth through various incentives. Secondly, to increase the amount of foreign talents and eventually to convince them to stay as permanent residents. To be clear, the crucial concern about an ageing population is the slowing of economic growth. Getting more permanent residents will ensure a sustainable and employable work force. However, in recent years, Singaporeans have increasingly expressed their unhappiness about the number of foreign talents and this has led the government to impose a limit on foreign talents. In my opinion, there are two main reasons for the unhappiness, namely biased opportunities for Singaporeans and delayed growth of infrastructure. Regarding biased opportunities for Singaporeans, the government has implemented various measures such as the National Job Banks and regulations requiring firms to advertise first for Singaporeans and then foreign talents. However, the unhappiness is still significant; hence, the main reason would be delayed growth of infrastructure. When the government opened the gates to foreign talents, they did not substantially increase their budget and expenditure to developing the infrastructure, such as the transport system, the housing estates and community facilities. This situation then resulted in overcrowding and caused unhappiness among the locals. However, after limiting the entrance of foreign talents, the government has been actively increasing expenditure on infrastructures. From 2011–2012, there were 32,689 housing units built as compared to 30,069 units from 2006–2010 (HDB Statistics, 2013). The government has also introduced new Mass Rapid Transit (MRT) lines and improved existing MRT lines. The new infrastructure will ease the overcrowding situation and hopefully, reduce Singaporeans' unhappiness with foreign talents.

An increase in foreign talents will not only help to mitigate the impact of ageing population but also to share the load of infrastructure development. With more foreign talents becoming permanent residents, the taxes that they pay will contribute to the development of Singapore and her infrastructure. The cost of development is shared among more people and hence, less individual cost. This will benefit Singapore greatly. Furthermore, immigration will aid the economy in both lower and higher skilled jobs. Most Singaporeans prefer to work in offices, financial sectors, estate management, investments and other white-collar jobs. However, there is still a need for workers in food centres, cleaning industries, landscaping industries and so on. For higher skilled jobs, the experience and skills of foreign talents will aid us to learn and gain new experiences and skills.

With the benefits that foreign talents bring and the risk of a decrease in the number of foreign talents coming to Singapore in the next 50 years, Singapore must work hard to assimilate foreign talents and to attract more into Singapore. Only by increasing the population will we be able to have a prosperous economy and not one that is decreasing in terms of the number of working-age individuals and labour. Without a sustainable pool of labour, Singaporeans can only try to venture into very specific service industries and research and development industries. There might still be growth but definitely at a much slower rate without foreign talents.

Tough Decisions and Happiness

On a previous visit to Singapore, American economist Bryan Douglas Caplan commented that Singapore frequently adopts policies that are "economically efficient but politically unpopular" (Caplan, 2009). Tough decisions usually come with immediate costs but results in long-term benefits and thus, making them politically unpopular. The general population, who mainly see the short-term costs and only the long-term benefits much later, will be unhappy with tough policies. Through the past 50 years, Singapore has had to make some tough decisions and the ability to make these decisions has contributed to the success of its economy today. In the past, Singaporeans were less educated and much poorer, with few university graduates, diploma holders and not having much to lose, they placed their trust in those in the government who were seemingly more educated and believed that the short-term costs were worth it. Furthermore, the government was formed mainly by a singular political party and hence, tough decisions could be made and implemented. The costs in the past were definitely worth the current success and urbanisation of Singapore. However, Singapore will continue to face situations in the next 50 years that will require her to make tough decisions.

In recent times, many personal blogs have been set up and many forums have been discussing the decisions of the government. Criticism of policies, expressions of unhappiness and demands for transparency have been frequent topics of discussion. With more education, Singaporeans are demanding to be more involved in the thought process of policies and that policymaking becomes more transparent. This is in stark contrast to when the government would decide among themselves which policies to advance. The short-term costs of tough policies such as the Central Provident Fund (CPF), which is a compulsory savings plan to fund, amongst other things, the retirement of Singaporeans and permanent residents, have resulted in the general unhappiness of some Singaporeans and they have demanded to be included in the debates regarding such tough policies. This has caused the government to tread lightly and to think twice before embarking on challenging decisions and sometimes, the government would even adjust their decisions on tough policies to accommodate the people. On one hand, this is a good situation as it causes the government to evaluate carefully before implementing policies but on the other hand, it results in a longer delay and handicaps the government in terms of implementing tough but important decisions. The government must not be trapped in addressing the people's short-term needs but rather, be able to identify and keep in perspective society's long-term needs and to convince the people of the long-term benefits of tough policies.

Since the general population is unable to see the long-term benefits but only the short-term costs, the government would need to bridge the knowledge gap between the government and the people. For example, the need for highly priced Certificates of Entitlement (COEs) for car ownership is deemed by the people to be an unnecessary policy but the general population does not see the need to limit the amount of cars, to prevent congestion and environmental damages. Hence, in order to bridge this gap between the government and the people, the government needs to carry out more educational talks and provide more information to the people and involve the citizenry, not merely limiting the debate among academics and politicians. The population too can play a part in bridging the gap, they must remain open-minded, listen to other views before determining their views and trust the government more. Only with the government and the people working together, will we then be able to make tough decisions that are supported by the people. Together, we can create a better Singapore in 2065.

Conclusion

In summary, I believe that Singapore will continue to thrive as a busy metropolis in 2065 with sufficient population to sustain its economy and excellent infrastructure. We may become a globalised financial hub with very few manufacturing industries where firms use Singapore as a headquarters to reach out to other parts of Southeast Asia and Asia. Singaporeans will be able to work hand in hand with the government and to implement economically efficient policies together. My strong belief stems from the fact that we were always able to get back on our feet, regardless of the challenges that we faced. When others said that we could never make it as an independent country, we did it and we will continue to make our mark in the world.

References

World Bank. (n.d.). GDP per capita (current US$). Retrieved October 24, 2014 from http://data.worldbank.org/indicator/NY.GDP.PCAP.CD.

Singapore Statistics. (2014, October 24). Retrieved October 24, 2014, from http://www.singstat.gov.sg/statistics/latest_data.html#16.

Housing and Development Board, Singapore (HDB). (2013). HDB Key Statistics 2013. Retrieved October 24, 2014 from http://www10.hdb.gov.sg/eBook/AR2013/keystatistics.htm.

Caplan, B. (2009). Singapore's Political Economy: Two Paradoxes. *Ethos, 6*, 65–72.

Singapore 2065 — Whither or Wither?

Khoo Shao Tze
Personal Advisor to Minister of Tourism
and Creative Economy, Indonesia,
H.E. Mari Elka Pangestu

Fifty years is a relatively long period and makes it difficult to predict macroeconomic trends due to rapidly changing demographic landscapes globally and the continuous myriad of technological advancements. Undoubtedly, Singapore's own development in the last fifty years is a testament to that. So where will Singapore be in 50 years' time? Will we still stay relevant economically in the global arena? And will our living environment and quality of life be impacted negatively? I will attempt to answer both questions here.

Whither Singapore's Economy in 2065

As one of the most open economies in the world, our economy in the future will be influenced greatly by global macroeconomic trends. Will Singaporeans maintain their current standard of living? As it stands currently, we already boast the third highest per capita GDP globally (PPP) and have consistently enjoyed unemployment rates below 2%. What will the global economic landscape look like for us in 2065?

Economic balance globally in 2065

I have opted to begin by segmenting the world geographically into six broad regions, being: (i) the Americas (including North America, Canada and

South America), (ii) Asia (including Australia), (iii) Europe, (iv) the Middle East, (v) Russia (including Central Asia) and (vi) the African continent.

Currently, based on the GDP (nominal) of the top 30 countries globally, the Americas and Asia are quite similar in size. This is followed by Europe which is almost 25% smaller than Asia. The other three regions do not even constitute 10% of the global economy. This percentage does not change much when we extrapolate it to the top 50 countries globally.

I opine that whether a region stays relevant economically; will depend on it possessing these five elements, which are (i) innovation, (ii) energy independence, (iii) food/agricultural independence, (iv) sizeable market, and (v) strong military prowess. These five elements are not cited in order of priority, and taken in totality, will help to influence if a region will become stronger economically. Without expounding in detail, currently only the Americas and Asia actually possess all five elements above. As such, I foresee both the Americas and Asia as pulling away in importance from Europe and becoming more dominant globally over the next few decades. I see the African continent and potentially even Russia gravitating towards Asia. This may tip the scale in favour of Asia, hence accelerating the advent of the Asian century, though more at the expense of Europe than the Americas.

Singapore's strategic position

Though Asia may be further segmented into say South Asia (India, Pakistan, Bangladesh), East Asia (Greater China, Korea, Japan), ASEAN and Australasia, Singapore is strategically placed in Asia, to not just capitalise but also leverage on the growth of Asia in the future. This strategic positioning is not just limited to our geographical location. It also extends to our ethnic composition and background which allows us to understand the cultural nuances of doing business in the above areas. Currently seven out of eight of our main export partners are already in Asia, and more than 70% of the portfolio held by Temasek Holdings (one of two of our Sovereign Wealth Funds) is also in Asia. As Asia grows in significance, so will Singapore.

Looking at our economy, currently we rely most heavily on the Services sector (70%), followed by Manufacturing (<25%) and Construction (5%). I do not see this composition changing much in the next few decades. Arguably, the contribution of our Services sector may even increase over the years. Since the Services sector is the main driver of our economy, what currently constitutes as the major components of our Services sector? They would be: Finance, Business Services, Trading and Tourism/Hospitality. Seeing this, I opine that for Singapore to stay relevant economically in 2065, it will depend very much on us remaining an open economy that is not just able to provide value-added services and contribute to the growth of the other Asian economies, but also depend on us being able to continue serving as a conduit and economic link between Asia and the Americas and also Europe. And whether we will continue to enjoy this privileged position will depend largely on whether we can safeguard our main strength. And Singapore's main strength is Freedom.

Singapore's main strength: Freedom

Did I say Freedom? Freedom is not just freedom of the press. It also includes freedom from poverty (HDB and CPF), freedom from disease (Medical), freedom from ignorance (Education), freedom from crime and invasion (Strong Army and Police), freedom from persecution (Religious Freedom and Racial Harmony), freedom from pollution (Good Living Environment) and, of course, economic freedom. The parts in parentheses are references to our strengths in the relative "freedoms."

Owing to the length of this essay, I will only expand on one example of why the above "Freedoms" are vital to us staying economically relevant in 2065: "Freedom from Ignorance." I have already explained that Singapore is strategically placed to leverage on the growth of Asia. A large part of this strength relies on our understanding of how the various areas in Asia operate. As they say: "Knowledge is Power." Thus far, we have been able to leverage on this knowledge to offer value added services, such as Finance and Business Services within Asia and to investors from the Americas and Europe. We have also been able to leverage on this knowledge to our benefit in Trading. So whether we will continue to prosper will depend on "how much we know." Our education sector will also play a key role in our advancement. Will our younger generation continue to embrace the importance of education? Will they understand how important it is to our economy to grow an external sector/wing? Will they see an overseas posting as being beneficial to their careers? All are important issues.

Ultimately, I opine that why Singapore is both relevant and attractive to the Asian economies and countries in the Americas and Europe, and is able to have a striving services sector, is primarily because of its ability to build and preserve all the above freedoms. This will be key to determining whether Singapore stays relevant economically in 2065.

Will Singapore's Environment "Wither" by 2065?

The length of my essay only lets me skim the surface here. I begin with my wish for Singapore's environment in 2065: To be a model city for sustainable and clean living globally. Though I acknowledge that this journey to becoming a Model City environmentally, may come at a "price" (and by which I mean higher costs and factors of production), I opine that we can afford this higher price and indeed must be prepared for it. In fact, a lot of whether we will remain an open economy that will also appeal to many to reside in, will depend on whether we will be "Free from Pollution."

Singapore: Model City 2065

Broadly speaking, our environment, being the air we breathe, the water we drink, and the living areas that we are surrounded with, is impacted by larger forces that may be beyond our control, especially given our small geographical size. We are very much affected by transboundary pollution and external environmental forces such as rising sea levels. That said, there is still much that we can do to improve our living environment and to become a Model City. In particular, we can improve our efforts in three broad categories, being (i) Energy Production, (ii) Transportation, (iii) Increasing Environmental Consciousness (including waste management, recycling efforts and sustainable and green building).

Energy production

Presently, we are still reliant on fossil fuels and even using thermal coal as a fuel to generate electricity. We should phase these out and switch to natural gas. I recognise that thermal coal (for example) may provide the best MEEP (Measure of Energy Efficiency Performance) and is the most cost efficient fuel for producing energy, and that switching to natural gas will lead to higher energy costs as a factor of production, and reduce our cost competitiveness. However, taken holistically, the benefit will be a better living environment that I opine many will gladly be willing to pay for, particularly when one considers that the environment in other cities may be more polluted and hence less liveable by 2065. We should also be more proactive in implementing more sources of renewable energy, such as solar and waste to energy.

Transportation

By 2065, I envisage a Singapore where electric cars have already replaced cars that still rely on fossil fuels. However, I hope that stronger steps can be taken in that direction now. To begin with, we should already mandate a biofuel mix in our petrol stations. This is already the case in countries like Germany. With the largest biodiesel plant in the world already situated in Singapore, and the abundance of biodiesel feedstock like palm oil close to us, there is no reason why we cannot already mandate the distribution of B20 biodiesel. We should also provide for more generous subsidies for hybrid and electric vehicles and provide for more charging stations island wide. The state of California is already charging (pun intended) ahead of us here and yet, they are far bigger than we are in size.

Environmental consciousness

I am heartened by the presence of green initiatives in our construction and building sector, and am particularly encouraged by our strong water resource management expertise. In the latter especially, Singapore has been consistently taking steps to ensure that we will be self-sufficient in water usage and management by 2065. To supplement our success here, more steps can be taken to accelerate and proliferate more recycling projects island-wide. This will also allow us to optimise our waste management, given our small geographical size, which may also lead to lower costs in construction of waste to energy power plants in the future. Environmental awareness campaigns and programmes can be rolled out in schools at an earlier stage, so that our younger generation will see recycling as part of their everyday lives.

Ultimately, Singapore's geographical size can be used to our advantage to develop and showcase our city state as a model of sustainable and clean living. Even though achieving this may lead to higher costs of living, a persuasive consideration for the present generation, is the living environment that we will be passing on to our future generations.

Finally, I will like to close with this note. As we turn 50 as a nation, and I reflect on my own life as a second-generation Singaporean, I cannot help but marvel at how far Singapore has come. So it is up to us to grow our economy and to protect this environment, to ensure that we can pass this blessing on for the next 50 years.

Singapore Economy and Environment in 2065

Hean Teik Ong
M Med (NUS), FRCP (Edin, Glas), FACC, FESC
Consultant Cardiologist
H. T. Ong Heart Clinic, Penang, Malaysia

Fifty years ago when faced with the fundamental question of what type of country they wanted, the founding fathers of Singapore decided to seek one that emphasised integrity and competency, where all ethnicities were equal and English retained as a uniting working language. This answer meant that ultimately Singapore could not be a part of Malaysia, where it had been decided that the royalty was to be retained and the founding social contract gave preeminence to the Malay race, language and religion. The shape of Singapore's economy and environment fifty years from now will be decided by the answers to four other equally fundamental questions, namely (i) will Singapore prosper or perish, (ii) is Singapore to be home or hotel, (iii) is society to be courteous and caring, or contentious and condescending, and lastly, (iv) can there be compromise, cooperation and consensus?

Will Singapore Prosper, or Perish?

This apparently profound question is in fact the easiest to answer scientifically and logically. Singapore's survival and sustainability is the result of its geographical location, and the different peoples attracted to it. Located strategically at the confluence of land, sea and now air routes, Singapore has always been a vibrant trading hub. Within 13 years of its founding in 1819, Singapore had supplanted Penang, a place discovered much earlier in 1786, as the capital of the British Straits Settlement.[1] In 1965, Singapore's per capita GDP placed it 3rd in Asia, below only Japan and Hong Kong.[2] In 2013, the International Monetary Fund ranks Singapore 8th in the world in calculated per capita gross domestic product, above the United States ($54,775 vs $53,101).[3] It only stands to reason that Singapore's economic performance, which has persisted over the last 200 years through world wars, deep depression and dramatic changes in political governance will continue for the next 50 years and into the foreseeable future.

Some point to global warming and the potential rise in sea level as a dire threat to Singapore, saying the island can disappear. Such doomsday scenarios ignore geographical realities. Singapore is located at the southernmost tip of the Malacca Straits, where the sea depth is shallow and usually only about 27 m deep, allowing for fairly easy land reclamation.[4] In fact reclamation activity has increased Singapore's land area by 23% from 581.5 km^2 to 710.2 km^2 over the period 1965 to 2008.[5] A detailed study of the threats to Singapore from climate change by the AAG Center for Global Geography Education shows that even a 5 m rise in sea level, calculated in a worst case scenario by combining the sea level 6,000 years ago with the occurrence of unusually high tide, will leave most parts of Singapore still intact.[6] By 2100, it has been postulated that rising sea-level could result in a loss of 4 to 17 km^2 of dry land, accounting for only 0.6% to 2.7% of Singapore's total land area. A system of protective sea-walls can

---

[1] British Malaya, Wikipedia. Retrieved January 21, 2015 from http://en.wikipedia.org/wiki/British_Malaya.

[2] World Economics. Maddison Historical GDP Data. Retrieved January 21, 2015 from http://www.worldeconomics.com/Data/MadisonHistoricalGDP/Madison%20Historical%20GDP%20Data.efp.

[3] List of countries by GDP (nominal) per capita, Wikipedia. Retrieved January 21, 2015 from http://en.wikipedia.org/wiki/List_of_countries_by_GDP_(nominal)_per_capita.

[4] Missing Malaysia Airlines Plane: 10 Key Facts about the Malacca Strait and Andaman Sea, *Straits Times* (March 12, 2014). Retrieved January 21, 2015 from http://www.straitstimes.com/breaking-news/se-asia/story/missing-malaysia-airlines-plane-10-key-facts-malacca-strait-andaman-sea-MH370#sthash.0Ye9YcVW.dpuf.

[5] Tan H. T. W., Chou L. M., Yeo D. C. J., and Ng P. K. L. (2009), *The Natural Heritage of Singapore*, 3rd Edition, Singapore: Prentice Hall-Pearson Education South Asia Pte Ltd.

[6] Chang C. H. (2010), Global Climate Change Case Study: How are Countries Adapting to Climate Change? In M. Solem, P. Klein O. Muñiz-Solari, and W. Ray (eds.), *AAG Center for Global Geography Education*. Retrieved January 21, 2015 from http://cgge.aag.org/GlobalClimateChange1e/cs-2/index.html.

effectively and economically mitigate the impact of such rise in sea-level.[7] Singapore is not the Maldives, a country in the middle of the deep Indian Ocean whose economy and existence is indeed threatened by climate change and rising sea-levels. The reality is that Singapore will not perish in the foreseeable future.

Is Singapore to be Home or Hotel?

As a small predominantly Chinese society in a post-colonial Southeast Asia emphasising its nationalistic predominantly Muslim characteristics, Singapore had to find a glue to unite its citizens and make them willing to defend their new country. Coincidentally, the housing needs of the population was a pressing issue 50 years ago with 300,000 people living in squatter settlements in the suburbs and 250,000 in squalid shophouses in the town centre.[8] Congested unhygienic living conditions no doubt played a significant role in outbreaks of fire, riots and infectious diseases. By investing heavily in building low-cost housing units to be then sold to its people, the government made Singapore a home-owning society and laid the seeds of nationalism in their fledging country. Home ownership made Singapore a place worth defending and resulted in general support for compulsory national service for all males introduced in 1967. There was no doubt that the early leaders saw Singapore as a home for its people, and worked hard to achieve their vision.

The concept of Singapore as a home may not be supportive of rapid development since a home is a happy place of relaxation and refuge whereas progress necessitates toil and anxiety. In an interview with Dan Buettner that was published in the book *Thrive*, Lee Kuan Yew had rated his own happiness at 5 when he was Prime Minister and 6 after elevation to Minister Mentor, and he said, "Nothing would take me to 9… Then I would be complacent, flabby, and walk into the sunset."[9] To ensure that "the spurs are stuck on the hinds" of Singaporeans, for continued economic

[7] Ng W. S. and R. Mendelsohn (2005), The Impact of Sea Level Rise on Singapore, *Environment and Development Economics, 10*, 201–215.

[8] B. Yuen (2007), Squatters No More: Singapore Social Housing, *Global Urban Development Magazine, 3*(1). Retrieved January 21, 2015 from http://www.globalurban.org/GUDMag07Vol3Iss1/Yuen.htm.

[9] D. Buettner (2010), *Thrive: Finding Happiness the Blue Zones Way*, Washington. D.C.: National Geographic Society, p. 84.

progress and to make up for the low reproduction rate, immigration is promoted with an especially warm welcome to the wealthy and capable.[10,11] Olympic medals were won by essentially transplanted Chinese players and naming rights to public institutions are given to philanthropists, even if they have no close bond to the institution receiving the contribution. Singapore began to resemble a hotel where its dwellers seek to profit from their stay. As David Marshall the pioneering Chief Minister lamented, "There is a very serious danger of promoting a society in which all merit is governed by gold; where the money in the bank account indicates the merit of the individual. There is a very grave danger that our youth is growing up with no morality except money."[12]

The Lehman collapse in 2008 clearly revealed the very adverse impact on society and country when American bankers pursue a profit at all costs policy. Singaporeans too seem to object to the newer government policy of constantly seeking strong economic growth. In the 2011 presidential election, in a crowded field of four, the candidate supported by the ruling PAP government was pipped to the post his second place rival, a man who had once been a PAP MP, by only 1.35% of total votes cast.[13] A White Paper planning for a 6.9 million population resulted in the largest public protest in recent times, although it mobilised only 4,000.[14] After winning just 60% of the popular vote in 2011, and losing two subsequent by-elections the government does seem to be responding to the needs of its voters. Over the last couple of years, an improved medical scheme promised Singaporeans cradle-to-grave insurance for all, and retirement safety nets are strengthened. Hopefully government and governed in Singapore will realise that a home is not merely a large, expensively furnished house, and in 2065 Singapore will truly be a happy home for its people.

---

[10] Transcript of Minister Mentor Lee Kuan Yew's interview with Mark Jacobson from National Geographic on July 6, 2009 (for National Geographic magazine Jan 2010 edition). SGPressCentre. Retrieved January 21, 2015 from http://www.news.gov.sg/public/sgpc/en/media_releases/agencies/pmo/transcript/T-20091228-1.html.

[11] Han F. K., Z. Ibrahim, Chua M. H., L. Lim, I. Low, R. Lin, and R. Chan, (2011), *Lee Kuan Yew: Hard Truths to Keep Singapore Going*, Singapore: Straits Times Press.

[12] Chew M. (1996), *Leaders of Singapore*, Singapore: Resource Press.

[13] Presidential Elections in Singapore, Wikipedia. Retrieved January 21, 2015 from http://en.wikipedia.org/wiki/Presidential_elections_in_Singapore.

[14] Rare Mass Rally Over Singapore Immigration Plans, *BBC News Asia* (February 16, 2013). Retrieved January 21, 2015 from http://www.bbc.com/news/world-asia-21485729.

Courteous and Caring or Contentious and Condescending

With the retirement of the hard driving founding leaders, there was talk of making Singapore a "kinder, gentler society." Singaporeans are generally supportive of the principle that every individual has to work hard and be self-reliant, with those successful deserving their reward and thus held up as worthy role models. Unfortunately, the successful are sometimes unable to understand and empathise with the anxieties of the struggling. Wee Shu Min, the 18-year-old daughter of a PAP MP, came under intense criticism when she called a blogger who voiced his anxieties about his future prospects a "stupid crackpot" belonging to the "sadder class" who should "please get out of my elite, uncaring face."[15] More recently, a British expatriate Anton Casey who belittled "all those poor people" travelling on public subway lost his job and subsequently left Singapore after facing intense anger and antagonism.[16] In competing for the limited number of scholarships or coveted positions, Singaporeans seem to have little time for pleasantries or patience for the less materially successful. In July 2013, speaking at a Raffles Institution Homecoming event, Emeritus Senior Minister Goh Chok Tong warned Singapore against developing into an elitist society.[17] Ngiam Tong Dow, a respected retired civil servant, expressed similar concerns when he wrote of being told by a Japanese investor that the educational quality of the Singapore workforce was very uneven. He called for a change in policy to raise the educational level of the masses to establish a high plateau instead of pursuing the development of tall solitary peaks.[18] Even the Dean of Law felt it necessary to call on his graduates, and society, to embrace failure so as to ultimately achieve more happiness.[19]

---

[15] Wee Shu Min Elitism Controversy, Wikipedia. Retrieved January 21, 2015 from http://en.wikipedia.org/wiki/Wee_Shu_Min_elitism_controversy.

[16] M. Tadeo (2014, January 27), Anton Casey Fired and Flees Singapore in Economy Class over "Poor People" Comments, *The Independent*. Retrieved January 21, 2015 from http://www.independent.co.uk/news/business/news/anton-casey-fired-and-flees-singapore-in-economy-class-over-poor-people-comments-9088199.html.

[17] Singapore Must Guard Against Elitism: Goh Chok Tong, *Today* (2013, July 28). Retrieved January 21, 2015 from http://www.todayonline.com/singapore/singapore-must-guard-against-elitism-goh-chok-tong?singlepage=true.

[18] Ngiam T. D. (2006), *A Mandarin and the Making of Public Policy: Reflections by Ngiam Tong Dow*, Singapore: NUS Press.

[19] S. Chesterman (2014, July 21), In Praise of Failure, *The Straits Times*. Retrieved January 21, 2015 from http://www.straitstimes.com/news/opinion/eye-singapore/story/praise-failure-20140721.

Singapore has consistently performed poorly in measures of happiness and positive emotions. In 2011, a Gallup poll of 148 countries puts Singapore at the very bottom of the scale, below even troubled Iraq.[20] The 2012 Happy Planet Index ranks Singapore 90 out of the 151 countries surveyed.[21] There is good scientific data to show that continued increase in income does not produce a corresponding increase in wellbeing beyond a certain point.[22] While there is no doubt that meritocracy is vital for Singapore, the type of meritocracy practiced will shape the behaviour pattern of society. In a society practicing competitive meritocracy that rewards only the top winners, people will not cooperate and may even engage in behaviour to sabotage fellow competitors. On the other hand, a meritocracy with a fixed "passing mark" that rewards all who cross this level will ensure fewer are left behind and may even promote cooperative behaviour.[23] Similarly, more will benefit if effort and industry, not grades and degrees, are rewarded.

Li Ka-shing, Asia's wealthiest man, writes that one should only buy meals for those who are "richer or more knowledgeable" and "when poor, spend money on others, when rich, spend money on yourself."[24] On the other hand, Leo Tolstoy, in answer to the three questions of "when is the best time to do something, who is the most important person to do it with and what is the most important thing to do" writes that there is only one important time and that is now, the most important person is the one with you at that moment and the most important activity is to make that person happy for that alone is the purpose of life.[25] Nobody knows what 2065 has in store, but if Tolstoy is read rather than Lee Ka-shing, Singaporeans will be score better in happiness index, being more caring and courteous.

[20] J. Clifton (2012, December 19), Latin Americans Most Positive in the World; Singaporeans are the Least Positive Worldwide, *Gallup World*, Retrieved January 21, 2015 from http://www.gallup.com/poll/159254/latin-americans-positive-world.aspx#1.

[21] Happy Planet Index. Singapore achieves a Happy Planet Index Score of 39.8 and ranks #90 of all the Countries Analysed. Retrieved January 21, 2015 from http://www.happyplanetindex.org/countries/singapore/#sthash.UlfLHxwo.dpuf.

[22] D. Kahneman and A. Deaton (2010), High Income Improves Evaluation of Life but not Emotional Well-being. *PNAS*, *107*(38), 16489–16493.

[23] D. Low (2014), Good Meritocracy, Bad Meritocracy, in D. Low and S. T. Vadaketh (eds.), *Hard Choices: Challenging the Singapore Consensus*, Singapore: NUS Press.

[24] Li Ka-shing on How You Can Buy a Car and House in 5 Years, *Asiaone*, February 19, 2014. Retrieved January 21, 2015 from http://business.asiaone.com/personal-finance/news/li-ka-shing-how-you-can-buy-car-and-house-5-years.

[25] Leo Tolstoy, The Emperor's Three Questions. Retrieved from http://textfiles.com/stories/emperor3.txt.

Conclusion — Can there be Compromise, Cooperation and Consensus?

Eddie Barker, Singapore Law Minister 1964–1988, spoke of being summoned to see PM Lee who demanded to know why Barker often and aggressively opposed Lee's proposals. Barker replied that he was previously instructed to speak honestly, and that if Lee wanted him to be a yes-man, he will make sure he supports Lee in future. Lee Kuan Yew's reply was to continue to speak openly.[26] Thus two intelligent, bold and forthright men were able to resolve their conflict, reach a consensus and continue their cooperation in the service of Singapore.

Singapore is a land of contrasting conundrums. Its universities rate very highly in world rankings, yet its tertiary enrolment at 40% is far below Australia's 86% or Thailand's 51% and just above Malaysia's 36%.[27,28] Foreign royalty seek medical treatment in Singapore, yet its hospitals are so short of beds that patients are sleeping in tents and corridors.[29] In 2013, 10% of Singapore households are millionaires making it the 3rd highest worldwide, yet wage share of GDP has stagnated over the last 20 years and at 42% is lower than many other high income countries and only above that of Ireland and Italy.[30–32]

---

[26] Tan K. Y. L. (1999), The Legalists: Kenny Byrne and Eddie Barker. In Lam P. E. and Tan K. Y. L. (eds.), *Lee's Lieutenants*. Australia: Allen & Unwin.

[27] Education: Gross Enrolment Ratio by Level of Education, UNESCO Institute for Statistics, Data Centre. Retrieved from http://data.uis.unesco.org/index.aspx?queryid=142&lang=en.

[28] Teo Z. (2013, March), Educational Profile of Singapore Resident Non-Students, 2002–2012, Statistics Singapore Newsletter. Retrieved January 21, 2015 from http://www.singstat.gov.sg/docs/default-source/default-document-library/publications/publications_and_papers/education_and_literacy/ssnmar13-pg1-7.pdf.

[29] S. Khalik (2014, January 8), Hospitals Facing Severe Bed Crunch Take Unusual Steps, *The Straits Times*. Retrieved January 21, 2015 from http://www.straitstimes.com/breaking-news/singapore/story/hospitals-facing-severe-bed-crunch-take-unusual-steps-20140108.

[30] B. Beardsley, J. Becerra, F. Burgoni, B. Holley, D. Kessler, F. Muxi, M. Naumann, T. Tang, and A. Zakrzewski (2014), Global Wealth 2014: Riding a Wave of Growth, *BCG Perspective*. Retrieved January 21, 2015 from https://www.bcgperspectives.com/content/articles/financial_institutions_business_unit_strategy_global_wealth_2014_riding_wave_growth/?chapter=2.

[31] Hui W. T. and R. Toh (2014), *Growth with Equity in Singapore: Challenges and Prospects*, International Labour Office, Conditions of Work and Employment Branch, Geneva: ILO. Retrieved January 21, 2015 from http://www.ilo.org/wcmsp5/groups/public/---ed_protect/---protrav/---travail/documents/publication/wcms_244819.pdf.

[32] Goh T. W. (2013), A Look at Wage Share and Wages in Singapore Workers, *Economic Survey of Singapore First Quarter 2013*. Ministry of Trade and Industry. Retrieved January 21, 2015 from http://www.mti.gov.sg/ResearchRoom/SiteAssets/Pages/Economic-Survey-of-Singapore-First-Quarter-2013/BA_1Q13.pdf.

Presently almost a quarter of Singaporeans over the age of 65 have to continue working, with fully 35% of these elderly workers earning less than S$1,000 a month.[33] 50 years ago, fault lines opened up because of race or religion. Today, conflicts more often arise between different economic classes or because of a different view about lifestyle issues. In fact Christians and Muslims in Singapore were recently united in demonstrating opposition to the "Pink Dot" movement.[34]

It is difficult to sail a tranquil ship in turbulent oceans. Fortunately, developments in Malaysia and Indonesia, Singapore's closest neighbours, suggest that they are transforming into societies that can weather economic challenges, demonstrative democracy and political transitions. Singapore's record of facing different but equally challenging problems also gives much hope that its pragmatic population is able to compromise, cooperate and come to a working consensus on what course is best for the country. There is much reason to feel that in 2065, consistent with its founding principles for a fair, meritocratic society emphasising integrity, industry and inclusiveness, Singapore will continue to be a thriving country.

[33] R. Basu (2014, August 25), 35,000 Older Workers Earn Less Than $1,000, *The Straits Times*. Retrieved January 21, 2015 from http://www.straitstimes.com/news/singapore/more-singapore-stories/story/35000-older-workers-earn-less-1000-20140825.

[34] Thousands of Singaporean Christians Wear White to Protest Pink Dot Gay Rally, Yahoo Newsroom (2014, June 29). Retrieved January 21, 2015 from https://sg.news.yahoo.com/thousands-of-singaporean-christians-wear-white-to-protest-pink-dot-gay-rally-143235694.html.

Against the Odds, Again

Benjamin C.W. Tan
NTU alumni

The year is 2065. It is 9.30 a.m. on a Saturday morning and I have just dragged myself out of bed. Turning to my right, I glance at a picture of my wife and children in an old 2010s photo frame by my bedside. Home is a 750-square-foot apartment in Pasir Ris New Island, previously known as Pulau Ubin. Pretty spacious by the day's standards, especially for retirees like my wife and I.

"Terrybot, this is Benjamin, activate screen, please," I said, half yawning. "What mode would you like, sir?" the voice command speaker responded, "Hologram mode, please."

The Hologram Output Multi-use Device (HOMD) screened the television programming from the output device in the ceiling. I switched to Channel NewsWorld, one of the many news channels owned by the now privately run CNA Corp, one of the global "Big Three" in broadcasting, along with Alibaba-CCTV Global Enterprise and Comcast-Warner. An interview with a Ministry of Manpower director on high wages affecting competitiveness was being screened. I started reflecting back on the days when I was a young officer working in what was then called the Civil Service, and now known as the People Service. Today, the People Service still employs many Singaporeans, maintains a high level of efficiency, attracting some of the best talents. In 2027, the government had greatly reduced the number of overseas scholarships, an internal alignment with the higher standards that Singapore's education institutions offered.

Nanyang Technological University was now 7th in the world, just ousting 8th-placed Hong Kong University of Science and Technology.

As a young person 50 years ago, I had never really shared my thoughts on the state of matters, but I felt things changing for Singapore. For 50 stellar years we had stable growth, economic stability, political stability and arguably, social stability. However, I had noticed signs that the tapering had started. A tapering to normalcy from the exceptional progress my small, resourceless island state had made. In some sense, a rift was steadily growing, but for which no one had dared to announce, for the markers were not on any map, but in the minds and thoughts of the people. Political and social issues, which were once dormant, had exploded onto the scene, catalysed by social media and the increased socialisation of ideas that the Internet had enabled. The frustration with a global economy that would be stuck in a low gear for some time to come did not help. Everybody had a voice, and they wanted to be heard, from the young to the old, from the proponents of the status quo to its opponents, from the informed to the misinformed. As a young person, I treasured the free voice, but also realised that no voice could be free if everyone were to have his or her way. A technical impossibility, I reckoned. Antagonisation and appeasement was the play of the day. The room for measures that sought to produce the most fruitful end was becoming narrower. I was worried about how Singapore would cope, and what the future would hold for my children. "Will they be as blessed with peace as I am? Will Singapore even be around in 2065?"

Back then in 2015, as the world was becoming increasingly connected at a pace faster than social and political structures could adapt to, megacities and hubs were becoming increasingly saturated by trade movements, labour movements and though largely ignored for some time: the movements of ideas. The middle class felt squeezed, leading to the increased dynamism (and perhaps, inefficiency) of political progress and the difficulty in justifying resource allocation. This was why I was worried. The impediments seemed too great and I was pessimistic about the potential and heart that my generation possessed. If there were no tolerance, how could we face the important challenges as a collective? Would we stand the test of great challenges we would inevitably face? I had feared not.

I could not be more wrong.

As change became the norm, Singaporeans adapted. As we made it through the 2020s and 2030s, Singaporeans became increasingly educated and thought more critically where their futures were concerned. Debate became fruitful. Arguments became discussions. Protests became discourse. Trust was built. We had created a new system that became a global example to follow and copy. Referendums were called to reveal our reserves, they were called for universal healthcare and unsustainable wage floor policies, but none passed despite how politically popular they all were. How was this possible? I felt ashamed for having had so little faith when I was a younger man. The common man was no longer the common man. He hungered for his wellbeing in a sane manner. He craved progress, and not effortless languor. He understood what it meant to debate, and was at the same time his own harshest critic.

As I flipped through *The Straits Times* on my HOMD, I read an article reporting how homegrown companies dominated our export statistics, with substantial value contributed by non-oil technology related goods/services. Singapore now has many large Singapore brands to boot, enterprises that are globally competitive in the technology, engineering, lifestyle and services space. Impressive, I thought.

I flipped to the next page and saw an advertisement for the latest self-driving car. In 2052, Singapore became the first city to have self-driven car lanes on the road, with the full infrastructure changes to boast. I briefly thought about how nice it would be to own a new one but reminded myself that the train station was merely 50 metres away from my doorstep.

Just then, my eldest daughter walked into the door with my wife, and trudged toward the dining table with our breakfast fix of *chwee kueh*, *nasi lemak* and *peh dan chok*.[1] "The *peh dan chok* is for you Dad, it is less oily," she said quickly, before I could protest. I thought for a moment, and decided not to contest her. I had packets of *keropok*[2] hidden that she did not know about anyway.

A thought then occurred to me "National Day is just around the corner. SG100 you know. Can you get tickets for me? I want to go."

---

[1] These are a steamed rice cake, rice dish, and century egg porridge, respectively, all of which are dishes that are much loved in Singapore.

[2] Deep fried crackers.

"Sure thing Dad, I will try, okay? If not *Kor*[3] might be able to. Mum was saying it'll surely be very crowded! Are you sure?" She was genuinely concerned, as I had hurt my back a month ago.

Chuckling, I replied, "Of course! What a celebration it'll be! In fact, I wish I could live to see another hundred years!"

I added, "You might not know this, but back in the day, we were only known as a little red dot."

[3] Hokkien for elder brother.

Musing about Prosperity in 2065 Singapore

Raymond Toh
A Singaporean born in 1981

There is a traditional Chinese saying, "富不过三代" (*fu bu guo san dai*), which means that the wealth of a family does not stretch beyond three generations. With each generation around 30–35 years, this implies that by 2065, that is, when Singapore celebrates her 100th year of existence, it may be the end of her journey of prosperity and wealth.

It is a morbid thought to imagine that Singapore may not survive for another 50 years especially since we are celebrating SG50, 50 years of Singapore's independence, at the point of writing. However, history taught us that great nations rise and fall and though big countries took centuries to decline, Singapore being an extremely small country is vulnerable to a quicker demise.

So even as Singapore celebrates its 50 years of nationhood, we are at the crossroads again and we have to re-examine, re-focus and re-engineer our nation, in order to survive and prosper for the next 50 years and beyond.

Starting Line

The genesis of Singapore is that she is a nation created out of necessity and circumstances of the day. Singapore was "kicked out" from Malaysia on 9 August 1965 and since then Singapore has marched on and seldom looked back.

I would attribute Singapore's success of becoming a First World nation to the Government's approach to its policy making which was hinged on practicality (what works and what needed to be done) and flexibility in response to the world demands and not due to any particular ideology or theory of development.

From the beginning, Singapore's economy was export-oriented, supported mainly by Multinational Companies (MNCs) and not import-substitution. It was first among the region to do so as many young nations preferred to grow its own industries.

The primary sector was totally removed because it was not high value adding to the economy and instead manufacturing was promoted. And when the cost of production increased to the level that it became too expensive for MNCs to operate, Singapore focused on retaining higher value manufacturing (e.g. silicone chip making) and transformed itself to be the regional headquarters for exiting MNCs. As such, the economy was given the opportunity to transform to become more service oriented, providing financial services to the companies. Singapore also changed to become provider of tourism and entertainment services to the world, through the integrated resorts, hosting of world class events such as the annual Grand Prix Night Race, and the gathering of the world's best culinary experience in this small island.

Crossroads

The earlier generation of Baby Boomers was able to enjoy such great prosperity because they worked hard and also because there was clear leadership. The paternalistic style of governing by the founding Prime Minister, Mr. Lee Kuan Yew, meant that there were no ifs, ands or buts, and only a no nonsense "Just Do It" attitude. If the Government decided that it was the right thing for Singapore, the decision makers would act upon it, and the people would follow.

Social policies were also implemented without hesitation. To clean up the city image and make Singapore a Garden City, the government initiated a "Stop Littering" campaign and slapped a fine of S$500 if people were caught littering. To promote increase in productivity, the government came up with the Productivity Bee and a jingle to go along with it. To encourage courteous behavior, Singa the Courtesy Lion was created to remind the citizens to act with kindness. This is the way of the government then.

As the leadership transited from the Baby Boomers to the Generation "X" and "Y" and as the pioneer generation fades away, things are starting to change. The Government approach things differently. It is a kinder and gentler Government and more consultative in policymaking. Feedback and consultations are taken into consideration before implementation. Traditional methods such as fines and prohibitions are no longer enforced with as much zeal as before. Even Singa the Lion had to "retire" from service (in nicer terms, in actual fact it "resigned") since it is no longer able to fulfill its function of telling the people what to do.

U-turns

So, it is not uncommon to see the government reverse its past policies nowadays to suit the needs of the people or the situation. One policy U-turn was the "Stop at Two" campaign which was to reduce Singapore's birth rates during the early 1970s–1980s. When the birth rate fell rapidly below replacement rate, in 1990s the Government quickly changed to the campaign to encourage "Three or More, if You Can Afford It" and even designed various versions of Baby Bonuses to encourage the citizens to reproduce.

Being born in the 1980s, I am affected by such policy changes. Because of the policy to discourage higher child birth and being the third born in the family, my parents were "discriminated" against — from not being given any priorities in the delivery ward, to higher taxes and less education subsidies, which effective penalised my parents for giving birth to me. But now, as I have my own children, I am flooded with cash incentives and tax rebates to encourage me to have more children.

Destination

So are U-turns in policies a sign of bad government and bad policy making?

I think they are not. Instead policy changes are a reflection of the Government's willingness to do what works. It is willing to learn from mistakes and acknowledge that things have gone wrong and this is a mark of humility. As Singapore re-examine, re-focus and re-engineer our nation, we must be prepared to take the necessary U-turns so that we can get to where we want to be. Things that no longer make sense or are no longer relevant must be forsaken.

Another Chinese phrase is relevant here: "适者生存" (*shi zhe shengcun*) which is the translation of the term "survival of the fittest" as coined by Herbert Spencer following Charles Darwin's theory of evolution. The English phrase seems to suggest that fitness has to do with strength or might. But the Chinese translation accurately highlights the subtle nuance — the survivors are those who are the most adaptable and willing to evolve with time. Indeed, if Singapore were to continue to survive and prosper for the next 50 years or even centuries after that, the willingness to change and remain flexible and nimble will be the key.

The world will not stand still for us. We must remain adaptable and flexible, otherwise the 50 years of enduring hardship, toil and sweat by the Singapore Pioneer Generation and the wealth and prosperity that we enjoy today would likely to be all for naught.

Race with Droids and Drones

Tony Yeoh
Vice President Global Technology
Asia Middle East Africa
Intercontinental Hotels Group

Without the scientist, there is no future.

Dr. Michio Kaku
Physics of the Future: How Science will Shape our Daily Lives by the Year 2100

At a time the world is clawing its way out of a global financial meltdown, it is hard to be optimistic and predictive of what the future holds when this so-called "jobless recovery" seems anaemic and uncertain at a global level, despite all the fiscal and monetary measures.

Scarcity or Abundance?

One school of thought, as exemplified by economists such as Robert Gordon, and Tyler Cowen in his latest book, *Average is Over: Powering America Beyond the Age of the Great Stagnation*, asserts that because of globalisation, ageing demographics and technology innovation plateauing, advanced economies are trapped in declining productivity, widening income disparity and low job creation. Graham Turner and Cathy Alexander, researchers from University of Melbourne, used computer simulation to prove that the 40-year-old book *The Limits to Growth* is true in its hypothesis that our civilisation is nearing collapse because the earth is finite and the scarcity of material resources cannot support the exploding population growth.

Recently, an opposing school of thought led by Erik Brynjolfsson and Andrew McAfee in their book *The Second Machine Age* submitted a more fascinating and promising view that the global economy is in fact at an inflection point of the next staggering exponential growth driven by smart machines tapping on technology advances in artificial intelligence (AI), digitisation and hyper-networks. Peter H. Diamandis and Steven Kotler in *Abundance: The Future is Better Than You Think*, world-renowned physicist Michio Kaku in *Physics of the Future* and Philip Auerswald in *The Coming Prosperity: How Entrepreneurs Are Transforming the Global Economy* offer an antidote view to the doomsayers and asserts that technology and entrepreneurism would prove right the adage that necessity is the mother of all invention.

Singapore will, once again, through rational pragmatism turn adversity into advantage, through technology turn scarcity into sustainability. In the next 50 years, Singapore will ride the next wave of technology to stay ahead.

Exponential Growth

Since the Industrial Revolution, economic growth cycles have been driven by successive breakthroughs in general purpose technology. Progress in human civilisation can be attributed to our understanding of the Four Laws of Nature which has continually helped us understand the Universe. The first Newtonian law of gravity explained mechanics and motion which led to the invention of the steam-powered locomotive that enabled mass production and marked the start of the industrial revolution. The second law of electromagnetic force let Thomas Edison explain electricity and magnetism which unleashed the electrical revolution that modernised and urbanised human societies. The third and fourth laws of weak and strong nuclear forces explained by Einstein forms the basis of quantum theory that helps us demystify the subatomic world which led to the discovery of transistors which are switches of electronic signals and electrical power. These transistors were later integrated and compacted into the silicon chip 50 years ago, and made in the form of computers saw the rise of the digital revolution. The silicon chip has been the foundation for growth and productivity especially in the services-led information and communication industry, but it has also made inroads through combinatorial technology, into many other industries like energy, environment, space and medicine. Much of this exponential growth supports Moore's Law which simply means that computer power doubles every eighteen months, but there is growing concern that this is reaching its plateau.

In the near term over the next 25 years, the price of silicon chips will drop to a cent. Haptics and sensors will be embedded in many devices and distributed everywhere. Everyone and everything in Singapore will be connected to the Internet, the Internet of Everything (IoE). Singapore, taking advantage of its size as a city-state, will conduct many live nationwide deployments of incubation technology, ranging from cashless payments to sensors for big data analytics. Retail will be transformed through the use of mobile location-based commerce and experience showrooms. The driverless vehicle pilots will become a pervasive reality. Robotic cars will be used on long stretches of highways and public transport may be able to reduce its dependence on labour. Wearable computing such as contact lenses will be fashionable and will provide instant access to information on the Internet, making the term "average" a misnomer. Flexible electronic paper will be the skins of many walls and objects for instant projection and lugging computers around will be a thing of the past. Facing labour shortages, drones will be used to assist security surveillance and logistics. Singapore will be a hyper-connected, hyper-aware city through the use of sensors. Singapore will be highly mechanised and machines will be a significant complement to the workforce.

The New Foreign Worker

The current generation of robots such as Honda's ASIMO or Sony's robot dog AIBO, while it appears intelligent and emotionally responsive, the reality is that it is limited by how much humans have to pre-programme ahead of time. In 1997 IBM's Deep Blue beat Garry Kasparov at chess, and in 2011 Watson won at Jeopardy. Although progress is encouraging, it is still lacking in closing the man-machine gap. Programmatic robots as we know today are still far from matching the power of the human brain which is a neural network that is massively parallel, and learns through experience, deductive reasoning and complex optical recognition.

In the early advent of computers, promises of high productivity and fears that it will cause huge job redundancies turned out to be more a disillusionment leading to Solow's paradox — "You can see the computer age everywhere but in the productivity statistics." However, there is recognition that technology does have an impact on work especially through mechanisation of blue-collar factory production and in clerical information processing based on rules and logic. Economists Frank Levy and Richard Murnane in *The New Division of Labor: How Computers Are Creating the Next Job Market* argue that the distribution of jobs will be polarised between one end of the wage spectrum consisting of lowest-paid service jobs versus the other end of highly paid jobs requiring creative expert thinking, complex communication, pattern recognition and just pure common sense. The biggest relative losses are occurring in the lower middle job distribution: assembly-line work, clerical jobs in bureaucracy, jobs that are heavy in information processing and can be programmed in rules and logic. However, in the near term of the next 25 years, programmatic rules-based robots and drones will assist humans in the "dirty, dull and dangerous" jobs. While huge strides have been made in Artificial Intelligence, autonomous robots are still not within reach in the near term due to computing power limitations. Therefore augmentation and assistance by machines, for example the use of exoskeletons and robots, are more likely to raise productivity than cause labour redundancies. Like the Digital Divide of the past, the future is a race between nations who can afford and are willing to embrace and adopt Machines as the new colleagues in the workplace. This bodes well for countries like Singapore with a declining and ageing population to have increasing mechanisation to complement its workforce and continue to strengthen its talent pool on a strategy of fewer but better quality.

The Next Silicon

Autonomous robots, unlike programmatic robots are self-learning; will they ever be pervasive at work and at home? Much depends on the power of computing and breakthroughs in Artificial Intelligence research. There is already increasing concern that the power of computing is beginning to be limited by how much can be packed into the silicon wafer. Theoretical physicist Dr. Michio Kaku believes that Moore's Law has only 10 years left; circa 2020 the world economy could be in the doldrums, unless a replacement is found for the silicon chip. Chief Product Architect John Gustafson from Advanced Micro Devices (AMD) believes the difficulties in transitioning from 28 to 20 nanometer chips, is the beginning of the end. Several novel architectures like parallel processing, or HP's new research in memory called memristors, or silicon photonics, the transfer of data inside a computer using light instead of copper wires, are temporary workarounds. But eventually the limits of physics will be reached in terms of density and excessive heat. The hope lies in the new realm of physics called quantum theory.

Nanotechnology based on quantum theory is the manipulation of matter at an atomic and molecular scale. This could be the second industrial revolution where we could manufacture new materials that are superstrong, superlight, superconductive and magnetic, solving much of the current energy loss through a frictionless infrastructure. Singapore's A*STAR is currently researching graphene, a single sheet of carbon no more than one atom thick. Nobel Prize Physics winners, Konstantin Novosclov and Andre Geim have managed to use electron beams to create graphene transistors, one atom thick and ten atoms wide which makes the prospect of quantum computers bright. Potentially this will mean more advanced robotics will be developed. Dr. Michio Kaku is pessimistic about the prospect of autonomous robots for the next 50 years. According to his estimates, it is more likely that by 2100 and beyond, robots with advance intelligence and perhaps even consciousness may then become true work colleagues.

The Next Frontier

By combining nanotechnology and new discoveries in genomic sciences, the next wave of exponential growth is likely to be in medicine. Nanobots are devices that will course through our bodies and will revolutionise cancer-fighting with more precision through such molecular hunters. The adverse effects of the carpet-bombing chemotherapy will be replaced by nanoparticles that are like molecular smart bombs that will seek and destroy cancer cells by delivering its payload more accurately, minimising collateral damage. DNA chips which are tiny sensors in our clothes, body, and bathroom will be ubiquitous, constantly monitoring our health and detecting diseases early.

In parallel, advances in genomic medicine, stem cell and gene therapy are not only fixing broken genes but by mid-century it may go to the extent of creating designer children by enhancing or improving looks and performance. Imagine "kiasu" Singapore parents wanting to give their child a head start in the brave new world will become possible.

Through the twin pillars of nanotechnology and genomic medicine, Singapore by 2065, would turn its ageing population into an advantage and tap on research in healthy active ageing into an economic pillar. Singapore would have an array of human organ and tissue engineering farms and will become an exporter of organs such as the kidney, liver, heart, skin, limbs, etc. Singapore would be a robust centre for gene therapy that can slow down its ageing population and fight diseases such as cancer or finally boost and overcome the procreation challenge. Factories to manufacture nanocarriers and bionic parts for implants using the latest nanotechnology will be a major export.

These new industries will spearhead economic growth and generate needed revenue to stay ahead of the next race by investing in education and renewing infrastructure.

Future Ready

Against this future backdrop, key institutions in government will be in the spotlight.

In the early 1980s, the Singapore government initiated an S$100 million programme to computerise the civil service. At that time, Singapore was ahead in the region, and much more has been poured in since to refresh and continually keep service relevant and efficient. By 2065, Singapore would have tapped into its reserves and invested billions to overhaul its transport, housing and environment to take advantage of nano-based materials and install frictionless magnetic infrastructure and superconductive buildings to become more energy efficient and mechanised.

Building on its respected legal framework, Singapore will be one of the first countries to evolve and adapt to respond to ethical, moral and social challenges new technologies will bring so as to maintain social harmony. It will enact legislation such as the Genomics Technology Act to govern the use of genomics and biotechnology to ensure ethical use that is consistent with its social values.

Many scientists predict an era of Singularity where intelligence will be increasingly fused between man and machine on quantum proportions that will surpass biological limits and accelerate creativity but potentially also threaten humanity. For those who fear the stranglehold of the robots and machines as in the Terminator movie series, fighting the inevitable tide is energy sapping. Instead the Singapore legal and education system would be transformed to start honing human comparative advantage against smart machines in qualities and attributes such as:

- curiosity, creativity and passion — retaining the child-like curiosity to question and not just accept and then to follow and pursue interests with a fierce passion;
- contextualising, seeing beyond the obvious and connecting the dots — if everyone can Google and have easy access to information and data, then those that are more able to see the big picture, dive deep into critical areas and connect the dots would be ahead;
- conceptualising points of view — absorbing facts and information is necessary but interpreting implications and formulating opinions is more important; knowing which year Singapore gained independence is relevant but knowing why is even more important.
- convincing others and collaborating — appreciating diversity, complex communication in selling, telling your story.

Singapore will lead the region with its School of Transformational Leadership which will focus on critical thinking and life hacking skills; and going beyond just doing, as more and more mundane tasks are increasingly being automated and mechanised. Interdisciplinary lifelong learning becomes a core habit rather than just striving for the classical institutional certification. Going to university will not be the only pathway for the next generation, techno-entrepreneurism will become the norm when safe is risky.

Science and technology is a double-edged sword and how it cuts depends on how it is handled. Singapore through pragmatism will punch above its weight and continue to strengthen its branding on the world stage.

Singapore's 50 Years of Socioeconomic Transformation: Notes and Quick Facts[1]

Hui Ying SNG
Lecturer
Division of Economics
Nanyang Technological University, Singapore

National Income

Singapore's GDP (at 2010 market price) grew from S$10.0 billion in 1965 to S$380.6 billion in 2014, an increase of 37 times. Real GDP grew at an annual average of 7.8% over the last 50 years. On a per person basis, per capita GDP (at 2010 market price) grew from S$5,325 in 1965 to S$69,580 in 2014, an increase of 12 times.

The increase in absolute affluence in Singapore also translates into an increase in relative affluence of Singapore in the world. In 1965, according to available data from the World Bank, Singapore ranked 41 in the world in terms of per capita GDP. By 2013, Singapore's ranking in the world had moved up to the 9th position.

A closer look at the GDP by industry reveals that Singapore was dominated by services producing industries (SPI) in 1965, with goods producing industries (GPI) contributing only 25% to GDP. Singapore's effort in promoting industrialization propelled this ratio to a high of 36% in the early 1980s. In particular, manufacturing's contribution to GDP increased from

Please refer to the accompanying table "Key Economic and Social Indicators, 1965–2014" for more detailed statistical information. Each sub-section of this article and its corresponding sub-table share the same sub-heading.

14% in 1965 to around 25% in the 1980s. The fortunes of GPI and SPI reversed from mid-1980s onwards as the finance and insurance industry and the business services industry expanded. The joint contribution to GDP by these two industries increased sharply from 13% in 1965 to 27% in 2014.

Expenditure on GDP is another set of interesting indicators that reveals the economic transformation of the Singapore economy. Firstly, despite being a very competitive exporting economy now, Singapore's net exports were running a deficit up till mid-1980s. Secondly, private consumption expenditure was steadily declining over the years. It was only 37% of GDP in 2014, one of the lowest in the world and much lower than the 68% registered by the US in 2013 (World Bank, 2015). Thirdly, gross fixed capital formation increased steadily during the earlier years of development, peaking at 46% of GDP in mid-1980s, and began its long descent thereafter as diminishing returns set in after Singapore accumulated a sizable amount of fixed assets. Lastly, government consumption expenditure had remained very stable in the last 50 years without showing any perceptible increasing trend.

Singapore's Net Income from Abroad (NIFA) has been negative since 2000. NIFA is the difference between the total values of the primary incomes receivable from and payable to non-residents. In other words, it is Gross National Income (GNI) minus GDP. As NIFA includes net labour income and net property and entrepreneurial incomes, the large negative NIFA is a reflection of the huge presence of foreign enterprises and foreign workforce in Singapore.

Singapore is well known as a country with high saving rates. Time series analysis of Gross National Saving (GNS) reveals that saving rates increased steadily since independent and remained at elevated level till today. GNS as a percentage of GDP stood at 48% in 2014, a reflection of Singapore's high levels of corporate and household saving and government budget surplus.

Balance of Payments

In 2013, Singapore's current account surplus of 18.3% of GDP was one of the highest in the world. In fact, it was much higher than other export-oriented economies such as China (2.0% of GDP), Germany (6.9% of GDP) and South Korea (6.1% of GDP) (World Bank, 2015).

However, Singapore was registering substantial current account deficits in her earlier years of development. In fact, it was only in the mid-1990s when her goods balance turned from deficit to surplus. Services balance, on the other hand, turned from a surplus to a deficit position in 1999, and had only registered one surplus balance in 2011 since then.

On the other hand, capital and financial account turned from surplus to deficit from mid-1990s onwards. A negative capital and financial account indicates net financial outflow. It shows that Singapore is a net creditor in the world, providing funds to the rest of the world.

Prices and Inflation

Singapore has managed to achieve a very low rate of inflation in the last five decades, with an annual average of only 2.9%. The only exceptions were 1973 and 1974, when inflation rates reached a high of 19.6% and 22.3% respectively. The oil embargo by the members of the Organization of Arab Petroleum Exporting Countries (OAPEC) during the height of the Arab-Israeli War saw oil prices quadrupling from US$3 to US$12 and resulting in worldwide high inflation. Excluding 1973 and 1974, the annual average inflation rate in Singapore since 1965 was only 2.1%.

On a lighter note, which of the following food items saw the largest increase in retail prices in the last five decades: (a) rice, (b) hen, (c) Spanish mackerel, (d) hen eggs, (e) cabbage, and (f) apples?

The correct answer is Spanish mackerel (increased by 417%), followed closely by rice (increased by 379%). On the other hand, prices of hen and hen eggs only doubled in the last 50 years. The price inflation of fish was significantly higher than that of hen!

External Trade (Goods)

Total merchandise trade (exports plus imports) in Singapore is very large relative to the size of her GDP. Singapore's total merchandise trade stood at 263% of GDP in 2013, second highest in the world after Hong Kong (423%). Belgium was at a distant third at 175% (World Bank, 2015).

Three characteristics of Singapore and her development policies shaped the trend of her external trade. Firstly, Singapore's lack of natural resources and her relatively small domestic production capacity (in terms of absolute capacity in the earlier years and range of varieties in the later years) necessitate importation of a wide range of goods, including food, mineral fuels, raw materials and various manufactured goods and machinery. Thus the size of her imports had always been large and had never fallen below 115% of GDP in the last 50 years. Secondly, since the founding of Singapore in 1819 by Sir Stamford Raffles as a trading post of the British East India Company, entrepôt trade had been, and still is, an important pillar of the economy. Re-exports was at a high of 65% of total exports in 1969 (first available data on re-exports), and fluctuated between 40% and 50% of total exports in the recent years. The importance of re-exports attests to the role of Singapore as the regional and global transportation and logistics hub. The high re-exports figures also contribute to the high imports figures of Singapore. Thirdly, Singapore pursued an export-oriented industrialisation policy since independence and the success of this policy is reflected in the non-oil domestic exports (NODX) figures. NODX was at a low of 31% of GDP in 1970. This figure climbed steadily in the 1970s and fluctuated between 70% and 100% of GDP in the last 35 years.

Tourism

In 1959, Professor Lim Chong Yah, then Second Assistant Economic Advisor, participated in a discussion with the then Finance Minister Dr. Goh Keng Swee on the formulation of economic development strategies for Singapore. Professor Lim suggested tourism as another strategy. As Professor Lim recounted, Dr. Goh, as an initial response, dismissed the idea, as "only drunken soldiers would visit Singapore as tourists."

Some years later, as domestic conditions improved, the economic prospect of tourist trade in Singapore also improved in tandem. The push to attract more tourists to Singapore led to the opening of the Jurong Bird Park in 1971 and the Singapore Zoo in 1973. Professor Lim Chong Yah recounted another anecdote of Dr. Goh Keng Swee selecting the Jurong Bird Park over the Singapore Zoo as the first major tourist attraction in the Singapore as "birds are small, they eat little; zoo animals such as lions and tigers are big, they eat a lot." Budgetary constraint was an important consideration then.

Singapore government's push to develop Singapore into a major tourist destination resulted in tourist arrivals in Singapore leaped from 98,500 in 1965 to 15.09 million in 2014, an increase of more than 150 times.

Shipping and Aviation Hub

One of the key reasons behind Sir Stamford Raffles' choice of Singapore as the trading post of the East India Company was Singapore's strategic geographical location. Till today, Singapore's geographical location continues to be her comparative advantage as Singapore develops into a shipping and aviation hub. The port of Singapore is among the world's busiest transshipment ports, container ports and seaports (by cargo tonnage). Sea cargo handled increased from 22.1 million tonnes in 1965 to 581.3 million tonnes in 2014, an increase of 25 times while container throughput increased from less than 2 million tonnes in 1985 to almost 34 million tonnes in 2014. Air cargo handled increased even more dramatically by 87 times from 0.21 million tonnes in 1970 to 1.84 million tonnes in 2014.

Banking and Finance

Singapore's Asian Dollar Market was officially established in October 1968 when approval was first given for a bank to operate an Asian Currency Unit (ACU). Since then, merchant banks have also been allowed to operate ACUs. Total assets/liability of ACUs stood at US$1,191 billion in 2014, overshadowing the already sizable total assets/liability of S$1,060 billion of the domestic banking units.

Singapore was on a fixed exchange rate system until 1973 when she switched to a managed float system. In 1981, Singapore adopted an exchange rate-centred monetary policy with the main objectives of maintaining price stability and preserving the purchasing power of the Singapore dollar. One key mechanism to moderate imported inflation is through an appreciating Singapore dollar, which is managed against a trade-weighted basket of currencies. Since 1965, Singapore dollar appreciated by 317% against the British pound, 165% against the Malaysian ringgit, and 132% against the US dollar. On the other hand, the value of Singapore dollar fell by 23% against the Japanese yen, largely due to the overall strength of the yen as a result of the Plaza Accord.

Labour Force

Singapore's total labour force in 2014 was characterised by the huge presence of foreign workers, which account for 38% of total labour force labour. Inflow of foreign workers grew rapidly during the economic boom years, allowing the Singapore economy to expand without facing supply-side constraints.

Despite the large increase in foreign labour force, resident labour participation rate had been on an up-trend since 1970, with female labour participation rate increased significantly from 28.2% in 1965 to 58.6% in 2014. The healthy economic growth in Singapore had kept unemployment rate in check, with resident unemployment rate at 2.7% in 2014.

Population

Singapore's total population grew at an annual average rate of 2.2% in the last 50 years, with the citizen population being augmented with increasing number of new citizens, permanent residents and foreign workers. In 2014, total population in Singapore consisted of 3.87 million residents (71% of total population) and 1.60 million non-residents (29% of total population). Residents refer to citizens plus permanent residents while non-residents refer to foreign workers holding work passes, dependents and international students.

In 1965, Singapore was a very youthful society with a median age, which is the age at which exactly half the population is older and another half is younger, of only 17.8. There was 20.8 persons aged 15–64 supporting every person aged 65 and above. Fast-forwarded to 2014, falling total fertility rate (TFR) coupled with increasing life expectancy have led to Singapore becoming one of the most rapidly ageing countries in the world. In 2014, median age had increased to 39.3 and old-age support ratio had declined to 6.6.

Households and Housing

The number of resident households increased from 0.38 million in 1970 to 1.20 million in 2014. Household size, on the other hand, experienced a decline from 5.35 persons per household in 1970 to 3.43 persons per household in 2014 as a result of falling total fertility rate (TFR) and increasing number of one-person households (mostly singles).

In 1968, in an attempt to build a stronger sense of belonging to the newly independent Singapore, home ownership was actively encouraged through allowing citizens to use a portion of their Central Provident Fund (CPF) savings for the down payment and mortgage payment for purchase of public flats. Home ownership rate in Singapore increased from less than 30% in 1970 to more than 90% in 2014.

The expansion of home ownership coincided with the expansion of building programmes of the Housing Development Board (HDB). When the HDB was formed in 1960, only 9% of Singaporeans lived in public flats. This figure increased steadily to a high of 88% in the late 1990s and had fallen somewhat to 80% in 2014. It is also interesting to note that the share of households living in landed properties had declined from 14% in 1970 to 5.8% in 2014.

Family Formation

The economic progress of Singapore, coupled with the anti-natalist "Stop at Two" campaign in the 1970s, had resulted in a sharply declining TFR in the early 1970s and continued dip in the TFR below replacement rate since 1975. TFR in Singapore stood at 1.25 in 2014, among the lowest in the world.

Singapore's low TFR can be partly explained by our declining marriage rate and the increasing median age at first marriage. In 1970, median ages of grooms and brides were 26.9 and 23.1 respectively. The figures had increased to 30.2 and 28.1 in 2013.

Education and Health

Key indicators on education and health improved in tandem with the advancement in Singapore's economic performance. The literacy rate of the resident population aged 15 and above increased from 60.2% in 1965 to 96.7% in 2014. The share of resident population aged 25 years and above with university qualification also increased dramatically from 1.9% in 1970 to 27.3% in 2013.

On the other hand, infant mortality rate dropped significantly from 26.3 per 1000 live births to only 1.8 in 2014, one of the lowest in the world. People are also living longer, with life expectancy at birth increased from 64.5 in 1965 to 82.5 in 2013.

References

World Bank (2015). World Bank Databank. Retrieved April 7, 2015 from http://data.worldbank.org/

Key Economic and Social Indicators, 1965–2014

National Income	1965	1970	1975	1980	1985	1990	1995	2000	2005	2010	2014
GDP at 2010 Market Price (S$m)	10,047	18,405	28,986	43,805	60,943	92,146	139,405	183,379	232,773	322,361	380,585
GDP at Current Market Price (S$m)	2,982	5,876	13,728	25,863	40,824	70,507	124,575	165,218	212,074	322,361	390,089
GDP by Industry (as % of GDP)											
Goods Producing Industries	25	29	33	36	33	31	31	32	30	26	24
Services Producing Industries	66	62	61	58	60	61	58	56	61	65	67
Expenditure on GDP (as % of GDP)											
Private Consumption Expenditure	79	67	60	51	45	45	41	42	39	36	37
Government Consumption Expenditure	10	12	10	10	13	10	8	11	10	10	10
Gross Fixed Capital Formation	21	32	35	40	41	32	33	32	23	26	25
Changes in Inventories	1	6	4	6	0	4	1	3	−2	2	2
Net Exports of Goods and Services	−11	−19	−9	−7	0	10	17	12	30	26	24

GNI at Current Market Price (S$m)	3,078	5,932	13,852	24,537	41,162	69,799	125,475	164,205	198,051	320,527	378,330
Net Income From Abroad (S$m)	96	56	124	−1,327	338	−709	900	−1,013	−14,023	−1,834	−11,759
Per Capita GDP at 2010 Market Price (S$)	5,325	8,872	12,811	18,147	22,274	30,241	39,553	45,527	54,567	63,498	69,580
Per Capita GDP at Current Market Prices (US$)	516	925	2,559	5,004	6,782	12,766	24,937	23,794	29,866	46,570	56,284
World Ranking[1,2]	41	40	39	43	34	34	19	23	32	15	9
Number of Countries Compared Against	115	128	132	147	156	183	191	199	199	192	185
Gross National Saving (S$m)	367	1,191	4,078	8,271	16,920	30,744	62,591	75,170	91,696	166,120	182,279
As % of GDP	12	20	30	32	41	44	50	45	43	52	47

Balance of Payments[3]	**1965**	**1970**	**1975**	**1980**	**1985**	**1990**	**1995**	**2000**	**2005**	**2010**	**2014**
Current Account Balance (S$m)	−150	−1,751	−1,385	−3,376	128	5,615	20,434	17,511	46,383	76,279	74,467
As % of GDP	−5	−30	−10	−13	0	8	16	11	22	24	20
Goods Balance	−760	−2,619	−5,693	−5,981	−3,340	−3,037	14,888	27,967	79,464	85,682	96,758
Services Balance[4]	659	778	4,318	3,885	2,571	10,124	5,915	−7,659	−16,206	−519	−1,427
Primary Income Balance[5]	n.a.	114	82	−1,022	1,231	−709	900	−1,013	−14,023	−1,834	−11,759
Secondary Income Balance[6]	−49	−24	−92	−258	−333	−763	−1,269	−1,784	−2,853	−7,050	−9,105

(Continued)

Balance of Payments *(Continued)*

Balance of Payments[3]	**1965**	**1970**	**1975**	**1980**	**1985**	**1990**	**1995**	**2000**	**2005**	**2010**	**2014**
Capital and Financial Account Balance[7] (S$m)	104.3	532.6	1,374.4	3,419	1,401	6,010	–7,630	–9,650	–26,427	–24,921	–62,864
Direct Investment	n.a.	283.4	1,448.4	2,437	1,780	6,418	6,605	15,283	10,822	29,586	34,037
Portfolio Investment	n.a.	n.a.	n.a.	27	385	–1,880	–21,232	–36,299	–1,542	–40,135	–67,023
Financial Derivatives	n.a.	n.a.	n.a.	n.a.	n.a.	n.a.	n.a.	n.a.	n.a.	4,904	15,670
Other Investment	n.a.	249.2	–74.0	924	–627	1,472	6,997	11,367	–35,706	–19,275	–45,549
Overall Balance[8] (S$m)	–14	565	966	1,419	2,942	9,893	12,174	11,844	20,397	57,480	8,618
As % of GDP	0	10	7	5	7	14	10	7	10	18	2
Official Reserves[9] (S$m)	14	–565	–966	–1,419	–2,942	–9,892	–12,174	–11,844	–20,397	–57,480	–8,618

Prices	**1965**	**1970**	**1975**	**1980**	**1985**	**1990**	**1995**	**2000**	**2005**	**2010**	**2014**
Annual CPI Inflation Rate (%)	0.3	0.4	2.6	8.5	0.5	3.5	1.7	1.3	0.5	2.8	1.0
Average Retail Prices of (S$)											
Thai Rice 100% Fragrant (per 5 kg)	2.73	3.06	7.44	5.25	5.54	5.35	6.35	7.87	7.65	12.43	13.07
Hen (per 1 kg)	2.96	2.69	3.70	3.95	4.53	4.16	4.46	4.41	4.83	5.54	6.14
Spanish Mackerel (Tenggiri) (per 1 kg)	2.20	2.38	4.46	6.17	8.39	8.31	8.31	8.75	8.58	10.15	11.36
Hen Eggs (per 10 pieces)	1.01	0.94	1.30	1.47	1.58	1.50	1.34	1.49	1.69	1.85	2.14
Cabbage (per 1 kg)	0.68	0.60	0.89	1.29	1.55	1.64	1.91	1.70	1.55	1.73	2.01
Apple (each)	0.20	0.20	0.18	0.30	0.29	0.32	0.34	0.33	0.33	0.37	0.45

External Trade (Goods)	1965	1970	1975	1980	1985	1990	1995	2000	2005	2010	2014
Total Trade (S$m)	6,811	12,290	32,028	92,797	107,996	205,012	343,828	470,001	715,723	902,063	982,702
Exports (S$m)	3,004	4,756	12,758	41,452	50,179	95,206	167,515	237,826	382,532	478,841	518,923
Oil	n.a.	n.a.	n.a.	14,534	16,452	17,295	13,858	23,062	57,414	103,511	122,862
Non-oil	n.a.	n.a.	n.a.	26,918	33,727	77,910	153,657	214,765	325,118	375,330	396,060
Domestic Exports (S$m)	n.a.	1,832	7,540	25,805	32,576	62,754	98,473	135,938	207,448	248,610	273,492
Oil	n.a.	n.a.	n.a.	14,180	15,840	17,137	13,721	22,867	52,798	75,011	106,986
Non-oil	n.a.	n.a.	n.a.	11,625	16,735	45,617	84,751	113,072	154,650	173,599	166,506
Re-exports (S$m)	n.a.	2,924	5,218	15,647	17,603	32,452	69,042	101,888	175,084	230,231	245,431
Imports (S$m)	3,807	7,534	19,270	51,345	57,817	109,806	176,313	232,175	333,191	423,222	463,779
Oil	n.a.	n.a.	n.a.	14,889	17,031	17,399	14,204	27,987	59,145	115,592	143,740
Non-oil	n.a.	n.a.	n.a.	36,456	40,786	92,407	162,110	204,188	274,046	307,630	320,039

Tourism	1965	1970	1975	1980	1985	1990	1995	2000	2005	2010	2014
International Visitor Arrivals[10] ('000)	99	579	1,324	2,562	3,031	5,313	7,137	7,691	8,943	11,639	15,087

Shipping and Aviation Hub	1965	1970	1975	1980	1985	1990	1995	2000	2005	2010	2014
Sea Cargo Handled (million tonnes)	22.1	43.5	55.2	86.3	105.8	187.8	305.5	325.9	423.3	503.3	581.3
Container Throughput[11,12] (million TEUs)	n.a.	n.a.	n.a.	n.a.	1.7	5.2	11.8	17.1	23.2	28.4	33.9
Air Cargo Handled[13] ('000 tonnes)	n.a.	21	66	182	300	624	1,106	1,682	1,834	1,814	1,844

(Continued)

Shipping and Aviation Hub *(Continued)*

Shipping and Aviation Hub	**1965**	**1970**	**1975**	**1980**	**1985**	**1990**	**1995**	**2000**	**2005**	**2010**	**2014**
Aircraft Landings[13] (No.)	8,767	17,113	32,191	37,956	36,600	48,803	78,134	86,853	102,035	131,769	170,680
Air Passenger Movements[13] ('000)											
Arrivals	233	682	1,647	3,141	4,324	7,237	10,920	13,546	15,364	20,486	26,669
Departures	234	689	1,677	3,151	4,398	7,166	10,823	13,419	15,356	20,437	26,620
Transit	137	304	712	1,003	1,135	1,217	1,453	1,654	1,710	1,115	804

Banking and Finance[14]	**1965**	**1970**	**1975**	**1980**	**1985**	**1990**	**1995**	**2000**	**2005**	**2010**	**2014**
Money Supply (M1)[15] (S$m)	891	1,574	3,472	6,135	8,785	15,261	25,349	33,262	46,086	112,487	160,228
Total Assets/Liabilities of Domestic Banking Units (S$m)	2,382	5,042	14,417	33,316	70,618	134,002	224,579	335,816	425,222	781,607	1,060,400
Total Assets/Liabilities of Asian Currency Units[16] (US$m)	n.a.	390	12,597	54,393	155,374	390,396	478,233	481,693	611,377	971,299	1,190,797
Exchange Rates											
S$ Per Unit of US Dollar	3.0600	3.0800	2.4895	2.0935	2.1050	1.7445	1.4143	1.7315	1.6642	1.2875	1.3213
S$ Per Unit of Pound Sterling	8.5766	7.3726	5.0381	4.9982	3.0312	3.3451	2.1884	2.5818	2.8717	1.9887	2.0563

S$ Per 100 Units of Japanese Yen	0.8479	0.8612	0.8161	1.0303	1.0508	1.2913	1.3744	1.5091	1.4189	1.5798	1.1060
S$ Per Unit of Malaysian Ringgit	1.0003	1.0008	0.9618	0.9441	0.8720	0.6461	0.5567	0.4557	0.4403	0.4175	0.3781
Domestic Interest Rates[17] (Percent Per Annum)											
Banks' Prime Lending Rate	8.00	8.00	7.08	13.60	7.20	7.73	6.26	5.80	5.30	5.38	5.35
Banks' 3-Month Deposit Rate	5.00	5.50	4.31	11.22	4.58	5.05	3.41	1.70	0.56	0.19	0.14

Labour Force	**1965**	**1970**	**1975**	**1980**	**1985**	**1990**	**1995**	**2000**	**2005**	**2010**	**2014**
Total Labour Force[18,19] ('000)	n.a.	702	867	1,112	1,288	1,563	1,749	2,192	2,367	3,136	3,531
Resident Labour Force Participation Rate[19] (%)	n.a.	55.3	57.3	63.2	62.2	63.2	61.9	63.2	63.0	66.2	67.0
Males	n.a.	81.2	78.4	81.5	79.9	77.5	77.2	76.6	74.4	76.5	75.9
Females	n.a.	28.2	34.9	44.3	44.9	48.8	46.8	50.2	52.0	56.5	58.6
Unemployment Rate[19,20] (%)											
Total	9.2	8.2	4.5	3.5	4.1	1.8	1.8	2.7	3.1	2.2	2.0
Resident	n.a.	n.a.	n.a.	n.a.	n.a.	n.a.	2.2	3.7	4.1	3.1	2.7

Population	1965	1970	1975	1980	1985	1990	1995	2000	2005	2010	2014
Total Population[21–23] ('000)	1,886.9	2,074.5	2,262.6	2,413.9	2,736.0	3,047.1	3,524.5	4,027.9	4,265.8	5,076.7	5,469.7
Resident Population[22,23] ('000)	n.a.	2,013.6	n.a.	2,282.1	2,482.6	2,735.9	3,013.5	3,273.4	3,467.8	3,771.7	3,870.7
Population Density[24] (Per sq km)	3,245	3,538	3,791	3,907	4,409	4,814	5,443	5,900	6,121	7,146	7,615
Sex Ratio[25] (Males per 1,000 females)	1,066	1,049	1,045	1,032	1,028	1,027	1,010	998	985	974	967
Median Age[25] (Years)	17.8	19.7	21.9	24.4	27.2	29.8	31.9	34.0	35.8	37.4	39.3
Old-Age Support Ratio[25,26]	20.8	17.0	15.6	13.8	12.8	11.8	10.8	9.9	8.9	8.2	6.6

Households & Housing	1965	1970	1975	1980	1985	1990	1995	2000	2005	2010	2014
Resident Households[27] ('000)	n.a.	380.5	n.a.	472.7	551.5	661.7	768.4	915.1	1,024.5	1,145.9	1,200.0
Average Household Size[27] (Persons)	n.a.	5.35	n.a.	4.87	4.52	4.25	3.96	3.70	3.56	3.50	3.43
Home Ownership Rate[27] (%)	n.a.	29.4	n.a.	58.8	n.a.	87.5	90.0	92.0	91.1	87.2	90.3
Type of Dwelling[27,28] (%)	100.0	100.0	100.0	100.0	100.0	100.0	100.0	100.0	100.0	100.0	100.0
HDB Flats[29]	n.a.	30.9	n.a.	67.8	81.3	85.0	88.5	88.0	84.4	82.4	80.4
Condominiums & Other Apartments	n.a.	4.8	n.a.	3.9	2.7	4.7	4.6	6.5	9.8	11.5	13.5
Landed Properties	n.a.	14.1	n.a.	8.5	8.0	7.0	6.0	5.1	5.4	5.7	5.8

Family Formation	1965	1970	1975	1980	1985	1990	1995	2000	2005	2010	2014
General Marriage Rate[30,2]											
Males (Per 1,000 unmarried resident males)	n.a.	51.6	62.1	55.0	54.4	52.6	55.2	48.1	44.1	39.3	40.5

General Divorce Rate[31,2]											
Males (Per 1,000 married resident males)	n.a.	n.a.	n.a.	3.7	4.5	6.1	6.1	6.5	7.7	7.5	7.3
Females (Per 1,000 married resident females)	n.a.	n.a.	n.a.	3.8	4.6	6.1	6.1	6.5	7.5	7.2	6.9
Median Age at First Marriage[32,2] (Years)											
Grooms	n.a.	26.9	n.a.	26.7	27.1	28.0	28.6	28.7	29.8	30.0	30.2
Brides	n.a.	23.1	n.a.	23.6	24.3	25.3	25.6	26.2	26.9	27.7	28.1
Total Fertility Rate[25] (Per female)	4.66	3.07	2.07	1.82	1.61	1.83	1.67	1.60	1.26	1.15	1.25

Education and Health	**1965**	**1970**	**1975**	**1980**	**1985**	**1990**	**1995**	**2000**	**2005**	**2010**	**2014**
Literacy Rate[33] (Percent)	60.2	68.9	76.2	82.3	85.7	89.1	90.8	92.5	94.1	95.9	96.7
Population with University Qualification[34,2] (Percent)	n.a.	1.9	n.a.	2.7	3.6	4.7	7.6	12.1	17.5	23.7	27.3
Mean Years of Schooling[35] (Years)	n.a.	n.a.	n.a.	4.7	5.7	6.6	7.7	8.6	9.3	10.1	10.6
Males	n.a.	n.a.	n.a.	5.6	n.a.	7.3	8.4	9.2	9.9	10.6	11.1
Females	n.a.	n.a.	n.a.	3.7	n.a.	5.9	7.2	8.1	8.8	9.7	10.1
Infant Mortality Rate[25] (Per 1,000 resident live-births)	26.3	20.5	13.9	8.0	7.6	6.6	3.8	2.5	2.1	2.0	1.8
Life Expectancy at Birth[25,2] (Years)	64.5	65.8	66.8	72.1	73.9	75.3	76.3	78.0	80.1	81.7	82.5
Males	62.8	64.1	65.1	69.8	71.5	73.1	74.1	76.0	77.6	79.2	80.2
Females	66.6	67.8	68.8	74.7	76.4	77.6	78.6	80.0	82.5	84.0	84.6

Source: www.singstat.gov.sg; CEIC database; Yearbook of Statistics (various issues); Singapore's Statistical Highlights (various issues)

Notes:

1) Source: World Bank Databank. Figures in the next row give the total number of countries with available data for that year.
2) Data for 2014 is unavailable and data for 2013 is given instead.
3) Data for 1965 are from *Yearbook of Statistics*, 1974/75. Data for 1970 and 1975 are from *Singapore Statistical Hightlights*, 2004. Data for 1980 onwards are from CEIC Database. Data for 1980 and 1985 are based on the BPM5 format (5th Edition of the IMF's Balance of Payments and International Investment Position Manual) which has been discontinued. Data from 1990 onwards are based on the BPM6 format. Data from different sources are not strictly comparable due to changes in classification.
4) Data on "Services Balance" for 1965 include "Investment Income" as a signifcant sub-component. "Investment Income" was later reclassifised under "Primary Income Balance."
5) "Primary Income" refers to receipts and payments of employee compensation paid to nonresident workers and investment income (receipts and payments on direct investment, portfolio investment, other investments, and receipts on reserve assets). Data on "Primary Income Balance" for 1970 and 1975 refer to "Net Income."
6) "Secondary Income" refers to transfers recorded in the balance of payments whenever an economy provides or receives goods, services, income, or financial items without a *quid pro quo*. An important component of secondary income in Singapore is workers' remittances. Data on "Secondary Income Balance" for 1965, 1970 and 1975 refer to "Net Transfer Payment" or "Net Current Transfer."
7) Data for 1970 and 1975 refer to only financial account balance; data on capital account balance are not available for 1970 and 1975.
8) Overall BoP Balance is Current Account Balance + Capital and Financial Account Balance + Net Errors and Omission.
9) Official Reserves consist of Singapore's official holdings of monetary gold and foreign exchange assets, as well as Singapore's special drawing rights and reserve position in the International Monetary Fund.
10) Excludes arrivals of Malaysians by land.
11) The container port commenced operations since 1972.
12) TEU stands for Twenty-Foot Equivalent Unit.
13) Figures refer to passengers and freight on commercial flights handled primarily at the Paya Lebar Airport (up to 30 June 1981) and Changi Airport (from 1 July 1981).
14) Data are as at end of period.
15) Money supply (M1) consists of currency in active circulation and demand deposits.
16) The Asian Dollar Market was officially established in October 1968 when approval was first given for a bank to operate an Asian Currency Unit (ACU). Since then, merchant banks have also been allowed to operate ACUs.

17) Prior to October 1975, the banks' interest rates were fixed by the Association of Banks in Malaysia and Singapore and thereafter by the Association of Banks in Singapore in consultation with the Monetary Authority of Singapore. After July 1975, when banks were permitted to quote their own interest rates on advances and deposits to customers, the rate refers to the average quoted by 10 leading banks.
18) Data refer to persons aged 15 years and over.
19) Data for 1970, 1980, 1990 and 2000 are from Population Censuses. Data for 1995 and 2005 are from General Household Surveys. Data for other years are from Labour Force Surveys. Data from the LFS are not comparable with those from the Censuses and the GHSs due to differences in coverage and methodology.
20) Unemployment data for 1965 are from Koh and Mariano (2006), *The Economic Prospects of Singapore*. Unemployment data before 1992 refer to non-seasonally adjusted unemployment rate in June; unemployment data since 1992 refer to annual average (simple average of quarterly figures).
21) Total population comprises Singapore residents (i.e. Singapore citizens and permanent residents) and non-residents.
22) Data before 1990 are based on *de facto* concept (i.e. the person is present in the country when enumerated at the reference period). Data from 1990 onwards are based on *de jure* concept (i.e. the person's place of usual residence).
23) Data from 2003 onwards exclude residents who have been away from Singapore for a continuous period of 12 months or longer as at the reference period.
24) Prior to 2003, data are based on Singapore's land area as at end-December. From 2003 onwards, data are based on Singapore's land area as at end-June.
25) Data refer to resident population. Prior to 1980, data refer to total population.
26) Population aged 15–64 years divided by population aged 65 years and over.
27) Data refer to resident households (i.e. households headed by a Singapore citizen or permanent resident), except for 1970 which refer to private households.
28) Data include other housing units (e.g. non-HDB shophouses).
29) Data include non-privatised Housing and Urban Development Corporation (HUDC) flats.
30) Data are based on resident grooms/brides and resident population, except for 1970, 1975 and 1980 which are based on total grooms/brides and total population.
31) Data are based on divorces and annulments. Prior to 1985, data refer to married males/females. From 1985, data refer to married resident males/females. From 2004 onwards, data are based on divorces and annulments where either or both spouses are residents.
32) Data refer to total marriages.
33) Data refer to resident population aged 15 years and over. Prior to 1980, data refer to total population aged 15 years and over.
34) Data refer to resident non-students aged 25 years and over. Figure for 1970 refers to total population aged 25 years and over.
35) Data refer to resident non-students aged 25 years and over.

About the Editor

Professor Euston Quah is presently Head, Division of Economics; Vice-Chair, Sustainable Earth Office and immediate Past Chairman of the Senate Committee on University Policy Matters at the Nanyang Technological University (NTU), Singapore. He was formerly Chair, School of Humanities and Social Sciences at NTU. Prior to joining NTU, Professor Quah was at the National University of Singapore (NUS) where he was Vice-Dean, Faculty of Arts and Social Sciences; Deputy Director of the Public Policy Programme (now called the Lee Kuan Yew School of Public Policy); and headed the economics department there. A prolific writer, Professor Quah had published over 100 articles including journals such as *World Development*; *Environment and Planning*; *Applied Economics*; *Journal of Economics*; *Journal of Public Economic Theory*; *Journal of Environmental Management*; *Impact Assessment and Project Appraisal*; *American Journal of Economics and Sociology*; *Bulletin of Economic Research*; *Education Economics*; *European Journal of Law and Economics*; *Theoretical Economics Letters*; and *International Review of Law and Economics*, among others. His most recent work is a paper in an international publication on cost-benefit analysis by Oxford University Press, 2013, and a forthcoming paper in the journal, *World Economy*. Two books on Cost-Benefit Analysis were published by Routledge, UK in 2007 (with E. J. Mishan) and 2012. His work on Cost-Benefit Analysis was made a reference reading by the US White House and Office of Management and Budget in their circulars for US Government agencies applying for research and project funds. He was also co-author of an Asian Edition of the best-selling *Principles of Economics* textbook with Harvard Professor Gregory Mankiw (former Chairman, US Presidential Council of Economic Advisors) published by Cengage (formerly Thomson, USA) , now with a second edition in 2013. He has books published by McGraw-Hill, Edward Elgar (UK), and Longmans. He has a forthcoming book (written with Jinhua Zhao) on the Economics of Transboundary Pollution to be published by Edward Elgar, UK, and was recently invited by Springer Verlag to be a Series Editor (with Parkash Chander) for books on Sustainable Development.

Professor Quah advises the Singapore Government in various Ministries and was a Member of the recent Prime Minister's Economic Strategies Sub-Committee on Energy and the Environment, and served on the Committee of the Fare Review Mechanism of the Ministry of Transport. He presently sits on the Boards of Energy Market Authority, the Energy Studies Institute at NUS; and the Complaints Committee of the Singapore Medical Council. He is also a Review Panel Member for the Bill and Melinda Gates Foundation project hosted by the Overseas Development Institute, London; and a Technical Reviewer for the National Research Foundation (Singapore), Humanities and Social Sciences Research Council (Canada), and the Australian Research Council. He has been a referee for many economics and interdisciplinary journals including the *Journal of Political Economy*, *Environment and Planning* (Series C and A), *Journal of Environmental Economics and Management*, among others. Professor Quah is Editor of the ISI (SSCI) journal, *The Singapore Economic Review* (since 2002), and the President of the Economic Society of Singapore (since 2009). In 2014, Professor Quah was elected as President of the Asian Law and Economics Association. He has been invited by Stanford University, Princeton University, the USA Inter-Pacific Bar Association, WWF for Asia, UNESCAP, Earth Institute of Columbia University (Asian Meetings), ADBI and ADB to speak at their functions and conferences. He was awarded the First Komai Fellowship by the Hitachi Scholarship Foundation in 1989. In 2014, Professor Quah was invited to give the World Economy Annual Asia Lecture at the international conference invited by the University of Nottingham, and sponsored by Wiley-Blackwell. Professor Quah has consulted for Price waterhouseCoopers; Economica (Canada); Gentings International; Singapore Government; IDRC Canada; World Bank and Asian Development Bank. In January 2015, Professor Quah was formally elected to be a fellow member of the prestigious learned society, the European Academy of Sciences and Arts. Professor Quah is often cited and interviewed by the local and foreign media on news, and documentary shows including CNA, Channel 5, BBC, Straits Times, Business Times, and foreign presses in France, Taiwan, Thailand, Malaysia, and Denmark. He is one of the most highly cited and influential university economists in Singapore.

About the Contributors

Singapore 50

Azmoon AHMAD

Azmoon Ahmad is currently Vice-President and Member of the Executive Management Board of Desay SV Automotive, China. His previous posts include the Managing Director and Executive Director Asia of ELMOS Semiconductor Singapore Pte Ltd, Managing Director of Continental Automotive Singapore Pte Ltd and Chief Executive Officer of Siemens VDO Automotive Pte Ltd (Singapore). He has extensive experience in international and diversity management, global customer orientation, and business financial management, with two international assignments in France and China. He graduated with a Master of Finance from RMIT University in 2005 and holds a Bachelor of Electrical Engineering (Major in Communications) from Nanyang Technological Institute Singapore in 1986. He also attended top training programmes such as the Top Management Course from Siemens @ Feldafing in 2007 and the Advanced Management Programme from Babson School of Business, US. Mr. Azmoon spends his free time contributing to the community through his voluntary position as a Board Member since 2003 and as Chairman of the Association of Muslim Professionals (AMP) Group since 2011. He also served as a Board Member of MERCU Learning Point, AMP's wholly owned subsidiary, from 2004 to 2011 and as Chairman of MERCU from 2010 to 2011.

Janet ANG

Janet Ang is the Vice-President of Systems of Engagement and Smarter Cities, IBM Asia Pacific, covering Australia and New Zealand, India, ASEAN and Korea. Janet is responsible for helping governments and organizations improve, integrate and add intelligence to systems such as transportation, public safety, water, energy, buildings, towns, citizen and employee engagement, and urban management that contribute toward achieving sustainable economic and community development. Prior to this role, Janet was the Managing Director of IBM Singapore from 2011 to 2015. In her 33 years in the industry, she has worked in Japan, China and Singapore, holding various senior leadership positions in management, sales, marketing and operations. Janet serves on the board of the Public Utilities Board (PUB), the InfoComm Development Authority (iDA), the NUS Institute of Systems Science (ISS), Singapore Press Holdings (SPH), the National Volunteer & Philanthropy Center (NVPC) and Caritas Singapore. She served on various committees including the Medishield Life Review Committee and the Women's Health Advisory Committee (WHAC). Janet is a member of Business China and is President of the International Women's Forum (Singapore chapter). Janet holds a Business Administration (Honors) degree from the National University of Singapore. She is happily married with four daughters.

Zulkifli BAHARUDIN

Zulkifli Baharudin is the Chairman of Indo-Trans Corporation, a logistics and supply chain company across Indochina. He is an Independent Director of Singapore Post Limited, Ascott Residence Trust Management Limited and data centre company, Securus. He is an Authority member of the Civil Aviation Authority of Singapore and Trustee of the Singapore Management University. In addition, Mr. Zulkifli is currently Singapore's Non-Resident Ambassador to the Republic of Uzbekistan and the Republic of Kazakhstan. He also served as Nominated Member of Parliament from October 1997 to September 2001 and was awarded the Public Service

Medal in 2005 and Public Service Star Medal in 2011. Mr. Zulkifli graduated from the National University of Singapore with a Bachelor of Science in Estate Management.

Vivian BALAKRISHNAN

Vivian Balakrishnan studied Medicine at the National University of Singapore after being awarded the President's Scholarship in 1980. He was elected President of the NUS Students' Union from 1981 to 1983 and Chairman from 1984 to 1985. After graduation, he specialised in Ophthalmology and served at the Singapore National Eye Centre (SNEC) and Singapore General Hospital. Dr. Balakrishnan has been a Member of Parliament since 2001. He is currently the Minister for the Environment and Water Resources. He is also the Minister-in-charge of the Smart Nation initiative. He previously held appointments as the Minister for Community Development, Youth and Sports, Second Minister for Trade and Industry, Minister responsible for Entrepreneurship, Second Minister for Information, Communications and the Arts and Minister of State for National Development. At MEWR, Dr. Balakrishnan has overseen the policy to build new hawker centres, the establishment of the Centre for Climate Research Singapore and the Department of Public Cleanliness, the implementation of a mandatory licensing scheme for the cleaning industry, and the adoption of higher air quality targets based on World Health Organization's Air Quality Guidelines as well as a revised air quality reporting index incorporating PM2.5. Dr. Balakrishnan has been married for 28 years to his wife, Joy. He enjoys spending precious time with his daughter and three sons. To keep fit, he runs and cycles. He is also a computer enthusiast and an avid reader.

Manu BHASKARAN

Manu Bhaskaran is a Partner of the Centennial Group, a strategic advisory firm headquartered in Washington DC and, as Founding CEO of its Singapore subsidiary Centennial Asia Advisors, he co-ordinates the Asian business of the Group. Manu is also Adjunct Senior Research Fellow at the Institute of Policy Studies in Singapore where his main interests are in analysing macroeconomic policy frameworks in Singapore. He was recently appointed as a Member of the Regional Advisory Board for Asia of the International Monetary Fund. He was educated at Magdalene College, Cambridge University where he earned an MA (Cantab) and at the John F. Kennedy School of Government at Harvard University where he obtained a Master in Public Administration. He is also a Chartered Financial Analyst.

Chun Sing CHAN

Chan Chun Sing is currently the Secretary-General of the National Trades Union Congress (NTUC) and Minister in the Prime Minister Office. He relinquished his previous duties in the Ministry of Social and Family Development (MSF) and Ministry of Defence on 9 April 2015 to join NTUC full time. At MSF, he was responsible for improving social service delivery, enhancing social safety nets and strengthening support for families in Singapore. On 8 April 2015, the NTUC Central Committee unanimously elected him to be NTUC Secretary-General from 4 May 2015 to help strengthen labour leadership at NTUC and the link between the Labour Movement and the Government.

David CHAN

David Chan is Lee Kuan Yew Fellow, Professor of Psychology and Director of the Behavioural Sciences Institute at the Singapore Management University (SMU). He is also Adjunct Principal Scientist at the Singapore's Agency for Science, Technology and Research (A*STAR) and Co-Director of the Centre for Technology and Social-Behavioural Insights jointly established by A*STAR and SMU. He has authored or edited five books and published numerous articles in psychology, management and methods journals. In 2000, he was ranked 9th worldwide in the list of Top 100 most published researchers of the 1990s in the top journals of Industrial and Organisational Psychology. His works have been cited over 3,000 times in various disciplines. He has received numerous international awards on scholarly achievement and scientific contributions. He has served as Editor or board member on several journals. He is Elected Fellow of four international psychological associations. He is a member on several national councils, advisory panels and boards of directors. He writes op-ed articles on social issues in *The Straits Times*. He is the consultant to the

Channel NewsAsia's "Social Experiment," which is a 5-part programme series that examines human behaviours using scientific experiments, and "Days of Disasters," which is a 5-part documentary series that examines previous disasters in Singapore. He does volunteer work as scientific advisor to the National Volunteer and Philanthropy Centre. He is a recipient of the Outstanding Volunteer Award from the Ministry of Social and Family Development.

Show Mao CHEN

Chen Show Mao is a full-time Member of Parliament of the Workers' Party serving the constituents of Aljunied (Paya Lebar division) in Singapore. Until his election in 2011, Show Mao was a partner of Davis Polk & Wardwell, one of the leading law firms in the world. He managed the China practice of the firm based in Beijing. He advised the Agricultural Bank of China on its 2010 US$22 billion initial public offering (IPO), which was the largest IPO in history. He advised the Industrial and Commercial Bank of China (ICBC) on its 2006 US$21 billion IPO, which in its turn was the largest IPO in history, and the first-ever global share offering that included a concurrent listing in China. He also advised China National Offshore Oil Company (CNOOC) on its proposed US$19 billion acquisition of Unocal, the largest attempted takeover of an overseas target by a Chinese company. Show Mao received much recognition for his professional accomplishments as a corporate lawyer, including most recently by The American Lawyer as 2010 Dealmaker of the Year before he left practice. Before he began legal practice, Show Mao worked at a number of research institutions such as the National Bureau of Economic Research (NBER). He was a Rhodes Scholar, and is an alumnus of Harvard, Oxford and Stanford Universities.

Jeanne CHENG

Jeanne Cheng was appointed Managing Director of SP Services Ltd in 2009. SP Services has about 780 employees and achieves an annual turnover of S$4 billion, providing convenient one-stop service and access to electricity, gas, water and other utility supplies. SP Services also facilitates competition in the deregulated electricity market. Mrs. Cheng is also a

Director of SGSP (Australia) Assets Pty Ltd, SP Group's subsidiary in Australia. Mrs. Cheng has been with the Singapore Power Group for 18 years and had held senior positions in Corporate Communications and Business Development before her appointment at SP Services. Prior to this, Mrs. Cheng worked as a media and communications specialist in both private and public sector entities. Mrs. Cheng graduated from the National University of Singapore with majors in Economics and Chinese Studies. She is Vice President of the Economic Society of Singapore Council. Mrs. Cheng is also an active grassroots leader and was awarded the Public Service Medal in 2009 for her community work. In 2012, she was voted Power Woman of the Year at the Asian Utility Industry Awards. Mrs. Cheng received the Work-Life Leadership Award at the Work-Life Excellence Awards 2014.

Soon Beng CHEW

Chew Soon Beng is Professor of Economics and Industrial Relations at Nanyang Technological University (NTU). He is author of *Small Firms in Singapore* (Oxford University Press), *Trade Unionism in Singapore* (McGraw-Hill), *Employment-Driven Industrial Relations Regimes* (Avebury), *Values and Lifestyles of Young Singaporeans* (Prentice-Hall), and *Foreign Enterprises in China: Operation and Management* (in Chinese). He has also published in journals such as *Singapore Economic Review*, China Economic Review and *China Economic Policy Review*. His recent publications include "Employment-based Social Protection in Singapore: Issues and Prospects" in the *ASEAN Economic Bulletin*, "Union Social Responsibility: A Necessary Public Good in a Globalized World" in the *International Journal of Comparative Labour Law and Industrial Relations*, and "Strategic Collective Bargaining" in the *Bulletin of Comparative Labour Relations*. Prof. Chew is founding director of the Master of Science in Managerial Economics programme (known as the Mayor's Class) at NTU. He is currently founding director of the Master of Science in Applied Economics.

Claire CHIANG

Claire Chiang pioneered the group's retail business and founded Banyan Tree Gallery. This year, it was awarded the Community Retailer Award by

Hong Kong Retail Industry Trade for its efforts in helping to sustain the livelihoods and skills of the artisans through gainful employment. She leads the acquisition of new hotel management contracts in China, and guides key strategic issues in the group's human capital strategy. She founded Banyan Tree Global Foundation, and steered the group's sustainability initiatives in building resilient communities. Ms. Chiang currently serves on numerous public and private Boards: as Justice of Peace, a Director on the Board of Mandai Safari Park Holdings and Wildlife Reserve Singapore Conservation Fund, Honorary Council Member of the Singapore Chinese Chamber of Commerce and Industry, Chairperson of National Book Development Council of Singapore, a member of ACCORD (Advisory Council on Community Relations in Defence), National Arts Council, the Tripartite Committee on Work-Life Strategy, the Board of Governors of Raffles Girls' Secondary School and a pioneering member of the Diversity Action Committee to build up the representation of women directors on boards of companies. Claire Chiang has served as a Singapore Nominated Member of Parliament for two terms (1997–2001). For her enduring service to community, Ms. Chiang has won national and international awards including the Public Service Star BBM in 2014.

Keen Meng CHOY

Choy Keen Meng is Principal Economist at the Economic Policy Group of the Monetary Authority of Singapore, where he heads the Economic Analysis Department. After obtaining his MSc (Econ) from the London School of Economics and his PhD from the National University of Singapore, he taught at universities in Singapore before joining the central bank. Trained as an econometrician, his research interests and academic publications are in the areas of forecasting, macroeconomics and business cycles. He is the co-author with Tilak Abeysinghe of a book on the Singapore economy based on a large-scale macroeconometric model. His collection of essays, entitled *Studies on the Singapore Economy*, was published by World Scientific in 2012.

Barry DESKER

Barry Desker is the Distinguished Fellow at the S. Rajaratnam School of International Studies (RSIS), Nanyang Technological University (NTU). He is a Member of the Presidential Council for Minority Rights, Singapore and a Member of the Board of Directors of the Lee Kuan Yew Exchange Fellowship. He was the Chief Executive Officer of the Singapore Trade Development Board from 1994 to 2000 and was Singapore's Ambassador to Indonesia from 1986 to 1993. He was the founding Dean of RSIS from 2007 to 2014 and was Director, Institute of Defence and Strategic Studies from 2000 to 2014. Ambassador Desker is currently also Non-Resident Ambassador of Singapore to the Holy See and Spain and Chairman of Singapore Technologies Marine. A President's Scholar, he was educated at the University of Singapore, University of London and Cornell University. He was awarded an honorary doctorate by Warwick University in 2012 and by the University of Exeter in 2013.

Grace FU

Grace Fu is the Member of Parliament for the Single Member Constituency of Yuhua. She currently holds the position of Minister, Prime Minister's Office, Second Minister for Foreign Affairs and Second Minister for the Environment and Water Resources. As Minister in the Prime Minister's Office, Ms. Fu has responsibilities in the National Talent and Population Division. She also heads the Municipal Services Office that was set up on 1 October 2014. She is the Chairperson of Women's Wing of the People's Action Party. She also sits on the boards of the Peoples' Association and the Chinese Development Assistance Council. She is or has been involved in a number of committees including the Ministerial Committee on Ageing, the Economic Strategies Committee, the Sino-Singapore Tianjin Eco-City and the National Integration Council. Before entering politics in 2006, Ms. Fu was Chief Executive Officer, PSA South East Asia and Japan. She joined PSA Corporation in 1995 and had taken on different responsibilities within the organisation. She began her career with the Overseas Union Bank as an Auditor. Ms. Fu is married with three sons and enjoys outdoor activities like rafting, swimming and hiking.

Min GEH

Geh Min (MBBS, FRCS, FAMS) is a staunch supporter and spokesperson for the environment. She was President of the Nature Society (Singapore) from 2000 to August 2008 and was sworn in as a Nominated Member of Parliament on 29 November 2004 with serving term from 1 January 2005 to 19 April 2006. She received the 2006 President's Award for the Environment and is currently a board member of Birdlife International (Asia) and a council member of The Nature Conservancy's Asia Pacific Council.

Gerald GIAM

Gerald Giam Yean Song is a Non-Constituency Member of Parliament and a member of the Workers' Party's (WP) central executive council. He contested the 2011 General Election as part of a five-person WP team in East Coast Group Representation Constituency. In Parliament, he has spoken on various issues of public concern, including healthcare, transport, housing, manpower and population policies. In 2013, he tabled an adjournment motion in Parliament on healthcare affordability, where he proposed various ways to ease the burden of healthcare expenses on Singaporeans and contain costs in the healthcare system. In 2010, he authored the book, *Singapore Version 2.0: Alternative Proposals for a Better Singapore* and continues to blog on policy issues at *geraldgiam.sg*. He was one of the founding members of the sociopolitical website, *The Online Citizen*, and was its deputy editor until 2009, when he joined the WP. Mr. Giam has an MSc in International Political Economy from the S. Rajaratnam School of International Studies at Nanyang Technological University and a BSc in Electrical Engineering (Computers) from the University of Southern California. He was schooled at Anglo-Chinese School (Independent) and Anglo-Chinese Junior College. He is married and has two young children.

Swee Keat HENG

Heng Swee Keat was elected a Member of Parliament for Tampines GRC and appointed Minister for Education in 2011. The Ministry of Education formulates and implements education policies on education structure, curriculum, pedagogy, and assessment. It oversees the management and development of Government-funded schools, the Institute of Technical Education, polytechnics and universities. MOE also funds academic research. Prior to this, Mr. Heng was Managing Director of the Monetary

Authority of Singapore (MAS). MAS serves as Singapore's central bank and an integrated supervisor of the financial services industry. Mr. Heng was named the Central Bank Governor of the Year in Asia-Pacific by British magazine, *The Banker* in 2010. He has also held appointments including the Permanent Secretary of the Ministry of Trade and Industry, Chief Executive Officer of the Trade Development Board and Principal Private Secretary to then Senior Minister Lee Kuan Yew. For his contribution to the public service, Mr. Heng was awarded the Gold Medal in Public Administration in 2001, and the Meritorious Service Medal in 2010. Mr. Heng graduated with an MA in Economics from the Cambridge University, United Kingdom. He also holds a Master of Public Administration from the John F. Kennedy School of Government, Harvard University.

Kwon Ping HO

Ho Kwon Ping is Executive Chairman of Banyan Tree Holdings, which owns both listed and private companies engaged in the development, ownership and operation of hotels, resorts, spas, residential homes, retail galleries and other lifestyle activities around the world. Born in 1952, Ho Kwon Ping was educated in Tunghai University, Taiwan; Stanford University, California and the University of Singapore. He worked as a broadcast and financial journalist and was the Economics Editor of the *Far Eastern Economic Review*. He joined the family business in 1981. In 1994, after the success of rehabilitating an abandoned tin mine into Laguna Phuket, Asia's first integrated resort, he launched Banyan Tree Hotels and Resorts. Banyan Tree has grown to more than 37 hotels and resorts, over 70 spas and over 80 retail galleries, as well as three golf courses. With a strong presence in China, Banyan Tree currently has over 20 projects under development. Mr. Ho has made numerous and significant contributions and has received accolades and awards in recognition of business innovations, creativity and leadership. His achievements and awards received include being named to the board of Daigeo, a British multinational company; 2012 CNBC's Travel Business Leader Award Asia Pacific; Top Thinker in Singapore, Yahoo! Singapore 9 Awards (2011); first Asian to receive the American Creativity Association Lifetime Achievement Award (2010); Singapore Government's Meritorious Service Medal, contribution in the founding of Singapore Management University as Chairman; Hospitality Life Achievement Award, China Hotel Investment in Shanghai (2009); CEO of the Year (2008), Singapore Corporate Awards; London Business School 2005 Entrepreneurship Award; being conferred an honorary doctorate by Johnson & Wales University (May 2000) among others. He is married to Claire Chiang, Senior Vice President, Banyan Tree Holdings Limited and is a father to two sons and a daughter.

Hian Teck HOON

Hoon Hian Teck is Professor of Economics and Associate Dean at the School of Economics, Singapore Management University. He obtained his PhD in economics at Columbia University in 1990. He specialises in macroeconomics, international trade, and economic growth. A major theme of his research focuses on understanding the big swings of economic activity — why nations experience slumps with elevated unemployment, for example — as well as business fluctuations. How Singapore managed to transit from Third World to First as measured by GDP per capita — completing the process of convergence without being caught in the middle-income trap — and figuring out what is needed to generate economic prosperity as a mature economy has occupied his mind in recent years. One theme in his research is the central role played by economic openness in explaining Singapore's catch-up growth and evolving income distribution. Since remaining integrated into the world economy brings both opportunities and threats, the question is how to structure institutions and policy to generate long-term gains across the whole of society while managing periodic external shocks. He is a past Vice President of the Economic Society of Singapore (2002–2004) and he has served as a co-editor of the *Singapore Economic Review* since January 2002.

Faizah JAMAL

Faizah Jamal served as Nominated Member of Parliament from Feb 2012 to Aug 2014 after a successful nomination by the Nature Society (Singapore), consistently speaking up for the environment, drawn from her 30-year involvement in environment advocacy. She had voted against the Population White Paper during the Parliament Debate in February

2013 on environmental grounds, making a strong call for compulsory and transparent environment impact assessments for major government projects, and calling for "a Singapore beyond GDP growth." Faizah has been a member of the Nature Society (Singapore) since 1984 and had served as Council Member, as well as Editor of its quarterly magazine, *Nature Watch*. Faizah found a second career as Adjunct Lecturer in Environment Education in tertiary institutions and schools in Singapore after giving up legal practice as a corporate lawyer. She obtained a Master's degree in Environment Law from King's College London in 1993 and was a recipient of the European Commission-ASEAN Post-graduate Scholarship for Environment Studies. She received her Bachelor of Laws degree from NUS Law School in 1984.

S. ISWARAN

S. Iswaran is Minister (Prime Minister's Office) and Second Minister for Home Affairs and Trade and Industry. He joined the Singapore Administrative Service in 1987. He served in the Ministries of Home Affairs and Education, was seconded to the National Trade Union Congress, and later to the Singapore Indian Development Association as its first Chief Executive Officer. Mr. Iswaran was Director for International Trade at the Ministry of Trade and Industry in the lead up to Singapore's hosting of the WTO Ministerial Conference in 1996. He then joined the private sector, as Director for Strategic Development at Singapore Technologies Pte Ltd. Later, as Managing Director at Temasek Holdings, he undertook investments, takeover, buy-out and merger transactions in the pharmaceuticals, biotech, hi-tech manufacturing, transport and logistics sectors. Mr. Iswaran has been elected as a Member of Parliament in four General Elections since 2 January 1997. Prior to his Cabinet appointment in 2006, he served on several Government Parliamentary Committees, and as the Deputy Speaker of Parliament from September 2004 to June 2006. Mr. Iswaran read Economics at the University of Adelaide and graduated with First Class Honours. He also holds a Master in Public Administration from Harvard University.

Basant K. KAPUR

Basant Kapur is a Professor of Economics at the National University of Singapore, where he has taught since obtaining his PhD from Stanford

University in 1974. From 1993–1998 he was also Head of the then Department of Economics and Statistics at NUS, and he served as President of the Economic Society of Singapore from 1996–1998. His teaching interests are in Macroeconomics (graduate and undergraduate courses) and International Economics (undergraduate courses). In the course of his career, he has researched and published in a broad range of areas, including (in approximate chronological order) financial repression and liberalisation in developing economies, open-economy macroeconomics, the Singapore economy, ethics and economics, and macroeconomic issues in developed economies. His recent and current interests are in endogenous growth models of closed and open economies. His articles have appeared in the *Journal of Political Economy*, *Quarterly Journal of Economics*, *International Economic Review*, *Journal of Development Economics*, *Social Choice and Welfare*, *Economic Theory*, *Journal of Economic Dynamics and Control*, and others, and he has also published a book *Communitarian Ethics and Economics* (Avebury, 1995). He has over many years also contributed articles and letters to the national press on a variety of issues of public interest in Singapore.

Er. Edwin Teck Fook KHEW

Er. Edwin KHEW Teck Fook is the Managing Director of Anaergia Pte Ltd, a global environmental waste-to-energy technology and management company with its headquarters for Asia in Singapore. He is also a former Nominated Member of Parliament (NMP) and currently the Chairman of the Sustainable Energy Association of Singapore (SEAS), the Vice President of The Institution of Engineers, Singapore (IES), a Supervisory Board Member of Solar Energy Research Institute of Singapore (SERIS) and Chairman of the Singapore Standards Council. Mr. Khew represents SEAS on the Asian Development Bank (ADB) lead Energy for All Partnership's (E4ALL) Steering Committee as its Co-Chair and Chairman of its Enterprise Development Working Group. He has an Executive MBA from the National University of Singapore; a Bachelor's degree in Chemical Engineering from the University of Queensland, Australia; is a Fellow of the Institute of Engineers, Singapore; a Fellow of the Institute of Chemical Engineers (UK); and a professional engineer of the Professional Engineers Board, Singapore.

Boon Hwee KOH

Koh Boon Hwee is the Chairman of the Board of Trustees of Nanyang Technological University. He is also Chairman of Credence Partners Pte Ltd, Sunningdale Tech Ltd, Yeo Hiap Seng Limited, Far East Orchard Limited, Rippledot Capital Advisers Pte Ltd, FEO Hospitality Asset Management, FEO Hospitality Trust Management Pte Ltd and AAC Technologies Holdings Inc. He started his career in 1977 at Hewlett Packard and rose to become its Managing Director in Singapore from 1985–1990. From 1991–2000, he was Executive Chairman of the Wuthelam Group. Boon Hwee was Chairman of the Singapore Telecom Group (SingTel) and its predecessor organisations from 1986–2001, Chairman of Singapore Airlines Limited from 2001–2005, and Chairman of DBS Bank from 2006–2010. Boon Hwee also served on the Board of Temasek Holdings Pte Ltd from 1996–2010. He is currently a director of the Hewlett Foundation and Agilent Technologies Inc. in the United States. Boon Hwee received his Bachelor's degree (First Class Honours) in Mechanical Engineering from the Imperial College of Science and Technology, University of London, and his MBA (Distinction) from the Harvard Business School.

Kheng-Lian KOH

Koh Kheng-Lian is Emeritus Professor of the Law Faculty, National University of Singapore. She was a founder member and former Director of the Asia Pacific Centre for Environmental Law from 1996–June 2013 . She was the IUCN CEL Regional Vice Chair for South and East Asia, and a member of its Steering Committee (1996–2004). She has been a resource person in various capacity building projects in environmental law with the Asian Development Bank, the Singapore Ministry of Foreign Affairs, United Nations Institute for Training and Research and Konrad-Adenauer-Stiftung. She served as a legal officer in the secretariat of the United Nations Commission on International Trade Law (UNCITRAL) in Vienna from 1980 to 1986. She is the 2012 Laureate, Elizabeth Haub Prize in Environmental Law conferred jointly by the University of Stockholm, Université Libre de Bruxelles and the International Council of Environmental Law, http://www.juridicum.su.se/ehp/news.html. She is an inductee to The Singapore Women's Hall of Fame 2014 for her pioneering work in the development of environmental law in the region, http://www.swhf.sg/the-inductees/17-environment-conservation/138-koh-kheng-lian She holds a PhD LLM (Singapore), *Diplôme de Hautes Études Internationales* (HEI, University of Geneva), LLB Hons (University of Malaya in Singapore), Advocate and Solicitor (Singapore).

Tommy KOH

Tommy Koh is Ambassador-At-Large at the Ministry of Foreign Affairs, Chairman of the Governing Board of the Centre for International Law and Rector of Tembusu College at the National University of Singapore. He is the Co-Chairman of the China-Singapore Forum, the India-Singapore Strategic Dialogue and the Japan-Singapore Symposium. He was Singapore's Permanent Representative to the United Nations in New York for 13 years. He was Ambassador to the United States of America for 6 years. He was the Dean of the Faculty of Law of NUS. He was also the President of the Third UN Conference on the Law of the Sea. He chaired the Preparatory Committee for and the Main Committee at the Earth Summit. He had served as the UN SecretaryGeneral's Special Envoy to Russia, Estonia, Latvia and Lithuania. He was also Singapore's Chief Negotiator for the USA-Singapore Free Trade Agreement. He has chaired two dispute panels for the WTO. In 1984, Yale University conferred on him an honorary degree of doctor of law. Prof Koh received the Elizabeth Haub Prize for Environmental Law in 1996 and was made a Champion of the Earth by the United Nations Environment Programme (UNEP) in 2006. He also received the Great Negotiator Award 2014 from Harvard University on 10 April 2014.

David Kuo Chuen LEE

David Lee Kuo Chuen is a Professor of Quantitative Finance at the Singapore Management University Director of the Sim Kee Boon Institute for Financial Economics, and the founder of Ferrell Asset Management Group. He is a Fulbright Scholar and a Visiting Fellow at Stanford University in 2015. He obtained his PhD from the London School of Economics and Political Science in 1990. He was a stockbroker, a specialist fund manager, Managing Director and Chairman of several listed companies, Private REIT manager and a property developer. He was the MD of OUE Limited, Auric Pacific

Limited, the Non-executive Chairman of MAP Holdings Limited, the Vice Chairman of Alternative Investment Management Association Singapore Chapter, a member of the Monetary Authority of Singapore Financial Research Council, and a member of the SGX Security Committee. Currently, he is the Independent Director of HLH Group Limited and SHS Limited. He is also a Vice President of the Economic Society of Singapore, a Board Member and Investment Committee Member for several charitable, professional and endowment funds. His interest is in Digital Currency, Branchless Banks, Financial Inclusion, Impact Investing, Internet Finance and Fintech Start-ups. His latest books are published by Elsevier on Asia Finance and Digital Currency.

Laurence LIEN

Laurence Lien is Co-Founder and CEO of the Asia Philanthropy Circle, a new non-profit initiative that convenes Asian philanthropists to learn, collaborate and catalyse new social interventions. He is also the Chairman of Lien Foundation and the Community Foundation of Singapore, Vice-President of the Centre for Non-Profit Leadership, and Board Member of the Lien Centre for Social Innovation at the Singapore Management University. Laurence was the CEO of the National Volunteer and Philanthropy Centre in Singapore from 2008–2014, when he founded the Community Foundation of Singapore. Under his leadership, Lien Foundation has become a philanthropic foundation well-regarded for its forward-thinking and radical approach. Prior to his work in the non-profit sector, Laurence served in the Singapore Government. Laurence holds degrees from Oxford University, the National University of Singapore, and Harvard University's John F. Kennedy School of Government. In 2010, Laurence was awarded the Eisenhower Fellowship. He was also a Nominated Member of Parliament in Singapore from 2012–2014.

Chong Yah LIM

Lim Chong Yah was the founding Head of the Division of Applied Economics, University of Malaya in Kuala Lumpur, prior to becoming the Head of the Department of Economics and Statistics and the elected Dean of the Faculty of Arts and Social Sciences of NUS. He was the President of the Economic Society of Singapore (1973–1991), founder of the Federation of ASEAN Economic Associations (FAEA), co-founder of the East Asian Economic Association (EAEA), and the Pacific Economic Co-operation Conference (PECC). He served as the Editor of the *Singapore Economic Review* (1978–1991). He retired from NUS as a Senior Professor in 1992, and was conferred the Emeritus Professorship of the University. NUS in 2001, through public donations, established a *Lim Chong Yah Professorship* in its Faculty of Arts and Social Sciences. He joined NTU in 1992 as Professor of Economics, and was promoted to Albert Winsemius Chair Professor of Economics in 2005. NTU also conferred on him the prestigious honorary position of Emeritus Professor upon his retirement in 2012. He has 29 books, 39 chapters in books, 51 articles in refereed academic journals and 74 international conference papers to his credit. Some of his academic publications have been translated into Chinese, Japanese and Malay. One has gone into Braille in Malaysia.

Linda Y. C. LIM

Linda Yuen-Ching Lim is Professor of Strategy at the Stephen M. Ross School of Business at the University of Michigan, Ann Arbor, where she was Director of the 55-year-old Center for Southeast Asian Studies from 2005–2009 and held other administrative positions in the International Institute. Linda holds degrees in economics from the universities of Cambridge (BA), Yale (MA) and Michigan (PhD). She has authored, co-authored or edited four books and published more than 100 other monographs, journal articles and book chapters on economic development, trade, investment, industrial policy, labour, multinational and local business in Asia. She has been writing about the Singapore economy since 1976, with five academic articles published in 2014–2015, and regularly contributes to *The Straits Times* and *Business Times* in Singapore. Linda teaches MBA courses and executive education sessions on The World Economy and Business in Asia. She has consulted for businesses, think tanks and international development agencies, is a Trustee Emeritus of The Asia Society, a New York-based non-profit, and serves on the board of the NUS America Foundation. She has a cumulative fifteen years' experience as an independent board director of two U.S. public companies in the tech sector with extensive Asia operations.

Selena LING

Selena Ling is Head of Treasury Research and Strategy in OCBC Bank. She is responsible for Treasury market research, forecasts, and trading recommendations for the bank, covering fixed income, interest rates, corporate credit, foreign exchange, and macroeconomic commentary. Her research writings has been extensively quoted and published by prominent media such as *Business Times*, *Straits Times*, *Today* newspaper, *Asia Money Magazine*, *The Edge* magazine, Bloomberg, Dow Jones, Reuters and Agence France-Presse newswires, MAS SGS website, as well as televised media including CNBC, Bloomberg, Channel NewsAsia, etc. Under her leadership, OCBC's research capabilities have been greatly valued by customers and highly ranked in surveys such as Best for interest rate research in Singapore, Best for FX Research and Market Coverage in Singapore, and 2nd best in regional best team for Asian macroeconomic research in the 2013 AsiaMoney Fixed Income and FX polls, amongst others. Prior to joining OCBC in August 2000, Selena was with the Fiscal Policy Unit under the Ministry of Finance (MOF), and the Economics Department in the Ministry of Trade and Industry (MTI).

Donald LOW

Donald Low is Associate Dean (Executive Education and Research) at the Lee Kuan Yew School of Public Policy. Besides leading the School's executive education efforts, he also heads its case study unit. His research interests at the School include inequality and social spending, behavioural economics, economics and public policy, public finance, and governance and politics in Singapore. Prior to his current appointment, Donald served 15 years in the Singapore government. During that time, he established the Centre for Public Economics at the Civil Service College to advance economics literacy in the Singapore public service. Donald also held senior positions at the heart of the Singapore government. He was the Director of Fiscal Policy at the Ministry of Finance from 2004 to 2005, and the Director of the Strategic Policy Office in the Public Service Division from

2006 to 2007. Donald is the editor of *Behavioural Economics and Policy Design: Examples from Singapore* (2011), a pioneering book which details how the Singapore government has applied ideas from behavioural economics in a number of policy domains. His most recent book, *Hard Choices: Challenging the Singapore Consensus* (2014), raises searching questions about the long-term viability of many aspects of governance in Singapore. He argues that a far-reaching rethinking of the country's policies and institutions is needed in light of new socioeconomic, demographic and political realities. Such rethinking — parts of which would have to be quite radical — is necessary even if weakens the very consensus that enabled Singapore to succeed in its first 50 years. Donald holds a double first in Politics, Philosophy and Economics from Oxford University, and a Master in International Public Policy from The Johns Hopkins University's School of Advanced International Studies. He is currently a Vice President of the Economic Society of Singapore.

Shawn LUM

Shawn Lum arrived in Singapore in 1989 to begin what was intended as a two- to three-year research project on tropical rainforests of Singapore and the region. The visit, hosted by the then Botany Department of the National University of Singapore, was to change the trajectory of his career in more ways than one. He joined the Nature Society in 1989 (then known as the Malayan Nature Society (Singapore Branch), today's Nature Society (Singapore)), and before leaving to complete his PhD thesis he applied to join the newly established biology faculty at the National Institute of Education, Nanyang Technological University. He remains a member of both today. Shawn's professional and civil society interests are related to his interest in ecology and nature conservation. His teaching centres upon plant diversity and forest ecology and management, while his conservation work uses biodiversity data as the basis for outreach work and stakeholder engagement. Shawn succeeded Dr. Geh Min as president of the Nature Society (Singapore) in 2008. Besides plants and nature conservation, Shawn's fate is tied to islands and to the Asia-Pacific. He was born in Japan, raised in Honolulu, Hawaii, and has spent his adult life in Singapore.

Kishore MAHBUBANI

Kishore Mahbubani has had the good fortune of enjoying a career in government and, at the same time, in writing extensively on public issues. He was with the Singapore Foreign Service for 33 years (1971–2004). He served as Singapore's Ambassador to the UN and as President of the UN Security Council in January 2001 and May 2002. He was Permanent Secretary at the Foreign Ministry from 1993 to 1998. Currently, he is Dean of the Lee Kuan Yew School of Public Policy, NUS. He is the author of *Can Asians Think?*, *Beyond The Age Of Innocence*, *The New Asian Hemisphere*, *The Great Convergence* (selected by *Financial Times* as one of the best books of 2013), and *Can Singapore Survive?* He was conferred the Public Administration Medal (Gold) by the Singapore Government in 1998 and the Foreign Policy Association Medal in 2004. He was listed as one of the top 100 public intellectuals in the world by *Foreign Policy* and *Prospect* in 2005; included in the 2009 *Financial Times* list of Top 50 individuals; and selected as one of *Foreign Policy's* Top Global Thinkers in 2010 and 2011. Most recently, he was selected by *Prospect* magazine as one of the top 50 world thinkers for 2014.

Ravi MENON

Ravi Menon was appointed Managing Director of the Monetary Authority of Singapore (MAS) in 2011. He is a member of the Financial Stability Board (FSB) Steering Committee and chairs the FSB Standing Committee on Standards Implementation. Mr. Menon was Permanent Secretary at the Ministry of Trade and Industry (2007–2011), where he led the ministry's work in economic strategy; industrial development; energy policies; research and development; international trade agreements; and regional economic integration. He chaired the APEC Senior Officials Meetings in 2009. Mr. Menon was Deputy Secretary at the Ministry of Finance (2003–2007), where he was responsible for fiscal policy and government reserves. He oversaw the preparation of the Annual Budget Statements; and led a review of the investment policy of the Singapore Government Investment Corporation. Mr. Menon began his career at MAS in 1987. During his 16 years in MAS, he was involved in monetary policy; econometric forecasting; organisational development; banking regulation and liberalisation and integrated supervision of complex financial institutions. Mr. Menon holds a Master's in Public Administration from Harvard University and a Bachelor of Social Science (Honours) in Economics from the National University of Singapore.

Yew-Kwang NG

Yew-Kwang Ng, Albert Winsemius Professor in Economics, Nanyang Technological University, Singapore, was born in 1942 in Malaysia. He obtained his BCom from Nanyang University in 1966, and PhD from Sydney University in 1971. He was a Professor of Economics at Monash University from 1985–2012 (and an emeritus professor since 2013) and has been a fellow of the Academy of Social Sciences in Australia since 1980. In 2007, he received the highest award (Distinguished Fellow) of the Economic Society of Australia. He has published over two hundred refereed papers in leading journals in economics, including *American Economic Review* (7 papers), *Economica* (6.5; joint papers counted fractionally), *Economic Journal* (6), *Journal of Economic Theory*, *Journal of Political Economy* (3), *Review of Economic Studies* (1.5), *Social Choice and Welfare* (12), and in biology, cosmology, mathematics, philosophy, psychology, and sociology. His recent books include *Common Mistakes in Economics by the Public, Students, Economists and Nobel Laureates* (Nova, 2011) (open access); *How Did the Universe Come About?* (Fudan University Press, 2011); *The Road to Happiness* (Fudan University Press, 2013); *Happinessism* (Wunan Publishing, Taiwan, 2015). His interests are Chinese couplets and poetry, and reading.

Max PHUA

Max Phua is the managing director of World Scientific, the largest privately owned publisher in Singapore and one of the leading professional and academic publishers in the world. He has a Master's degree from the London School of Economics and was an honours undergraduate student in economics and political science from the University of Rochester. Under his leadership, the company has broadened its products to include areas like research handbooks, general, economics and business books and journals. Mr. Phua has helped the company effectively move into digital media. More than 65% of the company's revenues are currently from digital products. Mr. Phua was the former honorary secretary of the Singapore Book Publishers Association and former council member of the Book Development Council of Singapore. He actively works with EDB, IE Singapore and MDA to raise the profile of media and knowledge industries in Singapore. He is also a member of the Young Business Leaders by Singapore Business Federation, former board member of the Singapore Economic Society, Advisory Panel of the National Youth Council's (NYC) Youth Expedition Project, board member of the Scientific, Medical and Technology Publishers International Association and member of the International Industrial Advisory Board of the Knowledge Management Laboratory at NUS.

Jose RAYMOND

Jose Raymond, a former multiple award-winning journalist who was named Mediacorp's Journalist of the Year in 2006, joined the Singapore Sports Council (SSC) in September 2007 after more than a decade in journalism. While at the SSC, Singapore's lead government agency tasked with developing a holistic sports culture for the nation, he held various appointments with the Sports Management Group and subsequently with the Sports Marketing Group. Jose also held concurrent appointments as the Head of Communications and IT for the 1st Asian Youth Games 2009 in Singapore. He was credited for strategising, formulating and executing a complete media and broadcast strategy for the inaugural Asian Youth Games. He also co-wrote the official theme song for the Games, "Asia's Youth, Our Future." Jose served as Press Secretary to current Minister of State for Trade and Industry, Teo Ser Luck, who was the Youth Olympic Village Mayor during the Singapore 2010 Youth Olympic Games and later served as Press Secretary to the Minister for the Environment and Water Resources Dr. Vivian Balakrishnan. He was appointed the Chief Executive Officer of the Singapore Environment Council on 15 September 2011. Jose is also an appointed District Councillor of the Northeast Community Development Council, where he is the Chairman of the Environment Standing Committee. He is also a member of the Cashew Constituency Citizens Consultative Committee. In June 2014, he was elected as the Vice-President of the Singapore Swimming Association. He has a Master in Business Administration from Murdoch University and has been accepted to pursue a Master in Public Administration at the Lee Kuan Yew School of Public Policy.

Edward ROBINSON

Edward Robinson is Assistant Managing Director (Economic Policy Group) and Chief Economist at the Monetary Authority of Singapore (MAS). He studied economics and econometrics at Monash University and the University of Melbourne. He has been with the MAS for about 20 years and currently heads the EPG which formulates Singapore' monetary policy. Edward has a particular interest in macroeconometric modelling and continues to be involved in the developmental work on the MAS suite of models, which are used for forecasting and policy analysis. He has also been involved in other areas of applied economic policy work including in the inter-Ministry Economic Monitoring Group reviewing the government's official economic forecasts and Economic Review Committee which looked at the structural challenges facing the Singapore economy. He was awarded the Public Administration Medal (Bronze) in 2002 and the Public Administration Medal (Silver) in 2014. He served on the Board of the Singapore Competition Commission in 2005-07.

Andrew TAN

Andrew Tan is Chief Executive of the Maritime and Port Authority of Singapore (MPA) and assumed his appointment in January 2014. Mr. Tan joined the Singapore Administrative Service in 1991. He has worked in various government agencies from the Ministry of Information and the Arts, Ministry of Defence, Ministry of Foreign Affairs, Ministry of The Environment and Water Resources, to the Ministry of Transport. Prior to MPA, Mr. Tan was the Chief Executive Officer of the National Environment Agency from 2009–2013. Mr. Tan was also Principal Private Secretary to the late Minister Mentor Lee Kuan Yew from 2002–2004 and worked on the Memoirs of Mr. Lee from 1994–1997. He was Founding Director of the Centre for Liveable Cities from 2008 to 2010 and remains a Fellow. Mr. Tan also sits on the boards of the Singapore Maritime Foundation, Singapore

Chamber of Maritime Arbitration, Singapore Maritime Institute, Tropical Marine Science Institute, Centre for Maritime Studies and the Competition Commission of Singapore.

Augustine H. H. TAN

Augustine H. H. Tan, PhD Stanford (Economics), is Practice Professor of Economics at the School of Economics, Singapore Management University. He was previously Vice-Provost [Research] and Deputy Director, Wharton-SMU Research Center, Singapore Management University. He was formerly teaching at the National University of Singapore (30 years) as well as serving as an elected Member of Parliament (21 years). He was Political Secretary to then Prime Minister Lee Kuan Yew and served as Chairman, Parliamentary Committee on Trade, Industry and Finance, Chairman, Estimates Committee and Chairman, National Productivity Board. He was also a board member of the Economic Development Board, Housing and Development Board and trustee of the Institute of Southeast Asian Studies (ISEAS). He has been consultant to the UN, World Bank, ILO, UNCTAD, ADB, ESCAP, Monetary Authority of Singapore, East-West Center and other bodies. His research interests are in international trade and finance and he has made contributions in the area of effective protection in general equilibrium with publications in the American Economic Review and Review of Economic Studies. He writes newspaper columns on the Singapore economy and other global and regional issues. He has won several awards including Outstanding Professor (MBA), Most Outstanding Professor (EMBA, three times), Teaching Excellence Award for Executive Education, and Mind Opener Instructor. Last year, Singapore Management University conferred on him the Distinguished Educator Award for his lifetime achievements in teaching and research.

Eugene K. B. TAN

Eugene K. B. Tan is associate professor of law at the School of Law, Singapore Management University (SMU) and co-director of the SMU Centre for Scholars' Development. An advocate and solicitor of the Supreme Court of Singapore, Eugene is a graduate of the National University of Singapore, the London School of Economics and Political

Science, and Stanford University where he was a Fulbright Fellow. His interdisciplinary research interests include constitutional and administrative law, the mutual interaction of law and public policy, the regulation of ethnic conflict, and the government and politics of Singapore. Eugene is an active analyst for the local and international media on Singapore politics, government, and society. He also writes commentaries for *TODAY* and *Lianhe Zaobao*. A strong believer in paying it forward and contributing to society, Eugene serves on the boards of the National Youth Achievement Award Council, Singapore Compact for Corporate Social Responsibility, and the Catholic Welfare Services. He also chairs the scholarship selection committee for the Tan Kah Kee Foundation Postgraduate Scholarship and the Tan Ean Kiam Foundation Postgraduate Scholarship. Between February 2012 and August 2014, Eugene served as a Nominated Member of Parliament in Singapore's 12th Parliament.

Kong Yam TAN

Tan Kong Yam is presently professor of economics at the Nanyang Technological University in Singapore and the Co-director of the Asia Competitiveness Institute at the Lee Kuan Yew School of Public Policy at the National University of Singapore. From 1985-88, he was the chief assistant to Dr. Goh Keng Swee, the late deputy Prime Minister of Singapore invited by Mr. Deng Xiaoping to advise China on economic development strategy. From June 2002 to June 2005, he was a senior economist at the World Bank office in Beijing. In 2004, he was a member of the World Bank expert group on the eleventh five-year plan (2006–2010) for the State Council in China. Prior to that, he was the chief economist of the Singapore government (1999–2002) and head of department of strategy and policy at the NUS Business School. He is a graduate of Princeton (1975–1979, class of 1931 scholar, Paul Volcker Thesis prize) and Stanford University (1980–1983). His research interests are in international trade and finance, economic and business trends in the Asia Pacific region and economic reforms in China. He has published ten books and numerous articles in major international journals on economic and business issues in the Asia Pacific region. He has also consulted for many organizations including Temasek, Citigroup, IBM and Bank of China.

Simon TAY

Simon S. C. Tay is Chairman of the Singapore Institute of International Affairs, ranked in global surveys as a leading Asian think tank. Simon is concurrently tenured professor of international law at the National University of Singapore and has also taught at Harvard Law School and Yale University. He also serves as advisor or independent director for the Mitsubishi United Financial Group of Japan and major Singaporean corporations, Far East Organization and Hyflux. He is Senior Consultant with WongPartnership a major Asian firm based in Singapore with practices across ASEAN and in China and the Middle East, and was previously corporate advisor to Temasek Holdings. He has served Singapore in a number of appointments including as chairman of Singapore's National Environment Agency, for three terms as a Nominated Member of the Singapore Parliament, and as the founding coordinator for the country's version of the Peace Corps. In 2006, he received a Singaporean National Day award. His commentaries feature regularly in leading international and regional media. He is also a prize-winning writer, having received the Singapore Literature Prize in 2010. Simon received his Masters in Law as a Fulbright scholar at Harvard, where he won the Laylin Prize for the best thesis in international law.

Josephine TEO

Josephine Teo was appointed Senior Minister of State for Finance and Transport on 1 September 2013. She was Minister of State for Finance and Transport from 21 May 2011 to 31 Aug 2013. A Member of Parliament since 2006, Mrs. Teo was formerly Chairman of the Government Parliamentary Committee for Education and Assistant Secretary-General of the National Trades Union Congress (NTUC). She represented the labour movement on the government-appointed Economic Strategies Committee and co-chaired the sub-committee on Fostering Inclusive Growth. Mrs. Teo was concurrently Chief Executive Officer of the not-for-profit organisation Business China, a platform launched by then Minister Mentor Lee Kuan Yew and then China Premier Wen Jiabao to strengthen Singapore's bicultural foundations, and remains a member of its Board. To enhance Singapore's position as a leading global air hub, Mrs. Teo was appointed to chair a multi-agency "Changi 2030

Steering Committee" in 2012. This Committee provides strategic direction for the long-term growth plans of Changi Airport. She currently co-chairs the Pioneer Generation Taskforce which oversees the Government's implementation of the Pioneer Generation Package to honour the 450,000 Singapore citizens who contributed to nation-building since the time of independence. She also chairs the Public Transport Tripartite Committee.

Leslie TEO

Leslie Teo is the Director of the Economics and Investment Strategy Department and Chief Economist at GIC. He oversees the economics and investment strategy team at the GIC. The team is responsible for asset allocation, total portfolio construction and identification of key long-term trends that would impact GIC's portfolio. Leslie holds a BA from the University of Chicago and PhD in economics from the University of Rochester. In addition, he is a certified Financial Risk Manager and a CFA charterholder. Prior to joining GIC, Leslie was at the International Monetary Fund. During his Fund career, he worked in the Asia Pacific, Monetary and Financial Systems, Policy Development and Review, and European II Departments. Leslie was also Head of the Financial Surveillance Division at the Monetary Authority of Singapore.

Jang Ping THIA

Thia Jang Ping is the Director of the Transformation Office, and the Security and Resilience Programme Directorate in the Ministry of Finance. His key responsibilities include overseeing the budget and manpower allocations to various Ministries, implementing transformation projects to improve public sector effectiveness, and the use of data analytics. He is also concurrently the Director (Social and Economics) at the Institute of Governance and Policy, Civil Service College. His key responsibility is to advance Public Economics and Social research, including use of behavioural insights in economic and social settings. Dr. Thia received his PhD in Economics from the London School of Economics. His main professional interest is in International Economics. His secondary interests include economic geography and population issues.

Kai Chong TSUI

Professor Tsui Kai Chong is Provost of SIM University. He is a member of the board of IP Academy Singapore, the National Community Leadership Institute and the National Council of Social Service. He received his PhD in Finance from New York University in 1988 and his Chartered Financial Analyst qualification in 1993.

Sudhir Thomas VADAKETH

Sudhir Thomas Vadaketh is a writer who in 2012 published his first book, *Floating on a Malayan Breeze: Travels in Malaysia and Singapore*, a socio-economic narrative on the two countries. In 2014 he co-authored a collection of essays, *Hard Choices: Challenging the Singapore Consensus*. He is currently working on a book about China and India. From 2006–2013 Sudhir worked for The Economist Group in Singapore, first as associate director of the Economist Corporate Network, then senior editor of *Economist Insights*. Sudhir has a BA (Geography), BA (South and Southeast Asian studies) and a BSc (Business Administration) from the University of California at Berkeley; and a Master in Public Policy from the Harvard Kennedy School. Sudhir lives in Singapore with his wife and two cats.

Aline WONG

Professor Aline Wong is currently an Academic Advisor in the President's Office of SIM University, Singapore. She was formerly Professor of Sociology at the National University of Singapore. Between 1984 and 2001, she was an elected Member of Parliament, and served for ten years as Minister of State for Health and for Education (1990–2001). Upon her retirement from politics, she was appointed as Chairman of the Housing and Development Board (2003–2007). She obtained her Ph.D. from the University of California at Berkeley, and has published widely in the fields of family sociology, women's studies, urban sociology and population issues

Lawrence WONG

Lawrence Wong was elected as the Member of Parliament for the West Coast Group Representation Constituency (Boon Lay Division) in the

2011 General Election. He is concurrently the Second Minister for Communications and Information, and also a member of the Board of Directors of the Monetary Authority of Singapore. Mr. Wong spent his earlier professional life as a civil servant. He was previously Chief Executive of the Energy Market Authority, and the Principal Private Secretary to the Prime Minister. Before that, he was the Director of Healthcare Finance at the Ministry of Health, where he implemented reforms to MediShield, to provide Singaporeans with better protection against large hospital bills. At the community level, Mr. Wong has been involved in youth work in church and voluntary organisations. He co-founded a voluntary organisation to develop and mentor youths called PromiseWorks, which received the Outstanding New Volunteer Initiative award in 2003. Mr. Wong was educated at Tanjong Katong Secondary School and Victoria Junior College. He obtained his undergraduate and master's degrees in Economics from the University of Wisconsin- Madison and the University of Michigan-Ann Arbor. He also has a Master in Public Administration from the Harvard Kennedy School.

Lam Keong YEOH

Yeoh Lam Keong is currently a private economic consultant and an Adjunct Professor at the Lee Kuan Yew School of Public Policy. He was Director of Economics and Strategy and Chief Economist at the Government of Singapore Investment Corporation for 10 years. Mr. Yeoh is a prominent economist in Singapore and is heavily involved in public policy research. He has advised a number of research institutes in Singapore, and is on the Singapore Management University (SMU) School of Economics Advisory Board. He has worked with major consulting firms, public and civic organizations and several key government ministries. He is well known policy analyst and social commentator and has published in international academic publications, as well as local policy journals and magazines, the press and recent notable books and conferences on public policy issues. He is also on the Advisory Board of Nuvest Capital, a Board member of Arohi Asset Management and a Board member of Bamboo Finance, (a leading microfinance and socially responsible private equity investment firm) and is a member of the National Council of Social Services Investment Committee.

Beyond 50: Journalists

Fiona CHAN

Fiona Chan is Deputy Political Editor for Singapore newspaper *The Straits Times*. Until recently, she was the paper's Tokyo-based Senior Economics Correspondent, analysing regional and global economic developments and their impact on Singapore's economy. In her eight years at The Straits Times, she has extensively covered a wide range of business and political news — from property and finance to political elections and economic policies — and has won a number of awards for her work in business journalism. In 2011, she co-authored *Sustaining Stability, Serving Singapore*, a book about the policies and history of the Monetary Authority of Singapore, the Singapore central bank and financial regulator. More recently, she contributed to *50 Things to Love about Singapore*, a collection of essays to celebrate Singapore's 50th birthday. Before assuming her role as Senior Economics Correspondent at *The Straits Times*, she was an investment banker at Bank of America Merrill Lynch, executing corporate finance transactions across Southeast Asia. Fiona is a graduate of the University of Pennsylvania and Harvard University.

Robin CHAN

Robin Chan is a manager in the Media Strategy and Analytics Division of Singapore Press Holdings. He was a journalist for *The Straits Times* from 2008 to 2014, where he covered economics, politics and finance, and last held the position of Assistant Political Editor. Robin is a co-author of *Hard Truths to Keep Singapore Going*. He has a bachelor's degree in International Economics from Georgetown University and grew up in Hong Kong and Singapore.

Mui Hoong CHUA

Chua Mui Hoong is Opinion Editor of *The Straits Times*, Singapore' biggest-circulation English language daily. She has been with *The Strait*

Times since 1991. She has a Bachelor of Arts in English literature from Cambridge University and a Master in Public Administration from the Harvard Kennedy School. She enjoys bird-watching and nature walks in her leisure time.

Zengkun FENG

Feng Zengkun has been with *The Straits Times* for almost six years. He is the newspaper's science and environment correspondent, specialising in issues like climate change, waste management and water supply and systems. He graduated from New York University with a bachelor of fine arts.

Salma KHALIK

Salma Khalik has been a journalist for more than 30 years — and has been covering health issues for the past 15 years. He started in *The Business Times* before moving to *The Straits Times*. He also spent five years in Singapore Press Holdings' (SPH) multimedia division and a year in Marketing where he helped launch the Recruit section. Among the things he has covered on health are the separation of Siamese twins from Nepal, the SARS outbreak, and the National Kidney Foundation saga. He was the only journalist to go into a SARS ward at the peak of the SARS outbreak. Mr. Khalik has won a number of awards at SPH, including Commentary of the Year (2014) — "Watchdog Must Be Fair to Patients Too", and Story of the Year (2012) — "Docs Upset Over HAS Safety Rule."

Vikram KHANNA

Vikram Khanna is Associate Editor of Singapore's financial daily, *The Business Times*, where he has worked since 1993, including as Economics Editor. He has been a columnist at the paper and also coordinates the prestigious Raffles Conversation interview series, under which he has personally conducted more than 200 one-on-one interviews with key personalities from around the world. He has also served on government committees, including the Entrepreneurship and Internationalisation subcommittee of the Economic Review Committee (2001), the Pro Enterprise Panel (2003–2006) and The Enterprise Challenge (2002–2005). Prior to joining *The Business Times*, he served at the International

Monetary Fund in Washington DC for seven years. Vikram has BA, MA and MPhil degrees in Economics from the University of Cambridge, UK.

Beyond 50: Foreign Contributors

Parkash CHANDER

Parkash Chander, Professor of Economics and Executive Director of Center for Environmental Economics and Climate Change at Jindal School of Government and Public Policy, is a Fellow of the Econometric Society, an Associate Editor of *Journal of Public Economic Theory*, a member of the Advisory Board of *Journal of Economic Surveys*, and a member of the International Advisory Board of *Singapore Economic Review*. He has previously held professorial positions at Indian Statistical Institute, Delhi and National University of Singapore (in reverse order). Also, he served as Head of Indian Statistical Institute, Delhi and as Head of Department of Economics, National University of Singapore. Professor Chander has researched primarily in the areas of microeconomics, public economics, environmental economics, and game theory and applications. He has held visiting appointments at Johns Hopkins University, California Institute of Technology, University of Pennsylvania, Vanderbilt University, CORE (Louvain-la-Neuve), the Autonomous University of Barcelona, and International Monetary Fund, among other institutions.

Jack L. KNETSCH

Jack Knetsch is Emeritus Professor of Economics at Simon Fraser University and has held recent appointments as a Senior Visiting Fellow at the Civil Service College, Singapore and the Nanyang Visiting Professor at the Nanyang Technological University. His research on behavioural economics and applications to policy issues, extending over three decades, has appeared in most leading international journals. His name continues to appear regularly on lists of the most cited economists.

Joergen Oerstroem MOELLER

Joergen Oerstroem Moeller was born in 1944 and has a Cand. Polit (Master of Science, Economics) from the University of Copenhagen

(1968). He joined the Danish diplomatic service on 1 February 1968 and worked with European integration for 26 years (1971–1997); and was State-Secretary from 1989–1997. He was the Danish Ambassador to Singapore and Brunei Darussalam (1997–2005) and from 2002 was also Ambassador to Australia and New Zealand, residing in Singapore. When he retired from the Danish Diplomatic Service in 2005, Mr. Moeller joined the Institute of Southeast Asian Studies (ISEAS), Singapore as Visiting Senior Research Fellow and the Diplomatic Academy as Senior Fellow. He is Adjunct Professor, Copenhagen Business School and Singapore Management University (SMU), Chairman of the Advisory Board, Asia Research Center, Copenhagen Business School (CBS), Honorary Alumni University of Copenhagen, Global Advisory Council of The World Future Society, and Board of Governors ASEF (Asia Europe Foundation). His major publications in English are: *The Global Economy in Transition, Debt and Resource Scarcities* (World Scientific, 2013); *How Asia Can Shape the World, From the Era of Plenty to the Era of Scarcities* (ISEAS, 2011); *Political Economy in a Globalized World* (World Scientific, 2009); and *European Integration: Sharing of Experiences* (ISEAS, 2008). He has published in a large number of journals and contributed columns to numerous newspapers and websites.

Richard L. SANDOR

Richard L. Sandor (PhD, Dr.Sc.h.c) is Chairman and CEO of Environmental Financial Products, which specialises in inventing, designing and developing new financial markets. He is the Aaron Director Lecturer in Law and Economics at the University of Chicago Law School and a Visiting Fellow with the Smith School of Enterprise and the Environment at Oxford University. He was honoured by the City of Chicago for his universal recognition as the "father of financial futures" and named one of TIME Magazine's "Heroes of the Environment" for his work as the "Father of Carbon Trading." In 2013, Dr. Sandor was awarded the title of Chevalier (Knight) in the French National Order of the Legion of Honour, for his accomplishments in the field of environmental finance and carbon trading. He holds an honorary degree of Doctor of Science, honoris causa, from the Swiss Federal Institute of Technology (ETH). He is the author of *Good*

Derivatives: A Story of Financial and Environmental Innovation and the lead author of *Sustainable Investing and Environmental Markets: Opportunities in a New Asset Class* (published by World Scientific). He received his Bachelor of Arts degree from Brooklyn College and holds a PhD in economics from the University of Minnesota.

Beyond 50: Associates

Pei Lin CHAN

Chan Pei Lin graduated from Raffles Girls' Secondary in 2010 and from Raffles Institution (Junior College) in 2012. She is a research assistant of Professor Euston Quah and is currently pursuing a degree in Economics at Nanyang Technological University.

Youngho CHANG

Chang Youngho is an Assistant Professor of Economics at the Division of Economics, Nanyang Technological University, Singapore. Apart from the academic affiliation, he is a member of Technical Committee for Clean Development Mechanism (CDM) Designated National Authority (DNA), National Environment Agency, Singapore. Dr. Chang specialises in the economics of climate change, energy and security, oil and macroeconomy, and the economics of electricity market deregulation. He has published his research output in internationally refereed academic journals and co-edited books on energy security such as *Energy and Non-Traditional Security (NTS) in Asia*, *Rethinking Energy Security in Asia* (both by Springer), *Energy Security: Asia Pacific Perspectives* (Manas Publications) and *Energy Conservation in East Asia: Towards Greater Energy Security* (World Scientific). Along with academic publications, he carried out consultation projects for the public and private sector. Dr. Chang has been interviewed and quoted by global and local media such as the *International Herald Tribune*, *The Strait Times*, *BBC*, *Bloomberg*, *Channel News Asia* regarding energy- and climate change-related issues. He was a degree fellow at the East-West Center, Hawaii and received his PhD in Economics (Environmental and Resource Economics) from the University of Hawaii at Manoa, US.

Cristian CHEN

Cristian Chen graduated from Nanyang Technological University in 2015 with a degree in Economics. His hobbies include reading, watching movies and playing the drums.

Roland CHEO

Roland Cheo is currently working at the Center of Economic Research, Shandong University in China where he heads the experimental economics laboratory. He received his PhD from Monash University, Australia. He has actively been involved in development projects in China working on projects looking at other regarding behaviour in teams, and promoting the right incentives in community driven development. He is often in China running laboratory or field studies. His latest field experiment looks at how the gender composition of village committees affects the types of aid they seek from aid agencies. Prior to working in China, Roland worked in the National University of Singapore. He has published in international refereed journals such as *Economics Letters*, *Economic Record*, *Education Economics* and *Applied Economic Letters*. He is also currently a handling editor for an upcoming issue of China for the *Singapore Economic Review*. He credits his ability to find balance in a world full of hectic schedules and constant activity to his wife, who is also an economist.

Wai Mun CHIA

Chia Wai Mun is Associate Professor of Economics at the School of Humanities and Social Sciences, Nanyang Technological University. Her research covers topics in international macroeconomics, housing economics and cost-benefit analysis. She is an associate editor to the *Singapore Economic Review*. She holds a PhD from Nanyang Technological University, an MSc from London School of Economics and a BSc from University of London, all in economics. Wai Mun is also a consultant to various government agencies in Singapore including the Singapore Police Force, National Environment Agency, Land Transport Authority, Ministry of Community Development, Youth and Sports and Building and Construction Authority.

William Henry CLUNE

William Henry Clune is a consultant, lawyer, and entrepreneur in Singapore, Sweden, and the US, whose work focuses on sustainable economic development and environmental protection. With projects and research related to global and corporate governance, legal frameworks, addressing the challenges and opportunities of urban development, and empowering individuals and communities, he has worked with corporations, governments, universities, and third sector clients. At NTU in Singapore, William is a Faculty Associate in the Division of Economics and the Policy Director at the Sustainable Earth Office. William graduated with distinction from Stanford University with degrees in Economics and English (BA). He obtained a Juris Doctor (JD) from The University of Chicago Law School. He completed a Master's degree (MSc) in Environmental Science at The University of Wisconsin, a Master's degree (MA) in Public Policy from The University of Chicago, and a Juris Magister (LLM) in European Law from Stockholm University.

Dannon HONG

Dannon Hong Xiuxian is majoring in Economics in Nanyang Technological University's (NTU) School of Humanities and Social Sciences. In his course of undergraduate studies, he is also active in the NTU Economics Society (NTU-ECSOC) and Overseas Volunteering Expedition (OVE). He was a business manager in the NTU-ECSOC Overseas Study Trip 2013 to Hong Kong and director for the NTU-ECSOC Overseas Study Trip 2014 to Shanghai, where he liaised and organised a study trip for students to private enterprises, government entities and universities. He also volunteered in the 2014 OVE to Vietnam and is the business manager for the 2015 OVE to Yunnan, which he sourced for sponsors and volunteered at the same time. He is also an economics researcher for the Head of the Economics department from his freshman year and has assisted the Head in multiple local and overseas conferences, such as the Beijing Humboldt Forum and the Singapore Sustainability Symposium. He is also active in the Economic Society of Singapore (ESS), assisting in events such as emceeing for the 2015 Annual ESS Dinner.

Shao Tze KHOO

Khoo Shao Tze served as the Personal Advisor to the Indonesian Minister of Tourism and Creative Economy H.E. Mari Elka Pangestu till the end of 2014 and was also responsible for the Indonesia Pavilion at the Shanghai World Expo 2010 (which won a Bronze Award) while she was the Indonesian Minister of Trade. After graduation, Shao Tze was in legal practice in Hong Kong and China until 2000, specialising mainly in China direct investments and corporate finance. He then ventured into business as an entrepreneur, founding two companies in the media and entertainment industries, focused on production and distribution of content and also advertising, targeting the Greater China and South East Asia markets. He exited the companies in 2005 before serving in senior management positions with several Asian conglomerates with businesses spanning mining and natural resources, renewable energy, manufacturing, media and property. Shao Tze is now with Genting Singapore Plc as the Vice President of Business Development of Resorts World Sentosa. He holds a LLB (Hons) and MBA from the National University of Singapore and an MBA from UCLA.

Hean Teik ONG

Ong Hean Teik graduated from the University of Malaya in 1983, and obtained the M Med (Int Med) from the National University of Singapore in 1988. Presently a consultant cardiologist at HT Ong Heart Clinic and a clinical lecturer at Penang Medical College, he writes mainly on academic subjects in the medical journals. After editing a book on the history of doctors and healthcare in Penang for the Penang Medical Practitioners' Society in 1994, he has become more vocal writing on social-political matters. Amongst his articles are "A Doctor's Duty is to Heal the Unhealthy: The story of Tun Dr. Mahathir Mohamad" (*Annals of the Academy of Medicine, Singapore, 34* (2005), 45C–51C), "Surviving the Cost of Medical Care" (*The Sun*, November 20, 2006, p. 24) and "Malaysia versus Singapore: Comparisons, 50 Years On" (*New Straits* Times, April 2, 2015, pp. 18–19).

Hui Ying SNG

Sng Hui Ying is Lecturer of Economics in the School of Humanities and Social Science at the Nanyang Technological University (NTU). She received her PhD (Economics) from NTU and her B.SocSci. (Hons) and M.SocSci. (Applied Economics) from the National University of Singapore. Her research areas include development economics, Singapore economy, and Southeast Asian economies. Prior to joining NTU, she was a broadcast journalist with Mediacorp News and a senior research officer with the Jurong Town Corporation. In 2002, she participated in a consultation project led by Professor Lim Chong Yah to advise the government of Mauritius on wage determination system and wage reform issues. She is the co-editor of the books *Singapore and Asia in a Globalized World: Contemporary Economic Issues and Policies* (2008), *Singapore and Asia: Impact of the Global Financial Tsunami and other Economic Issues* (2009) and *Crisis Management and Public Policy: Singapore's Approach to Economic Resilience* (2011). Her research monograph, *Economic Growth and Transition: Econometric Analysis of Lim's S-Curve Hypothesis*, was published in 2010. She has also published in refereed journals such as *World Economics* and *Journal of Economic Development* and contributed to *Regional Outlook: Southeast Asia* published by the Institute of Southeast Asian Studies.

Christabelle SOH

Christabelle Soh majored in Economics at Nanyang Technological University's School of Humanities and Social Sciences. In the course of her undergraduate studies, she was awarded the Ministry of Trade and Industry (MTI) Economist Service Book Prize, the Koh Boon Hwee University Scholar's Award, and the Lee Kuan Yew Gold Medal. She has co-authored articles on Economics and the environment that were published in *The Straits Times* and also authored a book chapter on Benefit Transfers in *Cost-Benefit Analysis: Cases and Materials*, a guidebook for Cost-Benefit Analysis practitioners. From 2011 to 2013 she taught Economics in Raffles Institution (Year 5–6) and is currently involved in evaluative studies. She is also an active member of the Economic Society of Singapore (ESS) and serves on the editorial team for the ESS Bulletin, a publication that aims to enhance Economics education amongst students and laymen, that will be launched in the second half of 2015.

Benjamin C. W. TAN

Benjamin Tan majored in Economics at Nanyang Technological University's School of Humanities and Social Sciences. In the course of his undergraduate studies, he was awarded the IE Singapore mid-term scholarship. Benjamin was the captain of the university tennis team in 2011, winning a gold medal in the team event (2011) and was the Singapore University Game's doubles champion in his senior year (2013). He was appointed a director in NTU's Economic Society, at one point organising the largest annual networking event for the society. He was also an economics researcher for the Head of the Economics department from his sophomore year, and is in the process of co-publishing his graduation thesis with the Head. Today, Benjamin is with IE Singapore's Natural Resources arm, assisting Singapore Oil and Gas companies with overseas business activities, catalysing market share acquisition overseas through partnerships, acquisitions, and conducting management consultancy analysis to propose internationalisation strategies for firms.

Tsiat Siong TAN

Tan Tsiat Siong graduated with a MSc (Applied Economics) from National University of Singapore and a BA (Economics) from Nanyang Technological University with First Class Honours. Tsiat Siong was a valedictorian nominee in NTU and a valedictorian in NUS.

Raymond TOH

Raymond Toh is a graduate from NUS in 2005 with a degree in economics. In the short span of 30-odd years, he has witness the many economic transformations that have taken place in Singapore. He is currently working as a Business Development Manager in a local firm.

Tony YEOH

Tony Yeoh is the regional Chief Information Officer (CIO) for a global hotel company, Intercontinental Hotels Group (IHG) responsible for technology in the Asia, Middle East and Africa region. IHG is one of the world's leading hotel companies whose goal is to create Great Hotels Guests Love, with over 700,000 rooms in more than 4,900 hotels in nearly 100 countries. In his role he is attuned to latest developments in technology ranging from consumer to corporate, used by hotel guests and colleagues. He is responsible for the technology services and infrastructure in corporate offices, BPO centre and also support hotel openings and systems operation in 250 hotels. Prior to joining IHG in 2006, Tony was leading the consulting and systems integration business for Hewlett Packard (HP) and worked in several practices in China, Taiwan, Thailand, Singapore and Malaysia. He started his career with the National Computer Board in its formative years when Singapore was tapping growth in computerisation. Tony holds an MBA from University of Auckland, New Zealand and a BSc from Monash University, Australia.

Printed in the United States
By Bookmasters